Windows® 2000 Security

New
Riders

Selected Titles from New Riders Publishing

Tim Hill: *Windows Script Host*
ISBN: 1-57870-139-2

Tim Hill: *Windows NT Shell Scripting*
ISBN: 1-57870-047-7

Dave Roth: *Win32 Perl Programming: The Standard Extensions*
ISBN: 1-57870-067-1

Dave Roth: *Win32 Perl Scripting: The Administrator's Handbook*
ISBN: 1-57870-215-1

Thomas Eck: *Windows NT/2000 ADSI Scripting for System Administration*
ISBN: 1-57870-219-4

Duncan Mackenzie and
Joel Semeniuk: *Exchange & Outlook: Constructing Collaborative Solutions*
ISBN: 1-57870-252-6

Luke Kenneth Casson Leighton: *DCE/RPC over SMB: Samba and Windows NT Domain Internals*
ISBN: 1-57870-150-3

Gary Nebbett: *Windows NT/2000 Native API Reference*
ISBN: 1-57870-199-6

Eric Harmon: *Delphi COM Programming*
ISBN: 1-57870-221-6

Paul Hinsberg: *Windows NT Applications: Measuring and Optimizing Performance*
ISBN: 1-57870-176-7

Peter G. Viscarola and
W. Anthony Mason: *Windows NT Device Driver Development*
ISBN: 1-57870-058-2

William H. Zack: *Windows 2000 and Mainframe Integration*
ISBN: 1-57870-200-3

Sean Deuby: *Windows 2000 Server: Planning and Migration*
ISBN: 1-57870-023-X

Todd Mathers: *Windows NT/2000 Thin Client Solutions: Implementing Terminal Services and Citrix MetaFrame*
ISBN: 1-57870-239-9

Eugene Schultz: *Windows NT/2000 Network Security*
ISBN: 1-57870-253-4

Edgar Brovic, Doug Hauger,
and William C. Wade III: *Windows 2000 Active Directory*
ISBN: 0-7357-0870-3

Gary Olsen: *Windows 2000 Active Directory Design & Deployment*
ISBN: 1-57870-242-9

Windows® 2000 Security

201 West 103rd Street,
Indianapolis, Indiana 46290

Roberta Bragg

Windows 2000 Security

International Standard Book Number: 0-7357-0991-2

Library of Congress Catalog Card Number: 00-100516

05 04 03 02 01   7 6 5 4 3 2 1

Interpretation of the printing code: The rightmost double-digit number is the year of the book's printing; the right-most single-digit number is the number of the book's printing. For example, the printing code 01-1 shows that the first printing of the book occurred in 2001.

Composed in Quark 4.0 and MCPdigital by New Riders Publishing

Printed in the United States of America

Trademarks

Warning and Disclaimer

Publisher
David Dwyer

Associate Publisher
Al Valvano

Managing Editor
Gina Brown

Product Marketing Manager
Stephanie Layton

Publicity Manager
Susan Petro

Acquisitions Editor
Theresa Gheen

Development Editor
Shannon Leuma

Project Editor
Jake McFarland

Copy Editor
Amy Lepore

Indexer
Larry Sweazy

Manufacturing Coordinator
Chris Moos

Book Designer
Louisa Klucznik

Cover Designer
Aren Howell

Proofreader
Debbie Williams

Composition
Amy Parker
Suzanne Pettypiece

Contents

About the Author

Roberta Bragg has run her consulting firm, Have Computer Will Travel, Inc., out of a laptop or luggable computer since 1985. In addition, she has worked as a salesperson, systems administrator, developer, author, university instructor, trade school teacher, and technical trainer. Current certifications include MCSE (Windows 3.51, 4.0, and 2000), MCT, MCP+Internet, and CTT. Mainframe moonlanding, 80 column cards, and Fortran are part of her ancient history. Virtual existence lies sometime in the future. You can find her on the Web as a security columnist at www.mcpmag.com, an instructor at www.spu.edu, and a security evangelist at www.peaceweaver.com.

About the Technical Reviewers

These reviewers contributed their considerable hands-on expertise to the entire development process for *Windows 2000 Security*. As the book was being written, these dedicated professionals reviewed all the material for technical content, organization, and flow. Their feedback was critical to ensuring that *Windows 2000 Security* fits our readers' need for the highest quality technical information.

David Shackelford is the overseer of network and computer operations at IRSC, a subsidiary of ChoicePoint, Inc. His background includes working as a beekeeper, screening submissions for a popular poetry journal, and teaching networking classes at Hewlett-Packard and Intel. He has been working in the computer industry for a decade in the capacity of instructor, systems engineer, network designer, and security administrator. David holds a master's degree in English, is a Microsoft-Certified Systems Engineer and Trainer, was a contributing author to the *Windows 2000 Essential Reference* published by New Riders, and was a technical editor for *Inside Windows 2000 Server* also by New Riders.

Mich Kabay began learning Assembler at age 15 and learned FORTRAN IV G at McGill University by 1966. In 1976, he received his Ph.D. from Dartmouth College in applied statistics and invertebrate zoology. In 1979, he joined a compiler team for a new 4GL and RDBMS in the United States and was responsible for developing the statistical syntax, writing the parser, error traps, and code generation for statistical functions in the command language. Dr. Kabay joined Hewlett-Packard in 1980 and became a performance specialist, winning the Systems Engineer of the Year Award in 1982. He has written security columns for *Computer World*, *Network World*, *Computing Canada*, *Secure Computing Magazine*, *NCSA News*, *Information Security Magazine*, and several other trade magazines. He attained the status of Certified Systems Security Professional (CISSP) in 1997. Dr. Kabay has published more than 220 technical papers in operations management and security and completed a college textbook, *The NCSA Guide to Enterprise Security: Protecting Information Assets* (ISBN 0-07-033147-2), published by McGraw-Hill in April 1996. He was director of education for ICSA Labs (formerly NCSA and then ICSA) from 1991 to 1999. In January 2000, he joined the INFOSEC Group of Atomic Tangerine, Inc. as security leader.

Brendan McTague is a senior systems engineer with the Global Financial Services division of Perot Systems Corporation. He currently manages a cross-platform Internet engineering team for the investment banking division of a major European bank. Brendan graduated with a bachelor of science degree in computer science from Temple University; he has been working with Windows NT through Windows 2000 for more than five years and received his MCSE in early 1995. When not working, Brendan prefers to spend his time with his wife and son in their home outside Chicago. Please feel free to send him comments at `brendan.mctague@mindspring.com`.

Dedication

To Jim, for what once was.

Acknowledgments

Thanks to those at New Riders who understood my need for a life outside of writing this book—and who bugged me anyway.

Tell Us What You Think

As the reader of this book, you are the most important critic and commentator. We value your opinion and want to know what we're doing right, what we could do better, in what areas you'd like to see us publish, and any other words of wisdom you're willing to pass our way.

As the Associate Publisher for New Riders Publishing, I welcome your comments. You can fax, email, or write to me directly to let me know what you did or didn't like about this book—as well as what we can do to make our books stronger.

Please note that I cannot help you with technical problems related to the topic of this book and that, due to the high volume of mail I receive, I might not be able to reply to every message.

When you write, please be sure to include this book's title and author as well as your name and phone or fax number. I will carefully review your comments and share them with the author and editors who worked on the book.

Fax: 317-581-4663
Email: nrfeedback@newriders.com
Mail: Al Valvano
          Associate Publisher
          New Riders Publishing
          201 West 103rd Street
          Indianapolis, IN 46290 USA

Introduction

Information systems security has become everyone's business. It's not enough anymore to understand the use of passwords and how to set file permissions. If you administer, design, implement, install, or use computer systems, you have a right and a duty to protect them and the information that resides on and moves through them in the best possible way.

Windows 2000 was designed with security in mind. Many new features exist, and technical enhancements have been made to familiar items. If these features are implemented appropriately and correctly, they can protect systems and data. It's not enough, however, to know these features and how to use them: You must know the why and when. You must know that there is no one "correct" way to utilize the new technologies. Finally, you must implement security in a manner that others can understand and maintain.

This book provides information on all aspects of Windows 2000 security. It is not meant to be your only guide to Windows 2000. Rather, its focus is on the facilities and tools that are available to secure your Windows 2000 network.

Who This Book Is For

Individuals who are charged with administering and supporting Windows 2000 networks, or who will be migrating to Windows 2000 networks, will find solid information on the security tools, features, and structures of Windows 2000 security. Windows NT 4.0 aficionados will find familiar ground to associate with, but knowledge of Windows NT or Windows NT security is not necessary to understand the concepts presented.

Meanwhile, knowledge of networking is assumed. Only basic introductory material is presented on the architecture of the Active Directory. It is assumed that readers who require more knowledge can find it in numerous sources including those listed in the appendix. However, knowledge of cryptography is not assumed. Thus, introductory material is presented in the first section of this book for people whose paths have not led them through this area before.

Individuals whose areas of specialization include information systems security and/or auditing will find all the details of Windows 2000 security presented. If you are not new to your field, you might want to skip the introductory material on cryptography; details of Windows 2000 implementations are presented in later sections.

How This Book Is Organized

This book is divided into four sections as follows.

Part I: Concepts and Definitions

This section includes chapters on basic security concepts, cryptography, security-related protocols, Public Key Infrastructure, and Kerberos. If the reader is intimately familiar with these subjects, he is advised to jump directly to the later sections in which specific Windows 2000 information is presented. In many conversations with Windows NT administrators and supporters of Windows infrastructures, however, I have found that a large number of them have no background in these subjects. They have not had to deal with Kerberos or PKI or make choices of cryptographic algorithms. That is why this introductory information is included in this book. Later sections, which discuss how Windows 2000 implements a standard or provides choices, do not have to be interrupted with verbose discussions, or worse, lose the reader because of a lack of knowledge about basic concepts. Any reader who possesses knowledge of these concepts can easily skip to Part II. Should an unfamiliar term or concept be mentioned, the reader can return to the introduction to find more information.

Part II: Securing the OS

The first step in any security program should be to secure the basic operating system. This section investigates common features of all versions of Windows 2000 and addresses the issue of security for standalone systems. Here is where you will find information on Kerberos authentication in Windows 2000, the Encrypting File System, NTFS, local computer-security policies, and security tools native to Windows 2000.

Part III: Securing the Local Area, Microsoft Network

Few computers are islands. Connectivity ranges from the home, telecommuter, or road-warrior system that connects via dial-up to corporate servers or the Internet, to wide area networks that integrate a multitude of operating systems. This section looks specifically at the pure Windows local area network. Information on Windows 2000 domain security administration and protection is addressed. In addition, there is information on securing down-level Windows clients and on the new Distributed File System.

Part IV: Securing Real World Networks

A large number of networks consist of multiple OSs and involve a large number of locations. This section explores the features that Windows 2000 possesses to assist in securing these real-world scenarios. Information can be found on securing remote access via RADIUS and RRAS, and on establishing a Public Key Infrastructure, Web security, and interoperability.

Conventions Used in This Book

Throughout the book, special "Best Practices" and "For More Information" sections are included. The "Best Practices" sections include Microsoft and author recommendations on the use of features and practices described in the chapters. The "For More Information" sections summarize the location of additional or related information on the subject in this book.

I

Concepts and Definitions

1

Basic Security Concepts

THE COMPUTER INDUSTRY IS FULL OF ACRONYMS AND words that everyone has heard but many have trouble defining. Information systems security is no exception. Worse yet, information systems professionals cannot always agree on the definitions of some industry terms. This chapter presents some basic security concepts and provides commonly accepted definitions of a number of security-related terms. Depending on your background, you might want to use this chapter in one of three ways:

- If you are new to security, this chapter is a must-read because I will be using these concepts and terms throughout the book.

- If you are new to Windows operating systems *and* to information systems security, it might be helpful if you examine the chapter while keeping in mind an operating system you do know because the concepts and definitions are not specific to Windows 2000. In addition, at the end of the chapter, you will find a section with chapter references for Windows 2000–specific information on these concepts. (For further information on the general aspects of Windows 2000, a number of excellent resources can be found in the Appendix, "Resources.")

- If you are new to Windows operating systems but not to information systems security, there is nothing about Windows here that is not covered elsewhere in the book. You will not find any startling new terms or radical interpretations of security concepts. However, you might want to use this chapter as an indicator of the definitions accepted for the purposes of this book, or you might prefer to merely visit the section at the end of the chapter that indicates where topics relevant to Windows 2000 are covered.

For the purpose of explaining the concepts and definitions in this chapter, I'd like to introduce you to some friends of mine named Alice and Bob. Alice and Bob are actually quite well known in some circles, and you might have met them before. Many people use the names Alice and Bob when explaining security concepts; it's a bit of a tradition. Alice and Bob are quite ordinary users, and I could have easily chosen to use the names Fred and Francine, Roberta and Luke, or David and Brendan. But Alice and Bob are much easier to type, and it's nice to work with someone familiar. Now let's get started.

The Three A's of Security

One common approach to security is called "the three A's of security." The three concepts being referred to are

- Authentication
- Authorization
- Auditing

Proponents of the three A's approach claim that if you implement the appropriate information system structures to manage these three concepts, then you have appropriately secured the computer system. If you ask security professionals to explain the three concepts, however, you might get different definitions. Most of these differences will be semantic, but occasionally you will find a true disagreement. What follows are definitions that I believe the majority of people in the information systems security industry agree on.

Authentication

Authentication is the capability of one entity (a computer, a person, or whatever) to prove its identity to another entity (a computer, a person, or whatever). For most people, it's easy to recognize the concept of being able to prove that you are who you say you are. When Alice wants to use her plane ticket to fly to Disney World, she will be asked to present a valid ID before she can obtain a boarding pass. She has to prove that she is the Alice for whom the ticket was issued; that is, she must authenticate herself to the airline agent. A good choice for such authentication is a driver's license, which represents proof of identity from someone the airline trusts (in this case, the state automobile licensing authority). A second authentication process also occurs at this time: The airline agent compares the photo on Alice's driver's license to Alice herself.

Another example of authentication occurs when Bob uses an Internet kiosk at the airport to access mail on a remote server. To do so, he must enter his user ID and a password. Bob is thus authenticating himself to the email server by giving it some kind of identification that was previously established with the server.

Both of these processes are authentication processes, but Bob's email access is more similar to the authentication process used by many computer systems. Each user of the operating system services must provide a user ID and a password. The operating system matches this password with the one in its database for the user's ID. Like the scenario in an old army movie, the security service stands guard at the perimeter and at any attempt to enter the camp hollers, "Who goes there?" If you know the password, you are allowed to pass. If not, you are refused. (Most computer security services don't shoot you if you don't know the correct password—at least not yet.)

Other authentication schemes involve mutual authentication, computer-to-computer authentication, authentication algorithms, the use of certificates, and the use of special devices such as smart cards or biometric devices.

Mutual Authentication

If Alice has an account and a password for a server, she uses that account and password to prove her identity to the server. The server is thus assured that Alice is who she says she is. Alice, however, does not really know that she has connected to the server. Think about this for a minute. When you visit http://www.microsoft.com, how do you know you are actually reading information from the company's servers? How do you know, when you log on to the server at the office, that you are really connecting to the server to which you think you are connecting?

The identity of the server could be proved if you could challenge the server and get a verifiable response. In the airport example, Alice accepts the identity of the airline agent because the agent is at the airline's booth at the airport. When you purchase a book from a Web site, however, how do you know you are sharing your credit card number with the merchant instead of an imposter?

Your Web browser is able to authenticate the server of the company from which you are making a purchase by verifying information it is given against information it already has. You are not explicitly aware of this. (However, you can verify that you are making a secure, authenticated connection by making sure https is used instead of http in the address line.)

Thus, authentication can be of the client by the server in some cases and of the server by the client in others. When both identification methods are used, the process is called *mutual authentication*. If Alice is going to use online banking, she probably would like to know that, in addition to the bank's server authenticating her access to her account, she can be assured that she is, indeed, connecting to her bank's server and not some impersonator.

Mutual authentication is an extremely valuable service in today's distributed systems. The boundary between the safe, trusted, private network of your organization and the hostile world is not as clear as it once was. Even when the utmost security practices are carried out, absolute protection is not assured. Indeed, even within the corporate network, systems are vulnerable to attack from authorized users of the network. Mutual authentication, then, offers an extra measure of defense.

Computer-to-Computer Authentication

In computer-to-computer authentication schemes, the computers share a secret. This information is used by one computer to identify itself to the other. You can think of this as one computer being the client and the other being the server, if this is the way it is being processed, or as mutual authentication if both computers are authenticating each other.

Authentication Algorithms

Windows NT 4.0 uses the NT LAN Manager Challenge and Response Algorithm (NTLM) for authentication. In this algorithm, a random string of characters, "the challenge," is given to any system seeking access. NT uses the user-entered password as part of the one-way encryption of the challenge and presents this "response" to the server. The server—because it has access to the challenge and the user's password information—can verify that the user is who she says she is. The password never travels across the network in clear or encrypted form.

To allow users of Windows 9x systems to authenticate to NT, NT can also use the LAN Manager Challenge and Response Algorithm (LM). The LM algorithm is similar to the NTLM algorithm, but for reasons that will be explained in Chapter 12, "Domain-Level Security," it is less secure. Windows 2000 is capable of using either of these algorithms to authenticate down-level clients (Windows 9X, Windows NT) and can also use NTLM as a backup authentication mechanism for Windows 2000 clients.

The Windows 2000 default authentication algorithm, however, is Kerberos. Kerberos is widely used in distributed computing systems and is recognized as a secure authentication algorithm. Kerberos uses a series of request and reply messages and a number of checks and balances to securely and mutually authenticate clients and servers. The advantages of using Kerberos include a more secure authentication system, the capability to have mutual authentication, and interoperability with other operating systems that use Kerberos V5 for authentication.

Of course, no system is perfect. In many systems (NTLM, LM, and Kerberos), we only need a user ID and a password to be authenticated. Should we be able to steal, guess, or otherwise obtain this information, the server is not able to distinguish whether we truly are who we say we are. Thus, any system of authentication is only as strong as its weakest point. In the user ID and password scheme, the weakest point is the password. If users write their passwords down, share them with fellow workers, or use simple passwords, even the most complex system can be compromised.

Kerberos does have a number of safeguards, however, that make password information, after it has entered the system, more secure from electronic attack. Mutual authentication is one of these safeguards because it makes it harder to impersonate a server and thus gain password information from a client request or to reuse captured packets that might contain authentication requests.

Other Authentication Schemes and Devices

Many schemes and devices attempt to deal with the all-too-vulnerable user ID/password scheme. Among them are certificates (data structures that assist in the distribution of encryption keys), smart cards (credit card–size devices with embedded chips that hold authentication information), biometric devices (which rely on some feature of human physiology for authentication), and security tokens (key fobs or cards that provide additional identification information).

Windows 2000 has built-in smart card capabilities—all that is necessary is the appropriate hardware. Certificate Services can be installed and implemented at no extra charge. Integrated biometric support is due in the summer of 2000, while third-party drivers and applications are already appearing.

Authorization

Although authentication proves you are the user you say you are, *authorization* is the process of discovering whether you have the rights or permissions to do what you have asked to do. In the Windows world, authorization might be called into play to check your permissions (such as Read, Write, Delete) on an object or to determine whether you have the right to perform an action (such as add a user or install an application).

At the airport, the agent authenticates Alice by comparing her picture ID to her face. Alice is authorized to board the plane after the agent finds her name on the passenger list. These two steps are actually separate even though they are accomplished at the same time.

Note

An object in Windows 2000 represents any item that can be assigned privileges including files, folders, users, printers, computers, and policies. Security can thus be established for any object.

Speeding Up Airport Lines

I've often wondered why airlines don't separate the picture authentication process from the boarding list authorization process. It would make everyone's airport check-ins much faster. Agents could travel up and down the waiting line of passengers and check their IDs. They could time-stamp the passenger's ticket or e-ticket notice or give the passenger something to present to the next agent—a ticket-granting ticket, if you will. The passenger would present this ticket-granting ticket to the agent, and the ticket agent could then check the passenger's name against the passenger list, check baggage, and assign seats. Much faster!

It is possible to have authentication with little to no authorization. For example, if I provide you with a user ID and a password but give you no file access, and if I carefully control the capabilities given to the default groups to which you belong, you might be able to successfully log on to a system but not run programs or copy or read files. In our airport example, Alice might be able to prove her identity to the airline agent, but if she has not purchased a ticket, she will not be allowed to board the plane.

Windows 2000 has an extensive array of capabilities to provide and control authorization. There are default groups that provide specific rights, object permissions that can be assigned to give a fine granularity of control, and the capability to add or remove rights from users and groups.

Auditing

Auditing is the process of checking to see whether something has been done the way it is supposed to have been done. To audit, you need to have a tool that can tell you what happened when.

Wouldn't you like to know what's been happening in your house while you're away? I, for one, would like to know what really happened one fateful Saturday night when I was out of town and my teenage son was at home—Sigh. With computer systems, it is not a question of relying on the neighbors; most enterprise-wide operating systems generate logs that enable you to track activity.

Auditing information systems requires the capability to log activity within a computer system. This allows administrators, auditors, and other approved personnel to determine who's been doing what. The degree to which the audit trail exists will vary for two reasons:

1. Different operating systems have different capabilities.

2. Some operating systems have a range of audit capabilities that must be selected.

Audit logs are useful in determining accountability (that is, who is responsible for what action). Want to know who has been accessing the payroll files? Who added Sally to the Administrators group? When was the check printer last used? Use the audit log.

Windows NT and Windows 2000 do not have auditing enabled by default. Windows 2000, however, provides the opportunity to develop an audit policy that defines the type of security events Windows 2000 keeps in the security log. This policy also can be automatically applied to other servers and workstations and can be centrally updated and maintained.

Security Policy

A Security Policy establishes the guidelines and responsibilities necessary to protect a company's information assets. It contains an expression of the disciplinary actions that will occur should the policy be ignored.

Many corporations use the Security Policy as a broad expression of intent, leaving supplementary policies to detail standards, procedures, and further guidelines. The Management Security Policy outlines the security devices, algorithms, and procedures for the system administrator to implement.

Security Policy, for example, might dictate that passwords consist of at least eight characters, be composed of uppercase and lowercase characters and numbers, be changed every 45 days, and not be repeated. The systems administrator is then responsible for implementing this policy as much as possible, using computer system settings and possibly third-party software. Managers are responsible for communicating the policy to their employees, and employees are responsible for following the policy.

Computer Security Objectives

If the list of the three A's of security seemed a little short to you, it may be because its focus on authentication, authorization, and auditing was initially developed during the use of the centralized computer systems of the past. Back then, there was less concern with data traveling from computer to computer because the connections between clients and servers often were more direct. A terminal, rather than an intelligent device, was used. The concern was with identifying the user, determining his privileges, and auditing his actions. The need to focus on the integrity of the data was determined by its location, which usually was on a single server.

As systems become more widespread, client workstations become closer in capability to the servers, and data becomes ever more distributed, our focus on data security becomes more distributed as well. Instead of looking at one computer, we examine multiple systems and the communication paths between them.

A more encompassing approach, then, specifies a list of computer security objectives. The objectives of computer security are to provide integrity, control, availability, and auditing. Because we already have discussed the auditing objective, this section will cover integrity, control, and availability.

Integrity

A computer system must be able to ensure accuracy, reliability, and confidentiality. The users of the system must have confidence that the data the system stores, and any data manipulation they request, is accurate and free from tampering. A system that guarantees the preceding is said to have *integrity*.

Accuracy is not just the process of being able to correctly add numbers. It is the process of ensuring that both the original number and the calculation results are protected from tampering. Unauthorized modification must not be allowed to occur, and all data must only be available, at any time, to those with approved access.

If Alice stores her scientific research on the server, she wants to be able to return to it later and not have to worry that it has been changed. If Bob uses a graphical user interface (GUI) to set permissions on files, he shouldn't have to worry about whether the graphical results he is getting represent what is actually set. If users copy data from one system to another or send it as an attachment to an email, they need to feel comfortable that nothing will happen to it during transport.

Damage to the integrity of a system can be caused by many things including

- Human error
- Physical errors during transmission of data
- Hardware problems (such as hard disk crashes)
- Software bugs
- Natural disasters (floods, hurricanes)
- Malicious intent (viruses, Trojan Horses, data and code tampering)

Many of these problems can be prevented, guarded against, or prepared for through good physical protection of the infrastructure, backup and contingency planning, virus protection, error- and tampering-detection techniques, and software-based data transport protection and access control.

To place these techniques in the context of day-to-day operations, we must divide the issue of integrity into the following four areas:

- Integrity of data maintained on the server
- Integrity of data during transport
- Integrity of operating system code
- Integrity of application code

Because two of these involve data integrity and two involve code integrity, they can be grouped into two discussions.

Data Integrity

The integrity of data maintained on a server is guaranteed by setting access controls, properly maintaining the hardware, and planning for failure by properly backing up data. Setting access controls encompasses physical security as well as digital access. You physically protect the server by maintaining it in an area separate from public work areas (such as in a server cabinet, closet, or room) and by preventing unauthorized access. Digital access is controlled by requiring authentication and authorization as previously described.

If the data leaves the server or is saved to the server from outside sources, you must maintain the integrity of data during transport. This is often referred to as *message integrity*. If a message has message integrity, it is guaranteed to be received as it is sent. This means that no insertions, duplications, modifications, reorderings, or replays appear in any received message. There is also no destruction of data.

Two types of protection are required:

- Error detection (Was some data lost or damaged during transport due to tampering or malfunction?)
- Protection of data during transport (Can tampering or data loss be prevented?)

Checksums and other more sophisticated techniques are used to detect transmission errors. In these cases, before the data is sent, a number is calculated by applying a formula to the data. The data and the number are transmitted. The receiving side performs the same calculation over the data again. The answer should match the received number. If it does not, an error has occurred and the data must be resent. You can see why this would not allow us to detect all forms of tampering. There is nothing to prevent a malicious user from modifying the data and recalculating the checksum.

More sophisticated techniques are used to determine whether data has been tampered with during transmission. These techniques will be examined in Chapter 2, "Cryptology Introduction," but put briefly, what if the results of the calculation done over the data to be transmitted were protected from tampering? That is, what if the result was modified in some manner such that only the properly authorized receiver could decode it? Or that only the authorized sender could have produced it? These methods could be used to guarantee freedom from tampering during transmission and thus to ensure the veracity, or integrity, of the data.

Windows 2000 has built-in features that assist in the maintenance of data integrity. The use of Kerberos for authentication, a built-in file encryption system, and the capability to granularly define file and folder permissions enable the protection of data on computer systems. Built-in capabilities for implementing Certificate Services, IP Security (IPSec), and virtual private networks (VPN) also assist in maintaining the integrity of data during transmission.

Code Integrity

Operating system code should be free from error and should not be vulnerable to accidental deletion or replacement. It should also not be possible to tamper with or change the way the operating system works. No one, for example, should be able to insert code that would prevent the activities of a particular account from being logged.

Administrative tools used to grant rights to operating system utilities should do so. That is, if Bob has been given the right to add users to the system, he should be able to do so. More importantly, no user—whether authorized or unauthorized to use the system—should be able to add users unless he has been granted that right.

Operating systems traditionally guarantee their integrity by preventing access to the operating system code itself and by running the operating system code in more protected, separate areas of memory from application code. By protecting code stored on the system (setting Read and Execution rights while reserving Write rights), the code base is protected. By separating processing of operating system code from application code, the system is protected from poor or malicious code that might otherwise interfere with or crash the system.

Windows 2000 runs operating system code in a protected mode and protects operating system code on the system by setting file and folder permissions. An additional protection device, the Windows File Protection (WFP) system, prevents the overwriting or deletion of protected system files.

Application code likewise can be protected by using operating system functionality—such as the capability to set access permissions on program files—and by using other techniques incorporated into the application itself. Application integrity responsibility is shared by the developers of the application, the developers of the operating system, and the administrators who implement the security features of the system on which the application is installed.

Control

Access to the computer system and the allocation of its resources should be under the control of management. All of the sophisticated protection devices and schemes in the world will not secure an information system, computer, or network if they are not used.

Who made Bob an Administrator of the XYZ computer system? Who said Alice could program the routers? Ultimately, the rights allowed on the system should be granted by management authority and only by this authority. There should not be a way to subvert, or bypass, this power. Information systems management is assigned by organization policy. Management of all information systems components and areas is then delegated.

Windows 2000 has a set of management roles and delegatable responsibilities that flow from the authority given to the initial Administrator account created during system installation. If Windows 2000 computers are joined in a logical collection called a *domain*, control of systems flows downward from the initial Administrator account of the first domain controller (a specialized function that maintains the central control structures of the domain).

Several domains can be collected in a hierarchical structure known as a *forest*. In this structure, domains are security boundaries (an Administrator in one domain has no rights or privileges in other domains), but a special group exists called Enterprise Admins. Membership in this group allows cross-domain management. The Administrator account of the first system in the forest (the root domain) becomes the first member of the Enterprise Admins group.

Access to and control of Administrator accounts ensures management control over the Windows 2000 network.

Availability

Availability means a system, application, or data file is ready to be used when an attempt is made to access it. To provide good availability, the system must be secured against any attack, disaster, error, or oversight that would deny its availability to authorized users. If authorized users cannot access the system when they need to, there is a problem. Work cannot be done; money and opportunity are lost.

Availability is often expressed in terms such as 24×7, meaning the system is always available to authorized users. This "always-up" availability might not be the definition of availability required by all of your systems, but whatever the stated availability time is, it should be upheld.

Some of the same problems that can compromise data integrity (hard disk crashes, hurricanes, human errors, viruses, and malicious attacks) also can prevent system availability.

Miscellaneous Security Terms

Many other terms are used when discussing computer security. Where possible and logical, they will be defined in the context of their usage. The following terms, however, should be considered basic to an understanding of computer security concepts:

- **Nonrepudiation.** Nonrepudiation means that the sender of a message cannot deny she sent the message and the receiver cannot deny he received it. The receiver can prove that the message was sent by the sender; the sender can prove that the message was received by the receiver. If I send you a message via email or even via the U.S. mail, how do you know it was really sent by me? How do I know you really received it? Unless we are both using software beyond the usually desktop messaging client (or mail techniques beyond the normal postal handling of a letter), we cannot know this for sure. It is amazingly easy to send a message that has a false return address. In most email and mail communications, we do not have nonrepudiation.

  Nonrepudiation in email systems, some say, cannot be accomplished. Others believe that cryptographic techniques can prove the origination of an email message. This is quickly becoming a legal issue and one for the courts to decide.

  An example of a system with nonrepudiation is the prosecution of a bank robber using tapes from the camera systems at a bank. It would be a little hard for the robber to deny that he robbed the bank (or for the teller to say it wasn't him) if the bank has videotapes that show him pointing a gun at the teller and receiving the bag of money from her.

- **Data origin authentication.** Data origin authentication is the capability to reliably determine where the data came from. This is more specific than just identifying who sent an email message. Data origin authentication is specific at a lower level. The system receiving the data can clearly identify and authenticate that the data came from another particular system.

In the U.S. mail system, data origin authentication would be the equivalent of being able to identify that a sack of mail received at the local post office and identified as coming from the regional post office actually came from the regional post office. In a computer information system using TCP/IP as the transport protocol, each packet is identified with the IP address of the sending device. Data origin authentication, then, might check that IP address against a list of possible addresses for the system that supposedly sent the packet.

- **Confidentiality.** There are two aspects of confidentiality. One is the protection of data content during data transmission, which involves keeping the content of the data stream private from attackers. This is usually accomplished using encryption. The second aspect is protection from traffic analysis. To have this type of confidentiality, an attacker must be prevented from figuring out the source and destination of the traffic, its frequency, its length, or other characteristics. In this form of confidentiality, not only is my message private, but to whom I'm sending it is also a secret.

- **Discretionary access controls.** Discretionary access controls provide the capability to limit and control access to systems, applications, and resources. Each person trying to gain access must first be authenticated, and then authorization must be given to access the resource, depending on some feature of the person's identity such as group membership. Each resource can then limit access according to group membership or user ID. The concept of discretionary access controls is part of the process of authorization described previously.

> **Note**
> In the ever-changing world of security, we often hear or read terms for which we don't have a definition. A good source of general definitions, concepts, and links to more information is AOL's Webopedia, available at http://aol.webopedia.com.

For More Information

This chapter introduced many concepts and techniques that are explained more thoroughly in other chapters of this book. The following list should serve as a reference for you in locating this information.

For more information on encryption and checksums, see Chapter 2, "Cryptology Introduction," and Chapter 3, "New Protocols, Products, and APIs."

For specific information on IPSec, see Chapter 16, "Securing the Network Using Distributed Security Services."

Information on the use of certificates in a Public Key Infrastructure can be found in Chapter 4, "Public Key Infrastructure (PKI)," while implementing a public key Infrastructure using Windows 2000 Certificate Services can be found in Chapter 17, "Enterprise Public Key Infrastructure."

Authentication as implemented in Windows 2000, including NTLM and Kerberos, is covered in Chapter 7, "User Authentication."

The specifics of IPSec and Virtual Private Networks are covered in Chapter 15, "Secure Remote Access Options," and Chapter 16, "Securing the Network Using Distributed Security Services."

Summary

This chapter explained basic security terms and concepts. It was not meant to be a primer on information systems and their security for the neophyte; rather, it was a simple introduction for those information systems administrators and managers whose education and employment has not provided it.

Where appropriate, the chapter also introduced some of the features and techniques by which Windows 2000 incorporates or allows the implementation of security. Finally, references stating where to find more information within this book were presented.

In the next chapter, "Cryptology Introduction," various techniques for fulfilling these concepts by protecting data will be explored.

2

Cryptology Introduction

CRYPTOLOGY IS A MATHEMATICAL SCIENCE THAT INCLUDES both *cryptography* (hiding the meaning of a message) and *cryptanalysis* (discovering the meaning of a message).

Cryptography began as the science of disguising or encoding words so they would not be readable by unauthorized persons. Today, it encompasses a range of techniques that provide a scientific approach to information security. The practice of cryptography includes the use of techniques that provide the following:

- Information confidentiality (Can the information be kept secret?)
- Data integrity (Can you be sure the data isn't changed?)
- Entity authentication (Are you really who you say you are?)
- Data origin authentication (Did the information really come from you?)

Cryptography includes the creation of mathematical algorithms that change the appearance of a message so it cannot be directly understood except by those authorized to do so. A cryptographic algorithm does many things. In the oldest and simplest meaning, it takes *cleartext*—that is, text that you and I can read—and uses a secret component to scramble it so you can't read it. The scrambled text is called *ciphertext*. *Encryption* is the scrambling process. *Decryption* uses the secret component, often called a *cryptovariable*, to unscramble the message.

Cryptanalysis is the process of breaking or cracking scrambled messages without knowing the secret or algorithm and sometimes without knowing either. Because today's algorithms rely on a large number of potential keys used with known algorithms, cryptanalysis is also defined as the process of determining the correct decryption key for a specific ciphertext.

This chapter presents a brief look at the history of cryptology, defines common cryptographic terms, and briefly introduces modern cryptographic algorithms and methods of attack. Its purpose is not to provide a large number of complex mathematical formulae or enough detail or pseudo code to implement the process, but to provide information that will allow an easier understanding of technologies specific to the Windows 2000 environment. My apologies to those mathematicians for whom precise formulae equate to the simplest and most exact explanation—for most of us, such formulae only create an unnecessary barrier to understanding.

Information specific to Windows 2000 will be presented in later chapters.

Historical Background

Until the 1970s, cryptanalysis was primarily a function of diplomatic and military groups. During World War II, a full-time cryptographic force was established, and President Truman later created the National Security Agency. However, scrambling data to confuse one's enemies was by no means a new idea at that time.

Picture yourself as a Roman general fighting ancient Celtic bands in the far-off land of Gaul. You need to get information to your lieutenants. "Marcus, attack their left flank! Franco, move your troops to the east—don't attack until you see the whites of their eyes! Esmeralda, I'll be at your side before the moon rises over the…" (Well, you get the picture.)

How do you get the word out? You have runners, but they might be captured and tortured. Write the message down? Certainly most of these heathens don't know Latin, do they? You must be sure that any intercepted message cannot be understood.

Obfuscated information on Roman troop movements is among some of the first-known examples of cryptography. Historical evidence shows that Romans relied on secret algorithms to hide data. Allies agreed on the algorithm so they could communicate. Enemies didn't know the algorithm, so they couldn't translate intercepted messages.

In fact, some evidence places the origin of message-hiding in Egypt 4,000 years ago, and some historians claim that seventh-century Arabs may have been the first to write about cryptanalysis as a science. However, Caesar's Cipher—a simple alphabetic substitution—usually gets credited as the earliest formal algorithm. This cipher replaces each letter in the alphabet with the letter, for example, three letters to the right.

(Other ways of rearranging the alphabet were also used.) To make it easy to encrypt or decrypt using this algorithm, a key was created by writing out the new alphabet below a copy of the old. For the preceding example, the key would look like this:

a b c d e f g h i j k l m n o p q r s t u v w x y z

d e f g h i j k l m n o p q r s t u v w x y z a b c

Thus, a simple sentence like "attack from their right flank" becomes "dwwdfn iurp wkhlu uljkw iodqn." Only one copy of the alphabet key is made. Because of this single alphabet key, Caesar's Cipher is the first monoalphabetic substitution algorithm.

As simple as this seems and as easy by today's standards as it is to crack, remember that there are 26 factorial—or 403,291,461,126,606,000,000,000,000—ways to arrange the 26 letters of the alphabet. All but one of these yields a nonstandard alphabet. In ancient Rome, discovering which way the alphabet was arranged presented a formidable exercise.

Other simple substitution or replacement algorithms were also used in ancient times. A special alphabet was created by replacing each letter with some calculated value. Writing a message was simply a matter of using this new "alphabet." To the enemy, it was unintelligible.

What's in an !

The use of an exclamation mark (!) after a number denotes the factorial expression of that number. For example, 5! = 5 × 4 × 3 × 2 × 1. The factorial of an argument (n) multiplies all the integers less than or equal to n. In general:

$$n! = n \times (n\text{-}1) \times (n\text{-}2) \dots 3 \times 2 \times 1.$$

An Early Cipher Device

One of the first recorded hardware-based encryption algorithms consisted of a long strip of paper and a stick of wood. You can try this yourself. Cut a strip of paper and spiral it around a stick of wood. (A pencil will do.) Write your message down the side of the paper-covered stick of wood. Unwrap the paper and try to decipher the message. For two people to exchange messages in this way, each one needs to have a stick of wood with the exact same circumference. This "stick and strip of paper" algorithm was used in ancient Sparta in the fifth century B.C. The stick of wood was called a *scytale*, or cipher device.

If you'd like to learn more about the history of cryptography, read the book *The Code Breakers: The Comprehensive Story of Secret Communications from Ancient Times to the Internet* by David Kahn (Scribner, 1996).

Today's Cryptographic Algorithms

To help you understand the protocols used with Windows 2000 and to help you make intelligent choices when securing your networks, you need to learn the basics of two types of cryptographic algorithms: symmetric key cryptography and asymmetric key cryptography.

Symmetric Key Cryptography

Symmetric key cryptography uses the principal of a shared secret; that is, the same key is used to both encrypt and decrypt the message. Generally, the algorithm—or how the data are scrambled—is well known.

Each instance of communication between two or more users is known as a *session*. Two different names—*session key* or *secret key*—are used to describe the key used during the session. This key, or *cryptovariable*, is used to make the data unreadable by any unauthorized person or process because knowledge of the key allows decryption. Without the cryptovariable, it should be impossible to decode the message.

You probably use symmetric algorithms without even knowing it. You use them during the user ID and password logon process to access your email and, in their simplest version, to lock the front door to your house when you leave and unlock it when you return.

Let's look at an example of how this might be used to encrypt data that may cross a network. We'll use those two champions of security, Bob and Alice.

Bob wants to send a message to Alice but doesn't want anyone else to know what he's telling her. Bob and Alice agree that, for all communications, they will use the secret key !@#$%^A&)(zT*&. Because this and all the words they will send to each other can be expressed as binary numbers, they can be scrambled and unscrambled in a mathematical calculation.

Bob never took graduate mathematics and doesn't care to learn it. No problem. Bob has a *magic box* that will do the calculation for him. Bob takes his message and the secret key and places them in the hopper of his magic box. The scrambled result is sent to Alice. Alice receives the scrambled message. She puts it, along with her copy of the secret key, in her magic box (it's identical to Bob's box) and receives the information Bob sent her. She composes a reply, places it and the secret key in the hopper, and sends the scrambled answer to Bob.

Magic Boxes

Today, when we speak of a *magic box*, we are referring to the implementation of a mathematical algorithm. There have been many cryptographic devices throughout history, however, including the Enigma engine of the Germans during World War II and a ciphering device created in the eighteenth century by Thomas Jefferson. Jefferson's device was a stack of 26 disks. The alphabet was printed around the edge of each disk, but each disk's alphabet was in a different order. To encode a message, 25 of the disks were rotated a standard distance. (The distance can be thought of as the cryptovariable.) Next, a bar was placed over the first letter of the message on the top disk. Finally, all the letters down the side of the stack, one from each disk, were written down. The bar placement and copy steps were repeated for each letter of the message. Thus, each letter of the message was represented by 25 characters. Decryption was accomplished by realigning the bar and matching up the letters to regain the original letters.

Fred, however, intercepts the message. To Fred, the message is garbage. Fred is resourceful, though; he knows there are a limited number of magic boxes. In fact, with a little checking, he learns which brand Alice and Bob are using and buys one of his own.

Now Fred has a magic box like Alice and Bob, but he doesn't have their secret key, so he can't immediately process the message and learn what it says. He doesn't give up, though. He begins the process of trying to guess the secret key. With any luck, Bob and Alice chose a key that is so large and hard to guess that Fred will never figure it out, or at least the data will be old and worthless when he does.

Because Alice's answer is missing (Bob never received it because Fred intercepted it), Bob and Alice decide to change their secret key and agree that it would probably be a good idea to do so periodically anyway. The time period between such key changes is known as the *cryptoperiod*.

This process is symmetric key cryptography. The same key is used for encryption and decryption. Isn't this like the ancient stick and paper algorithm or like Caesar's Cipher? Yes and no. Like the ancients, Bob and Alice rely on a shared secret (the dimensions of the stick or the offset in the alphabet), but unlike them, Bob and Alice's algorithm is well known (anyone can purchase the magic box).

Well-known algorithms are used today for two reasons. First, many people can study a well-known algorithm, and its faults can be found. If there is something about the algorithm that makes it easy to crack, the algorithm can be modified or its use dropped. A second reason for using well-known algorithms is that any secret algorithm will eventually be discovered. If the secrecy of the message relies on the secrecy of the algorithm, as soon as the algorithm is known, so is the secret. Today's well-known algorithms rely on the existence of a shared secret, or cryptovariable.

An example of a symmetric key algorithm used today is the Data Encryption Standard (DES), which will be discussed later in this chapter. Its key is 56 bits long. Is a 56-bit key large enough to keep a DES-encrypted message a secret? In June of 1997, a large number of computers were set up to work in parallel. They cracked the DES key in 140 days. DES was cracked in 45 days in 1998. It was cracked in a matter of hours in 1999. Today, DES is not considered a difficult algorithm to crack. A stronger variant of DES, Triple-DES, uses DES three times with three different, unrelated keys.

Asymmetric Key Cryptography

The basic premise of *asymmetric key cryptography* is the use of two different keys. One is used to encrypt; the other is used to decrypt. Think of a lock box with two keys. Each key is different, but either key can open the box or lock the box. If you and I each have one of the keys and I use my key to lock the box and send you the box, you can use your key to open the box.

Digital communications can use a *key pair*, known as the *public key/private key pair*. The *public key* is available, well, publicly. It can be freely distributed, included in a directory, recorded in an application, or enclosed in some communication. The *private key* should be known to only its owner.

In asymmetric key cryptography, Bob and Alice each have their own public key/private key pair. Neither Bob nor Alice (nor anyone else) knows or can get a copy of the other's private key. They each know the other's public key.

Bob uses Alice's public key to encrypt a message to Alice. (Once again, he has a magic box to do the actual math for him.) Alice receives the message and uses her private key and magic box to unscramble it. She uses Bob's public key to encrypt a response to Bob and sends it on its way.

It is important to note that, because Bob used Alice's public key, only Alice can decrypt the message because only she possesses her private key. Thus, he *must* use her public key because the key is part of a set. Only the corresponding private key can unlock the message encrypted with the public key. This is true of any public key/private key algorithm; only the corresponding keys can be used as encrypt/decrypt pairs. This use of public keys to encrypt messages and private keys to decrypt them is often referred to as *sealing*. Sealing is used to ensure that messages remain private.

Once again, however, Fred intercepts Alice's response to Bob, but because he does not have Bob's private key, he cannot decrypt the message. But can't Fred hack the private key—that is, guess it or deduce it? Although it is possible, this is much more difficult than determining a single symmetric key.

The opposite use of public key/private key pairs—that is, using an entity's public key to decrypt something the entity encrypted with his or her own private key—can also be done. It is often used to prove the identity of the entity or to prove that the message received was actually sent by the person who claimed to be sending it. (I will discuss this in greater detail in the "Digital Signatures" section.)

An example of such digital signing using a public key/private key pair can be seen in Web-based credit card transactions. Your browser issues the "Who goes there?" challenge and the server replies. Your browser takes a second step to verify a secure communication. Your browser says, "Prove it." The server answers by using its private key to encrypt a response. The answer and its encrypted version are returned to your browser. Your browser can use the server's known public key to decrypt the encrypted version to see if it matches the message. If it finds a match, it knows it has the right server.

Where does your browser get the server's public key? This information is in the form of a certificate that the server can provide in its answer to the question "Who goes there?" The certificate contains a lot of information including

- The name of the certificate issuer
- The name of the certificate holder
- The public key of the subject
- Time stamps (the actual time that some process, such as the certificate issuance, occurred)

So couldn't some unscrupulous person make up a certificate? Well, he could, but your browser is looking for a certificate signed by a party it trusts—the certificate issuer. Your browser will validate a certificate signed by a third-party Certificate Authority (CA), such as Verisign. You can set your browser to accept different CAs.

Public Key Infrastructure

The way that public key/private key pairs are implemented in your organization is referred to as your *Public Key Infrastructure(PKI)*. A Public Key Infrastructure can include a CA hosted by the corporation, by a third party, by trading partners, or by some combination of these.

Chapter 4, "Public Key Infrastructure (PKI)," covers public keys in more detail.

Digital Signatures

Bob doesn't always need to encrypt his message to Alice. Perhaps he wants to share information that doesn't need to be kept a secret. However, sometimes Alice would like to be able to verify that a message is really coming from Bob. This can be accomplished using a *digital signature*.

Bob uses a special algorithm or hash on the message to reduce it to a fixed size, or *message digest*. He then uses his private key to encrypt his message digest. He sends this encrypted message digest and the message to Alice. Alice hashes the message using the same algorithm and creates a new message digest. She uses Bob's public key to decrypt the encrypted message digest he sent and thus regenerates Bob's original message digest. When she compares the two message digests, they should match exactly. If there is a match, she knows the message came from Bob, and she also knows the message has not been changed. This message digest is known as a *digital signature*.

Try it, You'll Like it

Want to play with certificates and see how they work? You can obtain a trial certificate (good for a few days), which you can use to send secure email, from `http://www.verisign.com`.

Verisign often has interesting documentation and white papers and sometimes offers trial server certificates so you can learn how to secure transactions on a test Web server.

Digital Encoding

Another way of talking about today's cryptographic algorithms is to look at the two types of ciphers used: stream ciphers and block ciphers.

Stream Ciphers

Stream ciphers are continuous streams of plaintext represented by 1s and 0s. The bits of a stream cipher are encrypted one bit at a time. A *keystream generator* (some hardware device or black box) uses a key and an algorithm to produce a seemingly random stream of 1s and 0s that are added modulo 2, bit by bit, to plaintext to create the ciphertext stream. The result of a modular function is the remainder of integer division. (Integer division, as you probably know, does not express the result in decimals; it leaves the result in integer form.) So 7 divided by 2 is 3. 7 modulo 2 is 1 (the remainder of the integer division). 6 modulo 3 is 0.

Because the bits in my plaintext and my keystream can only be 1s and 0s, the largest number is 2. Thus, 2 modulo 2 is 0, 1 modulo 2 is 1, and 0 modulo 2 is 0. The ciphertext can be interpreted (unscrambled back to plaintext) by adding the bits of the ciphertext with the keystream bits.

To understand how a stream cipher works, imagine the tossing of a penny. First it might land heads up, then tails, then tails, then heads, and so on. Pretend that heads up represents a 1 and tails a 0. If I have a message that has been encoded into its binary representation, I toss the penny once for each bit in the message and add (modulo 2) the resultant 1 or 0 to the next bit in the message. If the first bit is a 1 and the penny toss is heads, first add the two numbers to get 2, then divide this modulo 2 to get the result 0. If my message, which is

    1 0 1 0 1 1 1 0

This is added modulo 2 to the results of my penny toss, which bit by bit and toss by toss is

    1 1 0 0 1 1 0 1

The result becomes

    0 1 1 0 0 0 1 1

XOR

Those of you familiar with logic tables will recognize the pattern described in this section. The results of combining 1s and 0s modulo 2 is the same as the results of XORing the bits. By understanding the process using modulo, you can translate your understanding to larger numbers. Thus, you might read an analysis of some cryptographic processes that require a combination of numbers, the result of which is processed modulo 64. The important point to make with stream ciphers is that the result of the combination of the cleartext with the keystream bits can be decrypted if you can reproduce the keystream bits.

If I have recorded the results of the penny toss (my keystream bits) and have given them to you along with the result, you can easily decode the message by adding modulo 2 the result with the keystream bits. Of course, the generation of the keystream bits is not done by tossing pennies; it is generated. To be able to encrypt a message on one computer and decrypt it on another, you must be able to reproduce the keystream bits exactly.

Although this process might seem straightforward, a few conditions are necessary for message sending and receiving:

- The equipment must use the same identical algorithms to produce the keystreams for encryption and decryption.

- The same cryptovariable must be used, and the machines must start in the same state (have the same settings). (See the sidebar "I'm in a State of Confusion…" for more information on states.)

- The system used for decryption must have knowledge of where the message begins.

Managing the distribution of the cryptovariable is known as key management. We will discuss key management in greater detail in Chapter 4.

Block Ciphers

Unlike stream ciphers, which work on one bit at a time, *block ciphers* encrypt a fixed-size block of data one block at a time and usually are generated in software. The block often corresponds to the word size of the computer used. For example, if the word size of the computer used is 8-bit ASCII, the block would be 8 bits long. In any block cipher of n bits, there are 2^n possible input blocks and output blocks. So for each 8-bit block, there would be 256 possible rearrangements of the bits. (Of course, one of them would be the original 8-bit block.) The relationship between each input and output block is considered a permutation or rearrangement. By definition, for any n items there are n! permutations.

I'm in a State of Confusion...

The word "state" is often used when discussing both logical and physical representations of equations, equipment, objects, and algorithms. Although we often think of a "state of mind" or a "state" in the United States, this kind of state represents a static definition of the item.

For example, if we consider a traffic light, we see that it has at least three states. Go (or green), stop (or red), and prepare to stop (or yellow). Its characteristics or properties might be defined differently depending on the state it is in. Likewise, the state of a computer before it is turned on is its "initial state."

To examine what this is like, use a smaller block size to make the number of permutations smaller. A good size block to use for our example is 3 (3 is used to make our problem simple; 3 would not be a good size to use for a block cipher). To take a 3-bit block and scramble it so you can't tell what it is, how many choices do you have? (Remember, the number of possible blocks from a single block of size n is 2^n; therefore, a block size of 3 translates into 2^3, or 8.) With only 3 bits, you can easily produce the results.

By definition, the number of bits in the output block must be the same as the number of bits in the input block. If the block is 101, then 101 can only become one of the following results:

000

001

010

011

100

110

111

If you then take each possible combination of the bits (the preceding list plus the original block) and prepare a table of possible permutations, it might look like Table 2.1.

Table 2.1   3-bit Block Cipher Table

Block	1	2	3	4	5	6	7
000	001	010	011	100	101	110	111
001	010	011	100	101	110	111	000
010	011	100	101	110	111	000	001
011	100	101	110	111	000	001	010
100	101	110	111	000	001	010	011
101	110	111	000	001	010	011	100
110	111	000	001	010	011	100	101
111	000	001	010	011	100	101	110

You could use the table to encrypt blocks by deciding to find your input block in the first column and then move over some number of columns to pick the output block. The number of columns you might go over could be called your key. If you and I decide the key will be 5, then 101 will always be 010, 110 will be 011, 111 will be 100, and so on.

If your message to me is "101000100111", you would first divide the message into blocks to obtain 101 000 100 111. Then, using the preceding table and the agreed-upon key, you would produce the output 010 101 001 100. To decrypt, I need to work your algorithm in reverse. 010 becomes 101 (I find 010 in the sixth column and look up my result in the first), 101 becomes 000, and so on.

Before you decide that this is trivial to crack, remember that although you and I know how to generate the table, how long the block is (3 bits), and what the key is (5 columns over), the person seeking to decode our message knows none of these. In this example, of course, the possibilities are not infinite, and every possibility could be tried until the result was found.

A useful block cipher would incorporate a larger block size (making the table much larger and the possibilities for its arrangement larger) as well as other techniques to prevent (or at least prolong) decryption.

Common Cryptographic Algorithms

An administrator or manager often must determine which encryption method to choose for a given process. The abbreviated descriptions that follow can assist in this choice by allowing even the novice to identify what kind of algorithm they are, where they can be used, and information regarding the complexity of their processing. Complete discussion of the relative merits of various algorithms and an extensive description of the mathematics involved is beyond the scope of this book.

DES

DES is a block cipher adopted in 1977 by the National Bureau of Standards (now the National Institute of Standards and Technology) as a Federal Information Processing Standard (FIPS). As we have discussed, DES encryption consists of multiple steps that involve 64-bit blocks of plaintext and a 56-bit key. Triple-DES (3DES) uses multiple keys and applies the DES algorithm three times.

How does DES work? A very complex algorithm is used to encrypt the text. The following steps give you the general idea:

1. The 64-bit plaintext is scrambled.

2. A complex function is applied 16 times using the key and the scrambled plaintext to produce a 64-bit output.

3. The two halves of the 64-bit output are swapped.

4. This result is operated on again to produce the 64-bit ciphertext.

Where Did DES Come from?

When the National Bureau of Standards (now the National Institute of Standards and Technology) first requested a proposal for a public cryptographic system in 1973, nothing suitable was submitted. In 1974, IBM proposed the Lucifer system, which eventually was adopted and became known as the Data Encryption Standard (DES). A contest is currently being held to find a more secure replacement algorithm for DES.

Although DES uses a key that is 64 bits long, 8 of these bits are parity-check bits (for simple error detection), so the effective length is 56 bits. The number of possible keys is therefore 2^{56}, or approximately 72,000,000,000,000,000 keys.

If, to crack DES, you attempt to try all possible variables (a brute force or exhaustion attack), you can begin to appreciate why it originally was thought that breaking DES was impossible. Just a few years ago, scientists thought it would take a very long time—even years. However, DES has been broken on several occasions, most recently in 22 hours 15 minutes by the Electronic Frontier Foundation's "Deep Crack" in a combined effort with distributed.net.

What we must keep in mind is that the Electronic Frontier Foundation's "Deep Crack" found only one key and still took more than 22 hours to do so. Breaking a longer code or one with multiple session keys used during its transmission would have taken longer.

But would the information gained be of any use once determined? It depends on the situation. If, for example, a person sent a message to a drug dealer to meet him or her in three hours, and you would like to catch that person buying drugs, the fact that you can decode the message in 22 hours is meaningless. The very fact that the seemingly impossible task of hacking DES can be accomplished, however, points out the need for longer keys and more advanced algorithms.

Cracking DES

The story of how the seemingly impossible task of cracking DES was accomplished is interesting. The Electronic Frontier Foundation (http://www.eff.org) is a nonprofit education organization dedicated to protecting rights and promoting liberty online. If you want to learn more about how the organization cracked DES, see the recently published book *Cracking DES: Secrets of Encryption Research, Wiretap Politics and Chip Design (How Federal Agencies Subvert Privacy)*, Electronic Frontier Foundation (O'Reilly, 1998).

http://www.distributed.net is a clearinghouse for distributed computing projects. One such project is to make available the computing resources of many machines.

If you are interested in the current status of DES hacks or in more information on attacks against the DES algorithm, visit the DES challenge site at http://www.rsasecurity.com/rsalabs/challenges.

For information on a hardware accelerator used in cracking DES, visit http://www.eff.org/descracker.html.

Proposed Replacements for DES

Several different encryption algorithms have been proposed as replacement algorithms for DES including IDEA and Blowfish.

IDEA

The International Data Encryption Algorithm (IDEA) is a symmetric block cipher that has been proposed as a replacement for DES. Developed by Xuejia Lai and James Massey, IDEA uses a 128-bit key to encrypt data in blocks of 64 bits. It is included in Pretty Good Privacy (PGP), which is both shareware and a commercial product that can be used to encrypt email. The IDEA algorithm steps are as follows:

1. The input is divided into four 16-bit subblocks.
2. Eight rounds of three operations on the subblocks produce a final set of four 16-bit subblocks. Each round uses six 16-bit subkeys.
3. The four subblocks are concatenated into a 64-bit block using four subkeys.
4. The 52 16-bit subkeys used in the encryption are generated from the 128-bit key.

Blowfish

Blowfish was developed by Bruce Schneier to run on 32-bit microprocessors quickly, to use limited memory (5KB), to use a variable key (up to 448 bits), and to be easily implemented. It is a symmetric block cipher that encrypts 64-bit blocks.

Ron Rivest Algorithms

Ron Rivest developed numerous symmetric key algorithms including RC2 and RC5.

RC2 is a symmetric key algorithm developed to run on 16-bit microprocessors. It uses plaintext and ciphertext blocks of 64 bits and a variable key size (8 to 1,024 bits). It is used in S/MIME with 40-, 64-, and 128-bit key sizes.

RC5 is a fast, simple algorithm that operates on full words of data. Its simple structure and low memory requirements make it suitable for running on microprocessors. Because it has as its parameters word length, number of rounds, and key length, it is adaptable to processors of different word lengths (16-, 32-, and 64-bit). In addition, its key length (0 to 2,040 bits) and number of rounds (0 to 255) in the calculation are variable, making for more rounds, higher security, and less speed. RC5 is incorporated into RSA Data Security Inc.'s BSAFE, JSAFE, and S/MAIL products.

Versions of RC5 are designated as RC5-word/number-of-rounds/number-of-bytes-in-secret-key. The nominal version suggested by Rivest is RC5-32/12/16, or RC5 with a 32-bit word length using 12 rounds and a 128-bit key.

CAST-128

CAST-128, one of a number of symmetric algorithms developed by Carlisle Adams and Stafford Tavares, uses a variable key of 40 bits to 128 bits. Sixteen rounds of calculation operate on 64-bit blocks of plaintext using two subkeys in each round to produce 64-bit blocks of ciphertext. Four different functions are used and vary depending on the round.

Diffie-Hellman

The Diffie-Hellman Key Exchange Algorithm was the first published public-key algorithm, and it is used by a number of commercial products. The algorithm, whose purpose is to allow the secure exchange of a session key, specifies only the key exchange technique. Its security is based on the difficulty of computing discrete logarithms, especially for large prime numbers.

RSA

RSA, developed by Ron Rivest, Adi Shamir, and Len Adleman, is the widely accepted and implemented public-key encryption algorithm. Its security relies on its use of the factors of very large primes. Just as RSA has publicly challenged the cracking of the DES algorithm, it also offers challenges for the factoring of ciphers with large key sizes including their own. Information on how the RSA-155 challenge and others were solved can be found at `http://www.rsasecurity.com/reslabs/challenges`.

No Script Kiddies Here

Factoring (finding the keys) for RSA-155 was not a problem hacked by script kiddies (individuals who rely on GUI-based scripts to do their hacking for them) or rogue hackers. Serious computing power, time (7.4 months), and mathematical expertise were required. One half of the 7.4 months, the equivalent of 8,000 MIPS years, was spent on one part of the process. It involved 160 175-400MHz SGI and Sun workstations, 120 300-450MHz Pentium II PCs, 8 250MHz SGI Origin 2000 processors, and four 500MHz Digital/Compaq boxes. This process produced a matrix (6.7 million columns × 6.7 million rows) that was then processed for 224 CPU hours on a Cray C916 using 3.2GB of memory. In comparison, the factoring of RSA-140 took just nine weeks.

Hash Functions

Hash functions take a message of any length and map it to a fixed-length sequence. A one-way hash function cannot be reversed; that is, a one-way hash can produce the same sequence for multiple input messages. Well-known hash algorithms include:

- **MD5.** MD5 (RFC 1321), developed by Ron Rivest, was until recently the most widely used secure hash algorithm. It produces a 128-bit message digest from a message of any length. MD5 is now considered vulnerable to brute-force attacks.

- **MD4.** MD4 (RFC 1320) was a precursor to MD5.

- **SHA-1.** SHA-1, the secure hash algorithm developed by the National Institute of Standards and Technology, is a federal information processing standard. It is based on MD4. SHA-1 creates a 150-bit message digest from a message of less than 2^{64} bits. SHA-1 is considered to be more resistant to brute force attacks than MD4 or MD5 due to the larger message digest.

Note

A hash algorithm's vulnerability can be measured by the difficulty of producing a given message digest (2^{128} for MD5 and 2^{160} for SHA-1) and/or the difficulty of producing two messages that have the same digest (2^{64} for MD5 and 2^{80} for SHA-1). A hash with a larger message digest, therefore, is stronger.

- **RIPEMD-160.** RIPEMD-128 was developed by the European RACE Integrity Primitives Evaluation (RIPE) project. Later, due to published attacks on MD4, MD5, and RIPEMD-128, H. Dobbertin and former RIPE members updated the algorithm. RIPEMD-160 produces a 160-bit message digest from a message of arbitrary length. Although derived from MD4 and therefore similar to MD5, RIPEMD-160, like SHA-1, was developed to be resistant to known attacks. It is more complex in function than SHA-1. Although all three algorithms perform well on a 32-bit processor, RIPEMD-160 is slower than MD-5.

- **MAC.** A Message Authentication Code (MAC) is created by a function using a message and a secret key to produce a small, fixed-length value. It is often known as the cryptographic checksum. The MAC is appended to a message. The intended recipient receives the message and the MAC and can verify that the message is intact by creating his or her own MAC from the message and the key and then comparing the received MAC and the calculated MAC. In addition, because no one else knows the secret key, the recipient knows the message is from the sender. A MAC function does not need to be reversible.

- **HMAC.** The traditional MAC is produced by using a block cipher. HMAC (RFC 2104) is created by using a secret key and an existing hash function. HMAC has several advantages over the traditional MAC. Hash functions generally are faster than symmetric block ciphers. In addition, code for hash function is readily available, and there are no export restrictions on cryptographic hash functions. HMAC can utilize a variety of hash functions including newer hash functions in the future. Its security is directly related to the security of the hash function used. HMAC is used in Internet protocols such as SSL and is implemented in IP Security (IPSec).

Future Promise: Elliptic Curve Cryptography

An elliptic curve is a collection of points in an equation of the form $y^2 = x^3 + ax + b$. This collection of points can be used as keys in complex cryptographic algorithms such as Diffie-Hellman. Some cryptographers claim that the computation of these keys is faster and yet the breaking of these keys would be harder. Others say enough research has not been done.

Other Forms of Obfuscation

Other ways of hiding information are also used, although not commonly by operating systems. One such method is *steganography*, the process of hiding messages by placing data within some normally transmitted data stream. Many objects, when transmitted across the Internet or in a radio broadcast, include extraneous bits of data, or noise. Typically, the noise is filtered at the receiving end. With steganography, the extra bits are used to transport the message. If you are expecting a message transported in this manner, you simply filter out the image to recover your message.

Another form of message-hiding is to place hidden meaning behind the seemingly innocent radio broadcast of a baseball game. If I know the code, I get the message. If I don't, I just hear a baseball game. Spy novels abound with tales of the use of microdots that contain thousands of words in a single micron-size chip.

Methods of Attack

To crack, or determine, the secret key or keys used to encrypt a message, several techniques can be used. Although it is beyond the scope of this book to discuss these techniques in detail, they include

- **Brute force or exhaustion attack.** This technique tries all possible variables.
- **Analytic attack.** This technique uses the weakness in an algorithm. Thus, the complexity is reduced through algebraic manipulation.
- **Statistical attack.** This technique uses a statistically determined weakness in the design. (For example, the possibility that the bios of a keystream generator are more likely to place 1s than 0s in the keystream.)
- **Implementation attack.** Although the algorithm might be very strong, this technique looks at the implementation of the algorithm for weaknesses. In 1995, a Berkeley student discovered that the Netscape implementation of encryption, although it uses a 128-bit cryptovariable, was using a seed value that was a function of the system time. Thus, using a system with a similar clock, he was able to generate keys and break the code.
- **Timing attack.** This technique attempts to determine a key by tracking how long it takes a computer to decrypt messages.

For More Information

This chapter introduced many concepts and techniques that are explained more thoroughly in other chapters of this book. The following list should serve as a referral source for you in locating this information.

For more information on asymmetric key algorithms, see Chapter 4, "Public Key Infrastructure (PKI)."

More details on Kerberos, a system that uses a symmetric key algorithm, are found in Chapter 5, "Kerberos in the RAW."

For Windows 2000 Kerberos implementation information, see Chapter 7, "User Authentication."

For information on Windows 2000 PKI, see Chapter 17, "Enterprise Public Key Infrastructure."

Summary

The study of cryptographic techniques is a large one. This chapter has briefly discussed the historical background of cryptography, has defined some terms, and has provided simple explanations for complicated processes. Its purpose was not to produce cryptologists, but to give some background for the uninitiated. This information can be used to provide reference and pointers to assist administrators and others in making choices during the implementation of services used in Windows 2000.

Although these choices are often made by policy, every administrator should know why it might be important to choose MD5 over MD4, why he should seek 128-bit encryption over 56-bit encryption, what the difference is between symmetric key algorithms and asymmetric key algorithms, and what the fuss is over DES.

Future chapters discuss the use of these algorithms by protocols and processes in Windows 2000. But first, we will look at new protocols, products, and APIs in Chapter 3.

3

New Protocols, Products, and APIs

T HE WINDOWS 2000 SERVER USES A LARGE ARRAY OF new protocols. However, many Windows NT 4.0 experts, a large number of whom are experienced administrators, have little experience with these protocols. This chapter introduces these protocols from a security perspective. Specifically, I will cover Web-related protocols, remote access protocols, secure dynamic DNS, IPSec, and Microsoft-specific protocols. If you are familiar with Windows NT, you will find some discussion of protocols and APIs with which you might already be acquainted.

Many of the protocols discussed in this chapter have corresponding Internet Engineering Task Force (IETF) Request for Comment (RFC) documents available for further study. Wherever possible, the RFC document is listed after the name of the RFC protocol in this chapter's heads. (Note that this chapter assumes an understanding of the basic networking protocols including the OSI Data Networking Model and the TCP/IP Logical Model.) Later chapters explore how Windows 2000 uses these protocols and the networks of which Windows 2000 is a part.

Just the Facts, Ma'am

Sgt. Friday's famous line helped calm witnesses and get to the crux of the matter. To get the facts about this chapter's protocols in more detail, visit http://www.ietf.org. For a handy site at which you can search by RFC number or by protocol name, visit http://www.rfc-editor.org/rfcsearch.html.

RFCs: Virtual Documentation and Standards

Requests for Comments (RFCs) were originally started in 1969 as a series of notes about computer communications including networking protocols, programs, concepts, and the results of meetings. These notes described processes followed on the Internet (then known as ARPAnet). Currently, all specifications defined by the IETF are published as RFCs.

RFC documents come in types or subseries. Documents are considered standards, drafts, proposals, or informational. You can usually tell the status of a document by looking at the three digits included in the name. STD indicates that the document is a standard protocol used on the Internet. FYI indicates that it is merely informational. BCP indicates that the RFC represents a statement of principle or conclusion about the best way to perform an IETF function. Other documents might be considered experimental.

RFCs are live documents and, as such, are continually revised. RFC 2026, "The Internet Standards Process—Revision 3" defines the Internet Standards Process and describes the process by which RFCs become standards. RFCs that are standards are listed in RFC 2600 (March 2000) and can be found at `ftp.isi.edu/in-notes/std/std1.txt`. To determine the status of a particular RFC, visit the IETF site.

To learn about activities of the IETF, including draft announcements and status, email *ietf-announce-request@ietf.org* and type the word **subscribe** in the subject line and message body.

Web-Related Protocols

Windows 2000 Server and Advanced Server include a copy of Internet Information Server V (IISV) that can be Secure Sockets Layer (SSL)–enabled. All versions of the operating system provide Web access via Internet Explorer, which also is SSL-enabled. The proposed standard Transport Layer Security (TLS) is also provided with IIS.

Secure Sockets Layer and HTTPS

Secure Sockets Layer (SSL) Protocol 3.0 was designed by Netscape to provide server authentication, data encryption, message integrity, and optional client authentication for TCP/IP connections. It requires an SSL-enabled server and an SSL-enabled browser. You can tell whether your browser is using SSL by looking for an s added to the `http` in your browser's address line. You can see this `https` when making a credit card purchase over the Web, for example.

Without SSL, most Web transactions, including credit card transactions, would travel over the Internet in the clear. The SSL protocol sits between the application layer and the transport layer in the TCP/IP protocol stack and is not limited to one protocol. Figure 3.1 shows this arrangement and also indicates that the SSL layer is broken into two layers: a message layer and a record layer. Each of these layers is in turn responsible for specific parts of the protocol.

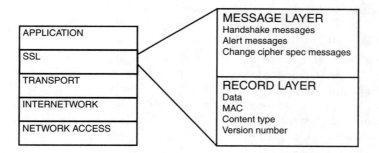

Figure 3.1   The Secure Sockets Layer protocol stack.

Server Authentication

So how does SSL work? Why is its use necessary? SSL is usually implemented as one-way server authentication. This is the opposite of the sentry challenging you at the gate. Instead, *you* get to issue the challenge. If you are going to give XYZ Company your credit card number, you want to be sure you are talking with a representative of XYZ Company. When you place a phone call or visit a restaurant or store, you feel comfortable that the person receiving your card number works for that company. But what if you are using the Internet? We've all heard about the exploits of slimy opera-tors who spoof, or masquerade as, someone else's Web site. We'd like to know that the server with which we are communicating is what it claims to be.

SSL uses public key cryptography to enable the positive identification of the Web site to which you are connecting. This thwarts the would-be imposter. I will discuss such public key cryptography in Chapter 4, "Public Key Infrastructure (PKI)."

Data Encryption

After server authentication, the browser and server negotiate the encryption algorithm, the Message Authentication Code (MAC) algorithm, and cryptographic key to be used for all data. As discussed in Chapter 2, "Cryptology Introduction," the browser passes a secret encrypted with the server's public key to the server, and the server uses its private key to decrypt it. This secret becomes the key used to encrypt all communi-cation between the server and the browser for this session. The session key is not reused. Because each session gets its own key, the effectiveness of a brute force attack is diminished. An attacker would have to capture the encrypted key, hack it, and use it while the current session is open.

Why don't the server and browser continue to use the server's public and private keys? Using key pairs is a cumbersome operation and slows down communication. (Public key/private key encryption is up to 1,000 times as slow as symmetric encryp-tion.) Thus, after authentication, a single key algorithm is used. To learn about single key algorithms, see Chapter 5, "Kerberos in the RAW."

Message Integrity

SSL can use both MD5 and SHA in tandem. To protect data, a MAC is computed using the MAC secret, the sequence number, the message length, the message content, and two fixed-character strings. The MAC secret is produced, as are the encryption keys, from a hashing of the session key with random numbers. The sequence number, of course, allows for the detection of message reordering, deletion, or substitution. The MAC itself is encrypted. Thus, an attacker would have to first break the encryption algorithm and then the MAC.

Client Authentication

Server authentication and data encryption are enough for most Web transactions. Public Web sites wanting to sell merchandise, however, are not the only spheres in which SSL is used. Many Web sites might want to ensure that they are providing confidential information to a select subset of people who connect to their sites. In this case, it is appropriate to insist on mutual authentication. Client authentication is thus optional with SSL, but it can be implemented.

To do so, a certificate must be issued to each client that wants to communicate with the secured server, and the server must make a challenge of its own. Client certificates can be obtained from a third-party Certificate Authority (CA), or your company might choose to host its own CA. Windows 2000 provides an optional CA that can be used for client, server, or mutual authentication. For more information on this CA, see Chapter 17, "Enterprise Public Key Infrastructure."

Transport Layer Security (TLS) Protocol (RFC 2246)

The Transport Layer Security (TLS) protocol, which is based on SSL, was developed to provide an Internet standard version of SSL. Like Netscape's SSL, it provides privacy and data integrity for client/server applications. It can be used for all communications between applications.

TLS varies from SSL in that it offers a variable padding length during the encryption process. That is, during encryption, if a block of data does not fit the requirements of the algorithm, the block is often padded to some standard size. TLS can vary this process, making the protocol more difficult to attack.

TLS supports SSL exchange technologies with the exception of the government standard Fortezza. (Fortezza is a standard required by many government installations. If this is a standard your organization requires, TLS cannot be used in its current form) Although TLS supports similar technologies and performs similar functions, it does so in a different way than SSL. SSL and TLS are not interoperable. It is too early to determine whether TLS will be widely adopted and whether it will replace SSL.

From the Horse's Mouth

If you would like to learn directly from Netscape about SSL and find other Web security information, including a way to obtain a test certificate, visit the company's Web site at http://www.netscape.com/security/techbriefs/ssl.html.

Examining Certificates

To see a list of certificates that your browser, and thus you, trusts:

1. Access the Tools menu in Internet Explorer and click Internet Options.

2. Click the Content tab.

3. Click the Certificates or Publishers buttons to display the list.

The TLS protocol consists of two layers:

- A *handshake protocol*, which establishes connection security
- A *record protocol*, which provides connection security

The handshake protocol uses public key cryptography to authenticate peers and to establish connection security. Thus, the negotiation of the session-shared secret is secure. The TLS handshake protocol can be used to negotiate DES, RC4, or other symmetric cryptographic keys, although other protocols can be used.

Secure hash functions (SHA, MD5, and so on) are used to compute a keyed MAC used for message-integrity checks. The TLS record protocol fragments data into blocks (and might compress the data), applies the MAC, encrypts, and transmits. When the data is received, it is decrypted, verified, decompressed, and reassembled.

TLS is application-protocol independent and is designed to work with future public key and symmetric key encryption methods.

Remote Access Protocols

For as long as computers have existed, people have needed to access them remotely. Somehow, the very essence of the personal computer seemed to belie this. After all, it was personal, not shared; people were fascinated by having such direct access. The computer was not some impersonal, mysterious box that existed elsewhere; it was here and in your face. Suddenly, an individual could have the data present on his desktop instead of having to connect to a database elsewhere.

Businesses have matured and so has the PC. People still want the personal computer experience, but they need and want access to every bit of data there is. People want to be where they want to be, not necessarily where the data is. Companies and communities also have a need to work together on projects and to share data. Years ago, companies leased private lines to share data with remote branches or distant divisions. A few telecommuters and some offices used remote dial-up access. PCs were used in this process.

Enter the Internet. Companies could not fail to notice the reduction in cost if this public access network were to replace private or leased lines. However, there was a price to be paid: privacy and security. To reduce this price, there has been an explosion in protocols that attempt to allow the use of the Internet for secure communication between multiple points. Some of these protocols merely establish remote communication with optional authentication and encryption; others are designed to provide only secure communication. These protocols, and the hardware and software that use them, create virtual private networks (VPNs). (For information on virtual private networking with Windows 2000, see Chapter 15, "Secure Remote Access Options.") This section will discuss a number of these protocols.

Serial Line Internet Protocol (RFC 1055)

The Serial Line Internet Protocol (SLIP) is an older protocol that can be used for dial-up access. SLIP can only transport TCP/IP. To configure SLIP requires knowledge of IP addressing and addresses. SLIP also transmits the user's password unencrypted and has no error-correction handling.

Point-to-Point Protocol (RFC 1661)

The Point-to-Point Protocol (PPP) was designed for simple links to transport packets between peers. PPP provides a Link Control Protocol (LCP) that is used to agree on encapsulation format options, to handle limits on packet size, to detect looped-back link and other configuration errors, and to terminate the link. Peer authentication and normal function determination is optional.

PPP can use multiple protocols (TCP/IP, IPS/SPX, and NetBEUI), and it was designed to be easily configured. It enables defaults automatically and can self-configure by conversation with its peer: All you have to know is the phone number, user ID, and password. Communication is established first with LCP packets for configuring and testing the data link and then with Network Control Protocol (NCP) packets to choose and configure network-layer protocols.

If peer authentication is configured, PPP uses the Password Authentication Protocol (PAP) or Challenge-Handshake Authentication Protocol (CHAP).

Password Authentication Protocol

The Password Authentication Protocol (PAP) is used to verify that the user attempting a connection is authorized to do so. The server maintains a database of authorized users, and the information entered by the caller (the client) is compared to the database before a session between the client and the server can begin. The authentication algorithm does not encrypt the password, and it is passed in cleartext over the network.

It might be necessary to use this protocol to connect to remote access servers that do not support other more secure protocols or to allow the use of third-party remote access client software to connect to Windows 2000. Its use, however, is not recommended if other possibilities exist. The reason, of course, is that the password is passed in cleartext and therefore might be captured and used by unauthorized individuals to access network resources.

Challenge-Handshake Authentication Protocol (RFC 1994)

The Challenge-Handshake Authentication Protocol (CHAP) is used by PPP to verify the identity of the peer (caller). If required, authentication is accomplished upon link establishment and can be repeated afterwards. CHAP is also supported by Internet Information Server and the Windows 2000 Internet Authentication Service.

When using CHAP, the authenticator (the server) sends a challenge to the peer (the client). The peer returns a value calculated using a one-way hash function. (In Windows 2000, MD5 is used.) The authenticator checks the response against its own calculation of the expected hash value. If the values match, authentication is acknowledged; otherwise, the connection is terminated. This provides protection against a playback attack because CHAP specifies the use of incrementally changing identifiers and variable challenge values. The secret (a password) is known to the authenticator and its peer and is not sent over the link. Authentication is one-way but can be negotiated in both directions to provide mutual authentication. The secrets used can be placed in a table to support more than one name/secret pair per system and to change the secret at any time within the session.

Optimal security in CHAP is maintained by

- Using a password that is the length of the hash value of the hashing algorithm chosen (that is, 16 octets for MD5)

- Making the challenge value unique and unpredictable

- Terminating the link upon authentication failure

Microsoft-CHAP Version 1 (RFC 2433) and Version 2 (RFC 2759)

Although CHAP is an authentication protocol used by many remote access servers, Microsoft-CHAP Version 1 (MS-CHAP-V1) was designed for compatibility with NT 3.5, 3.51, 4.0, and Windows 9x. MS-CHAP provides server-controlled authentication retry. The Windows NT–compatible challenge response uses a value that is encrypted by using a password hash. Attacks designed to defeat the password hash exist. The differences between MS-CHAP and CHAP are

- MS-CHAP is designed to work with Microsoft processes and mechanisms for remote access and password storage.

- Unlike some implementations of CHAP, MS-CHAP does not require the server to store a cleartext or reversibly encrypted password.

- MS-CHAP is the only remote access protocol provided with Windows 2000 that supports password change during the authentication process.

- MS-CHAP defines a Microsoft-specific set of reasons for failure, and codes are returned in the failure packet message field.

Microsoft-CHAP Version 2 (MS-CHAP-V2), as described in RFC 2759, is incompatible with MS-CHAP-V1. MS-CHAP–V2 uses fields for different purposes. MS-CHAP-V2 functionality is similar to MS-CHAP-V1 with the following exceptions:

- MS-CHAP-V2 provides mutual authentication.
- The calculation of the response in MS-CHAP-V2 includes the challenge and the client (peer) name.
- The MS-CHAP-V2 LAN Manager compatible challenge response subfield in the response includes the peer challenge and the client name.
- Two different change-password fields used by MS-CHAP-V1 are replaced with one change-password packet in MS-CHAP-V2. (Passwords can only be changed if a Password Expired error message is returned to the client by the authenticator.) This packet is supported by NT 4.0 Service Pack 3 and above and by Windows 9x.
- If the change-password mechanism is used in MS-CHAP-V2, MD5 is used to hash the password before it is encrypted and added to the change-password packet.

Point-to-Point Tunneling Protocol (RFC 2637)

The Point-to-Point Tunneling Protocol (PPTP) was designed by a vendor consortium (Ascend Communications, Microsoft, 3Com, ECI Telematics, and U.S. Robotics) to provide a protocol that tunnels through an IP network. A PPTP session connects two endpoints and creates a logical *tunnel*, or connection, across another network. The endpoints each exist on their own private networks. The tunnel enables secure communication between these two private networks. The data, therefore, travels across a public (or other) network but is not directly exposed to that network. The final destination and origination address is hidden from the other network. The routers along the way only see the addresses of the endpoints.

What's a Tunnel?

A tunnel is a logical structure created between two endpoints. Let's call these endpoints connection points on networks 1 and 3. Between these two endpoints lies a second network, network 2. By creating the tunnel, you can send packets using the protocol of network 1 across network 2 even if network 2 uses a different protocol. The packets of network 1 are encapsulated within packets recognized by network 2. The network 2 connections can thus be used. When the packets reach the other tunnel endpoint, the encapsulation can be removed, and the packet can now travel within network 1.

Figure 3.2 illustrates the additional layers placed on the PPTP packet to enable it to travel across network 2.

continues

continued

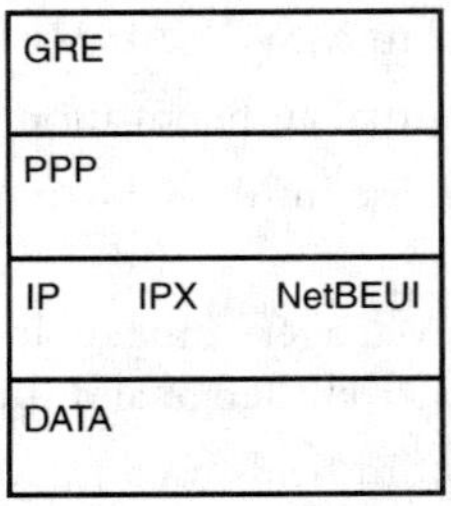

GRE
PPP
IP
IPX
NetBEUI
DATA

Figure 3.2 The PPTP protocol stack.

Figure 3.3 shows the packet and indicates the part of the packet that can be encrypted.

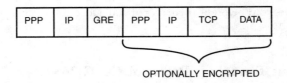

PPP
IP
GRE
PPP
IP
TCP
DATA
OPTIONALLY ENCRYPTED

Figure 3.3 The IP packet.

Figure 3.4 illustrates a logical expression of a tunnel across the Internet. The two shaded boxes represent the packet layers involved and the portion of them that represents the tunnel. The larger box, which cuts through both shaded boxes, indicates the existence of the tunnel, from NAS to NAS in this case.

Just as a tunnel underneath a large body of water can connect two cities, a logical PPTP tunnel connects two networks. Consider the network endpoints (network access servers) to represent the tollbooths on either side of the tunnel. You pay the toll and are allowed into the tunnel, which encapsulates you and keeps you dry as you travel through the water.

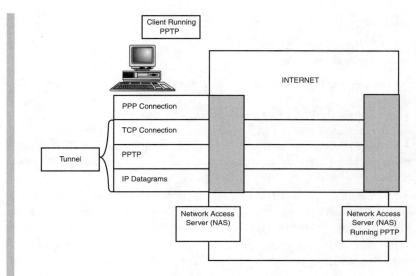

Client Running
PPTP

INTERNET

PPP Connection

TCP Connection

Tunnel

PPTP

IP Datagrams

Network Access
Server (NAS)

Network Access
Server (NAS)
Running PPTP

Figure 3.4   The PPTP tunnel.

PPTP also provides an easy way to create a virtual private network (VPN). The VPN can exist between a client and a server or between two servers.

A PPTP Network Server (PNS) can be a Windows NT or Windows 2000 server or another operating system. Meanwhile, the PPTP Access Concentrator (PAC), or client application, usually runs on a personal computer. PPTP connections are usually made through dial-up remote access, but a PPTP connection also can be made over a network. The PPTP server can control the PSTN or ISDN dial-in access or can initiate its own connection with other PPTP servers. Generic Routing Encapsulation (GRE) is used for flow and congestion control of the encapsulated datagrams. If a firewall sits between the client and the server, the firewall must be configured to allow both PPP and GRE protocols to pass.

To create a connection, two endpoints must exist. If multiple protocols are used (for example, NetBEUI on the client and TCP/IP on the remote network), the remote network endpoint must be running both protocols to allow multiprotocol routing and bridging. The network access server (a PNS) acts as one of these endpoints.

The processing of functions is divided between the PNS and the PAC. The PNS handles

- Logical termination of PPP network control protocols
- Management and aggregation of PPP multilink protocols
- Participation in PPP authentication protocols

The PAC handles

- Physical interface to PSTN or ISDN
- Control of modems or terminal adapters

The client or the server can handle logical termination of the PPP Link Control Protocol sessions.

Because both the physical interface to the network and modem control are client functions, the client process can be installed separately. A network access server (the PNS) will have both client and server software installed, while the client PC can install its own copy of the client software. In fact, client (PAC) software from another company can be used. In addition

- Users can maintain a single IP address and use different PACs as long as they use a common PNS. An enterprise network using unregistered addresses can rely on the PNS to assign meaningful addresses for the private network.
- Non–IP protocols can be supported for dial networks. Tunneling of Appletalk and IPX through an IP provider is possible. The PAC does not need to be able to process these protocols.
- Connections are made between the PAC and the PNS; therefore, no other device on the private or public network needs to implement PPTP.

Architecture

A tunnel is created between a PNS and PAC pair. The PAC may be on a server or on a client PC. Many sessions can be multiplexed in a single tunnel. A control connection manages the establishment, release, and maintenance of sessions and of the tunnel itself. The control connection is a TCP session. PPTP call control and management information is passed over this session. It is associated with but is separate from the tunneling sessions illustrated in Figure 3.4. If data encryption is implemented, the control session is not part of the encrypted data.

The GRE header contains a key that establishes the session to which a packet belongs. It also contains acknowledgement and sequencing information used for congestion control and error detection over the tunnel.

Messages are sent as TCP data on the control connection using port 1723. Any unused port is used as the source port.

Magic Cookie

PPTP control connection message headers contain a magic cookie. The term *magic cookie* comes from UNIX's use of magic numbers and a magic file (/etc/magic). Magic numbers are unique numbers assigned by the UNIX linker, and they are used during program execution to separate write-protected data from non-write-protected data. The magic file is used to determine the file type (ASCII or kernel subroutine, and so on). The Magic_Cookie field in PPTP headers is used to ensure that the receiver is synchronized with the TCP data stream. It is always the constant 0x1A2B3C4D. Other protocols, such as DHCP, also have a variable called magic_cookie.

Security Considerations

PPTP does not specify algorithms for encryption or authentication. Security of user data and authentication of PPP peers is managed by PPP. Several vulnerabilities are inherently present including

- PPTP control channel messages are not authenticated, or integrity protected, so an attack might hijack the TCP connection.

- False control channel messages or the altering of genuine messages might be possible and undetected.

- GRE packets are used to form the tunnel and are not encrypted. Eavesdroppers might modify these negotiations.

- The use of PPTP does not automatically mean that PPP packets are encrypted; thus, PPP data could be captured and read or modified.

Microsoft PPTP and L0pht Brouhaha

When Microsoft introduced its implementation of PPTP, there was an almost immediate attack on its security weaknesses. One such analysis was provided by Bruce Schneier (Counterpane Internet Security, http://www.counterpane.com) and Mudge (L0pht Heavy Industries, http://www.l0pht.com). Other commentaries also emerged, but the L0pht voice was the loudest. The attacks were directed specifically at Microsoft's implementation. The basic complaints were:

- **Weak encryption in both 40-bit and 128-bit modes.** The Microsoft Point-to-Point Encryption (MPPE) protocol can be used to encrypt PPTP packets. Because the shared secret used to encrypt the packets is generated from the password, MPPE encrypted packets are no more secure than the password.

- **Bad design decisions.** Connections through a firewall can be opened by abusing PPTP negotiations. Most of these abuses would be denial-of-service attacks. Spoofing of configuration packets can also force all name resolution through a compromised DNS server.

- **Crashes.** Mounting various types of attacks against the control channel crashed the Windows NT machine before the attacks could be carried out.

- **Protocol message information leaks.** The Windows 95 implementation of the PPTP client protocol leaks information in the protocol messages, and buffers are not reset to 0x00 as specified.

- Flip bits. Because MPPE does not authenticate packets, an attacker could flip bits (exchange a 1 for a 0 or a 0 for a 1) in the ciphertext. This would not require the attacker to know the encryption key or the client's password.

- **Possible spoofing.** Spoofing of the MPPE resynchronization requests or forging of MPPE packets with incorrect coherency counts (to initialize resynchronization requests) is possible.

- **Other information leaks.** The PPTP server announces publicly the maximum number of channels available; this information can be used to estimate the size of the PPTP server and to monitor its load. A new connection can be determined, as can usage patterns. Information leaks from the control channel might enable an eavesdropper to obtain sensitive data such as a client and server IP address, a client machine RAS version, NetBIOS names, an internal virtual tunnel IP address, an internal DNS server's address, and client usernames.

Note

For an analysis of the original Microsoft implementation of PPTP, see "Cryptanalysis of Microsoft's Point-to-Point Tunneling Protocol (PPTP)," by Bruce Schneier and Mudge, October 24, 1999. This document can be found in PDF form on `http://www.L0pht.com`.

Microsoft's Response

Although at first defensive, Microsoft implemented changes to its PPTP implementation. The protocol used for authentication in Microsoft PPTP was MS-CHAP-1. It was replaced by MS-CHAP-2. MS-CHAP-2 is available as a free upgrade to Windows 95/98 and Windows NT.

MS-CHAP-2 prevents several issues that weakened MS-CHAP-1. For example:

- MS-CHAP-2 no longer sends the weaker LAN Manager hash along with the NT hash.

- MS-CHAP-2 provides for server authentication.

- MS-CHAP-2 replaces the multiple-change password packets of MS-CHAP-1 with a single-change password packet. This prevents spoofing of MS-CHAP failure packets.

- PPTP V5 closes information leaks from the communications channel. Information that could be gained from this channel in the earlier version included client and server IP addresses, client machine RAS versions, NetBIOS names, internal virtual tunnel IP addresses, internal DNS server addresses, and client usernames.

- MPPE uses unique keys in each direction. This prevents XORing the text stream in each direction to remove the effects of encryption.

Tip

For a more secure PPTP, change the registry value of the SecureVPN entry to 0x00000001 to force the use of MS-CHAP-2 for VPN authentication (a simple dial-up connection is not affected). A server configured with this entry will refuse PPTP connections that do not request MS-CHAP-2 for authentication. A PPTP client configured with this value will always use MS-CHAP-2. The SecureVPN value is found at HKLM\SYSTEM\CurrentControlSet\Services\RasMan\PPP.

L0pht responds

A second document ("Cryptanalysis of Microsoft's PPTP Authentication Extensions [MS-CHAPv2]," by Bruce Schneier and Mudge, October 24, 1999) at the L0pht Web site admits that, "Microsoft's changes correct the major security weaknesses of their original implementation." The document appears to grudgingly admit that this version is resistant to denial-of-service attacks and closes information leaks.

However, L0pht claims that the MS-CHAP protocol is still weak. They claim that Microsoft's use of a very complicated, unique algorithm reduces the 128-bit security to the equivalent of 57-bit security. L0pht also claims that most people will not take the extra step to ensure the use of the newer, more secure algorithm because requiring a registry entry is just too difficult. (As an NT administrator, aren't you offended? Adding a registry entry is too difficult? I, for one, wouldn't hesitate to use a free upgrade on my clients.)

Finally, L0pht says that PPTP, like most security schemes based on a password chosen by a user, has a fundamental weakness: It is only as secure as the password chosen by the user. Unfortunately, most security schemes in use today are based on passwords, and this is a fault of all such schemes, not just PPTP.

Microsoft Point-to-Point Encryption Scheme (MPPE)

Microsoft Point-to-Point Encryption (MPPE) passes PPP packets in encrypted form. MPPE uses RSA RC4 with a negotiated session-key length. Session keys change throughout the transmission. The frequency of session-key change is negotiated, and session keys can be changed with every packet.

Layer 2 Tunneling Protocol (RFC 2661)

The Layer 2 Tunneling Protocol (L2TP) assists and extends the tunneling of PPP packets over a network. Like PPTP, L2TP operates at Layer 2 and negotiates session address assignment, encryption, and compression. Sensitive control-message data such as user passwords or user IDs can be encrypted if shared secrets are negotiated during tunnel authentication.

Two types of L2TP messages are used: control, which is sent over a reliable channel, and data, which is not. Both control and data packets use the same packet structure, which can be seen in Figure 3.5. The entire L2TP packet is sent within a UDP datagram. Because L2TP doesn't natively resend lost or dropped data packets, it is inherently unreliable if used over UDP, especially if compression and encryption are used.

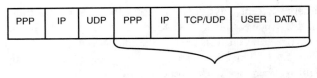

OPTIONALLY ENCRYPTED

Figure 3.5 The L2TP packet structure.

Figure 3.6 shows the division of the L2TP layer (shown unshaded) into two halves. On the right, a reliable channel is used to transmit L2TP control messages. On the left, L2TP moves data over an unreliable data channel. In a UDP/IP network, the entire packet is sent within a UDP datagram (one of the choices in the bottom shaded block). Because UDP is an unreliable transport protocol, the reliability of the control channel is implemented within the L2TP protocol.

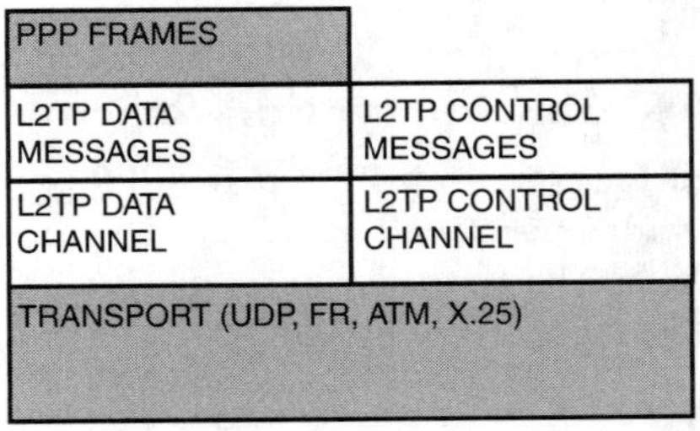

PPP FRAMES	
L2TP DATA MESSAGES	L2TP CONTROL MESSAGES
L2TP DATA CHANNEL	L2TP CONTROL CHANNEL
TRANSPORT (UDP, FR, ATM, X.25)	

Figure 3.6 The L2TP Sockets Layer IP packet/protocol stack.

L2TP, however, does not have many of the weaknesses of PPTP. Although both protocols use PPP to encapsulate the data and then apply headers used for transport across another network, L2TP is more secure than PPTP because

- PPTP requires that the other network be an IP network. L2TP, however, can use UDP for transport over IP, frame relay, X.25, or ATM.

- L2TP can use multiple tunnels between the same endpoints; PPTP creates a single tunnel.

- L2TP can use header compression; PPTP cannot.

- L2TP can provide tunnel authentication; PPTP cannot.

- Unlike PPTP, the L2TP tunnel includes its own control channel. This enables channel authentication and the hiding of communication information.

L2TP Architecture

The L2TP Access Concentrator (LAC) and the L2TP Network Server (LNS) are the two sides or endpoints of an L2TP tunnel. A remote connection can be made to the LAC (through a PPP link), or a client can natively run L2TP (a LAC client). The LAC is responsible for the outgoing calls, while the LNS is responsible for the incoming calls. Thus, the LNS sits on the home network. The LAC can be a network access point or can reside on the remote client. A network access server (NAS) can be an LAC, an LNS, or both.

The L2TP tunnel is created between an LAC-LNS pair and consists of a control connection and zero or more L2TP sessions. (The control connection establishes the tunnel before any sessions are negotiated.) The tunnel carries encapsulated PPP datagrams and control messages between the LAC and LNS.

An LAC client tunnels directly across the Internet, frame relay, or ATM cloud to the LNS to access the remote LAN. A remote system can use PPP across the PSTN to the LAC, which then tunnels to the LNS. In either case, client authentication, authorization, and accounting can be provided by the remote LAN.

In Figure 3.7, the center block represents the entire L2TP tunnel, which includes control and data sessions. The LAC and the LNS endpoints are the shaded boxes on each side of the L2TP tunnel. To the far left, a PC is using PPP over a dial-up connection to connect to the LAC and to use the tunnel. Note that the "call" block (which extends from the PC to the tunnel endpoint on the LAC) is not part of the L2TP tunnel. In this figure, the PC is not running L2TP.

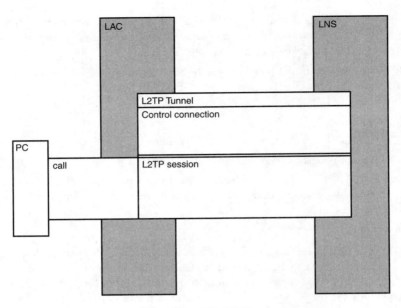

Figure 3.7 The L2TP tunnel.

Tunneling a PPP Session with L2TP

The tunnel can be used for multiple sessions, and multiple tunnels can exist between the same LAC and LNS. Sequence numbers are defined in the L2TP header for control messages and optionally for data messages. Sequence numbering in data messages is not used by L2TP to retransmit lost data messages. The sequence numbers can be used by other methods to detect lost packets and to restore the original sequence if necessary.

An L2TP tunnel and its control connections, control session, and data sessions are established using the following steps:

1. Prior to tunneling PPP sessions with L2TP, a control connection is established.

2. Tunnel authentication (during control connection) is established by using a shared secret.

3. The same secret is then used to encrypt the user ID and password of the L2TP messages.

4. Individual data sessions are then established.

5. PPP frames from a remote system are received at the LAC; are stripped of CRC, link framing, and transparency bytes; are encapsulated in L2TP; and are forwarded over the tunnel.

6. The LNS receives the L2TP packet and processes the PPP frame as if it were received on a local PPP interface.

> **Tip**
> L2TP uses the IANA assigned Port 1701. Because this port is also used by L2F (RFC 2341), the header version field (1 for L2F and 2 for L2TP) should be used, if appropriate, to indicate which protocol is being used. L2F is a tunneling protocol used primarily by Cisco routers.

Security Issues

Two security issues exist: a lack of data encryption and a lack of end-to-end security.

Tunnel establishment uses authentication procedures, but these only provide endpoint security. Malicious users can snoop the tunnel stream and inject packets. To obtain packet-level security, the underlying transport would need to provide encryption, integrity, and authentication services for all L2TP traffic.

> **Note**
> The IP Security protocol (IPSec) can be used with L2TP to provide these features. Be sure to review the "IPSec" section later in this chapter.

In addition, end-to-end security is not provided. Although data is protected within the tunnel, the data passed between the tunnel endpoint and the destination server is not.

IPSec (RFCs 2207, 2401, 2410, 2709, 2402, 2403, 2404, 2405, 2406, 2410, 2451, 1828, 1827, and 1829)

The goal of IPSec is to provide security services for traffic at the IP layer in both the Ipv4 and Ipv6 environment. The interoperable security services include

- Access control
- Connectionless integrity
- Data-origin authentication
- Protection against replays
- Partial sequence integrity
- Confidentiality (encryption)
- Limited traffic-flow confidentiality

Although provided at the IP layer, IPSec offers protection for IP and upper-layer protocols (TCP, UDP, ICMP, BGP, and so on). It was designed to operate in many host or security gateways and to provide protection to IP traffic.

IPSec is algorithm-independent. Its modularity enables the selection of different sets of algorithms without affecting other parts of implementation. Default algorithms are defined for interoperability.

IPSec enables the selection of required security protocols and the algorithms to use for service. Cryptographic keys are required. It can be used to protect a path between a pair of hosts, a pair of security gateways, or a security gateway and a host. (A security gateway is an intermediate system that implements IPSec protocols; it can be a router or a firewall.)

An administrator controls the granularity at which the service is offered. A single tunnel can be implemented for all traffic between security gateways, or separate tunnels can be created for each connection between hosts using the gateways.

Key Management

Determining secret keys and managing their distribution can be problematic. Two problems exist: The number of keys can be difficult to manage, and the process of secure distribution can be challenging. Although IPSec allows manual configuration and distribution of cryptographic keys by a system administrator, this is not practical in large, volatile implementations.

ISAKMP/Oakley is an automated key-management protocol designed for IPSec. Internet Security Association and Key Management Protocol (ISAKMP) is a framework for Internet key management. ISAKMP enables the use of a variety of key exchange algorithms. The Oakley Key Determination Protocol (a Diffie-Hellman–based key exchange protocol with added security), however, describes several modes of key exchange. It allows the use of digital signatures, public key encryption, or symmetric key encryption for authentication.

Internet Key Exchange (IKE), as described in the proposed standard RFC 2409, is a combination of Oakley, ISAKMP, and SKEME (another key-exchange technique). IKE's purpose is to provide authenticated keying material to be used by IPSec. During the establishment of each connection, IKE is used to define formats for exchanging key generations and authentication data.

Security Policy Database

A Security Policy Database (SPD) is used to define what is protected. It contains the rules that determine the disposition of all IP traffic inbound or outbound from the host or security gateway. The SPD is established and maintained by an administrator or application.

Each IP packet is selected for one of three processing modes. This decision is based on IP and transport layer header information, called IPSec selectors, that has been matched against SPD entries. When packets are processed, IPSec makes one of three choices:

- If no policy is found in SPD that matches the packet, discard the packet.
- If policy says the packet is allowed to bypass, the packet continues to normal processing (for that environment).

- If a processing ID is required: it is mapped to an Existing SA or SA bundle, or a new SA or SA bundle is created for the packet. Use the SA or SA bundle to do required IPSec processing (authenticate and encrypt—outbound; authenticate and decrypt—inbound)

IPSec, therefore, can act as if it is a broadcasting firewall. Although a firewall screens data that seeks to enter your network, IPSec policies screen data that seek to leave or enter a particular computer, thus protecting data on your network.

Tip

Your policy can be so secure that no traffic gets in or out! When setting up your SPD, remember that the SPD is used to control all traffic, including key-management traffic, from and to all entities behind the security gateway. So account for IKE traffic in your SPD or else it will be discarded!

Compression

IPSec supports compression negotiation (SMPT98). When encryption is employed within IPSec, however, effective compression is prevented by lower protocol layers.

Tip

Compression can be employed above the IP layer. For more information on compression and IPSec, visit the IETF Web site (`http://www.ietf.org`) and look for the work of the IP Payload Compression Protocol (IPPCP) working group. This group is working on the compression of the individual payload before the payload is encrypted.

Security Associations

A *security association (SA)* is a one-way connection that offers security services to traffic carried by it. The SA enforces Security Policy. The SPD maintains a Security Association Database (SAD) for each active connection.

IPSec implements an SA using one of two IPSec security protocols: Authentication Header (AH) or Encapsulating Security Payload (ESP). (See the section "Traffic Security Protocols: AH and ESP" later in this chapter.) AH is used for portions of the IP header and all portions of the tunneled packet. ESP is used for higher-level protocols. If both AH and ESP are required, there will be two security associations.

One SA is required for each communication direction. Thus, bidirectional communication would require two SAs, and bidirectional communication with both AH and ESP would require a total of four SAs.

An SA can be transport mode or tunnel mode. A transport mode SA is between two hosts, while a tunnel mode can be between any combination of a client, host, or gateway. An SA must be in tunnel mode if either end of the SA is a security gateway. Two hosts can use tunnel mode.

The type of protection that an SA offers depends on the security protocol selected, the SA mode, the endpoints of the SA, and the election of options and services within the protocol.

IP Stack Implementation

IPSec is implemented using several different methodologies:

- In new systems, IPSec can be implemented directly in the source code of the IP stack.
- Legacy systems require IPSec to be implemented *bump-in-the-stack (BITS)*. IPSec can be implemented underneath an existing implementation of the IP protocol stack, between the network drivers and native IP. No access to the IP stack source code is needed.
- An outboard crypto-processor (a processor dedicated to performing the crypto-graphic processing required by a security protocol) can be used to implement IPSec as *bump-in-the-wire (BITW)*. The crypto-processor can be a host or a gateway that is IP addressable. This is common in military environments.

Traffic Security Protocols: AH and ESP

IPSec is implemented using two Traffic Security Protocols:

- Authentication Header (AH), which offers connectionless integrity, data-origin (packet-authentication) authentication, and an optional antireplay service
- Encapsulating Security Payload (ESP), which offers confidentiality (packet encryption), limited traffic-flow confidentiality, connectionless integrity, data-origin authentication, and antireplay service

Figure 3.8 shows the AH and ESP packet structures when used in their different modes. Each structure indicates the part of the packet that is encrypted and authenticated.

Both AH and ESP are used for access control; they can be applied alone or in combination. AH and ESP also support a transport mode and a tunnel mode. The transport mode provides protection for upper-layer protocols, while the tunnel mode is applied to tunneled IP packets. In addition, both AH and ESP use cryptographic key-management procedures and protocols.

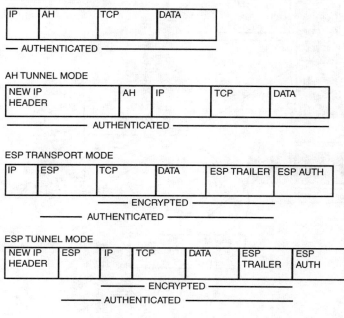

Figure 3.8 The IPSec protocol packet structure.

AH Modes

AH transport mode is used for authentication directly from client to server, while the tunnel mode is used for authentication between a client and a firewall or another intermediary server. The format of the packets varies as shown in Figure 3.8.

Figure 3.9 shows the potential uses of both AH modes. The first double arrow shows a client computer directly connecting to the server using the IPSec AH transport mode. The session is authenticated between the server and the client but is not tunneled. Both the client computer and the server are on the local LAN. The second double arrow shows a similar scenario except this connection is over the Internet. AH transport mode is still in use. There is no tunnel. Finally, the third double arrow shows AH tunnel mode being used across the Internet to a router or firewall. Authentication takes place at the firewall, which acts as an intermediary host.

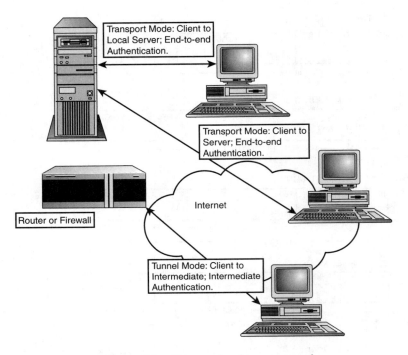

Figure 3.9 AH tunnel and transport modes.

Although AH and ESP can be used together, AH alone is appropriate when confidentiality is not required or is not permitted due to import or export restrictions on encryption. AH by itself provides data–origin authentication and protection against replay attacks. A *replay attack* is the reuse of data captured during transmission in an attempt to gain entry to a system or to utilize some service or feature to which the captured transmission had access. If AH is being used to authenticate the origin of data, an attacker might seek to either divert that data stream or pass false data to the server or client.

AH, however, uses a mandatory sequence number in each packet. The sender and the receiver track packet sequence numbers. Both the sender and the receiver's sequence number is set to 0 when a connection is established, and the sender's sequence number increases by one each time a packet is sent. The receiver then checks each incoming packet to make sure it has not received the packet's sequence number previously. If a sequence number is duplicated, the packet is discarded. Thus, an attacker attempting to reuse a captured packet will fail. An integrity check of the packet (checking to make sure the packet hasn't changed in transport) protects the packet from modification (and thus change in the sequence number).

ESP Modes

ESP uses transport mode for encryption and optional authentication between two hosts. Packet structures are shown in Figure 3.8. Tunnel mode is used to set up a virtual private network.

Figure 3.10 shows ESP transport and tunnel modes. Transport mode (the top part of the figure) is used to protect communications between two hosts. Data is encrypted. The bottom part of the figure shows the creation of ESP tunnel mode between three security gateways (labeled SG). These gateways can be routers or firewalls. The client connects to one of the gateways and is able to send secured and encrypted communications between any two security gateways.

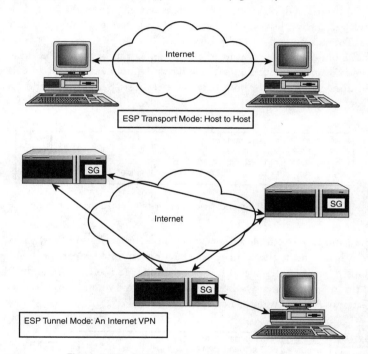

Figure 3.10 ESP tunnel and transport modes.

The confidentiality afforded by ESP depends on the strength of the encryption algorithm employed and the granularity of the SA. ESP can also provide authentication. ESP tunnel mode between two gateways can offer partial traffic-flow confidentiality; that is, IP headers can be encrypted and therefore conceal the identities of the originating traffic source and ultimate destination, and payload padding can be used to hide the size of packets. A fine granularity SA (one or few subscribers are carried) is more susceptible to traffic analysis than a coarse granularity SA that hosts many sessions. ESP is often used for mobile users in the dial-up and establishment of tunnel mode to a corporate firewall (security gateway).

SA Bundles

IPSec can create an SA bundle. An *SA bundle* is a sequence of SAs through which traffic must be processed to satisfy Security Policy. Tunneling can be iterated; that is, multiple layers of security protocol tunneling can be used with each tunnel originating or terminating at a different IPSec site.

One of the security issues with many tunneling protocols is the difficulty of providing end-to-end authentication and/or encryption. *End-to-end* simply means that all communication from host to destination and back is part of the protected process. When a host, or client system, uses some other protocol to access an encrypted tunnel that ends in some remote system, this provides communication security from tunnel endpoint to tunnel endpoint. While the data is traveling from the host to one end of the tunnel, and once it leaves the other tunnel endpoint, the communication is not protected. There is no end-to-end protection.

IPSec SA bundles enable you to create combinations of security associations that provide end-to-end security. Figure 3.11 shows a simple example of an end-to-end authentication, encryption, or both between two hosts. SA bundles reside at each host, one for each protocol mode.

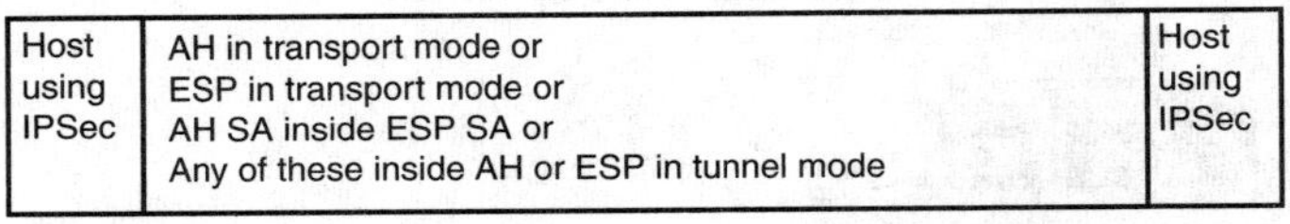

Host using IPSec	AH in transport mode or ESP in transport mode or AH SA inside ESP SA or Any of these inside AH or ESP in tunnel mode	Host using IPSec

Figure 3.11   IPSec end-to-end security associations, host to host.

Figure 3.12 shows an example of encryption and authentication between two security gateways. A host outside the security gateways on each side is part of the communication. If Host A sends a message to Host B, the message is encrypted and authenticated between the A and B Gateways, but it is not encrypted or authenticated between Host A and Gateway A or between Gateway B and Host B.

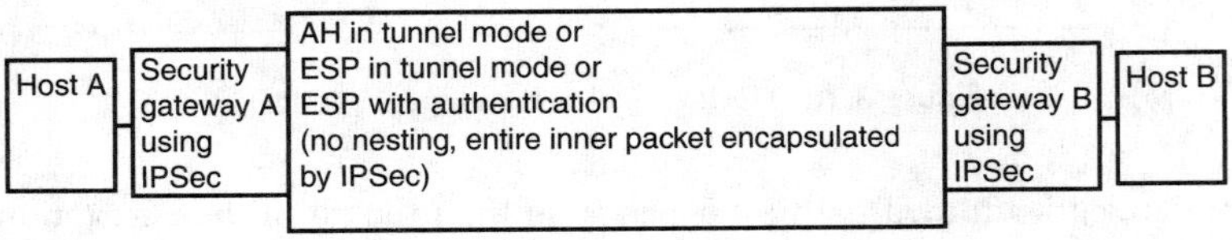

Host A	Security gateway A using IPSec	AH in tunnel mode or ESP in tunnel mode or ESP with authentication (no nesting, entire inner packet encapsulated by IPSec)	Security gateway B using IPSec	Host B

Figure 3.12   IPSec security associations, gateway to gateway.

A similar scenario exists in Figure 3.13, with one exception. Host A and Host B are using IPSec and have created an SA bundle with the security gateways. End-to-end security is present here. Messages between Host A and Host B can be secured.

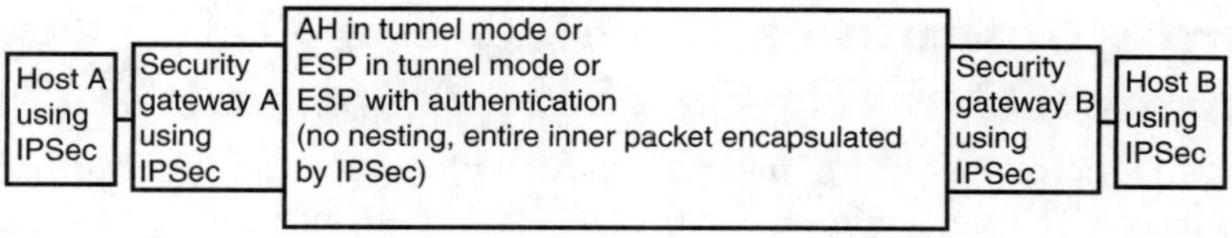

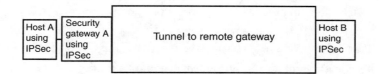

Figure 3.13   IPSec end-to-end security, host to gateway to gateway to host.

Finally, in Figure 3.14, Host B is tunneling through to a remote gateway using IPSec. On the other end, Host A has a secured connection to Gateway A. End-to-end security between Host A and Host B can be established using security bundles.

| Host A using IPSec | Security gateway A using IPSec | Tunnel to remote gateway | Host B using IPSec |

Figure 3.14   IPSec end-to-end security, host to gateway to host.

Performance Issues

More memory is necessary for IPSec code and data structures, computation of integrity check values, encryption and decryption, and added per-packet handling. These requirements might result in increased latency and reduced throughput. The use of key-management protocols, especially public key cryptography, adds costs. Hosts will not experience too great of a reduction in services. IPSec implemented in hardware devices might be more appropriate for security gateways (as they represent aggregation points) and some hosts.

Bandwidth utilization will increase at the transmission, switching, and routing components of Internet infrastructure. Even components that are not implementing IPSec will be affected due to the increase in packet size from AH and ESP headers, AH and ESP tunneling (a second IP header is added), and increased packet traffic with key-management protocols. This will be especially noticeable over a dial-up link that might have used compression previously.

Secure Communication Between DHCP and Dynamic DNS (RFCs 2535, 2136, and 2137)

Traditional DNS is composed of statically updated files. A dynamically updateable DNS system can reduce administrative time and inconvenience and can eliminate errors. Without a secure interface, however, a dynamically updateable server is open to attack, abuse, or stupidity. A malicious user could easily add incorrect information in the form of bogus name and address pairs or by changing existing information. A denial-of-service attack could be instituted by simply flooding the system with updates.

IPSec or some other mechanism can be used to implement securely updateable dynamic DNS. Other means for securing dynamic DNS are the use of public key/private key algorithms and the use of Kerberos to secure dynamic updates.

Public Key/Private Key Implementation (RFC 2535)

A public key infrastructure can be implemented and used for key distribution, data-origin authentication, and transaction and request authentication. New DNS request and response structures and new error codes would be required to implement secure DNS (DNSSEC).

The updating of any DNS record can be protected through the use of public key/private key pairs. In this scenario, to update records, a host or user must use a private key to sign the change. The DNS server can then determine whether the change is valid by using the public key of the authorized updating entity. Each key pair is authorized (signed) by the private key belonging to the DNS zone (a grouping of hostnames and their associated IP addresses) and is a way of determining whether the validity of the key pair is preserved.

The zone key would be stored in a signature resource record (SIG). In a broader hierarchical structure, other KEY resource records (RRs) would contain public keys for other zones or for various resource record types. These records would be called KEY records. In addition to the public key, they would include the type of RR being signed, the name of the signor, the time the signature was created, the time it expires, the time when it no longer is believed, the time to live, the cryptographic algorithm in use, and the actual signature.

Because there is one SIG resource record associated with each resource type (or for an entire zone), SIG RRs can be used to provide secure resolution of DNS requests. A security-aware resolver (a DNS client) can obtain the public key from the SIG and then validate that the information it has been given is truly the correct address.

An additional RR of type next (NXT) can be used to associate keys with DNS names and allows the use of DNS for public key distribution.

A KEY resource record includes an algorithm identifier, the actual public key and its parameters, and flags that help identify the type of entity. Security-aware DNS servers attempt to return KEY resources as additional information along with RRs requested to minimize the number of queries needed. KEY RRs are stored in their superzone and subzone servers, if any. So a secure DNS tree of zones can be traversed by a security-aware resolver.

A dynamic secure zone is a secure DNS zone that contains at least one KEY resource record that can authorize dynamic updates.

A zone that permits dynamic updates is still less secure than a static secure zone maintained offline. To limit damage done from the breach of a dynamic zone's security, the dynamic RRs can be isolated from zones holding mostly static resource records.

DHCP Authentication Via Kerberos 5 and the Secure Updating of DNS Using DHCP

Two proposed standard RFCs, 2136 "Dynamic Updates in the Domain Name System" and 2137 "Secure Domain Name System Dynamic Update," discuss secure, dynamic updating of DNS via Dynamic Host Configuration Protocol (DHCP). The IETF drafts "draft-hornstein-dhc-kerbauth-02.txt," "draft-ietf-dhc-dhcp-dns-12.txt," and "draft-whr-dnsext-secure-online-update-00.txt" also discuss dynamic DNS. The combination of DHCP and Secure Dynamic DNS will further reduce administrative costs. Currently, a formal definition of secure DHCP is limited to a DHCP working group internet-draft.

> **Note**
>
> Drafts are the working documents of IETF and can be updated, replaced, or obsoleted by other documents at any time. Although they should not be used as a reference, they are helpful in understanding how such authentication might work. Drafts can be located and read on the IETF Web site.

The rationale behind secure DHCP is the need for mutual authentication and a guarantee of packets in transit to and from the DHCP client and the DHCP server. This can be implemented using a Kerberos session key to compute a message-integrity check value. For more information about Kerberos, see Chapter 5.

Securing communications between the DHCP server and its clients can prevent rogue DHCP servers from providing incorrect addresses and rogue clients from obtaining them (via theft of service, exhaustion of CPU, or exhaustion of valid addresses). It would also prevent unintentionally (or intentionally) instantiated DHCP servers from misconfiguring clients (denial of service). Validation and authentication would include the following:

- The client includes an authentication request option in its DHCPDISCOVER message along with an option to ID itself to the server.

- The client validates any DHCPOFFER message that includes authentication information. The client discards messages that fail to pass validation.

- The client includes authentication information encoded with the secret used by the server in the DHCPOFFER message.
- The client validates the DHCPACK message from the server.

To use this secure DHCP to securely, dynamically update DNS, the client can give the DHCP server its fully qualified domain name (FQDN). The DHCP server can use this to update DNS. The DNS can be configured to only accept updates from authenticated DHCP servers. Other proposals enable the client to establish authentication with the DNS server to update its own record.

To learn how Windows 2000 can provide you with secure, dynamically updateable DNS, see Chapter 7, "User Authentication."

Microsoft-Specific APIs and Security Protocols

Microsoft-provided APIs and protocols are

- Server Gated Cryptography
- CryptoAPI
- Authenticode
- Secure Support Provider Interface (SSPI)
- LM, NTLM and NTLMv2

Server Gated Cryptography

This Microsoft technology enables the controlled use of 128-bit encryption technology. Banks whose offices are outside the United States and that are required to prove controlled use of 128-bit cryptography (due to previous U.S. export restrictions) have made use of this technology.

CryptoAPI

CryptoAPI provides a standard framework for programs to obtain cryptographic and certificate services. Win32-based application developers can add security based on cryptography to their applications. This API includes functions for encoding and decoding ASN.1, hashing, encrypting and decrypting data (session or public and private key pairs), authenticating using digital certificates, and managing certificates in certificate stores. Applications can be created that exchange documents and other data in a secure environment over nonsecure media such as the Internet. Developers can use the functions without knowing the implementation details. The functions work with a number of Cryptographic Service Providers that perform the actual cryptographic functions. These include

- **Microsoft Base Cryptographic Provider.** Basic cryptographic functionality that can be exported.
- **Microsoft Strong Cryptographic Provider.** Available with Windows 2000 and later; for use in the United States and Canada.

- **Microsoft Enhanced Cryptographic Provider.** Longer keys and additional algorithms; for use in the United States and Canada.

- **Microsoft DSS Cryptographic Provider.** Hashing, data signing, and signature verification capability using Secure Hash Algorithm (SHA) and Digital Signature Standard (DSS) algorithm.

- **Microsoft Base DSS and Diffie-Hellman Cryptographic Provider.** Superset of the DSS cryptographic provider that supports Diffie-Hellman key exchange, hashing, data signing, and signature verification using secure hash algorithm ShA-1 and digital signature standard DSS algorithms.

- **Microsoft DSS and Diffie-Hellman/SChannel Cryptographic Provider.** Supports hashing, data signing with DSS, generating Diffie-Hellman keys, and exchanging and exporting keys. Supports key derivation for the SSL3 and TLS1 protocols.

- **Microsoft RSA/SChannel Cryptographic Provider.** Hashing, data signing, and signature verification. SSL 3.0 and TLS 1.0 client authentication. Supports key derivation for SSL2, PCT11, SSL3, and TLS1 protocols. Available for Windows 2000 or later.

- **CryptoAPI Tools.** Used to digitally sign files to be used with Microsoft Authenticode and to view and manage certificates, Certificate Revocation Lists (CRLs), and Certificate Trust Lists (CTLs). Requires I.E. 4.01.

To learn more about CryptoAPI 2.0, visit `http://msdn.microsoft.com/library/psdk/crypto/portalapi_3351.htm?RLD=290`.

ASN: Moving Data Across Phone Lines

Abstract Syntax Notation One (ASN.1) is an ISO/ITU standard for encoding and decoding data that travels across dissimilar communication systems. It is used to encode data traveling from the application layer to the hardware layer and to decode data moving from the hardware layer to the application layer.

Authenticode

Authenticode enables corporate administrators to preconfigure security zones and to customize CAs. System policies can be created and restrictions can be set to control whether users can modify their security settings.

Authenticode also provides users with a means to trust code published on the Internet. It allows the attachment of digital signatures to files. Digital signatures are created and verified using CryptoAPI. They can be used to sign .EXE and cabinet files (multiple files that are compressed into one file that is expanded during program installation). Digital thumbprints can be used to ensure the integrity of .OCX, .DLL, and .CTL (certificate trust list) files.

Secure Support Provider Interface (SSPI)

The Secure Support Provider Interface (SSPI) is Microsoft's implementation of the Generic Security Services API (RFC 1509, 1961, and 1964), or GSS API. (More information on SSSPI can be found in Chapter 16, "Securing the Network Using Distributed Security Services.")

The Generic Security Services API provides security services. It is implemented over other cryptographic mechanisms. GSS enhances these underlying mechanisms in the following ways:

- It allows the authentication of an identity associated with a peer application, it delegates rights to a peer, and it adds confidentiality and integrity on a per-message basis.

- It allows delegation of authentication to an application. An application might require a set of credentials to prove its identity to other processes. This might be some global identity and not necessarily the local username under which the application is running.

- Two communication applications can use a pair of GSS API data structures that share state information. This information enables the applications to establish a joint security context, which can include mutual authentication.

- Messages can be signed or sealed by GSS API to apply integrity and data-origination authentication.

- A GSS API can be used at the end of a session to delete the security context.

Is CryptoAPI a Standard?

Although Microsoft CryptoAPI does not represent the implementation of any IETF standard, an RFC dated June 1999 (RFC 2628) provides a proposed cryptographic API standard. This standard defines cryptoplugins, cryptolibraries, and wrappers. Cryptoplugins are shared libraries, drivers, and modules that provide cryptographic function and would provide a standard interface. Cryptoplugins are composed of cryptolibraries or APIs, which provide cryptographic functions and wrappers. These functions and wrappers in turn provide an interface between the CryptoAPI and OS specifics.

LM, NTLM, NTLMv2

Long, long ago and far, far away, Microsoft and IBM cooperated to develop the LAN Manager product. The product was expected to serve small LANs. The authentication protocol developed was called the LAN Manager Challenge and Response protocol, or LM. As networking functions were added to MS-DOS and as network clients (Windows for Workgroups, Windows 95) were developed, the LM protocol client was included as part of their code.

When Windows NT was developed, a stronger protocol, the NTLM Challenge and Response protocol, was developed. To allow authentication by clients that were not NT, however, the LM protocol was included as well. Each transmission of the challenge and response includes both the old LM hash and the more secure NTLM hash. This has enabled the development of password-cracking tools that can crack passwords both in the SAM database and traveling across the wire.

A new, more robust, and stronger challenge and response algorithm, NTLMv2, has been available for some time, but it is rarely implemented due to lack of knowledge and the perceived requirement of pure NT networks. (NTLMv2 must be configured before it is used.) Although it is true that to use only NTLMv2 you must have a pure NT network, some benefits can be obtained by allowing NT clients to use it with NT servers while allowing down-level clients to use the LM protocol. Windows 2000 provides a Directory Services client that includes an implementation of NTLMv2 for Windows 9x. For a description of how to implement NTLMv2, see Chapter 13, "Securing Legacy Windows Clients."

MSV1_0 Authentication Package

Users in Windows NT are authenticated using an authentication package. The default package is MSV1_0. This package uses the SAM database as its database of users and supports pass-through authentication. MSV1_0 resides in two halves: one half on the client and one half on the server.

> **Note**
>
> Remember, each Windows NT system contains both a client and a server service. When authentication is local, the client and server service on a single system is used.

LM Challenge and Response

The LAN Manager password is based on the OEM character set and is not case sensitive. Passwords are forced to uppercase before encryption. The password can be up to 14 characters long. The first 7 bytes of the password are used to compute the first 8 bytes of the 16-byte LAN Manager One-Way Function (OWF) password. The second 7 bytes of the password are used to compute the second 8 bytes of the OWF password. (Thus, the password can be attacked in 7-byte chunks.) A constant is encrypted using the cleartext password and DES.

During network logons, the client is given a 16-byte challenge, or *nonce*. The LAN Manager client encrypts the 16-byte challenge with the 16-byte LAN Manager OWF password to produce a 24-bit response. This challenge-response is passed to the NT Server.

The NT server half of the MSV1_0 authentication package is passed the domain name, the username, the original challenge, and the LAN Manager challenge-response. The MSV1_0 authentication package computes its own challenge-response using the LM OWF password from the SAM and the challenge. If the result matches the challenge and response passed to it, the client is authenticated.

NTLM Challenge and Response

The NT password is based on the Unicode character set. It is case sensitive and can theoretically be up to 128 characters long. (The NT interface limits the actual password to 14 characters.) An NT OWF password is computed using RSA MD-4 encryption to compute a 16-byte message digest of the password.

Network logon works much the same as for the LAN Manager client except the MSV1_0 authentication package on the server is passed the NT OWF in addition to the LM OWF. The MSV1_0 authentication package computes its own challenge-response using the NT OWF password from the SAM. Because the SAM stores both an LM OWF and an NT OWF, case sensitivity can be enforced when using NT, but the inclusion of both passwords allows backwards compatibility. It is this storage of the LM OWF and the passage of the LM OWF across the network that then allows cracking of NTLM passwords.

NTLMv2 Challenge and Response

NTLMv2 has been available since NT Service Pack 4 (1998). The keyspace in NTLMv2 is 128 bits. It enables clients to control whether the LM OWF is created and/or used by the client and/or the server. It can prevent the LM challenge. Sessions between SP4 NT clients and SP4 NT servers can require negotiation of message confidentiality, message integrity using separate keys and the HMAC-MD5 algorithm (RFC 2104), 128-bit encryption, and NTLMV2 session security. These controls are implemented with registry entries.

For More Information

This chapter discussed services for which complementary information exists in other chapters of this book. The following should serve as a referral source for you in locating this information.

Information on Public Key Infrastructure can be found in Chapter 4, "Public Key Infrastructure (PKI)." Microsoft's Windows 2000 implementation is discussed in Chapter 17, "Enterprise Public Key Infrastructure."

For a discussion of the Kerberos standard, see Chapter 5, "Kerberos in the RAW."

Microsoft's implementation of dynamically updateable DNS is in Chapter 7, "User Authentication," while Chapter 15, "Secure Remote Access Options," covers such options.

For a description of how to implement NTLMv2, see Chapter 13, "Securing Legacy Windows Clients."

More information on SSSPI can be found in Chapter 16, "Securing the Network Using Distributed Security Services."

Summary

This chapter introduced several new protocols used in Windows 2000. These protocols were discussed primarily from the standpoint of their standard RFC description. Some of the older protocols, however, such as PPTP and NTLM, were discussed in reference to the many complaints about their true and perceived weaknesses and what has been done in response to these complaints. The knowledge presented here should provide you with enough background to benefit from Windows 2000–specific information as well as implementation and design suggestions to be found in later chapters. As promised, the next chapter will deal specifically with PKI.

4

Public Key Infrastructure (PKI)

"DO I REALLY HAVE TO GO TO ALL THAT TROUBLE TO KEEP communications confidential?" a student asked me when I was first explaining the ins and outs of Public Key Infrastructure (PKI). Her question stopped me. I really didn't think I had made it seem like a chore. The product we were looking at was all point-and-click.

What I had forgotten was that, although the process is simple, understanding what is going on is not. In my desire to make this process clear, I had obscured the ease of implementation and use. Now when I teach PKI, I try to separate implementation from understanding the underlying theory. (Guess that means you're in for the hard part now, right? Right.)

When a company embraces new technology, the installation and initial implementation can be a challenge. The move to a new operating system or to new networking equipment can seem complicated and difficult. After the system is up and running, however, the process of using the infrastructure is transparent to the user. The same is true of a PKI. Just as your network infrastructure has components that work together to produce this feat, your PKI also has components including

- A Certification Authority (CA)
- Certificates and keys
- A Certificate Repository
- A Certificate Revocation List (CRL)

- An optional Registration Authority (RA)
- A trust model
- PKI clients (the end user, computer, or application that requires a public key/private key pair and has a certificate, which has a copy of the public key and private key assigned to it.)
- Client software (including a Personal Security Environment—the local trusted storage in which the client stores his private key and information necessary to use it)
- A set of maintenance processes including:
  - Time synchronization
  - Certificate lifecycle procedures
  - Procedures and process for certificate revocation
  - Key backup and recovery
  - Key update
  - Maintenance of key history
  - Cross certification

In this chapter, I will discuss the basics of PKI including many of the preceding items. Chapter 17, "Enterprise Public Key Infrastructure," will provide you with information on implementing a PKI using Windows 2000.

Certification Authority

A Certification Authority (CA) is responsible for issuing certificates. The certificate contains the public key as well as other information of a nonsensitive nature. The certificate is digitally signed by the CA after examination of the public key holder's credentials. This process of identity verification is why you trust that the certificate holds the public key of the party it says it does. If you can trust the CA, you can trust the certificate.

What's in a Name?

Is it Certificate Authority or Certification Authority? RFC 2510, a proposed standard that describes PKI certificate-management protocols, defines the CA as the Certification Authority. However, Verisign (http://www.verisign.com) defines the CA as Certificate Authority. Such are the growing pains of a still-maturing standard. Which should you use? Use what's accepted by your community of peers and don't worry about it.

So who should we trust to be our CA? Many PKI implementations utilize an internal CA. (That is, many companies operate their own CA.) There are also publicly operated CAs such as Verisign (`http://www.verisign.com`), Entrust Technologies (`http://entrust.net/index.htm`), Internet Financial Transactions (`http://www.ift.net`), and Digital Signature Trust (`http://www.digsigtrust.com`). If many companies place their trust in such a company, they can participate in a broader PKI—a public, Public Key Infrastructure (PPKI). Companies that manage their own CA might develop other external structures, or trust hierarchies, to securely communicate with business partners. I will discuss trust hierarchies in more depth later in this chapter.

You can install a CA for your company using Windows 2000 Certificate Services, which is included in your purchase of Windows 2000 Server and Advanced Server. We will discuss this in detail in Chapter 17.

Registration Authority

Delegation of some of the CA's duties is often given to a Registration Authority (RA). This can offload processing from the CA that has to support a large number of users. An RA also can be used to assist you in securing the CA. The RAs, or Local Registration Authorities (LRAs) as they are sometimes called, can be responsible for

- Verifying the identity of an individual applying for a certificate
- Acting as an intermediary with the CA for groups of individuals during the initialization process
- Initiating revocation requests
- Performing key recovery

The CA alone issues certificates and Certificate Revocation Lists (CRLs). (CRLs are lists of revoked certificates managed by the CA. We will discuss these in greater detail later in this chapter.) The separation of duties can be used to protect the CA. Protecting the CA is necessary because a compromised CA could be used to issue certificates to irresponsible parties or to deny or revoke the certificates of authorized individuals.

In a secure implementation, the RA can be present for reasonable public access. For example, an RA could be available from a Web site and be used to request a certificate. The issuance of the certificate might be handled by a CA, which is not exposed to the Internet but is in a more secure, protected environment.

Certificates and Keys

The certificate serves as the binding between a user and an assigned public key. There are different kinds of certificates including

- X.509 public key certificates
- Simple Public Key Infrastructure (SPKI) certificates
- Pretty Good Privacy (PGP) certificates

X.509 Certificates

The X.509 certificate contains the information necessary to identify a server or individual and to provide the public key of a public key/private key pair. It is created and digitally signed by a trusted CA and has a limited lifetime. It is expressed as a data structure. Every programming language uses different types of variables to hold data used in a program. Some programs define data structures that provide a way to manage related variables by collecting them in one structure. Arrays, strings, and C-language structs are data structures.

The current version of the X.509 certificate is Version 3 (V3). When most people discuss PKI, they are referring to the X.509v3, RFC 2459, "X.509 Public Key Infrastructure Certificate and CRL Profile," certificate.

As you will recall from the discussion of asymmetric cryptography in Chapter 2, "Cryptology Introduction," information is provided in a certificate to identify both the holder of the certificate and the certificate issuer and to provide a copy of the public key. A list of X.509v3 certificate fields is shown in Table 4.1.

Table 4.1 **The X.509v3 Certificate Fields**

Field	Definition
TbsCertificate	The name of the subject and issuer, the public key associated with the subject, valid period.
SignatureAlgorithm (algorithmIdentifier)	The identifier for the cryptographic algorithms used by the CA to sign the certificate. (Supported algorithms are MD2, MD5, SHA-1.)
SignatureValue	A digital signature computed on the TbsCertificate.
Version	Version 3 certificates use the value 2; Version 2 certificates use the value 1; Version 1 certificates do not have a value.
SerialNumber	A unique integer assigned by the CA for each certificate.
Signature (algorithmIdentifier)	Identifies the algorithm used. (RSA and DSA are the most popular.) The one-way hash function specified in SignatureAlgorithm is used to prepare the signature and then encrypt it with the RSA or DSA algorithm. RSA works with MD-2, MD-5, or SHA-1. DSA only works with SHA-1.

Issuer Name	The x.01 distinguished name (another standard that specifies the composition of an identity) of the signer issuer of the certificate.
Validity	A time period during which the CA guarantees it will keep information about the status of the certificate.
Subject	Entity associated with the public key contained in the certificate.
Public Key	The algorithm with which the public key is used.

Note

Version 2 and Version 3 also contain extension fields.

Simple Public Key Infrastructure (SPKI)

An alternative to the X.509 certificate structure, the Simple Public Key Infrastructure (SPKI), is a proposed Internet standard that is easy to use and understand. Its focus is on authorization, not identity. In the absence of demand, it does not seem to be widely implemented. For more information, look up RFCs 2692 and 2693. You can read more about it at `http://www.ietf.org/html.charters/spki-charter.html`.

X.509

X.509 is a widely used standard for issuing certificates. This standard is an International Telecommunications Union (ITU) recommendation. The ITU serves as a clearinghouse; it forms technical study groups, studies proposed standards, and makes recommendations. These recommendations are non-binding standards. The goal is to have worldwide consensus on these standards; however, organizations are free to implement the standards any way they want. Organizations often will specify that they are "compliant" with a certain ITU recommendation (that is, they have implemented their product using all the specifications of the recommendation). This information is useful because it can help us determine their interoperability.

ITU standards documents are not easily obtainable; however, you can obtain a copy of the IETF RFC from the IETF Web site. RFC 2585 and 2510 detail the Internet PKI. In addition to describing the X.509 certificate, these RFCs contain information on CAs, management tasks, certificate use in secure Web communications, secure email, and IPSec applications.

Pretty Good Privacy (PGP)

As previously discussed, Pretty Good Privacy (PGP) is a commercial software product. Each copy of the software generates its own certificates to the PGP standard. Certificates are exchanged to be used for communications. For PGP to secure communications, the user needs to have an understanding of security and PKI concepts.

The PGP product is available for purchase. (Shareware and freeware versions are available as well.) Two resources for a list of sites with products and information are `http://www.hauert.net/pgpwins.html` and `http://dir.yahoo.com/Computers_and_Internet/Security_and_Encryption/PGP__Pretty_Good_Privacy/`. More information about PGP can be found in the "User Trust" section later in this chapter.

Certificate Validation

How do we know that the certificate is good? How do we know that a party we trust issued it? *Certificate validation* is the process of determining whether a certificate should be used. In its simplest form, validation means that we only accept certificates found in the usual maner; meaning in the repository. A more vigorous system looks for the digital signature of a trusted CA, checks the validity period, and checks a CRL.

Certificate Repository

Where does Bob go to find Alice's public key? To locate her public key, he needs to find a copy of her certificate. He could ask her to send him a copy; indeed, in some (especially very small) PKIs, this might be the distribution method of choice. Larger PKIs need some central place that can be a repository for all certificates, some place that anyone can go to find and examine Alice's certificate.

The process of publication, then, is the posting of certificates in a widely known, publicly available, and easily accessible location. The repository or database of certificates can then be accessed to find the certificate of any user—even that of a user unknown to the other party. Repositories can be central Lightweight Directory Access Protocol (LDAP) servers. Some implementations use

- DNS servers that follow RFC 2538, "Storing Certificates in the Domain Name System"
- Web servers or FTP servers that follow RFC 2585, "Internet X.509 Public Key Infrastructure Operational Protocols: FTP and HTTP"
- Corporate databases
- Embedded attributes of certificate entities in information system directories

Read access is provided to all authorized users. A public repository would give Read access to anyone. A private repository might restrict any type of access to those authorized. The repository should be protected from Write access except by digitally signed communications.

Certificate Revocation List (CRL)

When a certificate is issued, it is given a validity period (that is, a normal expiration date). So, presuming a certificate meets all other requirements for validity, you might assume that checking a certificate's validity period would be enough. There might be times, however, when a certificate needs to be invalidated before it has expired. Remember that a certificate refers to an electronic identity, not to a person. A person with multiple user IDs could have multiple certificates. Suppose, for example, that Joe has a user ID of joe@techsupport.SmallestCorp.com. Suppose Joe changes departments or leaves his job at SmallestCorp for another job (and a new user ID) at MegaCorp. Or maybe Joe suspects that his private key has been compromised. For a whole range of reasons, a certificate can be invalidated. It is for these purposes that a certificate revocation process is an important part of a PKI. A common way of implementing this function is to publish a CRL—a list of revoked certificates.

The CRL is digitally signed by the CA or some other authority. Each entry in the CRL lists a certificate ID (usually the serial number), the name of the issuer of the certificate, the known or suspected date of invalidity, and a reason code. Reason codes may include

- Key compromise
- CA compromise
- Affiliation change
- Superseded
- Cessation of operation certificate hold
- Removed from CRL
- Unspecified

Querying for Certificate Status

The Online Certificate Status Protocol (OCSP) (RFC 2527—a proposed IETF standard) is an online mechanism for Internet access to revocation information. OCSP responses are digitally signed. The protocol does not specify how the revocation information is collected or how up-to-date its information will be. Other query forms exist such as LDAP, HTTP, FTP, and so on.

Although the original X.509 standard defined the CRL, Version 2 and later versions are considered more secure because they are designed to protect against substitution attacks. (A substitution attack replaces a valid CRL with an invalid one.)

In a small enterprise that manages its own CA, a single CRL is appropriate. In a larger enterprise or for a public CA, other techniques—including CRL distribution points where many CRLs are posted and incremental posting of certificate revocation information (Delta CRLs)—are usually used.

If two or more CAs form some sort of a trust, they must also develop a way to share certificate revocation information between them. One possible solution is to issue indirect CRLs. Indirect CRLs enable revocation information from many CAs to be issued within a single CRL.

Options for Revocation Lists

CRLs are issued to give certificate users knowledge of certificates that are invalid before they expire. A CRL is usually published at a regular time. How frequently it is published is up to the designer of the CA infrastructure, the time it takes to get the CRL distributed, and the limitations of the CA products.

Suppose the previously mentioned company, SmallestCorp, establishes a one-year validity period for user certificates. SmallestCorp publishes a CRL each month. If any certificate becomes invalid for any reason, before it becomes invalid, the SmallestCorp certificate users might be able to determine this by looking at the CRL. Because the CRL is only published monthly, it is possible that a revoked certificate is not on the list. SmallestCorp has decided that this is a risk it can take, and the company feels it can always issue an immediate CRL (one that is issued under administrator command rather than automatically when the monthly date arrives). Another company might decide that this monthly publication is too long of a period and might set it to be shorter, say every two weeks.

Certificate Revocation Trees

Valicert (http://www.valicert.com) has developed a unique solution to the problem of multiple CAs. Instead of using a list, information from cooperating CAs is placed in a hash tree data structure. Information that identifies the CA and the serial numbers of revoked certificates is used in the Merkle hashing algorithm. The advantage of the Certificate Revocation Tree is the efficient manner in which a large amount of revocation information can be stored and retrieved. Instead of a list that grows to the size of the number of revoked certificate, the tree structure reduces the size to Log_2N. The ValiCert product can be purchased as a tool kit for use by any company that wants to develop such a structure. Meanwhile, Valicert claims it will support OCSP when the standard is completed.

The Valicert process is in turn used by Thawte (http://www.thawte.com) to manage the developer certificates it sells to software developers for code signing.

Companies can also control the currency of validity information by setting the validity period to a shorter length of time. If the validity period is very short, there might be no need ever to revoke a certificate. If the CRL is published very frequently in a large PKI, however, a lot of extra work is required. It might be difficult to generate and distribute a new CRL before yet another new CRL is required. So if you make the period too short, unnecessary work might be generated, or work that never results in complete publication might result. If the period is too long, invalid, revoked certificates will remain in use.

If, however, the time is set to match the validity period of your certificates, there is no need to ever revoke a certificate; it will expire before you could ever produce the CRL. A certificate could still become compromised before it has expired, but no matter the frequency with which the CRL is published, there will always be some latency in reporting involved. As long as a CRL must be published and distributed, there will always be a time during which an invalid certificate could exist and not be part of the current list.

This situation is similar to the issue of valid driver's licenses. A driver's license is usually issued for a period of several years. If, due to careless driving, physical disability, death, or any other reason, a driver's license is revoked, there might be a period of time before that information becomes available to law enforcement individuals.

Some institutions, such as some banks, might maintain validity information directly with their customer account information. All transactions are validated from the customer account information, and certificates, if issued, are only used to identify the customer. (If I possess the private key, I am identified as the authorized person on the account.) In this case, there is no reason to publish revocation information in the form of a CRL to consumers. The certificate might be invalid because I have closed my account, but the bank knows this and so do I. If I, or anyone else, attempt to use that private key and the certificate information to obtain money, I won't get any. If the bank, or I, thinks the certificate is compromised (someone stole my laptop, for instance), the account is closed or a new certificate is issued and mapped to the account. The old certificate is invalidated and cannot be used. Possession of the private key that matches the old will not get the user anywhere.

Certificate Trust Models

Many CAs already exist. If life were simple and there were one root CA, determining whether to trust a certificate would be easy. This is not the case, however, because there are many different root CAs. To determine whether to trust a certificate, you must be able to establish trust in the root CA.

The system of the public key/private key pair seems like the ideal solution for private communication between members of companies, between companies, or even between individuals and companies. It has but one fatal flaw: You must be able to determine whether the organization owning the CA and thus issuing the certificate is under the management of an evil, malicious vermin or is an honest enterprise. Whom and what you trust becomes a question of whether you trust a particular CA. How far you trust it is another decision. Trust of many CAs needs to be determined. You must determine whether to trust your company's CA, a public CA, a business partner's CA, and possibly, a competitor's CA. That's just the beginning. You must also determine whether a particular certificate can be trusted. To determine this, you must decide whether the CA that issued it should be trusted.

Determining whether to trust a particular CA is difficult. Fortunately, if trust between CAs needs to be established, there are a ways of doing so. In fact, there are several models, which I will discuss in the next sections.

Hierarchical Trust Model

In a hierarchical trust model, one CA—the root CA—represents the beginning point for trust. The root can certify a number of CAs, which then certify other CAs, which then certify other CAs; eventually, at some level, CAs certify non–CA entities (users, computers, applications, and so on).

This is a structure we are familiar with. In an army, for example, a general delegates authority to his or her lieutenants and they to their sergeants so that work can be carried out efficiently. People in an army trust that an officer's authority comes from the general; that is, the army follows a chain of command.

In the top-down hierarchical PKI trust model, although each entity is certified by a CA above it, all entities have the public key of the root CA; that is, their trust is anchored by the root CA. Alice, who has a copy of the root's public key, can verify the certificate of the CA that issued her certificate and on up and down the tree to verify any other certificate that she wants to trust and use.

The entire structure looks like a tree and is shown in Figure 4.1.

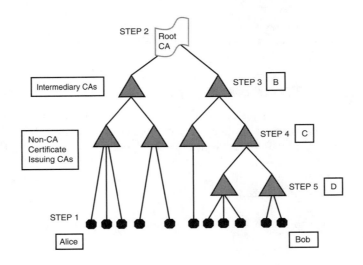

Figure 4.1   The hierarchical trust model.

At the top of the upside-down tree in Figure 4.1 is the root CA. Underneath the root are intermediary CAs (represented as triangles). The root CA and the CAs in the level just below it only issue CA certificates to other subordinate CAs. In the second row below the root CA, one CA only issues certificates to other CAs while the other CAs, and the two CAs in the last row, issue certificates to other types of entities—the octagons (users, computers, applications, and so on). Numbers on the figure represent points at which the following activities occur:

1. Alice holds a trusted copy of the root CA public key.

2. Alice can verify the certificate of CA B and can obtain a copy of B's public key.

3. Alice uses this to verify the certificate of CA C and to obtain a copy of C's public key.

4. This public key is used to verify the certificate of CA D and to obtain a copy of D's public key.

5. D's public key is then used to verify and extract Bob's certificate and thus obtain Bob's public key.

If this is your organization's PKI or if you trust the root of this hierarchy, you can determine the validity of all certificates issued under its authority. If this is the hierarchy of an e-commerce site and you have a copy of its root certificate in your browser, you can determine the validity of a certificate that is part of this hierarchy. Whether or not you choose to trust it with your credit card transaction is up to you.

Distributed Trust

Unlike the hierarchical model, which relies on everyone trusting a single root CA, the distributed trust model describes trust relationships between two or more CAs. Each of these CAs can be a root CA in a hierarchical trust.

In the distributed trust model, shown in Figure 4.2, Alice has a copy of her CA's root public key; Bob has a copy of his. Because it can be determined that the two root CAs trust each other, Alice and Bob can trust public keys from either CA. CA policies and design determine how these trusts can be made and the limitations of the trust between them.

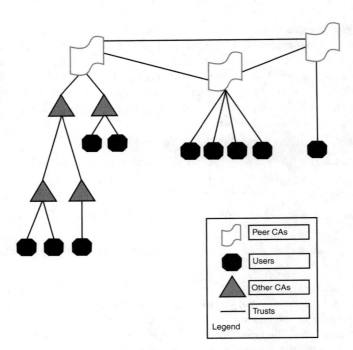

Figure 4.2   The distributed trust model.

Web Trust

In the Web model, CA public keys are preinstalled in off-the-shelf Web browsers. These keys represent the initial root CAs that the browser will trust. This does not represent an Internet version of a distributed trust model. The list of CAs says nothing about whether they trust each other. In effect, the browser vendor acts as a root CA and certifies the CAs it lists in its browser. Figure 4.3 illustrates this concept.

A certificate for each root CA trusted by your browser is indicated by the certificates within the oval in Figure 4.3. Server certificates issued by the root CA reside on Web servers or other servers at many locations. Only a few are pictured here. The validity of the server certificates can be examined because a copy of the root server certificate is held by the browser. This certificate has a copy of the root server's public key; this copy can be used to verify the digital signature made with the root server's private key on the Web server's certificate.

Finally, in the bottom row, there are end users with certificates issued by the root servers or by their subordinates. These user-level certificates could be used by the end users that possess them to digitally sign or seal email.

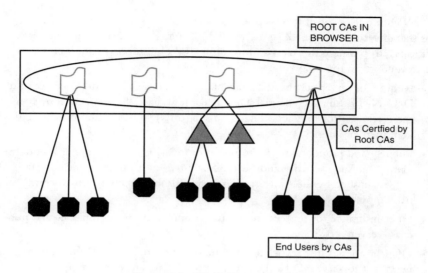

Figure 4.3   The Web trust model.

There are a number of security issues regarding the Web model:

- If one of the root CAs listed is compromised, there is no way to notify all the browser's owners and change the list.

- If one of the CAs fails to follow good practices in certification and maintenance of its certificates, there is no practical, efficient way to revoke the original CAs. The owner (user) of the browser can modify the list, but few users have the sophistication or diligence to manage their own list of trusted CAs.

- Even if information about a compromised CA could somehow be communicated to the millions of browser users around the world, can you imagine all of them responding by editing that browser list?

- If Alice wants to communicate with someone she doesn't know and she finds a certificate that can be validated by Company X, whose root CA is listed in her browser, she might believe she has the certificate of someone she knows and share confidential information. She has no way of knowing that Company X, while once upstanding, has now become poorly managed and does not check out applicants for certificates. Alice might not be communicating with who she thinks she is.

- If you want to purchase items from Company Y and you give your credit card information over the Web, you might think your transaction is secure until you find a large number of charges to your account that you did not make.

In the Web model, a lot of trust is placed in the root CAs. There are laws and regulations that govern the commercial use of PKI including who may be issued server certificates. To promote this trust and to fulfill legal obligations, major Web server certificate vendors do the following:

- Require of server certificate applicants and customers a valid Dun & Bradstreet D-U-N-S Business credential. They make it available for extraction by users of the certificate for transaction decision support. (D-U-N-S numbers are unique identifiers of business.)

- Publicly and proudly display the results of security audits by major accounting firms. One such security audit is the Statement of Auditing Standard 70 (SAS 70), established by the American Institute of Public Accountants to certify trusted practices.

- Offer insurance for protection against economic loss for companies that purchase server certificates.

- Offer businesses free revocation and replacement of server IDs. If a business suspects that its server ID has been compromised, it can receive a new ID. (Remember, it is the certificate vendor's root certificate that is in the browser, not the business's certificate. The certificate vendor, when called upon to validate a server certificate, will reject the old certificate.)

- Require evidence of U.S. residence and/or nonresidence in specific countries, depending on encryption strength requested and other legal considerations.

- Offer training, security auditing, and performance-measurement services to server certificate numbers.

- Reference customer programs such as government PKI contracts (Department of Defense, IRS, and so on).

User Trust

In a user trust model, each user is responsible for determining which certificates are valid. Usually, the list of certificates is a set of those of friends, family, colleagues, and business relationships that the user personally knows or that have been provided by someone the user knows and trusts.

PGP follows the user trust model. This model is appropriate for technical communities or private communications among individuals. It is more difficult to implement in large enterprises or in enterprises in which you need control over user trust. Furthermore, the user needs to have an understanding of security and PKI concepts to securely use the product.

In Figure 4.4, lines connecting the PCs represent trust relationships established between them. Any user can encrypt and send email to any other user with which they have established trust.

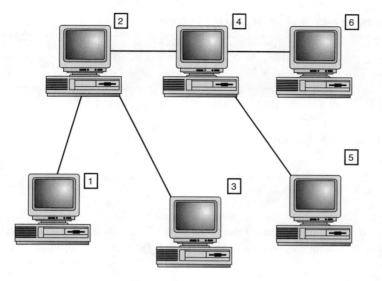

Figure 4.4   The user trust model.

According to the figure, user 2 and user 3, and user 2 and user 4, can share encrypted email, as can user 4 with user 5 and user 6. However, user 2 cannot send and receive encrypted email with user 5 unless user 2 and user 5 exchange copies of their certificates.

Cross Certification

The binding of two unrelated CAs (CAs that are not related by being in the same hierarchy) for the purpose of enabling secure communications between their communities of users is called *cross certification*. In the hierarchical model of trust, a CA will typically cross certify a one-way relationship. That is, CA-A will sign the identity and public key of CA-B, but CA-B will not sign the identity of CA-A.

Two companies can agree to have a mutual cross certification between their CAs. That is, CA-A and CA-B will each sign the identity and public key of the other. This can be used in both the distributed trust model and the Web model. In the user model, each user is essentially his or her own CA, so each other user that is trusted could be considered to be part of a cross-certification relationship. In essence, user A trusts user B and user B trusts user A.

Thus, cross certification is the recognition that one CA is authorized to issue certificates. If Alice and Bob each hold certificates from CA-C and CA-D, respectively, they initially have no way of validating each other's certificate. After CA-C and CA-D cross certify, Bob and Alice now have a way to validate each other's certificates.

Clients and Client Software

We've seen how the Web trust model relies on a browser as its client software and how a third-party product (in this case, PGP) implements the user trust model. Client software must contain sufficient processing to be able to validate trusted certificates, obtain a certificate, and use certificates in various processes that use certificates provided and managed by the PKI. For example, client software in the hierarchical model would have to be able to

- Obtain, notify the CA to revoke, maintain, and renew its own certificates
- Provide secure storage for its private key and information necessary to use it
- Validate other certificates presented to it in some communication or process that needs to be performed

One of the elements here, the secure storage, is often referred to as the trusted local storage or the Personal Security Environment (PSE). Any evaluation of the PKI product should include questions about the location of the storage of the private key. Obviously, the private key should never be stored in an area available to public access.

PKI Procedures

A PKI is more than a combination of structures and certificates. A PKI must have procedures for issuing, revoking, and managing certificates and setting up trusts. You must be able to back up, update, and recover keys. Key history must be maintained, and time synchronization must be provided for. Finally, client software must exist.

Time Issues

Imagine what would happen if time were not synchronized between the CA and its clients and the CA did not have reliable time. How could any software reliably determine whether a certificate were valid? The validity period of the certificate may or may not be current. A CRL could not be verified as being the latest. Secure time stamping and the issuing of time-sensitive data—both of which rely on authenticity and integrity—could not occur.

For these reasons, a trusted time authority should be established within the PKI. This trusted time authority can synchronize with a public time synchronization server.

> **Note**
>
> A number of timeservers are available via the Internet. Lists of public timeservers and statements on their use can be found at http://www.eecis.udel.edu/~mills/ntp/servers.htm.
>
> Typically, timeservers serve a geographical region and are listed as closed or open access. You should check the list carefully because some timeservers require prior arrangements or prior notification before you use them.

Key/Certificate Lifecycle

The key/certificate lifecycle is a concerto in three parts:

- Origination
- Lifetime
- Cancellation

Use Figure 4.5 and the following information to examine this process.

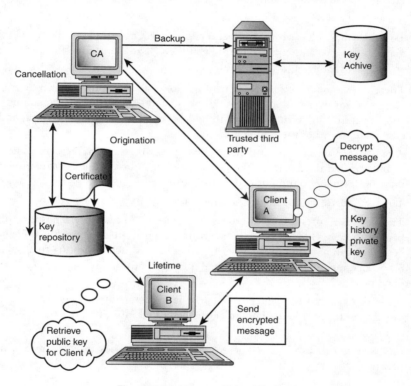

Figure 4.5   The certificate life cycle.

Cryptographically Secure Time?

RFC1305 describes a secure network time protocol and outlines a methodology for cryptographically authenticating the identity of the sender and for verifying the integrity of data in a Network Time Protocol Message.

Origination

In origination, the entity must register, the key pair must be generated, and the certificate must be created and distributed. The upper-left corner of Figure 4.5, which shows the CA, and the middle of the right side, which displays the client, illustrate origination. The client requests the certificate, and the CA issues and stores the certificate in the key repository (located below the CA in the figure). Backup is required with the trusted third party (the computer in the upper-right corner). The process might be completed in the following manner:

1. A user requests a registration form.

2. The CA sends the form to the user. The form might include some shared secret that can serve to authenticate the user to the CA at a later time in the process.

3. The user submits the properly completed form.

4. The CA follows an established certificate policy to verify the identity of the user. It might use existing, preregistration, shared secrets (imagine obtaining another certificate from a bank with which you already have an account and a certificate) or other methodologies.

5. A public/private key pair is generated either within the CA, the client software, or by a trusted third party. If the key is generated outside the CA, the public key must be securely communicated to the CA.

6. The CA creates the certificate and includes the public key.

7. The CA distributes the certificate to the end user, to a remote repository (database or directory), or to both. The certificate, which must be readily available to be useful, can also be disseminated by other means such as posting to a public repository, including it in secure email messages, or using some form of out-of-band posting.

8. If the key pair was not generated at the client, the private key must be securely distributed to the client. (The process is described in RFC 2510 and RFC 2511.)

9. Key backup can also be done at this point including backup by a trusted third party.

Who's Backing Up Your Private Keys?

A private key should be private. Some people, however, question whether it should be backed up. Others insist that it should be and state that backup is necessary in case something happens to corrupt your copy of the private key. The decision to back up private keys should be a policy decision made before implementation of the PKI and can depend on the perceived usage of the keys. It might be desirable in most instances to be able to recover keys if there has been corruption or damage. (If the key is on your computer but the email is on the server, if the hard disk crashes without key recovery, you will not be able to decrypt messages.) If the private key is issued for *digital signatures only*, however, then it should never be backed up. If it is, how could nonrepudiation (or the capability to argue that, because the private key had to be used, the digital signature is proof positive of the message's origination) be implemented? The same argument supports the practice of generating keys only within the client so that there is never a copy of the private key at any other location at any time.

Lifetime

During its life, the certificate must be retrieved, backed up, validated, possibly recovered, and updated.

Alice wants to send a secure message to Bob. (This process is indicated in Figure 4.5.) Client B sends Client A an encrypted message. Alice, or more correctly Alice's client software (Client B), performs the process of certificate retrieval and validation as follows:

1. A repository is located that has a copy of Bob's certificate. (This is represented by the double arrow between Client B and the key repository.)

2. The certificate is retrieved.

3. The certificate is examined to determine the CA that has issued it.

4. If this CA is the same as Alice's CA, then the certificate is validated.

5. If the CA is not Alice's CA, then the software examines trust relationships between the CAs. CA certificates are examined until validation can occur or until it is clear that no relationship can be found.

6. If the certificate is validated, the public key is extracted and is used to encrypt the message.

7. The message is sent to Bob.

For example, let's say Bob wants to read the message he received from Alice. Bob has just purchased a new laptop, and although he has installed the PKI client software, he has no access to his private key, which is on his desktop at the office. Because he is able to authenticate to the CA, he is able to use the key-recovery process to obtain his private key (the one he uses for secure communications, not the one he uses for digital signatures) and can thus read Alice's message.

Alice continues to work for the same company. At some point, her current certificate will expire. Her PKI either updates the certificate or renews it. Certificate update is the issuance of a new public/private key pair and certificate. Certificate renewal places the same public key into a new certificate with a new validity period. Renewal usually occurs automatically well before the end of the validity period and is transparent to Alice. She just knows she can continue to securely communicate with Bob.

It is possible for certificates to be valid only for certain purposes such as file encryption/decryption, email, or IPSec. They also can be valid only on certain servers or be accepted only by certain processes. If an employee changes job functions, he or she might need a new certificate, or changes might need to be made to the old certificate. If a more secure algorithm is to be used to issue key pairs, perhaps an update is possible, or perhaps new certificates will be required. Certificate processes exist that will update certificates. Whether they are used or not should be a policy decision. If updates are not allowed, the old certificates can be revoked and new certificates issued.

Another policy decision is whether to allow certificate renewals. When a certificate expires, there must be a policy to handle what happens next. If the employee is still employed, perhaps the certificate should be renewed. In a more strict security environment, a new certificate is issued before the old one expires.

Issuing a new certificate instead of updates or renewals requires more processing time and effort, but it provides a more secure alternative to simple renewal or updating.

Cancellation

At some point, the certificate will be cancelled due to either expiration or revocation. An end user might also request cancellation, perhaps because of a suspicion of private key compromise. If Bob's laptop gets stolen, he should request that his certificate be cancelled. The certificate is added to the CRL.

Key data should be stored even after expiration. This key history is to ensure recovery of encrypted material. The key data can be stored either locally with the user or by the CA or another trusted party.

A key archive can also be established to act as long-term storage of keying material to be used for audit and to dispute resolution purposes. The key archive typically is stored by the CA or some trusted third party.

For More Information

This chapter discussed services for which complementary information exists in other chapters of this book. The following should serve as a referral source for you in locating this information.

Chapter 17, "Enterprise Public Key Infrastructure," will provide you with information on implementing a PKI using Windows 2000.

A discussion of asymmetric cryptography is provided in Chapter 2, "Cryptology Introduction."

For information on how Windows 2000 synchronizes time and to learn how to set Windows 2000 to recognize an external SNTP server as authoritative, see Chapter 12, "Domain-Level Security."

Summary

This chapter presented the basics of a PKI as outlined in standards documentations and drafts. Understanding this information is critical to an understanding of Microsoft's implementation and to helping you determine whether Microsoft and other PKIs are compatible. Before beginning a discussion of Microsoft Windows 2000 security specifics, one more generic discussion is necessary. The next chapter, "Kerberos in the RAW," provides this background.

5

Kerberos in the RAW

Aʟʟ ɴᴇᴛᴡᴏʀᴋ ᴀᴅᴍɪɴɪsᴛʀᴀᴛᴏʀs, sᴇᴄᴜʀɪᴛʏ ɢᴜʀᴜs, ᴀɴᴅ ɪɴꜰᴏʀᴍᴀᴛɪᴏɴ auditors agree on one point: Communication over a network must be secured. How can this be done in a network in which you cannot guarantee that every node is friendly, nor can you assure that no outsider can get in?

The most common way is by building a database of users and passwords and requiring all users to log on to the network. The server then uses the user's logon information and the database for authentication.

But, you may ask, how do you make sure the database is secure? Can you keep the password from being sniffed as it travels over the network? Even if you disguise, encrypt, or obscure the information, how can you guarantee that someone won't be able to crack the passwords? How do you make sure that each server to which the user connects can validate the user? Can your client software be sure it's connecting to the real server? That is, is there a way to authenticate the server as well as the client?

Kerberos was developed to answer these questions. Computer scientists at the Massachusetts Institute of Technology (MIT) are a creative lot; they imagined early on that curious students, once given access to computer resources, would figure out ways to access all servers in the institution's network. Although no system can guarantee against every possible form of attack, the MIT scientists developed Kerberos with many attack scenarios in mind. In addition, it has been through several development and testing cycles and is used worldwide. It is considered by most to be a very good, strong authentication protocol.

Understanding the general methods by which Kerberos creates a secure environment is not difficult, and peeling back the layers and discovering the intricacies of its design and the ways in which it prevents improper access is a fascinating journey.

Note

RFC 1510, "The Kerberos Network Authentication Service (V5)," provides more than 100 pages of Kerberos details. If you want to write your own Kerberos system, want minutia of the details, want to verify the exact steps that make up the algorithm, want to find a description of every error message, or just want to memorize the names of the data structure fields, you can obtain a copy of the RFC at
http://www.ietf.org.

To use Kerberos, you must understand its terminology and protocol. Each object in the protocol has field names, and the message-structures names are strange-sounding. To the uninitiated, learning the protocol can be like trying to follow a roadmap written in a foreign language—the cacophony obscures even the familiar-looking terrain. To keep culture shock to a minimum, in this chapter I'll explain the Kerberos protocol using familiar terms and processes. Specifically, this chapter will present an explanation of the Kerberos algorithms that includes

- A brief description of the authentication process
- Definitions of the components of Kerberos
- A detailed, analogous clarification of the process
- A discussion on why features of Kerberos are implemented in the way in which they are

If you are already familiar with Kerberos and just want to learn about the Windows 2000 implementation, see Chapter 7, "User Authentication."

Kerberos in the RAW

Before you begin the study of Microsoft's implementation of the Kerberos standard, and certainly before you compare their implementation to those from other vendors, it is important to study the standard itself, uncooked—in the raw.

Kerberos Basics

Kerberos has three basic functions or, in the terms of its RFC, three *message exchanges*. The functions are called message exchanges because they consist of at least two messages: a request and a reply. The message exchanges are

- The Authentication Service Exchange
- The Ticket-Granting Service Exchange
- The Client/Server Authentication Exchange

Numerous error messages exist as well.

These messages allow secure authentication of clients and servers on an open network. The basic steps are outlined in the following list and are illustrated in Figure 5.1. (The numbers on the figure reflect the numbered steps in the list.) I will discuss basic Kerberos terminology later in this chapter.

Figure 5.1   Obtaining authentication credentials: the big picture.

Logon Authentication: The Authentication Service Exchange

Before any activity can occur, the client must request authentication. In the standard, several options for how this may occur are listed. For this introductory figure, we will reduce the possibilities.

1. The user Alice logs on by entering a user ID and a password.

2. The Kerberos client software prepares a message by combining this information (the password is never sent in cleartext across the network) with details about the client and the Kerberos server(s). The message is sent to the Kerberos Authentication Server (AS). This message is the KRB_AS_REQ, the Kerberos Authentication Server Request message of the Authentication Service Exchange.

3. The Kerberos Authentication Server looks up the client in its database, the Kerberos Key Distribution Center (KDC). The AS uses this information, as well as information in the message, to determine how it should respond.

4. If everything is okay, the Kerberos server prepares a response (the Kerberos Authentication Server Reply, or KRB_AS_REP) that includes a ticket and returns it to the client. In the standard, the ticket is either one that is useful for accessing an application server or one that can be used with a Ticket-Granting Server (TGS) to obtain a ticket to be used with the application server. The type of ticket returned depends on the implementation of the protocol and possibly the request made by the client. The difference in the tickets is in how they are used, how they are identified, and how they are encrypted. (We will cover this in greater detail later in the chapter.)

   In the figure, the ticket is represented by a Ticket-Granting Ticket (TGT) accompanying the reply sent back to the client.

The reply data includes a ticket and some additional information. Part of the reply (the ticket) is encrypted using the key of the server to which it will be presented, and part of the response is encrypted using the client's key. The client can use the ticket and cache it for the user later or can cache it at this time.

Getting a Ticket to Ride: The Ticket-Granting Service Exchange

If the ticket returned is a TGT, then other steps must be taken for Alice to complete her logon and work with resources on the network. (Note that if the ticket returned can be used to access a resource directly, the Ticket-Granting Service Exchange step is not necessary. Instead, Alice's Kerberos client can skip to the Client/Server Authentication Exchange as explained in the next section.)

5. Alice attempts to access a file or another resource on the network.

6. The Kerberos client submits the previously cached ticket to a TGS along with a request for a ticket to connect to the server that holds the file. This message is the KRB_TGS_REQ, the Kerberos Ticket-Granting Service Request.

7. The TGS can decrypt the ticket provided by the client because it is encrypted using its key. It validates the information and, if the requested server is in its realm, provides a ticket to access the server in a KRB_TGS_REP (Kerberos Ticket-Granting Service Reply).

Accessing a Resource: The Client/Server Authentication Exchange

The whole purpose here is to allow properly authorized access to resources. That process, however, first requires proof that Alice has the right to access the network, and then to pass those credentials on to the file server.

8. Finally, with the appropriate ticket in hand, (included in the Kerberos Client/Server Request, or KRB_AP_REQ), the client heads for the file server.

9. After validating the ticket, the file server allows the connection. It can decrypt the ticket because the ticket has been encrypted with its key.

> **Note**
>
> Authentication does not imply authorization; the two actions are interdependent but separate. Alice's request to access a file is not approved or denied by the Kerberos exchange. The file server checks to see whether Alice has permission to access the file. There is a Kerberos Client/Server Reply (KRB_AP_REP) message type, but the protocol does not demand that it be issued. After all, if Alice gets the file, that's reply enough.

Kerberos Components and Algorithms

In the Kerberos Realm (a logical collection of Kerberos servers and clients), TGSs and Authentication Servers can access the Kerberos database through the KDC to find keys of application servers. Certain application servers require special tickets before they'll consider a conversation with clients. Clients know their own key. They have either a hard-coded reference to the location of the Authentication Server or some methodology for finding out (for example, Windows 2000 Kerberos uses DNS service records).

The process sounds simple enough, but you might wonder why it's separated into a three-ring circus. Why would you have to get a ticket to get a ticket? It seems more efficient to give out the ticket that enables you to access any resource right away. You also might wonder what configuration is necessary on clients and servers and how the protocol is written to minimize or prevent its compromise. In the following sections, you'll see the parts of the messages and how the conversations are knit together in an attempt to prevent even the most determined attacker from unraveling network security.

Components

Many Kerberos components already have been described in action; for clarity, all components are briefly defined in the following list:

- **Authentication Server (AS).** A server used to provide authentication of Kerberos clients.

- **Authenticator.** The client must provide a new authenticator for each message request it issues. The authenticator contains information that can be used to verify that the response comes from a valid server in the realm and to prove to the server that the client knows the session key. The authenticator includes the client's current time and is encrypted by the client using the session key. Remember, the ticket can be reused; the authenticator cannot. More information on the makeup of the authenticator and how it is used is provided in the section "The Authenticator" later in this chapter.

- **Kerberos Administration Server (KADM).** The server used to administer the KDC and its database. The KADM and the KDC (and database) can exist on the same system, but it is not necessary that they do so. The KADM is used to add, delete, and change principal information and to set configuration parameters.

- **Kerberos policy**. How configuration parameters are set—and whether certain activities are allowed—is considered to be the Kerberos policy for the realm. RFC 1510 recommends the following policy settings:
    - Minimum lifetime (5 minutes)
    - Maximum renewable lifetime (1 week)
    - Maximum ticket lifetime (1 day)
    - Empty client address field (only if authorization data is restrictive)
    - PROXIABLE and other flags (allow)

- **Kerberos ticket**. A data structure that includes client credentials and session keys. It is used to authenticate the client to the resource servers or to the TGT. In this way, the user (principal) does not have to enter his or her ID or password again.

- **Key Distribution Center (KDC).** The Kerberos service that manages the key database. This database contains the user and server identification information, passwords, and other items. A record for each principal includes the following:
    - The principal's identifier
    - The principal's secret key
    - The principal's key version
    - The maximum lifetime for tickets
    - The maximum total lifetime for renewable tickets
    - The expiration date
    - Possible additional attributes
    - The time stamp of the latest modification

The specification calls for encoding of the principal identifier and allows for encryption of the principal's secret key by a Kerberos master key. If a master key is used, a field in each record indicates which version of this master key was used to encrypt the principal's secret key.

A record for every server in the realm is included in the database. These servers may be Kerberos Authentication Servers, administrative servers, Ticket-Granting Servers, or application servers (sometimes referred to as resource or service servers).

- **Message exchange.** As previously described, several Kerberos subprotocols or message exchanges dictate the exchanges between clients and servers and between servers and servers.

- **Message reply.** Each message exchange has a portion that describes the processing of the answer.

- **Message request.** Each message exchange has a portion that describes the request made and its processing.

- **Principals**. Users and servers.

- **Realm**. A logical collection of Kerberos clients and servers. The realm name is used by the client and server to identify the locations of the resources.

- **Session key**. A randomly generated, unique key used to encrypt parts of the message and to carry on encrypted conversations. The session key is generated by the Authentication Server and is provided to the client in the encrypted part of the response. It is provided to the destination server in the encrypted part of the ticket.

- **Ticket-Granting Server (TGS).** A Kerberos server that can validate a TGT and can provide tickets allowing access to resource or application servers.

If the Server Key Changes, Is My Ticket Invalid?

What if a key is changed for an application server? Does that mean my ticket is no good? Older keys are retained in the database. Tickets include the version number of the server key used. The ticket can be decrypted and is not automatically made invalid. The latest key is used for encryption, but the older keys remain available for decryption. Server keys and user keys, however, can be given expiration dates. If the key given to a user expires, then a ticket using this key would be invalid.

Kerberos Algorithms

How should you approach the details of Kerberos? Think of the network as you would the world within which a multinational conglomerate functions. Both the network and the business have resources (servers, applications, and data on one hand; buildings, people, and information on the other). Both entities want to protect these resources. Because there is no way a company or network of size can operate as a closed system, the company needs a strategy for ensuring that only authorized users can access the resources.

Anyone can walk in the front door of a complex, but only people who can prove their identity and who have legitimate business there can get past the front desk. Once inside, there may be some resources that anyone who has entry can use (an inner lobby, restrooms, pay phones) and other resources (offices, phones, computers) that are restricted. In each facility, a security officer keeps track of who can use what. If you've worked for such a company or visited a jail, an army base, or my grandmother's sewing room, you know how this type of security works.

Let's carry this analogy a little further. Think about how modern businesses manage confidentiality and integrity while their parts are thousands of miles from each other, and you have the rudiments of Kerberos.

In a large business, no one can know every employee. If the business has many locations, this is even truer. A large business thus controls entry by issuing ID badges. On an employee's first day at work and periodically thereafter, he or she presents his or her credentials. These credentials are checked, and the employee is thereafter issued a new ID badge. The ID badge itself identifies the employee to the person at the front desk. In a large, security-conscious industry, the badge is validated each time the employee uses it.

The following sections present an example business scenario that parallels the three Kerberos message exchanges previously discussed. To simplify this, I've assumed in this scenario that a TGT, not a service ticket, is issued by the Authentication Server.

Philadelphia: The Authentication Service Exchange

Phil Potts has just been hired as a courier for Fancy Feet Socks, and he works out of the Philadelphia office. Phil is asked to travel to the Fancy Feet Socks location in Pittsburgh to pick up a new million-dollar contract from Mr. Smith. Table 5.1 compares the experiences of Mr. Potts to the steps taken in the Kerberos Authentication Service Exchange. Figure 5.2 is a flow chart that outlines the process. The numbers in the flow chart correspond to the steps found in the second column in Table 5.1.

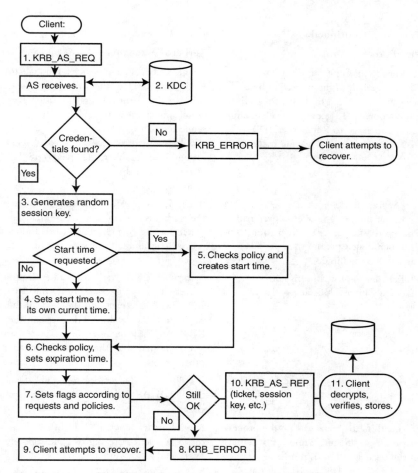

Figure 5.2 Authentication Service Exchange.

Table 5.1 **Authentication Service Exchange**

Phil Potts	**Kerberos Exchange**
Because he's just been hired at Fancy Feet Socks, Phil has no company credentials. (He can certainly *travel* to Pittsburgh without them, but he'll be stopped at the company door.) Pittsburgh does not have access to the Philadelphia employee database, nor does it have any way to verify that Phil is Phil.	A client in a Kerberos realm needs to prove that he is who he says he is.

continues

Table 5.1 **Continued**

Phil Potts	**Kerberos Exchange**
Phil needs an employee ID badge. The badge helps Phil prove that he is who he says he is (Phil Potts, Fancy Feet Socks courier). To get an ID badge, Phil sends a message to Kay Server, ID badge maker, asking for a badge. He includes his employee number.	1. The Kerberos client sends a message, the KRB_AS_REQ, to the server. This message includes the client ID, the ID of the server to which the client wants access, options, requested dates, and so on. (I will discuss this process in greater detail in the "KRB_AS_REQ" section later in this chapter.)
Kay Server checks her database and finds that there is a new employee named Phil Potts. She gets the information about Phil including a picture that was taken the day he was hired.	2. The Kerberos Authentication Server checks the Kerberos Distribution Center database. If a match for the client's credentials is found, the process continues; if not, an error message is issued.
Phil's badge is placed in his company mailbox, which is locked.	3. through 7. The Kerberos Authentication Server checks policies and other information, and a TGT is returned to the client if the client is found in the database. The message, the KRB_AS_REP, includes the ticket, a session key to be shared by the client, the server, and other details. (I will discuss this process in greater detail in the "KRB_AS_REP" section later in this chapter.)
If something happens to stop the process (for example, if Phil's name is not found in the database), Phil is notified.	8., 9. If errors occur, a KRB_ERROR response message is sent instead. Error messages are not encrypted.
If the process runs smoothly, Phil picks up his badge and checks the spelling of his name, the expiration date, and the start date.	10., 11. If the process runs smoothly, the client checks the name and client realm fields (and the server name and server realm fields), to make sure they match those requested. The client uses its secret key to decrypt the message.

Although this exchange has the Kerberos client getting a TGT, with small changes it can be used at the beginning of a login (to get credentials for an application server) and for password-changing services. These processes will be described later in this chapter.

KRB_AS_REQ

The KRB_AS_REQ format provides information necessary to process the client's request for authentication. Included fields are

- The protocol version number
- The message type
- The preauthentication data (`padata`), which is used before credentials are issued to authenticate the client
- The request body, which includes
  - Options (the request side of response flags)
  - The client name
  - The server name
  - The realm
  - The requested expiration date (can be empty)
  - The nonce (if used, a randomly generated number)
  - The desired encryption type for the response
  - The legal client addresses

KRB_AS_REP

The Authentication Server uses information from the request in its response, which is the KRB_AS_REP. There are two main parts to the response:

- Information about the ticket to help the client store and use it
- The ticket itself

The ticket information can be further divided into *encrypted* and *unencrypted* parts. Many of the parts in the encrypted ticket parts are duplicated in the client key encrypted response, which Figure 5.3 illustrates.

Padata

According to the specification, `padata` is left out of most KRB_AS_REQ messages. Some implementations, such as Microsoft, use it. It also can be used to support the implementation of Smart cards. For more information, see the "Preauthentication" section later in this chapter.

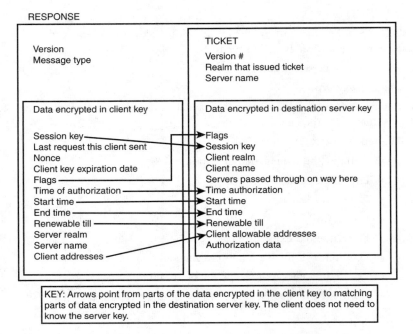

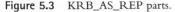

Figure 5.3   KRB_AS_REP parts.

In the figure, the largest box represents the KRB_AS_REP. The smaller right–hand box within the largest box represents the ticket part of the response. The smaller bordered box to its left represents the information encrypted in the client's key. The bordered box within the ticket box on the right represents data encrypted in the destination server key. The arrows show matching fields in the client and server encrypted sections. (The information is duplicated because the client cannot access information in the ticket. You should recall that the ticket is encrypted using the key of the server with which the ticket will be used. Because the client does not know the server's key, some information must be provided outside the ticket for the client's use.) The informational parts that *are* encrypted in the client key are

- The session key
- The last request this client sent
- The nonce

Note

The nonce can be the system time of the client or a random number that the client generates. The nonce is placed in request and response messages and is never reused by the client. When the Kerberos sever includes the nonce in its response, the client can tell that the response was generated recently and is not a replay attack.

- The client key expiration date
- Flags
- The time of authorization
- The start time (the ticket is good starting at this time)
- The end time (the ticket expires at this time)
- The renewable till
- The server realm
- The server name
- The legal client addresses

The version number and message type are not encrypted.

The Kerberos Ticket

An employee's corporate ID badge might be just a card with his or her picture, name, and photo ID, or it might have an embedded chip that provides more information. The Kerberos ticket may be more than it seems as well.

The purpose of the ID badge is to identify the employee to other employees of the company. The purpose of the Kerberos ticket is to help the user authenticate to an application server or a TGS. The Kerberos ticket does *not* include a copy of the user's password, nor does it include a hash of the password. Instead, it acts as proof to any server that the bearer has been authenticated by the proper network authority (the Kerberos Authentication Server).

The Kerberos ticket, like the message response, is also composed of encrypted and unencrypted parts. Parts that are encrypted in the server's key are

- Flags
- The session key
- The client realm
- The client name
- Servers passed through on the way
- The time of authorization
- The start time
- The end time
- The renewable till
- The client allowable addresses
- Authorization data

The version number, the realm that issued the ticket, and the server name are not encrypted.

Common Processing

The three major message exchanges all have some elements of their processes that are similar—even some of the same fields are used. The following sections present details that are common to more than one exchange.

Trusting Tickets

To make the process work, each party has to trust that

- The only possible holder of the ticket is the authenticated client (Phil).
- No one could steal the ticket and pretend to be the client (Phil).
- No one could give the client (Phil) a fake ticket.

Doing this requires a little bit more than just printing a badge.

Other systems of identification have built-in ways of aiding in their validity. For example, when you get a driver's license, your picture is put on it. And in many states, when your license is ready for you, it is mailed to your home. This process accomplishes a couple of things: The picture on the license helps people identify that you, the presenter of the badge, are the person identified on the badge. In addition, because the badge is mailed to you, it establishes that the address on the license is valid. A driver's license also has some other security techniques. It often is printed on special paper with stamps and seals to make it harder (but not impossible) to duplicate.

Likewise, the Kerberos ticket and its message have additional information to assist in security. Table 5.2 compares the Kerberos TGT to a driver's license and another form of identification many of us have, an insurance card.

Can You Trust a Kerberos Ticket?

The Kerberos process of using a ticket instead of providing the client password to each server is not new, and it is not foreign to us. After all, we use it every day. When you travel, you trust it with your life. At the airport ticket counter, you submit your driver's license and maybe your credit card, answer some security questions, and are given your boarding pass. You pass through a security barrier where you and your carry-on luggage are scanned with varying degrees of efficiency and sensitivity. To board the airplane, you must hand over your boarding pass, not the original ticket.

Table 5.2 **TGT Compared to Other Identification**

Kerberos TGT	Drivers License	Insurance Card
Random session key		
Start time (can be requested by the client; may be set to the server's time)	Date of issuance	Valid from XX/XX/XX
		(An agreed-upon start date after the payment of some fee)
End time/expiration time (can be requested by the client; might be start time plus maximum lifetime; can be by policy for an individual)	Renewal date	Valid until XX/XX/XX
Client address information	Name and address	Name and address
Server name, address	State ID	Insurance company ID

A portion of the Kerberos ticket is encrypted using the key of the server to which it will be sent. This part of the ticket includes

- Flags
- The client name
- The requested start and end times
- A possible list of valid addresses for the client
- Some additional authorization data

Flags contain special requests (renew this ticket, I want mutual authentication, and so on) that the client included in its request message. The authorization data may be specific to the service being requested.

But I Thought it Was About Authentication

Kerberos is designed for authentication, not authorization. The specification does, however, include a way that authorization data can be included in a Kerberos message. Microsoft uses this part of the plan to include authorization data (user and group security IDs) in its Kerberos implementation in Windows 2000. As you might know, resource objects (files and so or) have lists of the user and group security IDs that are authorized to access them. By including the data in this field, a comparison can be made with the objects' lists. That process, or authorization, is not done by Kerberos. Kerberos merely enables some of the necessary data to accompany the authentication process.

If the ticket included in the message response is a TGT, its encrypted portion is encrypted with the TGS's secret key. If the ticket is for a particular service server, then it is encrypted with that server's secret key.

Where do these keys come from? The Authentication Server, or the TGS, creates the ticket; these servers have access to the KDC, which contains a record for each server in its realm.

Start and End Times

The Kerberos realm specifies a ticket lifetime. The ticket lifetime assists management because tickets will eventually expire; thus even a hijacked ticket will become invalid. In many installations, the lifetime will be the amount of time—perhaps eight hours— that users are logged on. In networks with heightened security risks, the time period can be shorter. A hacker can intercept a conversation and spend a couple days working on decrypting it for use in an attack, but the keys and tickets no longer will be valid by the time the hacker is done.

Two ticket fields determine the ticket lifetime: the end time and the start time. The end time minus the start time gives a valid lifetime for a particular ticket. Because a ticket can only last so long, there must be a mechanism to grant one in the future. Kerberos policy can determine how far in the future this can be set. Postdated tickets are marked INVALID. They must be validated by the TGS before they can be used.

Policy also sets the requirements for continued authentication of clients. Each time a ticket is presented, the request can be checked against a current database and be rejected if no longer valid. The process of using tickets prevents the ceaseless and continued authentication process each time a user wants to access a new resource. However, this convenience must be balanced against the need to periodically revalidate a user.

Revalidation is accomplished partially by the normal work cycle of logging on at the beginning of the day and logging off at night. It also is enforced by expiring tickets. If I forget and leave my workstation logged on, my tickets will expire anyway. When the tickets expire, they cannot be used. Even if someone happens to find my unsecured desktop, he or she will not be able to access network resources after the tickets expire without knowing my password. There is, of course, the small chance that the person will happen by before the tickets expire, but the risk of unsecured access is greatly reduced. Depending on the implementation, Kerberos policy also can be set to allow tickets to automatically renew, in which case the problem of unsecured access persists.

Policy, therefore, can help servers in the Kerberos realm determine whether a ticket is valid. The combination of the start date and time and the original authentication time (both of which are included in the ticket) might show that the ticket couldn't have been issued by a valid server because there is too much time between when the ticket was issued and its valid start date. Policy could even reject a ticket that was issued at some time that has been determined to be around the time a valid Kerberos server was compromised.

Individual application servers also can have their own version of ticket lifetime and can reject tickets that are still valid according to the endtime but that are too old for the particular service. For example, a check-printing print server could reject a ticket that wasn't issued in the last 30 minutes, even though the ticket lifetime in the realm as a whole is for eight hours.

Client and Server Network Addresses

The ticket may include a list of valid addresses for the client. This list of valid addresses can be considered the only addresses from which the ticket can be used. If an otherwise valid ticket is used from an address not in the list, the server will reject it. By policy, a server can be told to accept a ticket without the client's address listed in this field (the ticket is good if used from any address) or to reject it.

How can this prevent an attack? To steal a ticket and use it, an attacker needs to know the session key. The session key is not transmitted in cleartext, so a mere capture of information is useless. Perhaps the attacker has obtained the session key in some other manner, however, and could then steal the ticket. The use of the ticket from some address other than the valid client address(es) would not be possible. If the thief got control of the client machine and used the ticket from there or if the thief spoofed (or faked) the client's valid network address, he could get around this check. Using a list of valid addresses, like any security effort, makes his job harder but not impossible.

Because a TGT will be used to identify the user to the TGS, which is going to give it credentials to access other servers or resources, you might think that it would possible for a Kerberos client to formulate a fake ticket. Such a fake ticket has the format of a real ticket but has not been issued by a true server. If the client could create this fake ticket, perhaps it could be used to obtain a "real" ticket from the TGS to another server.

A program can be written, of course, to create an object that emulates a ticket, but there are problems with this. First, even if the Kerberos client does have a model to go by and from which to steal parts, that only puts the Kerberos client in the same position as the hacker who captures the packet as it flows across the wire: Both still need a valid session key. The client has access to a session key; it's encrypted with the client's secret key. The session key, however, is only good for one session. The client could make one of its own; however, the client does not have access to the unencrypted server key. The client cannot decrypt that portion of the ticket. Because the Kerberos client cannot decrypt that portion of the ticket, he or she would have to copy it into his or her fake ticket. Because it contains outdated information or only provides authentication to servers to which he or she already has legitimate access, it's worthless.

Ticket Flags

As previously noted, various flags can be included in the ticket. These flags are used to convey the specifics of this ticket. Their use depends on the type of ticket (a TGT or a ticket for a service) and the requests that the client made at the time of authentication. Flags used most by the TGS include

- FORWARDABLE and PROXIABLE flags, which tell a TGS if it can issue new TGT or other tickets with new network addresses
- MAY-POSTDATE flags, which indicate that a postdated ticket can be issued
- INVALID flags, which tell an application server to reject the ticket
- RENEWABLE flags, which ask that the ticket be renewed without asking the client to authenticate again

Other flags, such as PROXY, FORWARDED, and INVALID flags, tell the TGS and the service servers information about the status of the ticket. The PRE-AUTHENT flag tells service servers that the client was authenticated before a ticket was issued, and the HW-AUTHENT flag indicates that authentication was based on expected hardware.

Policy and, alternatively, protocol specification determine the use to which this information is put; for example, the Kerberos protocol specifies that INVALID tickets be rejected. Your Kerberos policy might specify that no RENEWED tickets be considered valid.

Pittsburgh: The Ticket-Granting Service Exchange

Our traveler, Phil, makes it to the plant in Pittsburgh. Here he has to obtain additional credentials before he can get to his desired destination. Likewise, the Kerberos protocol allows the AS Exchange to provide a ticket for accessing a service directly. The alternative, which allows a broader range of access across multiple realms, involves an intermediate step. This process sends the client to the TGS with a TGT. The KDC holds copies of the secret keys of all the TGSs in its realm. Its response to the client's request becomes the TGT.

The client must present this ticket, along with an authenticator, to the TGS. The TGS can access the KDC to obtain the secret key of servers in its realm. It can also obtain interdomain keys for other realms with which its realm has a trust. (Kerberos trusts are explained in the section "Kerberos Trust Path" later in this chapter.) The TGS can use the interdomain key to pass on requests for server access in another realm.

In essence, the TGS receives a request for a ticket to some service, attempts to authenticate the request, and if valid, supplies a ticket that grants access to the service. Note that neither the AS nor the TGS checks to see whether the client is authorized to use the service; that is left up to the service itself. The TGS merely provides a pass to the service. The TGS can also be used to renew its TGT, to obtain a proxy ticket, and to VALIDATE a POST-DATED ticket.

In Table 5.3 and Figure 5.4, the steps of the Ticket-Granting Service Exchange are described. Table 5.3 compares Phil's experience to the exchange. Steps in the figure's flow chart correspond to the numbered steps in the second column of the table.

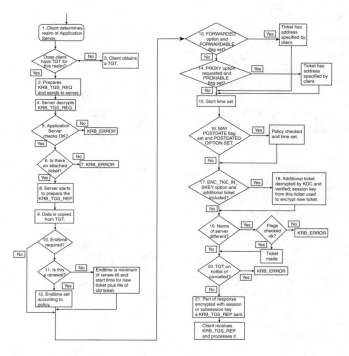

Figure 5.4   The Ticket–Granting Authentication Exchange.

Table 5.3   **The Ticket–Granting Authentication Exchange.**

Phil Potts	Kerberos
Phil finds the location of the plant and goes there.	1. The client determines the realm of the application server.
Phil enters the plant in Pittsburgh. He asks to see Mr. Smith. He presents his employee ID, and he enters the time and date in the logbook at the desk.	2. The client issues a KRG_TGS_REQ message to the TGS. The message includes the TGT, an authenticator, and some other information.
Because Phil is visiting a plant within his division, the ID badge is considered valid. If he were coming from a different division, a mechanism would have to be in place to provide him with some identification that's valid in the other division.	3. If the request is for access to another realm, the TGT might not be valid for that realm. The TGS might be able to issue a TGT for the other realm, or it might issue one for a TGS in a realm that is along the trust path to the desired realm.
	(Kerberos trusts and the Kerberos trust path are discussed in greater detail in the "Kerberos Trust Path" section later in this chapter.)

continues

Table 5.3   **Continued**

Phil Potts	**Kerberos**
The clerk checks Phil's ID badge against the list for his division.	4. If the ticket is from its own realm, the Kerberos TGS uses its secret key to decrypt the ticket. If it is for another realm, an interrealm key will be used.
The clerk makes sure Phil's name is not on the list in the book of invalid IDs.	5. The TGT uses a checksum provided in the client authenticator to verify the request. The ticket is checked against a list of canceled tickets.
Phil also has a letter from his boss to Mr. Smith, authorizing him to receive the contract. The letter is locked in a pouch and only Mr. Smith has the key.	6. The authorization data, if present, is decrypted.
If the pouch, the letter within, or the ID badge has been tampered with, Phil is not allowed to see Mr. Smith.	7. If any of the data has been tampered with (if the checksums don't match, for example), the request is rejected.
Phil is given a Security Pass that allows him to travel to the sales office.	8. through 21. A KRB_TGS_REP is sent. It includes a ticket for the requested server.

KRB_TGS_REQ

The KRB_TGS_REQ message includes the fields in the KRB_AS_REQ message as well as some new ones. These new fields might include encrypted authorization information for the application server and possibly additional tickets if required. *Padata*, the preauthentication data field, is now included to hold the authenticator.

How does the client know the realm of the application server? The Kerberos protocol offers suggestions including making it part of the principal name of the server, storing the information in a name server, or finding it in a configuration file. If a name server is used and the name server is not authenticated, there is risk of misdirection, spoofing, and the use of a realm that has been compromised.

The contents of the KRB_TGS_REP are similar to the contents of the KRB_AS_REP. The encrypted part of the response is encrypted in the subsession key from the authenticator (if present) or with the session key from the TGT. The client's key expiration data and key version fields are not present. Otherwise, the fields of the KRB_AS_REQ are the same as the KRB_AS_REP previously described.

Getting the Contract from the Sales Manager: The Kerberos Client/Server Authentication Exchange

Phil uses his ID badge to get a local security badge and heads for the sales department.

Table 5.4 compares the steps he takes to the Kerberos exchange. Figure 5.5 details the Kerberos exchange. The numbers in the second column of the table correspond to those in the figure.

Table 5.4   **The Client/Server Authentication Exchange**

Phil Potts	Kerberos
Phil uses his employee ID badge to get a local Security Pass. The pass is time-stamped when he receives it.	1. The AS or TGS exchange is used to get a ticket and a session key, which can be used to authenticate the client to the application server. The ticket is retrieved from the client secure storage.
Phil walks through the building to the sales department. He now has the pass to the right department. Note: He can use the pass again, but it must be time-stamped each time he uses it.	2. through 4. A KRB_AP_REQ message is sent by the client to the application server. The message includes the ticket, an authenticator, and other information. Note that, although a ticket can be reused until it expires, a new authenticator must be presented each time. The authenticator is described in greater detail in the "Authenticator" section later in this chapter.
The sales department personnel check Phil's security ID. They look for information to confirm that it is valid including its color and format.	5. The application server checks the version on the message. If the version is wrong, the message is rejected.
The sales department checks the name of the person who signed the ID to make sure it is still a valid signature.	6., 7. The application server looks at the session key. If it is old or invalid, the message is rejected.
The sales department checks from which desk the ID was issued. (There are several entrances into the building; each entrance has its own pass code, and the ID will be marked with that code.)	8. The server checks the realm indicated in the ticket. The server may be able to accept tickets from several realms. If so, it needs to know the realm from which the ticket was issued to select the right key to use to decrypt the ticket.
The ID pass is swiped through a reader, and the code for the desk of issuance is entered. If the ID pass has been altered, it is rejected.	9. The server decrypts the ticket. If it detects modified ciphertext, it will reject the ticket.
Phil's pass is checked for tampering. If the pass has been altered, security is called and Phil is detained.	10. The authenticator is decrypted using the session key from the decrypted ticket. If the authenticator has been modified, the ticket is rejected.
Phil is asked for his name and home office information. It is compared to that on the Security Pass.	11. The realm and name of the client is compared between the authenticator and the tickets. A mismatch requires rejection.
If Phil's address was included, it is checked against that on his home office badge.	12. If the address field is used, it is checked against the network address reported by the operating system for the client.

continues

Table 5.4 **Continued**

Phil Potts	Kerberos
The timestamp on the pass is checked against the current time. By policy, the timestamps can't be off by more than 15 minutes—more than enough time for Phil to walk down the hall.	13. The difference between the Application Server's time and the client's time in the authenticator is compared to the *clock skew time*. The skew time is set by policy. If the two times vary by more than the allotted time, the ticket is rejected.
Phil's name and the times on his pass are compared to a list of recent visitors to the desk. If the list says Phil was just there, Phil is detained. Someone is masquerading as Phil.	14. The server checks its list of connections, looking for one that matches the client and server times on the authenticator and the client name. If it finds one, it knows that this is a replay and rejects it. Its list of connections is kept for at least the length of the allowed clock skew.
If the security ID contains a sequence number (it would be used for later communication), the number is noted.	15. If a sequence number is present, it is recorded so it can be used in later communications such as in encrypted exchanges between the client and the server.
If a subkey is present, it is recorded for later use or is replaced by some key the department chooses.	16. A subkey may be present to be used for later tasks. If so, it may be kept by the server or be replaced by one of the servers chosen.
The age of the ID badge is checked. This can be found by comparing the current time to the time on the ID badge. The valid time on the badge cannot be earlier than the arranged time to account for differences in clocks.	17. The age of the ticket is calculated from the server time and the start time of the ticket. The start time must not be later than the current time plus the allowed clock skew.
Phil is now okayed by the sales desk. He gets to talk to Mr. Smith. Mr. Smith will examine the authorization data (the locked bag containing the letter) and decide whether he will give the contract to Phil.	18. through 20. If all the tests are passed, the server authenticates the client and returns a verification message, the KRB_AP_REP, or if the client also included his resource request, the server might not reply.

Kerberos doesn't believe that every ticket bearer is a good guy. Kerberos uses the ticket as a substitute for transmittal of a user's password multiple times across the network, but it does not allow the presence of a ticket to automatically authenticate that user to every server in the realm. When the Kerberos client presents the ticket to a server, that server checks the ticket nine ways from Sunday. There are a multitude of checks and balances built in to the protocol; it's as if two paranoid security chiefs sat doing the "what if" routine every time the poor protocol designer presented a new version.

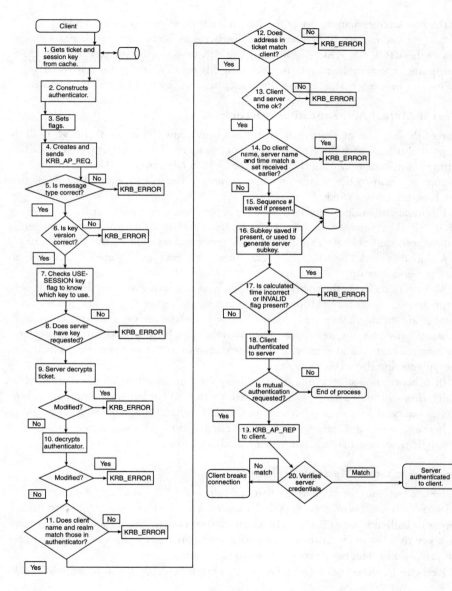

Figure 5.5

Because later exchanges verify the information presented to them, the initial exchange (Authentication Service) of the Kerberos protocol does not demand validation of the KRB_AS_REQ by checking the client password. The exchange can do that, and in many implementations (including Microsoft's), it is done that way. I will discuss this in greater detail in the "Preauthentication" section later in this chapter.

What if Mutual Authentication is Required?

One of the beauties of Kerberos is that it not only allows for the authentication of the client, it also allows for the authentication of the server. The client can verify that he is getting his information from the server from which he requires it. Thus, even an attempt at a man-in-the-middle attack, or a substitution of the required server by the attackers, can be thwarted.

If mutual authentication is required, the application server must return a KRB_AP_REP message. In this reply, the client's authenticator-provided time stamp and microsecond field are used. A randomly generated session key and a subkey might be included as well. The KRB_AP_REQ message is encrypted using the session key from the encrypted part of the ticket.

The client decrypts the message using the session key and verifies that the time-stamp and microsecond fields match those sent to the server. If a subkey and sequence number are included, they are saved for later use. To fake the information, an attacker must not only have the session key and the server key, he must also have intercepted the original request and extracted the information from the authenticator, which is encrypted using the server secret key.

If authentication successfully occurs, the application and the client have a secret key, which they can use to keep private any activity they might generate. Another session key for encrypted messaging between them can be chosen from the subkeys in the reply message and the authenticator. It is the application that does the choosing, or the implementation may include a negotiated key session.

Key Usage: Other Message Exchanges

There are two uses for keys. In the first use, which we have just seen, the client and the server can use their secret keys and a session key provided by the Authentication Server to authenticate each other. In addition, they can use the session key to negotiate a key to be used for further communications. This enables the application to ensure the privacy and integrity of its messages to the client.

Kerberos provides two other messages that can be used by the application. These messages are

- KRB_PRIV, which provides for privacy (encrypted communications) and integrity (verification that the message hasn't been changed in transit)
- KRB_SAFE, which provides message integrity

The Authenticator

The authenticator contains information that helps both parties determine the validity of the message including

- The client's system time
- Possibly an application–specific checksum
- An initial sequence number and/or session subkey that can be used to negotiate a session key unique to this particular session
- A possible request for mutual authentication or use of a session key–based ticket

Because the authenticator is encrypted with the session key, it tells the server that the client knows the encryption key in the ticket. The server can use the timestamp information to detect a replay. In exchange requests, it can compare the client times in the authenticator with the current timestamp.

Because a new authenticator must accompany each use of a ticket, an old timestamp has to represent an invalid request, possibly a replay. Per specification, the client time in the authenticator is compared to the local server time. The time difference cannot vary by more than the clock skew time set by policy. The server uses the client timestamp (placed in the nonce field) in its response, and the client can use this information to determine whether a valid server is responding to its request. A valid server knows the client's key and uses it to encrypt the response. In a KRB_PRIV or KRB_SAFE message, the included sequence number can be used. Message with numbers that are not in the sequence can be considered to be invalid.

Preauthentication

The Kerberos RFC does not specify that the client's ID and password be validated directly by the Kerberos Authentication Server during the AS exchange. It states that the AS checks the KDC for a record matching the ID presented and encrypts its response in the key of that principal.

Because only a client with knowledge of that key can decrypt the response and put it to use, this is where the validation of the password occurs. A side effect of this arrangement is that the user password does not pass over the network, even in an encrypted form, when the client requests a ticket. Because the password is not used in this exchange to encrypt anything in the request, a rogue server could not take an intercepted request and crack the password.

Could anyone with knowledge of a valid principal ID ask for and receive a ticket without knowing the key? Yep. But without the password, the person couldn't decrypt the information necessary to use the ticket.

The Kerberos RFC does, however, allow implementers to use an optional feature—preauthentication—if they want clients to present passwords and IDs before a ticket is issued. Preauthentication can be handled during the Authentication Service Exchange. Evidence of preauthentication is contained in the ticket flags. Three flags involved are:

- INITIAL (a ticket was issued during the AS Exchange, not the TGS Exchange)
- PRE-AUTHENT (a ticket was preauthenticated)
- HW-AUTHENT (a ticket was preauthenticated using expected hardware)

If the ticket was issued by the AS exchange, the PRE-AUTHENT- or HW-AUTHENT-flagged ticket will also have the INITIAL flag set. Preauthentication, simply put, means the client presented evidence that it knows its key in the KRB_AS_REQ. The password does not traverse the network in the clear. For more information, see the "Encryptions and Checksums" section later in this chapter.

Kerberos Trust Path

So far, I have talked about Kerberos almost as if the whole world were part of a single Kerberos realm. Surely, this is not even true within the same company. How then can cross-realm authentication be accomplished?

The Kerberos protocol specifies how realms can set up *trusts*. Essentially what happens is that the TGS of one realm becomes registered as a principal in the other. The TGSs in both realms share an interrealm key. The concept of trust means that cross-realm authentication is possible. It does not mean that wide-open access to all resources across all trusted realms is automatically granted. I do not have to have a different principal name and password for every realm I might need to access. I do not have to enter this information needlessly. The TGS in my realm can pass my request along to another realm by providing me with a TGT for that realm's TGS.

Trust does not have to be explicitly created between each and every realm. Trust in Kerberos is transitive. That is, if Realm A trusts Realm B and Realm B trusts Realm C, then Realm A trusts Realm C and vice versa. Figure 5.6 shows this relationship. In the figure, Realm A trusts Realm B and Realm B trusts Realm C. The trust is two-way. A bold, double-pointed arrow is meant to illustrate this point. Realm A also trusts Realm C, even though a specific trust relationship has not been implemented. A dotted, double-pointed arrow indicates this.

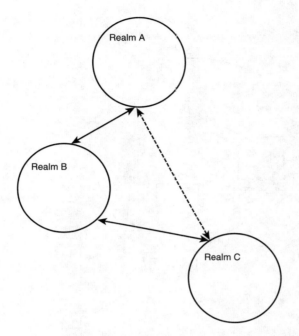

Figure 5.6 Kerberos transitive trust.

For Alice to get a file on Server B in Realm B, she must first acquire a TGT for Realm B. Figure 5.7 illustrates the following steps:

1. Alice does whatever her OS or application requires to identify the file and its location.

2. Her Kerberos client uses a KRB_AS_REQ to request a ticket for Server B.

3. The AS in her realm notes that the request is for another realm and sends Alice's client a TGT for her realm's TGS.

4. Alice's client sends the TGT to the TGS.

5. The TGS notes that the requested ticket is for a server in another realm. It finds an interrealm key for that realm and uses it to create a TGT for that realm.

6. The TGS sends the new TGT to Alice's client.

7. Alice's client sends the TGT to the TGS in Realm B.

8. The Realm B TGS validates the TGT and sends Alice a ticket for Server B in its realm.

9. Alice's client uses this ticket to access Server B.

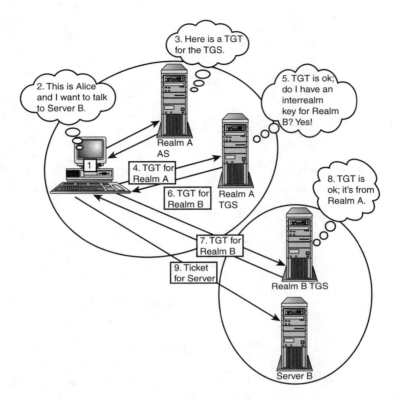

Figure 5.7 Interrealm access.

What if the server is not in a realm for which the TGS has an interrealm key? This is not a problem because of the transitive nature of Kerberos trusts. You can think of the realms as being part of a linked list of realms. Requests can be passed up or down the list of servers until one that can issue a TGT for the correct realm is found. The path they follow is called a trust path. The name *trust path* is also used to identify possible pathways for authentication.

Realms also can be organized hierarchically, and trust paths that travel up and then down another part of the hierarchy can be defined. Figure 5.8 shows such an arrangement. In the figure, each circle represents a realm. Black arrows identify trusts; darker, double-lined arrows identify the trust path from B2A2 to C2. Realms that directly trust each other (double-pointed arrows) share interrealm keys. Realm B2A2 and C2 do not share interrealm keys. To determine whether there is a trust relationship between them, a trust path must be constructed. If this can be done, a client in realm B2A2 is able to obtain a ticket for a server in Realm C2.

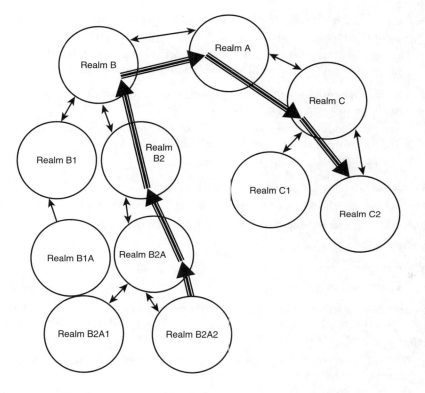

Figure 5.8 Hierarchical realm organization showing trust paths.

Encryptions and Checksums

The Kerberos protocol is modularly designed. The choice of encryption, encoding, or checksum algorithms is kept separate from the algorithms of the message exchanges themselves. RFC 1510 lists a variety of choices. As vulnerabilities to current crypto functions are found and newer, better ones replace them, the Kerberos protocol can be adapted to use them. To recap, the RFC 1510 specifies the following:

- The AS exchange uses the principal's secret key to encrypt its response to the request for a ticket.

- The TGS exchange uses the shared session key to encrypt its response to the request for a ticket.

- The principal's capability to decrypt the response and send a ticket and a valid authenticator to a server validates the identity of the principal.

- If a DES key is generated from a password, the password has the realm and the principal's name appended (password + realm name + name).
- The encrypted data field in a message includes information on which encryption type was used, an optional key version number, and the ciphertext.

To prepare the ciphertext, you must first prepare a string to hold the checksum and the data with the following steps:

1. Generate a random string to be used for the confounder (a zeroed-out octet string that is a placeholder for the checksum and the data).

2. Concatenate the confounder.

Next, calculate the checksum and replace the placeholder.

3. Calculate the checksum over this new string (confounder + placeholder + data).

4. Replace the zeroed-out placeholder with the calculated checksum.

5. Add necessary padding.

Finally, encrypt the string.

6. Encrypt the new string.

The encryption system used in a Kerberos implementation can vary, so the specification has provided for the inclusion of the encryption type used in the message. Systems specified in the RFC for Kerberos are

- Null (no encryption and no checksum, confounder, or padding; ciphertext = plaintext)
- DES in CBC mode with a CRC-32 checksum
- DES in CBC mode with an MD4 checksum
- DES in CBC mode with an MD5 checksum

Checksums are further classified in the specification by the properties of collision-proof and keyed. If two different plaintexts, when encrypted, generate the same ciphertext, a collision occurs. If this is possible, then it might be possible to substitute data in a message that requires integrity and get away with it. Because this is not the result desired, a checksum algorithm should be chosen that is regarded as collision-proof. (It is almost impossible to generate the same ciphertext from two different plaintexts.)

If a checksum is not considered to be collision-proof (such as CRC-32), the specification requires that it be used only where the result will be encrypted. Encryption of the checksums makes them more tamperproof. Keyed checksums, as you know, require a key to create them. Nonkeyed checksums should not be used unless they are encrypted.

RFC 1510 identifies and recommends RSA-MD4 using DES, RSA-MD5 using DES, and DES cipher-block chained checksum alternative as being keyed and collision-proof.

For More Information

This chapter discussed services for which complementary information exists in other chapters of this book. The following should serve as a referral source for you in locating this information.

An introduction to symmetric encryption can be found in Chapter 2, "Cryptology Introduction."

Many of the hash functions and cryptographic functions mentioned were first described in Chapter 3, "New Protocols, Products, and APIs."

To learn how Windows 2000 implements Kerberos, see Chapter 7, "User Authentication."

Summary

This chapter presented Kerberos algorithms and information separate from implementation specifics. The design of Kerberos, like the study of Kerberos, must have been fun but frustrating. It's a rich protocol with many intricacies. The rationale behind each detail becomes clearer the more you study it. If you have not done so already, obtain a copy of its specification, RFC 1510. I guarantee that you will find new evidence of its excellent design.

A wise man once said, "The devil's in the details." I like to think that's only true if you don't understand them and that maybe it's God who put them there. In any case, having studied Kerberos in the RAW, you will find your study of Windows 2000 and Microsoft's implementation of Kerberos much easier.

II

Securing the OS

6

Security from the Get-Go

PROFESSIONAL, SERVER, ADVANCED SERVER—ALL OF THESE VERSIONS share common security features. In this chapter and in Chapters 7 through 9, you'll learn about these security features. In this chapter, we'll start with the most important new aspect of Windows 2000 security: security from the get-go.

Windows NT is often criticized for its out-of-the-box openness. That is, to secure NT servers and clients, you have had to make registry entries, write systems policies, configure file-system ACLs, and badger Microsoft into responding with tools and processes and knowledge. Windows 2000, in contrast, provides more security features from the get-go, installs by default with improved security, and shares its security setup secrets with anyone who cares to study the online help files, download documentation, or attend a Microsoft-sponsored workshop, seminar, or class. There is even an official Microsoft security certification exam in the Windows 2000 MCSE track.

The out-of-the-box Windows 2000 default settings and processes include default file system and registry settings that secure sensitive areas, new defined users and group scopes, and a finer granularity available to rights and privileges assignments. Kerberos is the default methodology for authentication, and a new Encrypting File System is available to protect your files and folders with a click of the mouse. In addition, Windows 2000 has many new features available including smart card integration, Active Directory, security configuration tools, system file protection, and a new Recovery Console. A Public Key Infrastructure (PKI) is easily integrated into the new Active Directory. The default interface varies significantly from client to server, and new tools make it possible to define, maintain, and audit system security from a central location and let it flow to the outermost reaches of the enterprise.

To understand the impact of these changes as a whole, you must first examine each individual part. Meanwhile, before you can begin making the changes that will properly address security issues in your enterprise, you must learn the details of the defaults. This chapter will help you begin that journey by

- Describing default users and groups and their rights
- Examining the increased security applied to system files and registry keys
- Introducing the Encrypting File System
- Describing the Windows File Protection Service

Two other security features, Group Policy and Security Configuration and Analysis, are referred to in this chapter but are fully explored in Chapter 9, "Security Tools," and Chapter 16, "Securing the Network Using Distributed Security Services." These tools have default security settings right out of the box and can be additionally configured for powerful security control. Smart card integration is first described in Chapter 7, "User Authentication," and is more fully explained in Chapter 17, "Enterprise Public Key Infrastructure." The recovery process is described in Chapter 8, "Lifecycle Choices."

Users and Groups

If you understand how to properly use Windows NT groups to manage access and authority on your systems, you will be able to build on that knowledge in Windows 2000. There are new groups, rights, and permissions—and several new tools to help you take advantage of them. If you were frustrated by the lack of granularity in administrative roles, take heart; you have new options. Those who develop knowledge of the subtleties of group membership in Windows 2000 will be able to use them to secure their systems and to select, write, and implement programs that work without having to degrade security. However, if your company has ignored recommended assignments, strategies, and documentation—and instead of learning about the rights and privileges of group membership, has given everyone membership in every group or has gradually added memberships and privileges to somehow make its systems work—Windows 2000 will not miraculously repair the problems you might have with excessive rights or improper access.

Groups in Windows NT are either local or global. Groups in Windows 2000 are first divided into two classifications: security groups, which are used to assign or deny rights and permissions, or distribution groups, which are used to send email messages. Security groups are further distinguished by scope: local, domain local, universal, or domain global. (To learn more about group scope, see the section "Introduction to Group Scope" later in this chapter.)

Users and Groups on Standalone Systems

Standalone systems are Windows 2000 Professional, Server, and Advanced Server systems that are not joined in a domain. The range of default local users and groups available on these systems is different from those available on domain controllers. The scope that they may operate in is also different. These local users and groups can only have local scope; that is, they can only be assigned rights and permissions on the local system. Default local groups are

- Administrators
- Users
- Power Users
- Guests
- Replicator
- Backup Operators

During installation, only two accounts are created: Administrator and Guest.

Administrators

What can an Administrator do? What kinds of Administrators are there? Windows 2000 has three administrative groups: Domain Admins, Enterprise Admins, and Administrators. Two of these, Enterprise Admins and Domain Admins, do not exist if you do not have a domain. One of these, the Enterprise Admins group, is new with Windows 2000. I'll discuss all three groups thoroughly later.

To be more precise, our question should be: What can a local Administrator (on a Server or Professional system) do on that single system? The answer might seem confusing to those knowledgeable about Windows operating systems. In Windows 2000, the following rules apply:

- By default, the local Administrator can do anything she wants. For example, although she might not be granted access to some registry keys, files, or folders, she can take ownership of these objects and give herself those privileges.

- The Administrator can even grant herself additional privileges above those granted by default. For example, she can give herself the right to Act as Part of the Operating System.

- An Administrator can restrict another Administrator's privileges. For example, an Administrator can be kept from adding members to the Administrators group.

It is the third rule that challenges beliefs. The concept that an Administrator's absolute authority can be modified might not seem right, but it allows granularity in administrative control. This concept is explored in later discussions on security policies concerning restricted groups and on delegation of authority.

Another question to ask is this: What can an Administrator do that a User can't? Only an Administrator can

- Install applications that require the installation of services
- Install operating system components (such as drivers) and services
- Install service packs, hotfixes, and Windows updates
- Repair the OS using the Recovery Console
- Configure machine-wide OS parameters (password policy, kernel mode driver configuration, access controls, and audit functions)

Some legacy applications also require Administrator privileges to run them. This has more to do with the improper design of the application (it has to access files and registry keys that Users shouldn't be able to) than with a bug in the OS.

Administrators Should Never Log on

What? you ask. Then how can they do their work? Administrators should never log on using their Administrator account; they should log on using their user account (you did give them one didn't you?) and then use the RUNAS command to launch trusted administrative programs under their administrative account context. They can use the following command:

RUNAS /u:computername\administrator cmd

Applications launched here will inherit the parent access token. To use the RUNAS command through the shell, select the executable, press Shift, and right-click.

When the application thus started is closed, any administrative privileges are gone as well. The next action you take will execute under the context of your user account. Unlike the UNIX su command, with which you might be familiar, the RUNAS command does not start a session with administrative privileges from which you then run programs. RUNAS does not give your every point and click administrative command thereafter. RUNAS simply enables you to run the application you started with the RUNAS command with the privileges and access rights of the account for which you provided a user ID and password. Other commands or programs that you run under the context you logged on with. Close the application and you do not have any special privileges.

Users

What can a User do? It's easier to say what one *can't* do. If you do a clean install onto an NTFS partition, Windows 2000 is designed, by default, to keep a User from screwing with the OS and its installed applications. Unlike Windows NT, for which many critical registry and folder paths were marked Everyone Full Control, Windows 2000 implements restrictions on sensitive paths. Users cannot change registry settings that could impact the entire machine. Users cannot change operating system files or program files. Users cannot install programs for others to run. In the ideal Windows 2000 world, Users can run programs installed by Administrators, Power Users, and themselves, but they cannot run programs installed by other Users. (One more protection against Trojans.) A User cannot access another User's private data.

To keep this new out-of-the-box-style security secure, you have to do your part. Put end users in the Users group only. Deploy programs that they can run. Look for programs that have the *Windows 2000 Application Specification*.

Note

Applications that meet the *Windows 2000 Application Specification* will run successfully under this context. Microsoft Office 2000 meets the application specification. Consult the Windows 2000 application catalog for a list of compliant applications at

> http://www.microsoft.com/windows/compatible

and read the specification itself at

> http://msdn.microsoft.com/winlogo/win2000.asp.

Until all programs are written to standards, there will always be some standard programs that Users need elevated permissions to run. Many legacy applications will not be accessible to the Users group. You might have to consider placing some Users in the Power Users group.

Power Users

Power Users have essentially the standard settings that Users had in Windows NT. In addition, Power Users:

- Can install applications that do not install system services. (Installation of some legacy applications will fail because they might attempt to replace operating system files, which Power Users cannot do.)
- Can adjust system-wide resources such as System Time, Display Settings, Shares, Power Configuration, Printers, and so on.
- Cannot access other users' data if that data is stored on an NTFS partition and is properly protected.

Power Users also have more access to system folders and registry keys than Users do.

By default, the Power Users group has no members. If Users could run an application on NT Workstation, they might not be able to run it on Windows 2000 Professional. The problem is not a User privilege or right but rather the improved registry and system file restrictions (or the attempts of the application to modify system files now protected from overwriting). The Power Users group is granted the same registry and system file access that Users were granted in Windows NT. This makes it likely that members of the Power Users group will be able to run these applications. You might want to make users who need to run legacy applications members of the Power Users group or relax registry restrictions to keep from giving Users the additional rights that Power Users have.

Guests

The Guests group includes the Guest account, which is disabled by default. It has limited access to the system but does allow someone without a user ID and password to log on.

Replicator

The Replicator group can be used to support the File Replication Service (FRS) provided by a domain. It is not used on a standalone system.

Backup Operators

Backup Operators have the right to back up and restore files and folders.

A Summary of Implicit User Rights

User rights are defined explicitly by the basic rights and privileges given to them. Additional built-in or implicit rights are given to built-in groups, as described in Table 6.1.

Table 6.1 **Implicit Group Rights**

Implicit Right	Group
Create local users and groups	A, PU
Create, modify or delete any account	A
Modify users and groups that they have created	A, PU
Create and delete non-admin file shares	A, PU
Create, manage, delete and share local printers	A, PU

A = Administrators/PU = Power Users

Introduction to the Active Directory

Because the security boundaries in Windows 2000 are different from those in Windows NT, a brief introduction to Active Directory concepts is necessary. Basic definitions and domain modes are introduced here. A more thorough discussion of Active Directory will have to wait until Chapter 12, "Domain-Level Security."

Active Directory Infrastructure

Several Active Directory infrastructure concepts need to be defined:

- **Namespace.** Windows 2000 has adopted the DNS nomenclature and structure as the backbone of its directory. Thus, a Windows 2000 tree will have a DNS namespace.
- **Domain.** A logical grouping of computers under a centralized control.
- **Tree.** A hierarchical structure of domains in the same namespace.
- **Directory.** A listing of the objects that exist in a forest.
- **Class.** The logical definitions of any number of items that can exist in the directory including domain controllers, computers, users, and groups.
- **Object.** An actual thing. An object exists, while a class is just a description. For example, Bob's user account, which can operate within the domain, is an object; the class "user account" merely is a description. The class defines what any user account might look like once created.
- **Attribute.** Elements that describe an object. An object will have many attributes or features. A user account, for example, includes attributes such as first name, last name, department, telephone, member of, and so on.
- **Schema.** The classes and attributes that can exist in a forest.
- **Forest.** A collection of trees that share the same schema but that exist in different namespaces.
- **Site.** Whereas a domain is a logical collection of computers, a site represents the physical collection (that is, a subnet or group of subnets).
- **Organizational unit.** A collection of users or computers that exists entirely within a domain.

In Figure 6.1, the triangles represent Active Directory domains. The first triangle is enlarged simply to show the organizational units (OUs), represented by circles, and the member computers and users in the OUs. Domains to the left make up one tree; domains to the right are another. The entire figure represents a forest. Domains are named appropriately to illustrate the namespace.

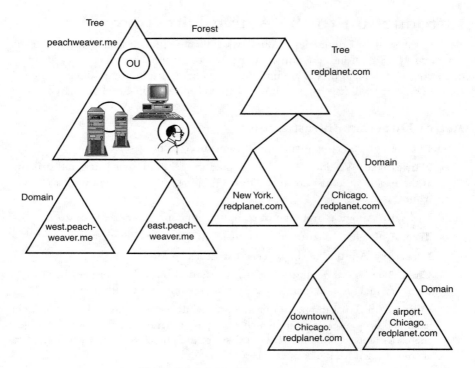

Figure 6.1 Active Directory concepts.

Trust is defined differently in Windows 2000 than in Windows NT. Whereas trust relationships must be established in Windows NT and are one-directional and non-transitive, trust in Windows 2000 is implicit, bidirectional, and transitive in the forest.

Domain Modes

Active Directory domains are in one of two modes. In mixed mode, which is the default mode, Windows NT 4.0 domain controllers can be part of the Windows 2000 domain. In native mode, domains cannot contain any Windows NT 4.0 domain controllers. A domain in either mode can have Windows NT 4.0 servers and Windows NT 4.0 workstation computers as members. Although Windows 9x computers cannot be joined in the domain, their users can log on to Windows 2000 domains in either mode.

The main point to remember here is this: A native mode Windows 2000 domain can include Windows NT servers and workstations; it just cannot have any Windows NT domain controllers. It is a commonly held misconception that Windows 2000 native mode domains can only include Windows 2000 computers.

Introduction to Group Scope

To understand the uses and capabilities of domain groups, you need to examine group scope. Group scope is not a new concept to Windows operating systems. Windows NT global groups can be assigned access and rights to computers in domains and trusting domains. NT local groups only have meaning on the machine on which they exist.

In Windows 2000, group scope has been expanded to include two new group scopes: universal and domain local. Local machine groups and domain global groups still exist. Universal group scope is only available if the domain is in native mode. It is easiest to understand the new group scopes if you realize that scope is really just an indication of where a group can be granted permissions and where a group's membership can come from. Permissions for groups are displayed in Table 6.2. The possible membership of each group is defined by whether the Windows 2000 network is in mixed mode or native mode. Table 6.3 lists those features.

Table 6.2 **Scope and Permissions**

Scope	Group Can be Granted Permissions in
Domain local	The domain in which it exists
Global	All domains in the forest
Universal	Any domain in the domain tree or forest
Local	The machine on which it exists

Table 6.3 **Group Membership**

Scope	Membership Can Consist of	
	Native Mode	**Mixed Mode**
Domain local	User accounts, global groups, and universal groups from any domain in the forest; domain local groups from the same domain.	User accounts, global groups from any domain.
Global	User accounts, global groups from the same domain only.	User accounts from the same domain.
Universal	User accounts, global groups, other universal groups from any domain in the forest.	Not applicable. Universal scope does not exist in mixed mode.
Local	User accounts, global groups, and universal groups from any domain in the forest; domain local groups from the same domain.	User accounts, global groups from any domain in the forest.

> **Note**
> Group nesting, or the membership of groups in other groups, does not exist in a mixed mode domain except for the placement of global groups in local groups. Group nesting is a valuable technique for more easily managing permissions and rights in an enterprise, and it is a valuable feature of native mode domains.

Understanding the true implication of group scope and how to select this scope when creating new groups is easier to understand when you have had more experience with, and understanding of, the Active Directory. In a small, single-domain, mixed mode Windows 2000 network, group scope consists of domain global and local groups, just as it did in a pure Windows NT network. Users are placed into global groups, and these groups are placed into local groups on resources where they need the privileges and/or access assigned to the local groups. In a large, Windows 2000 enterprise, user accounts are still placed in global groups, and then global groups are placed into local groups. When universal access is necessary and a domain is in native mode, universal group scope can be employed. A discussion on creating these larger groups' architectures and determining group scope can be found in Chapter 16.

In sum, a domain is required before global groups can be considered; a domain must be in native mode before universal groups exist. A Windows 2000 Server or Professional system that is not part of an Active Directory infrastructure (that is, it is not joined in a domain) does not have global groups, universal groups, or domain local groups.

Default Domain Groups

Windows 2000 domains have a number of default global and domain local groups. Most default global groups do not have inherent rights; they are given rights by virtue of their inclusion in domain local groups or by specific assignment. If you create a new global group, you can give it rights by adding it to domain local groups or by explicitly assigning it rights.

As previously mentioned, a new default global group in Windows 2000 is Enterprise Admins. In mixed mode, Enterprise Admins is a global group. When the domain is changed to native mode, the Enterprise Admins group becomes the first universal group. The Enterprise Admins group is for Administrators who need to control the entire network. The first domain created in a forest, the forest root domain, includes this group and gives it membership in the Domain Admins group. The Administrator of this first domain is the only default member of the Enterprise Admins group. Each new domain in the forest will automatically include this group as a member in its local Administrators group. You can give other Administrators far-reaching capabilities by adding them to the Enterprise Admins group.

Groups in a Windows 2000 domain can be managed from the Active Directory Users and Computers console. Groups are located in two of its subfolders. Groups with domain local scope are primarily located in the Built-in folder. Groups with global scope are located in Users folder.

User Folder Groups

Groups in the Users folder are

- **Domain Users.** Users in the domain
- **Domain Admins.** Administrators of the domain
- **Domain Guests.** Guest accounts in the domain
- **DNS Administrators.** Administrators allowed to administrate DNS servers
- **Enterprise Admins.** Administrators with forest-wide privileges
- **Group Policy Creator Owners.** Those that can create Group Policy
- **Schema Admins.** Those that can modify the schema

Windows 2000 also introduces a new group concept: computer groups. Computer groups are used to collect computers with the same responsibilities into a more easily manageable structure. A computer group implicitly grants rights to computers placed in these groups.

Computer groups in the Users folder are

- **RAS and IAS Servers.** Servers that can access remote access properties of users
- **Domain Controllers.** All domain controllers in the domain
- **Domain Computers.** All member servers and workstations joined in the domain
- **DnsUpdate Proxy.** DNS clients allowed to update DNS for other clients
- **Cert Publishers.** Agents for certification and renewal

Group membership for User groups in the Users folder is described in Table 6.4.

Table 6.4 **User Groups in the Users Folder**

Group	Default Membership	Default Group Membership
Domain Users	Administrator	Users,each new Domain User
Domain Admins	Administrator	Administrators
Domain Guests	Guest	Guests
DNS Administrators	None	None
Enterprise Admins	Administrator	Administrators
Group Policy Creator Owners	Administrator	None
Schema Admins	Administrator	None

Table 6.5 identifies the scope and default membership of computer groups.

Table 6.5   **User Folder Computer Group Scope and Membership**

Computer Group	Scope	Default Membership
RAS and IAS Servers	Domain local	None
Domain Controllers	Global	All DCs in domain
Domain Computers	Global	All member servers and workstations joined in the domain
DnsUpdate Proxy	Global	None
Cert Publishers	Global	None

Built-in Folder Groups

Domain local groups are in the Built-in folder. The privileges and the default membership for these groups are listed in Table 6.6.

Table 6.6   **Built-in Groups**

Group	Privileges	Default Membership
Administrators	All administrative tasks on all domain controllers and the domain	Administrator, Domain Admins global group
Account Operators	Create, delete, and modify user accounts and groups. Cannot modify the Administrators group or Operators group.	None
Backup Operators	Back up and restore all domain controllers using Windows Backup.	None
Print Operators	Set up and manage network printers on domain controllers.	None
Server Operators	Share disk resources and back up and restore files on a domain controller.	None
Guests	Tasks that they have granted Rights for, resources they have assigned permissions, cannot make permanent changes to their desktop environment.	Guest User, Domain Guests global group, Domain Users
Users	Tasks they have granted rights for, resources they have assigned permissions.	Domain Users
Replicator	File replication in a domain.	None
Pre-Windows 2000 Compatible	This backward-compatible group allows Read access on users and groups in the domain.	None

Implicit or System Groups

In addition to default groups that you can manage, Windows 2000 creates a number of implicit groups. Membership in these groups cannot be controlled. Their membership is determined by the activity in which a user is engaging. These groups are

- **Everyone.** All security principals including anonymous users
- **Authenticated Users.** All security principals who have been authenticated (does not include anonymous users)
- **Interactive.** Security principals who are logged on locally
- **Creator Owner.** The security principal who created, and thus owns, the object
- **Network.** Security principals whose logon was across the network
- **Anonymous Logon.** No identified Windows 2000 or Windows NT user account such as access to a printer by a user on a UNIX system
- **Dialup.** Users accessing resources through an RAS server

In Windows 2000, implicit groups are not given wide permissions or file and registry access. Instead, only groups that can be directly controlled by an Administrator are used.

Application Service Account Catch-22

What group membership is needed by application service accounts? This depends on whether the application meets the new standards. If the application meets the new standards, the install program should place the service account in the appropriate group. Legacy applications and applications that are not written to standard might need to have the default group membership changed. If the application doesn't run, it might need the account used to run its service account placed in the Power Users group. (Accounts that run under the context of the local systems account are not affected by stricter user rights in Windows 2000.)

Rights and Privileges

Although the implicit and default rights of users and groups already were introduced, many rights and privileges need to be defined. In addition, the concept of logon rights versus privileges is important.

Logon rights are granted by default to multiple groups. Logon rights do not give users privileges to perform other activities. Logon rights are just that: the right to log on. All other rights (such as the right to add workstations to a domain or to back up files and directories) are categorized as privileges.

Windows 2000 logon rights are described in Table 6.7. Privileges are described in Table 6.8. In the tables, several abbreviations are used:

- A = Administrators
- AO = Account Operator
- BO = Backup Operator
- E = Enterprise Admin
- G = Guest
- PO = Print Operator
- PU = Power User
- SO = Server Operator
- U = User

Table 6.7 **Logon Rights**

Logon Right	Default Groups or Users that Hold this Right	Definition
Access this computer from a network	A, PU, U, G, BO	Connects to computer over the network
Log on locally	A, PU, U, G, BO— Professional, A, PU, BO—Server A, E, SO, AO, PO—DC	Accesses the computer from the local console
Log on as a batch job	A	Logs on using a batch-queue facility
Log on as a service	Local Systems Account only	Establishes a security context
Deny access to this computer from the network	None	Explicitly denies access to this computer even if granted due to membership in some group

Logon Right	Default Groups or Users that Hold this Right	Definition
Deny logon as a batch job	None	Explicitly denies access to log on as a batch even if granted this right due to membership in some other group
Deny logon as a service	None	Explicitly denies access to log on as a service even if granted due to membership in some other group
Deny local logon	None	Explicitly denies access to log on locally even if granted due to membership in some group

Table 6.8 **Privileges**

Privilege	Group	Definition
Back up files and file folders	A, BO, SO	Supercedes file and folder permissions
Bypass traverse checking	E	Moves between folders to access files even if the user has no permission to access the parent folder
Change system time	A, PU, SO	Sets internal time clock of computer
Create page file	A	No effect
Debug programs	A	Debug low-level objects (threads)
Force shutdown from remote system	A, SO	Shuts down remote computer
Increase scheduling priority	A,PU	Boosts execution priority of a process
Load and unload device drivers	A	Installs and uninstalls device drivers

continues

Table 6.8   **Continued**

Privilege	Group	Definition
Manage auditing and security log	A	Specifies types of resource access (file access, and so on) that are to be audited, views and clears the security log, does not allow setting system audit policy
Modify firmware environmental variables	A	Modifies system environmental variables stored in nonvolatile RAM
Profile a single process	A, PU	Performs performance sampling
Restore files and file folders	A, BO	Restores backed up files and folders, supercedes directory permissions
Shut down the system	A, BO, E, PU, U—Professional A. E—Server and DC	Shuts down Windows 2000
Take ownership of files or other objects	A	Take ownership supercedes permission protecting objects

User and Group Management Tools

In a Windows 2000 Active Directory infrastructure, users and groups are managed with the Active Directory Users and Computers console, with the Security Configuration and Analysis Microsoft Management Console (MMC) snap-in, and or with Group Policy. For information on the Security Configuration and Analysis snap-in, see the section "Using the Security Configuration and Analysis Tool Set" in Chapter 9. For information on Group Policy, see Chapter 12.

Users and groups on Windows 2000 Professional and Windows 2000 Servers that are not joined in the domain are managed by using the Computer Management console and the Local Computer Policy console. The steps for group management are the same as in Windows NT:

1. Determine the privileges needed.
2. Determine the resources needed to access and at what level.
3. Examine default groups to see if they meet needs.
4. Create additional groups to meet additional needs.
5. Assign users to groups.
6. Give groups the privileges and access necessary.

Sound like a lot of work? The good news is that most privilege decisions boil down to a decision between two basic default groups: Administrators or Users.

First, decide who should be an Administrator and who should be a User. This isn't hard. Probably about 1 or 2 percent of your company population will have some administrative responsibilities and will therefore need administrative authority. The rest of the employees will start and complete their Windows 2000 lifecycles as Users. Keep in mind, however, that all Administrators need a User-level account as well. They will do much of their work as Users, and they only need the administrative account for specific, administrative duties.

Some Users will need additional privileges, somewhere in between Users and Administrators. Several default groups might fit their needs; otherwise, you'll create your own groups to provide granularity and control resource access.

After you have decided who belongs to which group, take each group and further divide its membership. Not all Administrators need to have full administrative powers. Perhaps their responsibilities will lie in one predefined area such as creating accounts or managing passwords; maybe they only need privileges in some small section of your enterprise. It could be that they only need to be Account Operators, Print Operators, or Backup Operators. On Windows 2000 Professional or standalone servers, they might be happily employed as Power Users.

Beware the Guest

Beware and be aware; the Guest account is a member of the system group Everyone. This means that any default privileges and access—and any access you assign to the group Everyone—are also available to the Guest account and any other account you assign membership in the Domain Guests group. Although the Guest account is disabled by default, you should carefully restrict the group Everyone and restrict the Guest account. To increase security, assign a strong password, deny logon hours 7×24, deny remote access, and if you have to have keep the NetBIOS protocol, restrict the Guest account logon to a nonexistent workstation.

The Microsoft Management Console

The Microsoft Management Console (MMC) is a tool that can be used to open, save, and create sets of administrative tools. A snap-in is one of these tools and can include objects that can be administered as well as functions used in administering them. Extension snap-ins can be added to extend the function of another snap-in.

Windows 2000 NTFS

Windows 2000 NTFS adds additional security features including an Encrypting File System and easier implementation and management of the Distributed File System.

> **Note**
>
> Information on securing the Distributed File System is located in Chapter 14, "Securing the Distributed File System." We will discuss the Encrypted File System later in this chapter.

Some of the most notable changes to the NTFS, however, are not in its new features but in the default security settings implemented when Windows 2000 is installed (not updated) on an NTFS partition. To understand these settings, you must first examine the sets of access permissions allowed.

File Permissions

To manage permissions on an object in Windows NT, you grant a specific type of access, give no access by simply not including the account, or explicitly define access by using the No Access permission. Windows 2000 increases the granularity by giving you the choice of Allow or Deny for each type of permission possible on an object. This is true of permissions set on printers, registry keys, and other objects as well as on files and folders.

File and folder permissions are grouped into categories; each category can include the permission sets of other categories. Categories are

- Full Control (includes Modify, Read & Execute, List Folder Contents, Read, Write)
- Modify (includes Read & Execute, List Folder Contents, Read, Write)
- Read & Execute (includes List Folder Contents, Read)
- List Folder Contents
- Read
- Write

Each category is a collection of permission sets. These permission sets can be viewed and selected individually on the Advanced page of the Security tab of the file or folder object properties page.

Each category and permission can be set to Allow or Deny for a particular user or group. This granularity allows a user to be denied Write permission, for example, on a file that a group to which he belongs has Write permission. In Windows NT, this cannot be done; it is either lose all permission or create even more groups.

Default Security Settings

During a clean installation, default security settings are applied. These default security settings are listed in Table 6.9. A number of abbreviations are used in this table to describe the permissions that various groups have. They are

- FC = Full Control
- RX = Read and Execute
- R = Read
- L = List Folder Contents
- W = Write

Table 6.9 **Default File and Folder Permissions, Windows 2000 Standalone Server**

File	Administrators	Power Users	Users	Authenticated Users	Everyone
System files: Boot.ini, ntdetect.com, ntldr, ntbootdd.sys	FC	RX	None	None	None
\ProgramFiles	FC	Modify, RX, L, R, W	RX, L, R	None	None
\WINNT	FC	Modify, RX, L, R, W	RX, L, R	None	None
\WINNT*.*	FC	RX,	R RX	None	RX, R
\WINNT\addins	FC	Modify, RX, L, R	RX	None	None
\WINNT\config*.*	FC	Modify, RX, L, R, W	RX, L, R	None	None
\WINNT\Connection Wizard	FC	RX, L, R	RX, R	None	None
\WINNT\cursors*.*	FC	Modify, RX, R, W	RX, R	None	None
\WINNT\fonts*.*	FC	Modify, RX, R, W	RX, R	None	None
WINNT\help*.*	FC	RX, R	RX, R	None	None
WINNT\inf*.* (installation files)	FC	RX, R	RX, R	None	None
WINNT\java	FC	RX, L, R	RX, L, R	None	None
WINNT\media*.* (sounds)	FC	Modify, RX, R, W	RX, R	None	None

continues

Table 6.9 **Continued**

File	Admini-strators	Power Users	Users	Authenti-cated Users	Everyone
WINNT\msagent (those annoying helpers)	FC	RX, L, R	RX, L, R	None	None
WINNT\repair (Registry files from setup, may contain more recent copies)	FC	Modify, RX, L, R, W	L	None	None
WINNT\security (templates and databases for security configuration)	FC	RX, L, R	RX, L, R	None	None
WINNT\speech	FC	Modify, RX	RX	None	None
WINNT\system*.*	FC	RX, R	RX, R	None	None
WINNT\Temp	FC	Modify, RX, L, R, W	None	None	None
WINNT\twain_32 (scanner files)	FC	RX, L, R	RX, L, R	None	None
WINNT\Web (Web printer info)	FC	RX, L, R	RX, L, R	None	None
System32	FC	Modify, RX, L, R, W	RX, L, R	None	None
System32*.I* (Inf and others)	FC	Modify, RX, R, W	RX, R	None	None
System32*.dll	FC	RX, R	RX, R	None	None
System32*.exe	FC	RX, R	RX, R	None	RX, R
System32\CatRoot	RC	RX, L, R	RX, L, R	None	None
System32\config (Registry location)	FC	L	L	None	None
System32\dhcp	FC	RX, L, R	RX, L, R	None	None
System32\dllcache (system DLL backup)	FC	None	None	None	None
System32\drivers	FC	RX, L, R	RX, L, R	None	None
System32\ias (radius database)	FC	None	None	None	None
System32\mui (scripts)	FC	RX, L, R	RX, L, R	None	None
System32\OS2*.*	FC	RX, R	RX, R	None	None
System32\OS2\DLL*.*	FC	RX, R	RX, R	None	None
System32\RAS*.*	FC	RX, R	RX, R	None	None

File	Administrators	Power Users	Users	Authenticated Users	Everyone
System32\ShellExt	FC	RX, L, R	RX, L, R	None	None
System32\wbem (Windows management instrumentation [WMI] files)	FC	RX, L, R	RX, L, R	None	None
System32\wbem\mof	FC	Modify, RX, L, R, W	RX, L, R	None	None
User profile folder (documents and settings)	FC	RX, L, R	RX, L, R	None	RX, L, R
Users own profile	FC	None	None	None	None
All Users	FC	Modify, RX, L, R, W	RX, L, R	None	RX, L, R
All Users\Documents (shared documents location)	FC	R	Modify	None	R
All Users\Application Data (shared application data location)	FC	Modify, RX, L, R, W	R	None	R

Resource Access

Designating permissions for users and groups to files and other objects adds an access control entry (ACE) to the Discretionary Access Control List (DACL) for that object. An ACE contains the security identification (SID) of the user or group, the permission the user or group has been granted, and whether it is an Allow or Deny permission. During the authentication process, an access token is built for the user. The token includes the user SID for that user and the SID for the groups of which she is a member. When a user attempts to access a resource, the SIDs in her access token are compared to the DACLs on the resource. If the permission required matches one of the ACEs, access is allowed. If access is specifically denied, this takes precedence.

Special Permissions

Files installed during the text-mode setup portion of the operating system installation cannot be modified by any user. On a Windows 2000 Professional system and a stand-alone or member server, the local Users group is given Read & Execute, List Folder Content, and Read access to the folders that include these files. The local Power Users group, on the other hand, can write new files in some folders for which it cannot modify files installed during text-mode setup. Thus, legacy applications can write files into the system directories if installed by Power Users. (Power Users cannot install Windows 2000 services.) The folders that are protected in this manner are:

- WINNT and its subdirectories: Config, Cursors, Fonts, Help, Inf, Media, and System
- System32 and its subdirectories: OS2, OS2\DLL, RAS

Power Users are given Modify on certain directories and subfolders and RX on the files in those directories and subfolders. The creator of the file becomes its owner, not the Power Users group. This enables a Power User to create new files in these directories but prevents the new files from being altered by other members of the Power Users group.

In sum, Users have full control over their own User Profile folder. They have Modify Permission on All Users\Documents and All Users\Application Data access. Users have Read Only or less access to the rest of the system.

Root directory permissions are not set by installation. By default, format sets Full Control to the group Everyone. If root directory permission were set more restrictively at installation, the Windows 2000 DACL inheritance would recursively attempt to configure all subdirectories of the root. If other, non–Windows 2000 applications were already in existence, this might have untoward effects.

Administrators should change the root permission to reflect the access requirements at the root, but first they should change the inheritance settings on subfolders to prevent the new, restrictive permissions from being propagated elsewhere. This enables Administrators to secure the root and yet have appropriate, relaxed control where necessary to allow programs to run and authorized users to access files.

Making Default Install More Secure!

We can all understand why default install doesn't set more restrictive DACLs on the root: Windows 2000 might overwrite other data access permissions in folders already present on the partition. But what if we know our installs are going to be on virgin partitions?

You can modify the default access control settings by modifying the default security templates used during setup or by applying default templates after install but before use. These templates can be modified by using the Security Templates MMC snap-in. The default templates defltwk.inf or defltsv.inf can be applied using the Security Configuration and Analysis console.

Differences from Previous NTFS Versions

Several differences in capabilities from previous versions of NTFS are present in Windows 2000.

- **Managing file permission inheritance.** You can set file and folder permissions in Windows 2000 so that they do not inherit permissions. This is an extension to inheritance in Windows NT. Normally, when setting permissions on a folder, you select this folder only in the Apply onto section. However, if you want to prevent future changes from propagating to certain files and folders, you can clear the Allow Inheritable Permission from Parent to Propagate to this Object check box.

- **Caching of material in the shared folder can be allowed for offline viewing.** This is enabled by default but can be disabled. It is recommended for folders containing user documents. Users must manually indicate which files they want available offline.

- **Encrypting of files and folders.** Windows 2000 allows encrypting of files and folders.

- **Support for mounting a local drive at any empty folder on a local NTFS volume.** This enables you to mount a CD-ROM drive on your computer to an empty folder with the path c:\CD-ROM. The CD-ROM could then be accessed through the path CD-ROM. The drive letter previously used by the CD-ROM can be freed. Mounted drives add flexibility to data storage management.

- **Distributed link tracking.** Enables client applications to track linked sources that have been moved. If a linked database location changes, a client application will still be able to access it.

- **Distributed authoring and versioning.** Remote authors can edit, move, or delete files, file properties, and directory properties over an HTTP connection. (See Chapter 19, "Web Security.")

Shared Folder Publication: Security from Obscurity?

Shared folder permissions are Full Control, Change (open, read, edit, and run programs), and Read (read files and execute programs). The default permission is Everyone Full Control—change it! Permissions can be given or explicitly denied.

In a native-mode Windows 2000 domain in which NetBIOS has been disabled, users cannot browse servers to find shares. Shares must be published in the Active Directory for users to locate them. First the share is created in the normal manner. (Right-click the folder, click Sharing, click Share the Folder, name it, and set permissions.) Then the share is published in the Active Directory. If a user does not have at least Read permission, she will be unaware of the share.

Default Registry Permissions

In addition to the stricter default file and folder permissions applied when Windows 2000 is installed on NTFS partitions, a number of critical registry keys are also assigned default permissions. They are listed in Table 6.10.

A number of abbreviations are used in this table to describe the permissions that various groups have:

- FC = Full Control (all of the following plus Create Link, Write DAC, Write Owner)
- S = Special (Query Value, Set Value, Create Subkey, Enumerate Subkeys, Notify, Delete, Read Control)
- R = Read (Query Value, Enumerate Subkeys, Notify, Read Control)

Table 6.10 **Default Registry Key Permissions**

Registry Key	Admins	Power Users	Users	Restricted	Everyone
HKEY_LOCAL_ MACHINE	R, FC			R	R
\Software	R, FC	S	R		
\Classes\helpfile	R, FC	R	R		R
\Classes\.hlp	R, FC	S	R		R
\Software\Microsoft	R, FC	S	R		
\Command Processor	R, FC	R	R		
\Cryptography\OID	R, FC	R	R		
\Cryptography\Providers\ Trust	R, FC	R	R		
\Cryptography\Services	R, FC	R	R		
\Driver Signing	R, FC	R	R		
\EnterpriseCertificates	R, FC	R	R		
\Non-Driver Signing	R, FC	R	R		
\NetDDE	R, FC	None	None		
\Ole	R, FC	R	R		
\Rpc	R, FC	R	R		
\Secure	R, FC	R	R		
\SystemCertificates	R, FC	R	R		
Software\Microsoft\ Windows\CurrentVersion\ RunOnce (also Run and RunOnceEX)	R, FC	S	R		

Registry Key	Admins	Power Users	Users	Restricted	Everyone
\Software\Microsoft\ windows NT\Current Version	R, FC	S	R		R
\Drivers32	R, FC	R	R		
\Font Drivers	R, FC	R	R		
\Font Mapper	FC	R	R		
\Image File Execution Options	FC	R	R		
\IniFileMapping	FC	R	R		
\Perflib	FC	R (interactive)	R (interactive)		
\SeCEdit	FC	R	R		
\Time Zones	FC	R	R		
\Windows	FC	R	R		
\Winlogon	FC	R	R		
\AsrCommands	FC	R	R		
\Classes	FC	R	R		
\Console★	FC	S	R		R
\EFS	FC	R	R		
\ProfileList	FC	R	R		
\Svchost	FC	R	R		
\PolicyGuid ★	FC	S	R		R
\Policy	FC	None	None	R	
System\Current Control Set\Control	FC	R	R		
\SecurePipeServers\winreg ★	FC	R	R		
\Session Manager\Executive	FC	S	Read		
\TimeZoneInformation	FC	S	R		
\WMI\Security ★	FC	None	None		
HKLM\Hardware	FC	None	None	R	R
HKLM\SAM	FC			R	R
HKLM\Security	S	None	None	None	None
HKEY\USERS	FC		R		
USERS\.DEFAULT		Read	Read	R	R

continues

Table 6.10   **Continued**

Registry Key	Admins	Power Users	Users	Restricted	Everyone
USERS\.DEFAULT\ SW\MS\NetDDE ★	FC	None	None	None	None
HKEY_CURRENT_USER		FC	FC	R	
Users portion of directory					

★CREATOR OWNER is given Full Control on SUBKEYS ONLY.

File ACL and registry permissions on domain controllers support a broad number of groups including Account Operators and Server Operators. The Power Users group does not exist on domain controllers.

Default Power User Permission Allows Trojans!

You might have noticed that, by default, Power Users have permission to modify access to the Program Files directory, can modify access to many locations in the HKEY_LOCAL_MACHINE\Software registry hive, and have Write access to most system directories. This is necessary to allow them to run legacy applications and perform per-machine installs of applications that do not modify system files. These permissions, however, also enable them to plant Trojan Horses and make system-wide operating system and application changes that affect other users of the system. You might be reluctant to include the interactive group in the Power Users group. In fact, you might not want to give anyone Power User group membership, but you might have legacy applications that require it. What a conundrum!

You do have other choices. One choice is to have users install the application themselves. (Users can install applications that only they use. The applications are installed in their users' profile directory and would modify only HKEY_Current user REGISTRY SETTINGS.) Your second choice is to create a group for the application, determine the minimum file DACLs and registry access that the application needs, and apply them. You might still have users with elevated privilege levels, but you can succeed in isolating or reducing their access, and you can have fewer users with this privilege.

Soft Protection and Windows File Protection

Soft protection is the appearance of HTML screens in the Windows Explorer interface when the user selects the system folder and/or <system folder>\system32. Windows File Protection protects system files from deletion or modification.

Soft Protection

Soft protection is meant as a warning to users that files in these folders are system files and shouldn't be tampered with. The screen can be removed by clicking the Show Files statement on the screen. The HTML screen is in Figure 6.2. This soft protection HTML screen can permanently be closed by disabling Web View on the General tab of the Folder Options dialog box.

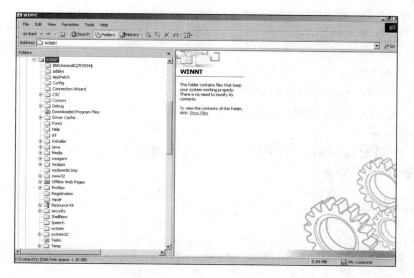

Figure 6.2   The Soft Protection screen.

Many files in these folders (and elsewhere) have the Hidden attribute set and will still not be visible. You make these files visible by selecting the Show Hidden Files and Folders option on the View tab of the Folder Options dialog box under Tools \Folder Options. System files are further protected by a second view option: Hide Protected Operating Systems Files. Checking Show Hidden Files and Folders will not expose these operating system files and folders; the second option must also be checked.

Windows File Protection

Windows File Protection (WFP) protects systems files (.SYS, .DLL, .OCS, .TTF, .EXE, and some .FON) from being replaced. In the past, the replacement and deletion of system files, inadvertently or by design, has meant system crashes and application failure. WFP won't allow applications or users to permanently delete, modify, move, or replace these files. This will also help protect these files from systemsviruses and Trojan Horses.

System files can only be replaced by Windows 2000 service packs, hotfix distributions, OS system upgrades, and the Windows update service. When you attempt to replace a file, the file system detects that change. WFP monitors the file system, and when the file system detects a change, WFP checks for a digital signature on the file. If the signature is missing or incorrect, the modified file is overwritten with an original copy from the dllcache folder.

Try this experiment for yourself:

1. Open Windows Explorer.

2. Navigate to your system folder \system32.

3. Select sol.exe (the solitaire game).

4. Delete it and watch the window.

You will see the sol.exe file reappear. This is WFP at work.

The Windows 2000 Encrypting File System (EFS)

As previously stated, the Encrypting File System (EFS) is a feature new to Windows 2000. Any authorized user can encrypt or decrypt his own files and folders that reside on a Windows 2000 NTFS partition. To encrypt a file requires that either the encryption property of the file be set or the file be placed in a folder whose encryption property has been set. The actual process of encryption and decryption is transparent to users. After the encryption property has been set, users continue to use their files normally. They do not have to decrypt or apply encryption each time they want to access a file. The next section describes various aspects you need to understand to manage EFS.

EFS Basics

Files or folders encrypted with EFS can only be decrypted by the user who encrypted them or by the EFS Recovery Agent. By default, the local administrator account is the Recovery Agent. The EFS was not designed to enable users to share. If Alice and Bob are Users and not Recovery Agents, Alice can encrypt a file and email it to Bob, but Bob will not be able to decrypt it. EFS is meant to be a personal encryption product.

EFS uses the Expanded Data Encryption Standard (DESX) 56-bit encryption algorithm. North American users can obtain 128-bit encryption by ordering the Enhanced CryptoPAK from Microsoft. The 128-bit encrypted files cannot be decrypted, accessed, or recovered on a system that only supports 56-bit encryption.

The encryption property is set from the Advanced Attributes property page. If you encrypt a folder, all files and subfolders created in the encrypted folder are automatically encrypted. Only files and folders on an NTFS partition can be encrypted. Although most files and folders on Windows 2000 NTFS partitions can be encrypted, system files cannot.

Encryption Persistence

Files remain encrypted when moved or copied to another NTFS folder or partition even if the destination folder is not marked as encrypted. Unencrypted files will be encrypted if moved or copied from an unencrypted folder to one that is encrypted.

If you copy or move the files to a volume that is not NTFS, the files are decrypted. If you copy files to a floppy disk, the files will be decrypted. However, if you use the Windows 2000 Backup program to back up an encrypted file and then copy the backup to a floppy disk (or another FAT media), the file remains encrypted. When the file is restored to an NTFS partition, it remains encrypted. If Alice backs up one of her encrypted files, Bob will not be able to restore it to a FAT partition and thus read the file.

> **Note**
>
> Encrypting does not protect against deletion. If Alice and Bob share the same computer and both have Modify permissions on a folder, Bob may not be able to decrypt and read a file that has been encrypted by Alice, but he can delete it.

I recommend that you encrypt the temp folder and any folder in which temporary files might be placed by documents; that way, the temporary files will be encrypted, too.

Remote Storage of Encrypted Files

If a folder on a remote Windows 2000 computer has been enabled for encryption and you have permission to use the folder, you can encrypt or decrypt files located on this folder. You should be aware that, when you open these files or save a file to this folder, data will be transmitted in the clear. The file is decrypted before being transported. If you were to copy an encrypted file from your system to the remote folder, the file is decrypted before it leaves your system and is encrypted when it is stored on the remote system. Use SSL/PCT or IPSec to encrypt data over the wire.

To enable remote encryption, the Windows 2000 server must be designated as trusted for delegation. This is done in Active Directory Users and Computers and is a property of the server.

How the Encrypting File System Works

Each file has a unique file encryption key (FEK), much like the session or bulk private key in the symmetric encryption algorithm described in Chapter 2, "Cryptology Introduction." The file encryption key is used to encrypt the file; the key itself is encrypted using the user's public key. To decrypt the file, the user's private key must first be used to decrypt the file encryption key. Then the file encryption key is used to decrypt the file. The FEK is also encrypted with the public key belonging to the Recovery Agent. The Recovery Agent can thus also decrypt the file.

The EFS uses both public/private key and session key algorithms. A public/private key pair ensures that only the user and the Recovery Agent can decrypt the session key used to encrypt the file.

Private keys are kept in the user's key store, not in the SAM or in a separate directory. The private keys can be exported to a floppy disk and kept for backup or recovery purposes. It is recommended that the recovery agent's key be exported and then removed from the Windows 2000 Professional system.

Default keys are self-signed; that is, there is no Certificate Authority to manage them. This is an awkward and potentially risky system because users do not usually understand the need to back up keys or secure them, and management of multiple keys by administrators is an awkward if not impossible task. To properly manage keys, you should provide an Enterprise (Active Directory–integrated) Certificate Authority. For more information, see Chapter 17, "Enterprise Public Key Infrastructure."

EFS can be disabled using Group Policy.

The FEK is stored in a Data Decryption Field (DDF) attached to the EFS file. Because the private key is needed to decrypt the bulk key and no one other than the user can access the private key, no one else can do so. Each time the file is saved, a new DDF is created. The FEK key is also encrypted with the Recovery Agent's public key and is placed in a special field called the Data Recovery Field (DRF). The DRF can contain info for multiple Recovery Agents.

Figures 6.3 and 6.4 illustrate the encryption/decryption process. In Figure 6.3, the right-hand box represents the encrypted file and its DDF and DRF fields. The processes of encryption and decryption are also described following each figure.

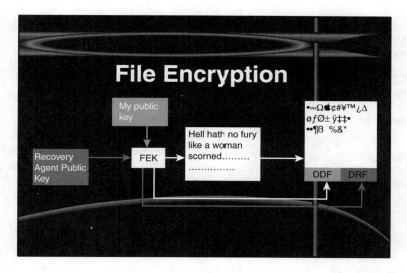

Figure 6.3 EFS encryption.

The EFS encryption process is as follows:

1. The unencrypted file is encrypted with the FEK.

2. A copy of the FEK is encrypted with the user's public key and is stored in the DDF.

3. A copy of the FEK is encrypted with the Recovery Agent's public key and is stored in the DRF.

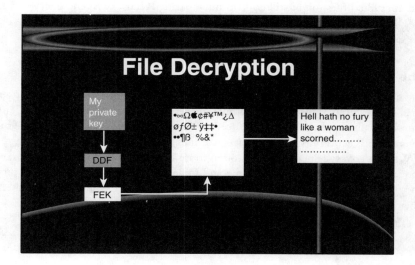

Figure 6.4 EFS decryption.

The EFS decryption process is as follows:

1. The user's private key is used to decrypt the DDF, or the Recovery Agent's private key is used to decrypt the DRF. Either action produces the FEK.

2. The FEK is used to decrypt the file.

Advantages of Providing a Certification Authority (CA)

Although not necessary, you can use a Certification Authority (CA) to generate and manage Recovery Agents and user certificates. If a CA is available, the EFS will request certificates from it rather than generate its own. There are several advantages to providing a CA.

- **Centralized management of keys.** Without a CA, each Windows 2000 system stores the keys for all users that have accounts on the system. The local administrator account for each system becomes the Recovery Agent. Any responsible backup or management of keys can quickly become a difficult chore.

- **Centralized management of key Recovery Agents.** In addition to the problem of a large number of Recovery Agents, the issue of who can decrypt the files of users is often a large one. Anyone who can use the local administrator account can decrypt any encrypted files stored on the system.

- **The capability to generate a Certificate Revocation List (CRL).** If a Recovery Agent private key becomes compromised, a way to prevent this key from being used becomes possible if a CRL can be issued.

- **The capability to issue new user certificates.** If a user's private key is compromised, only a CA can issue new EFS certificates and keys.

Old encrypted files might still contain out-of-date, Recovery Agent–encrypted keys in the DRF field. If you use a CA, keep a Recovery Agent archive so that these older files can be recovered.

The *Cipher* Command

The cipher command can be used to display or alter the encryption of folder and files on NTFS volumes. This is useful to bulk encrypt or decrypt files and folders. The same EFS rules apply. You can only decrypt files and folders that you encrypted unless you are the Recovery Agent for that set of files and folders.

When recovery is necessary, it is often more convenient to use the cipher command than to visit each individual file and folder and modify the encryption property. The cipher command parameters are defined in Table 6.11. The following statement provides the command syntax:

```
Cipher [/e ¦ /d][/s:dir][/a][/I\i][/f][/q][/h][pathname[…]]
```

Table 6.11 *Cipher* **Command Parameters**

Parameter	Action
/e	Encrypts
/d	Decrypts
/s:dir	Applies action to folders in the folder and all subfolders
/a	Applies action to files with specified names
/I	Continues performing even after error messages (by default, cipher stops after an error)
/f	Forces encryption or decryption (by default, already encrypted files are skipped)
/q	Reports only essential info
/h	Displays files with hidden or system attributes (by default, these are not encrypted or decrypted)

Cipher Command Examples

Encrypt the subfolder January in the folder Budget by typing

```
Cipher /e Budget\January
```

Encrypt all the subfolders in the folder Budget by typing

```
Cipher /e /s:Budget
```

Encrypt the file Houston.xls by typing

```
Cipher /e /a budget\January\Houston.xls
```

Note that multiple folder names (separated by a space) and wildcard characters can be used.

Recovery Policy and EFS Administration

Windows 2000 provides a built-in recovery policy. A recovery policy must be in place before a user can encrypt files. As previously described, data recovery is made possible by the designation of a Recovery Agent (by default, the Administrator). This agent has a certificate and an associated private key that allows data recovery for a scope of influence (that is, the site, domain, OU, or in a workgroup, the local disk).

The recovery policy can be changed through the Group Policy snap-in in the MMC. The Local Computer Policy\Public Key Policies\Encrypted Data Recovery Agent's path will enable you to add additional Recovery Agents, create a new file-recovery certificate, and delete the recovery policy. Deleting the recovery policy at the local computer level removes the capability of users on that computer to encrypt files.

On standalone computers, the policy is configured locally; for a domain, it is configured at each domain, OU, or individual computer level and is applied to all within the scope of influence.

EFS can be administered in the following ways:

- EFS can be disabled by removing the recovery policy.
- EFS can be disabled at the domain level, but EFS can be left available locally by making the domain-level recovery policy be empty. A domain-level policy configuration will override any local policy, but EFS will be available locally.

The Windows 2000 security subsystem handles enforcing, replicating, and caching of the recovery policy. Encryption can be implemented on a system even when it is offline.

Best Practices

Microsoft has several recommendations concerning the use of EFS:

- The recovery agent certificate and associated private key should be exported from the Certificates snap-in. This backup should be stored in a secure location. The private key should then be deleted from the system. If you need to perform recovery operations for a user, import the recovery certificate and its associated private key to a secured, designated recovery station (a Windows 2000 system). The files to be recovered are also placed on this system and are then decrypted. After recovering the data, delete the certificate and private key from the recovery station. This additional security measure will help protect sensitive data. Because the private key is not available on the client system, the local administrator account cannot be used to decrypt the file.
- Encrypt the My Documents folder if this is where you save most of your documents. All documents will then automatically be encrypted when saved.
- Encrypt your temp folder. Many applications use the temp folder to store interim saved copies of files in memory. By encrypting the temp folder, you are preventing the possibility that unencrypted copies of sensitive files might become available to unauthorized users.
- Encrypt folders, not files. All files placed in the folder will be encrypted. There will be a lot less work to do.
- Use NTFS permissions to further protect files. Remember that encrypted files are not safe from deletion.

Gotcha!

If you delete the certificate that has been created by the computer that designates the local Administrator as the default Recovery Agent and you do not have another policy in place, you have just created an empty recovery policy. A computer with an empty recovery policy cannot support encryption. Any encrypted files on the computer might be unrecoverable. You should never change the policy without having a backup of the original recovery certificate.

For More Information

Related information and more detailed discussion of many topics mentioned in this chapter can be found in other chapters in this book.

Encryption algorithms are described in Chapter 2, "Cryptology Introduction."

Smart card integration is first described in Chapter 7, "User Authentication," and then is more fully explained in Chapter 17, "Enterprise Public Key Infrastructure."

The recovery process is described in Chapter 8, "Lifecycle Choices."

Information on Group Policy and Security Configuration and Analysis is in Chapter 9, "Security Tools," and Chapter 16, "Securing the Network Using Distributed Security Services."

Active Directory is revisited in Chapter 12, "Domain-Level Security."

The Distributed File System is discussed in Chapter 14, "Securing the Distributed File System."

Discussion on creating larger group architectures and determining group scope also can be found in Chapter 16, "Securing the Network Using Distributed Security Services."

Good security practices for IIS can be found in Chapter 19, "Web Security."

Summary

Many new default settings and features make Windows 2000 more secure from the get-go, and many new features are available with little to no configuration. If you are aware of these features, you will not be frustrated by their actions and can incorporate them into your vision of a secure enterprise or can relax them to attempt compatibility with legacy applications. This chapter described such features as well as default users and groups, privileges, and logon rights. It also explored the Encrypting File System and Windows File Protection.

7

User Authentication

ALTHOUGH KERBEROS IS THE DEFAULT AUTHENTICATION MECHANISM for access to network services, Windows 2000 has many ways to manage authentication including Secure Socket Layer/Transport Layer Security (SSL/TLS), Lan Manager (LM) and NT Lan Manager (NTLM) for compatibility with down-level computers, certificates, and smart cards. In addition, to control remote access, Remote Authentication Dial-in User Service (RADIUS) can be selected instead of Windows authentication methods.

SSL/TLS authentication is supported by mapping SSL/TLS certificates to user accounts in the Active Directory (AD). Information on this process, connection with these services on IIS 5.0, and other SSL/TLS-related issues are discussed in Chapter 19, "Web Security." RADIUS and other remote access authentication processes are described in Chapter 15, "Secure Remote Access Options." Certificate authentication documentation can be found in Chapter 17, "Enterprise Public Key Infrastructure."

This chapter primarily reviews how Kerberos is integrated into Windows 2000, with notes on logon by non-Windows 2000 clients and by Windows 2000 clients to a Windows NT 4.0 domain. In particular, I will discuss

- LM and NTLM authentication
- Kerberos in Windows 2000
- Network logon
- Smart card integration with Kerberos

LM and NTLM Authentication

Although Kerberos is the default authentication method for network logon between Windows 2000 systems, LM and NTLM authentication is supported as well. LM and NTLM support is included so that Windows 9x and Windows NT clients can also authenticate to a Windows 2000 system. NTLM also serves as a backup network authentication method that can be used by Windows 2000 if Kerberos fails. The authentication method chosen depends on which operating system is on the domain controller and which is on the client. Table 7.1 defines what is used when.

Table 7.1   **Default Authentication Methods**

Client	Server	Authentication Method
Windows 2000	Windows 2000	Kerberos (NTLM if Kerberos fails)
Windows 2000	Windows NT 4.0	NTLM
Windows 9x	Windows NT 4.0	LM
Windows 9x	Windows 2000	LM
Windows 9x with Active Directory client	Windows 2000	LM (can be configured to use NTLM or NTLMv2 instead)
Windows NT 4.0	Windows NT 4.0	NTLM (can be configured to use NTLMv2)
Windows NT 4.0	Windows 2000	NTLM (can be configured to use NTLMv2)

> **Note**
>
> Windows 2000 beta timeframe reports from Microsoft seemed to indicate that it would be possible to eliminate the use of NTLM within a Windows 2000 domain if the domain were in native mode and only Windows 2000 systems were used. This is not the case with the shipping product. Even a 100-percent Windows 2000 native mode domain still has the possibility of NTLM being used for authentication.

Authentication of a Windows NT 4.0 domain user account requires the following:

- That the user enter his or her user ID and password
- The NTLM process
- SAM credentials
- That access be granted to the local computer and the domain
- That access potentially be granted to other workgroup computers and domains

Because LM and NTLM are still part of a Windows 2000 domain and because they often have been criticized as being weak, it makes sense to learn the best way to manage them. For information on securing down-level clients, see Chapter 13, "Securing Legacy Windows Clients."

Kerberos in Windows 2000

In Chapter 5, "Kerberos in the RAW," you learned how Kerberos works. Kerberos implementation in Windows 2000 closely follows the IETF specification defined in RFC 1510. The message format for passing security tokens follows the RFC 1964 specification for GSS-API. In this chapter, you will learn the details of how Kerberos works in Windows 2000, concentrating on

- Kerberos benefits for Windows 2000
- The role of the Active Directory
- Authentication steps
- Kerberos tickets
- DNS name resolution
- Interdomain activity
- Kerberos integration with the WinLogon service
- Using Kerberos tickets for access control information
- Kerberos integration with service accounts
- Kerberos extension for public key

Kerberos Benefits for Windows 2000

Kerberos provides a wide range of benefits for Windows 2000, including

- **Efficiency.** NTLM authentication requires an application server to contact a domain controller to authenticate each client. Kerberos provides the client with credentials; no application server contact with a domain controller is necessary.
- **Mutual authentication.** NTLM authenticates clients. How do the clients know they have the real server? Kerberos allows mutual authentication.
- **Delegated authentication.** Kerberos has a proxy service that enables a service to impersonate a user, to access resources, and to connect to other services. NTLM can only impersonate a user to access resources.
- **Simplified trust management.** By default, it is two-way and transitive.
- **Interoperability.** It is interoperable with other Kerberos version 5 installations.
- **Assumption of an open network.** It assumes an open network where clients and servers can be impersonated and used for attack.

The Role of the Active Directory (AD)

The Kerberos Key Distribution Center (KDC) is implemented as a domain service. It is a process that includes two services: the Authentication Service (AS) and the Ticket-Granting Service (TGS). The AD is used as the account database. The Kerberos realm in Windows 2000 is the domain. Each domain server has a KDC; therefore, any domain controller can accept authentication requests and ticket-granting requests addressed to the domain KDC. The KDC runs in the process space of the Local Security Authority (LSA). Ticket-Granting Tickets (TGTs) are issued to authenticated security principals (that is, users, machines, and services).

As you read the following discussion on Kerberos in Windows 2000, keep in mind the structure of the AD: It is the backbone on which Kerberos is implemented. Remember that domains are security boundaries and have their own policies but have two-way, transitive trusts with other domains in their own forest. The transitive nature of Kerberos trusts makes it unnecessary to create any other trusts.

Because each domain controller has a writable copy of the directory, changes made to one replica of the directory are propagated to the others. Knowledge of the new trust is thus passed along (as are new accounts, passwords, and so on) This is multimaster replication over a secure channel that has been established between replication partners. Windows 2000 does not implement the Kerberos replication protocol; it uses its own replication process.

Kerberos is divided into three protocols: the Authentication Service (AS) Exchange, the Ticket-Granting Service (TGS) Exchange, and the Client/Server (CS) Exchange. The next sections follow the Windows 2000 implementation of these protocols as Alice, a fictional user, logs on.

Authentication Step 1: Obtaining a Logon Session Key

Figure 7.1 illustrates the process in the following list.

1. Alice enters her user ID and password.

2. The Kerberos client on Alice's Windows 2000 Professional computer converts the password to a cryptographic key using a one-way hashing function. (The Kerberos standard is DES-CBC-MD5, and it is used by Windows 2000 as DES-CBC-CRC.) The key produced is known as Alice's long-term key. The client stores this key in its credentials cache. (This process only takes place at the logon for this session.)

3. Windows 2000 uses DNS Lookup to locate the nearest available domain controller. This domain controller will serve as Alice's preferred KDC during this logon session.

4. The client contacts the KDC to ask for a session key to be used for authentication during this logon session. The client uses the Kerberos Authentication Service Request (KRB_AS_REQ) message. It includes Alice's user ID, the name

of the service (the TGS), and preauthentication data that proves Alice knows the password. This is a time stamp encrypted with Alice's long-term key.

5. The domain KDC receives the request and looks up Alice in its database. It gets her long-term key, decrypts the authentication data, and evaluates it.

6. After validating Alice's identity, the KDC creates a session key and encrypts the server copy of the session key in its long-term key and the client copy of the session key with Alice's long-term key. Both keys are available in the KDC database in the AD. (If the client key is not available, the process ends here.)

7. The KDC sends a Ticket Granting Ticket (TGT) and the client-key-encrypted session key to the client in a KRB_AS_REP message. The TGT includes a copy of both (encrypted) session keys and information about the client. The TGT is encrypted with the server's key. Note that only the client can decrypt its copy of the session key, and only the server can decrypt the TGT to read its contents. The server does not retain a copy of the session key.

8. The client receives the TGT and the session key. The client uses its cached copy of its long-term key to decrypt its copy of the session key. This session key is now known as the logon session key. The logon session key and the TGT are cached in the Kerberos credentials cache (in volatile memory, not on disk). The client can discard its copy of its long-term key because it is no longer necessary. (All the rest of its exchanges with the KDC can use the logon session key.)

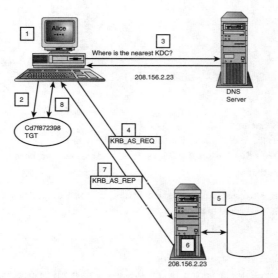

Figure 7.1 Authentication step 1: obtaining a logon session key.

Authentication Step 2: The TGS Exchange—Getting a Ticket for a Particular Server

After the client has preauthenticated and received a TGT, it is ready to request access to resources. During logon, the resource required is the desktop. The process that follows is the same whether Alice's system is attempting to display the desktop on her machine or is responding to a request for file resources on a remote server. Figure 7.2 illustrates the process in the following list.

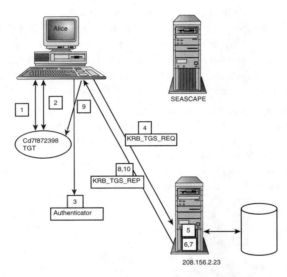

Figure 7.2   Authentication step 2: the TGS exchange.

The Credentials Cache

The Kerberos credentials cache is an area in volatile memory on the client machine. The LSA protects this area. This area is never paged to disk. The objects stored here are destroyed when a security principal logs off or the system is shut down.

The credentials cache is managed by the Kerberos Security Support Provider (SSP), which runs in the LSA's security context. If tickets need to be cached, obtained, or removed, the LSA calls the Kerberos SSP to do so.

The LSA, the SSP, and Cached Passwords

The LSA keeps a copy of the interactive user's hashed password. If a TGT expires during a logon session, the Kerberos SSP uses this copy to obtain a new TGT without asking the user.

Cached passwords for computers and services are stored in a secure area of the registry, as are hashed passwords for user accounts on the local system. These passwords, however, can only be used to access the local system; they are not used for network access.

1. Alice wants to read a file on the SEASCAPE server. She needs access to SEASCAPE's server service. The Kerberos client checks its credentials cache for a session ticket to that service.

2. If the client does not find one, it checks for a TGT.

3. If it finds a TGT, it retrieves the logon session key from the cache and uses this to prepare the Authenticator. The Authenticator is a copy of the current client time. The client encrypts the Authenticator with its copy of the logon session key.

4. The client then sends the KDC its credentials: the ticket (still encrypted with the server's key), its name, its Authenticator, and a request for a session ticket for the SEASCAPE server service (KRB_TGS_REQ).

5. The KDC decrypts the session ticket (TGT) with its long-term key, extracts the logon session key, and uses this key to decrypt and validate the client's Authenticator.

6. If the Authenticator is validated, the server has verified that the credentials were issued by the KDC. It extracts Alice's data from the TGT and invents a session key for the client and the requested service to share.

7. The KDC encrypts one copy of the session key with the client's logon session key. It embeds this and another copy of the session key in a ticket and encrypts this with the service (SEASCAPE) server's long-term key.

8. The KDC returns this service ticket and the copy of the session key encrypted with the client logon key to the client (KRB_TGS_REP).

9. The client uses its logon session key to decrypt the session key to use with the service and stores the ticket and the session key in its credentials cache.

10. If the client has asked for mutual authentication, the server encrypts the time-stamp from the client's Authenticator with the session key and returns it to the client as the server Authenticator.

Authentication Step 3: Using the Session Ticket for Admission—The CS Exchange

Finally, the client uses the session ticket to access the resource. Figure 7.3 illustrates the following list.

1. The client requests service from the server by sending a Kerberos Application Request (KRB_AP_REQ) to the server. It contains an Authenticator encrypted with the session key for the service, the session ticket for the server, and a flag indicating whether mutual authentication is desired. The use of this flag is an option in the Kerberos configuration; Alice will never be asked.

2. The service receives the request, decrypts the ticket, and extracts the user authorization data and the session key. The session key is used to decrypt the Authenticator and then the Authenticator is evaluated.

3. If it is validated, the mutual authentication flag is checked. If set, the service uses the session key to encrypt the time from the client Authenticator and returns this in a Kerberos Application Reply (KRB_AP_REP).

4. If the client receives a KRB_AP_REP, it uses the session key to decrypt the Authenticator and to validate it by comparing the timestamp with the one it sent.

During the session, the session key can be used to encrypt the application data.

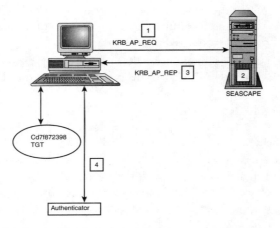

Figure 7.3   Authentication step3: the CS exchange

Tickets

When a client receives a ticket, how can it store and retrieve the ticket in its credentials cache? What does it know about the ticket? The first few fields of the ticket are not encrypted. The session key and other related information is in a data structure that includes these ticket fields and flags: `authtime`, `starttime`, `endtime`, and `renew-till`. This structure is encrypted with the client's key. It is returned with KRB_AS_REP and KRB_TGS_REP.

> **Note**
> See Chapter 5 for a detailed description of the RFC standard and a description of the Kerberos ticket fields.

DNS Name Resolution

The IETF Kerberos RFC specifies IP transport for all messages. The Windows 2000 Kerberos SSP needs the DNS name of the server where the KDC service is running. The KDC service runs on every Windows 2000 domain controller, as does the LDAP server service. Both services have registered DNS service locator records (SRV resource records). Clients query DNS for SRV records using *ldap*.tcp.dc._msdcs.DnsDomainName. The KDC service can be found by querying for the SRV with *Kerberos*.udp.DnsDomainName. If a client does not support the SRV record type, its DNS Resolver can query for a host record with the name of their domain.

If the KDC server to be used is not on a Windows 2000 domain controller, the client is participating in a non–Windows 2000 realm, and the name for the KDC will be stored in the client computer registry. The SSP will look in the registry for this name and then query DNS for an IP address. Figure 7.4 illustrates this process. The PC in the upper-left corner understands how to use SRV records and makes a request of the ocean.com DNS server for the address of any KDCs. The DNS server returns two IP addresses, and the client contacts one of them using TCP. The bottom-left PC does not understand resource records. It uses the stored name of the domain controller (or realm) to query the DNS server. It also returns an IP address. This client is a non–Windows 2000 client and uses UDP to contact the KDC.

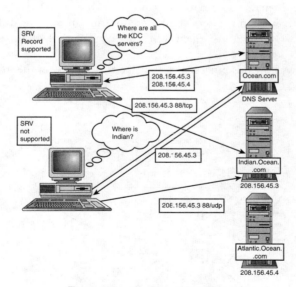

Figure 7.4   Locating the KDC server.

RFC 1510 specifies that the client send a UDP datagram to port 88 on the KDC's IP address when communicating. The KDC responds to the sending port at the sender's IP address. UDP is a connectionless protocol. This is not a good choice in a Windows 2000 domain because Windows 2000 authentication messages can easily exceed 1,500 octets, the limit for an Ethernet UDP datagram. When participating in a non–Windows 2000 realm, the extra Windows 2000 information can be omitted from the data; thus, the packet size is okay. A UDP datagram can be used. Windows 2000 domains, however, use TCP. The use of TCP has been proposed as a revision to RFC 1510 (draft–ietf–cat–kerberos–revisons–03, November 1998).

The session ticket can be used more than once by the client to authenticate to the server it wants to access. Session tickets have an expiration date and can be revoked before then if necessary. The expiration date is a function of Kerberos policy for the domain. For more information, see Chapter 11, "Securing Windows 2000 Server."

Interdomain Activity

What happens if the client process is on a computer in Domain A and the user's credentials are from Domain B? Authentication can be completed across domain boundaries. It is enabled by sharing an interdomain key. This automatically happens when a trust is established between two Windows 2000 domains. The ticket-granting service of Domain A is registered as a security principal with Domain B's KDC and vice versa. Then the Ticket-Granting Service in each domain can treat the other as just another service that authenticated clients can request and for which they can receive session tickets.

Figure 7.5 shows how this process proceeds and is described in the following list.

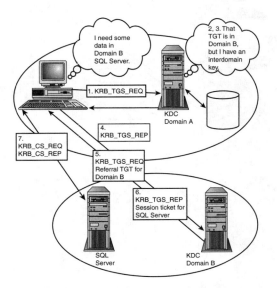

Figure 7.5 Kerberos trust relationships.

1. The client in Domain A wants to access a service in Domain B. It sends its request for a session ticket to the ticket-granting service in Domain A.

2. The ticket-granting service (TGS) of the KDC in Domain A notices that the service resides in Domain B.

3. The TGS encrypts a TGT with the interdomain key it shares with Domain B.

4. It sends this TGT, known as a referral ticket, to the client.

5. The client uses the referral ticket and sends a request for a session ticket to the TGS in Domain B.

6. The TGS in Domain B uses its copy of the interdomain key to decrypt the referral ticket. If this is successful, it sends the client a session ticket to the service in its domain.

7. The client uses the session ticket to access the resource.

On networks with more than two domains, the process is more complicated. Domains do not store interdomain keys for every domain. Each domain stores an interdomain key for the domains one step above and one step below it in the AD tree. When necessary, a referral path (also known as trust path) can be generated that enables the client to obtain referral tickets, one after another, until it obtains one for the domain it needs. Figure 7.6 illustrates the process, which is outlined in the following list.

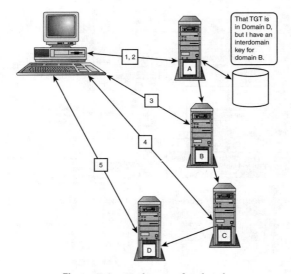

Figure 7.6   Kerberos referral path.

1. A request is made for a resource in Domain D. The client system is joined in Domain A.

2. The Domain A KDC produces a TGT for the KDC in Domain B.

3. The Domain B KDC produces a TGT for the KDC in Domain C.

4. The Domain C KDC produces a TGT for the KDC in Domain D and returns the TGT for Domain D to the client.

5. The client uses this ticket to request a session ticket for a resource in Domain D.

Kerberos Integration with the WinLogon service

Windows 2000 Kerberos does not invent an entirely new process of authentication for Windows. The Kerberos implementation is integrated with the WinLogon service. The flowchart in Figure 7.7 is further described in the following list.

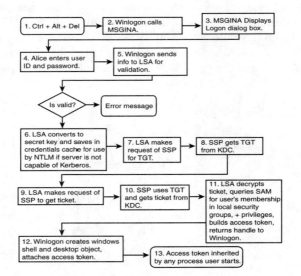

Figure 7.7   Kerberos integration with WinLogon.

1. Alice presses Ctrl+Alt+Delete (SAS or secure attention sequence).

2. WinLogon service calls the MS Graphical Identification and Authentication (MSGINA).

3. MSGINA.DLL displays the standard Logon dialog box.

4. Alice types her name and password in the dialog box.

5. MSGINA returns info to WinLogon, which sends the information to the LSA for validation.

6. If valid, the LSA converts the cleartext password to a secret key and saves the result in the credentials cache, where it can be used by NTLM (for servers that are not capable of Kerberos authentication) for TGT renewal or in case Kerberos fails.

7. The LSA makes a request of the Kerberos SSP for a TGT so that it can access the TGS.

8. The LSA works with Kerberos SSP, which exchanges messages with the KDC. SSP gets the TGT from the KDC.

9. The LSA requests a ticket from SSP.

10. SSP uses the TGT and gets the session ticket from the KDC.

11. The LSA gets the session ticket, decrypts it with the computer's secret key, and extracts authorization data. It then queries the local SAM to determine the user's membership in local security groups, as well as any special privileges, and adds any related SIDs. Lastly, it builds an access token and returns the token handle to WinLogon.

12. WinLogon creates the Window's shell and desktop object, attaches the access token, and starts the shell process Alice will use.

13. The access token is inherited by any application process that Alice starts.

Trusted for Delegation

A domain administrator holds, and can grant delegation of, authentication to a user or computer account. This privilege is necessary in an N-tier application because the user will authenticate to a middle-tier service. The middle-tier service will need to be able to authenticate to a backend data server on behalf of the user. A middle-tier service that acquires this privilege is known to be Trusted for Delegation. Trusted for Delegation is a property that the administrator can set for Windows 2000 servers.

An N-tier application might consist of a client accessing a server front end, which then must access a database backend. It could also be the combination of a browser client accessing a Web site, which then must obtain data from a third computer elsewhere.

Using Kerberos Tickets for Access Control Information

Kerberos is used for authentication, not authorization. It does not determine which files and other security principals clients are authorized to access. Authorization is left to other mechanisms already present on the system.

Remember that the initial logon to a computer does not give the client network access; it only gives the client access to the domain authentication service. This TGT can be used to request session tickets for other services in the domain. Computers joined in a Windows 2000 domain have their own accounts in the domain. Think of them as service accounts like the server service. When you want to access these services across the network, you must submit a request to the server service. Interactive users need to submit a request to access the workstation service. To access any service on the local computer, a session ticket for that computer must be presented.

Although Kerberos does not perform authorization, a field is provided for including authorization data in Kerberos tickets. This is part of the RFC. There is no specific requirement in the RFC, however, as to the form of the data or how servers should use it.

If applications are written to use their own private list of authorized names, integration with Kerberos can be a simple process of placing the names in the ticket's authorization field. This is called *name-based authorization*.

Windows 2000, however, uses user security IDs (SIDs) and security group SIDs for authorization. The KDC adds information to the authorization field in the form of a list of SIDs that identify a security principal and the principal's group memberships. The list of SIDs is accumulated in the following circumstances:

- When the KDC prepares a TGT, the KDC in the user's domain queries the AD. The user's account record includes the user's SID and the user's group membership SIDs. This list of SIDs is placed in the TGT's authorization data field. In multiple-domain environments, the KDC will query the Global Catalog for any universal groups of which the user or one of his groups is a member and will add those SIDS to the list as well. The list is signed by the KDC.

- When the user requests a session ticket for a server, the KDC in the server's domain copies the TGT's authorization data to the session ticket authorization data field. If the user's domain is different from the resource domain, the KDC queries the AD to find any local domain group memberships and includes those SIDS as well.

This use of the authorization field is included in the Proposed Standard RFC 1510 and reiterated in the draft (all ietf drafts are considered works in progress and not standards) draft–ietf–cat–kerberos–revisions–05, March 10 2000. This and other such documents can be found at `http://;search.ietf.org/serach/brokers/internet-drafts /query.html`.

Kerberos Integration with Service Accounts

When a client uses a service, the service acts on the client's behalf. For the service to do so, it must take on one of the client's characteristics: the client's level of authorization or security context on the system. This process is known as impersonation. Figure 7.8 displays the steps in the following list.

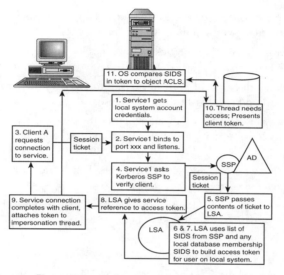

Figure 7.8   Kerberos and service accounts.

Why is the Authorization Data Signed?

If a rogue service is installed by a user with a legitimate network account but limited authorization on the computer, the user could request a session ticket for the service, and the service could decrypt the ticket, modify the authorization data by adding the SID for a privileged group, encrypt the altered ticket, and present it to the LSA. This would elevate the user's authorization level on the computer where the service is running.

The data is signed by the KDC before being stored in the session ticket to prevent tampering. The LSA on W2K always checks the validity of this signature when session tickets are presented by untrusted services.

The LSA trusts calls from services running under the local system account and thus does not need to check the signature. The local system account is used by services installed with OS by the server service. Other services can be configured to use the system account, but the administrator must do so.

Trust is not extended by the LSA. The LSA does not trust services that use other accounts. The LSA asks the KDC to verify the signature on the ticket authorization data via a RPC netlogon secure channel to the DC. Session tickets are also always issued and are authorized by the KDC for the target computer's domain.

1. At service start time, the service uses the Secure Support Provider Interface (SSPI) to obtain its credentials: the key for the account under which it runs.

2. The service binds to a communication port and listens for messages from prospective clients.

3. A client requests a connection to the service by sending a session ticket to the communication port.

4. The service asks the Kerberos SSP to verify the client credentials and passes the client session ticket and a pointer to the service's session key.

5. The Kerberos SSP verifies the ticket's authenticity, opens it, and passes the contents of the authorization data field to the LSA (its parent process).

6. If the data includes a list of domain SIDs, the LSA uses these SIDs as well as the user's SID to build an access token to represent the user on the local system.

7. The LSA queries its database to see whether the user or one of his groups is a member of a local security group. If found, the LSA adds these SIDs to the access token.

8. The LSA notifies the calling service that the client ID is authenticated, and includes a reference to the access token.

9. The service completes its connection with the client and attaches the access token to an impersonation thread (a body of executable code that will now use the client's security context).

10. When the thread needs access, it presents the client token.

11. The OS compares the SIDs in the token to SIDs in the object ACLs. If it finds a match, it checks the level of access granted to that requested.

Kerberos Extension for Public Key

Windows 2000 extends the Kerberos specification by permitting authentication using public key certificates rather than shared secret keys. This is how support for authentication with a smart card—and the use of certificates for IPSec authentication—is obtained. An IETF draft specification discusses this extension of the standard (draft-ietf-cat-kerberos-pk-init, often referred to as PKINIT). This draft recommends that a 512-bit RSA public key be required. To satisfy export regulations, however, Windows 2000 uses a PKCS #7 standard for encrypted data.

For more information on the implementation of this extension, see the section "Get Smart! Using Smart Cards with Windows 2000" later in this chapter.

The Big Picture: Network Logon

Even in a native mode Windows 2000 domain, Kerberos is not the only SSP for the entire network. Clients other than Windows 2000 clients will log on using other network authentication protocols. If the domain does not include any clients other than

Windows 2000, NTLM still is available in case of Kerberos failure. So how do the different authentication protocols fit in?

The design of Windows 2000 is modular and allows for flexibility here. Applications built for Windows 2000 can build in an authentication process that does not have to be aware of the details of any authentication protocol. The client/server application will make calls to the SSPI. The SSPI handles the details.

During local logon, the logon process creates a security context. It is within this security context that every action you take occurs. You cannot do anything that you have not been approved to do. You cannot access any data or run any application that you do not have authorization to run. Part of this security context is the access token, which includes your SID and the SIDs of groups to which you belong. When a client/server application you are running needs to run processes or access resources on the server, there is no ready-made security context available. The program, which does not know or need to know the authentication protocols, must ask the SSPI to create that context for you. The SSPI works on both the client and server side of the application with an SSP to get the job done. It's as if you have arrived at a foreign port and need to offload your cargo. Not only are skilled union laborers the only ones who can touch the equipment to move the cargo, you cannot ask for the union laborers help; the port authority must manage the entire operation. You are, by the way, greatly relieved that you do not have to learn the thousand languages or customs of the unloading crews.

SSPs for Kerberos, NTLM, and SChannel are included with Windows 2000. Although an application can specify a particular SSP, it also can allow the SSPI to negotiate for the most secure protocol available. Figure 7.9 and the following steps show how it would pan out.

1. Peter logs on to his workstation.

2. Peter opens a document on the file server Mayberry in Microsoft Word.

3. Word I/O calls to the OS on the workstation.

4. The OS sees that the document is not local and passes the request to the Redirector.

5. The Redirector connects to the remote server.

6. The server chooses the most secure SSP available on both the client and itself. (Windows 2000's preference is Kerberos, then NTLM, then SChannel.)

7. If both client and server are running Windows 2000, Kerberos is selected.

8. The Redirector calls SSP to get Peter's credentials (the TGT).

9. The Redirector calls SSPI and passes a handle to TGT specifying Mayberry.

10. A Kerberos KRB_TGS_REQ with Peter's TGT is generated and is sent to the KDC in Peter's domain.

11. The KDC returns a ticket for Mayberry.

12. The Kerberos SSP caches the ticket.

13. The Redirector asks again for a security context.

14. The Kerberos SSP generates KRB_AP_REQ including a ticket encrypted in secret key that the server shares with KDC and an Authenticator encrypted in the session key that Peter shares with the server. This message is returned to the Redirector.

15. The Redirector includes the Kerberos message as an authentication token and sends it to the server services of Mayberry.

16. The Mayberry server service receives the message and creates a local security context for the client by calling the SSPI.

17. The Kerberos SSP on Mayberry opens KRB_AP_REQ, extracts the ticket, takes the session key, and uses it to validate Peter's Authenticator.

18. If the Authenticator is valid, the SSP gets Peter's authorization data (from the session ticket) and passes it to the LSA on the server.

19. The Mayberry server service sends a KRB_AP_REP as data in a Server Message Block (SMB) message to the Redirector on the workstation.

20. The Mayberry server service impersonates Peter on Mayberry; his access token is attached to a thread in the service process. It can therefore act on Peter's behalf to open the file.

21. The Redirector receives a KRB_AP_REP and gives it to the Kerberos SSP on the workstation to validate the server's identity. The SSP uses its session key to decrypt the server's Authenticator. The timestamp is compared to the one sent. If they don't match, the Redirector breaks the connection.

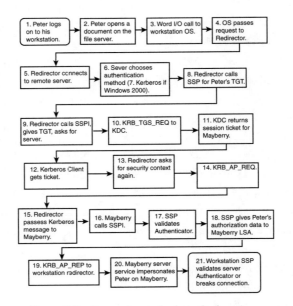

Figure 7.9 Logon in a mixed-mode domain.

Get Smart! Using Smart Cards with Windows 2000

In our super-security-conscious world, in which GUI programs exist to aid the immature and the immoral in cracking passwords, what's a person to do? We are reminded all the time that our security is only as safe as our password, and our passwords aren't safe. Security based on a secret is not so hot if someone can steal the secret.

Security based on something we share, as well as something you physically have, is a lot more secure. One way this is possible is by using smart cards. Smart cards are small, credit card–size devices that can contain powerful processors or a memory chip. If smart cards are used for authentication, at a minimum they store a private key that can be used with a special personal identification number (PIN) to authenticate a user.

Smart cards protect the private key. Not only do I have to have my card, which contains my private key, my computer also has to have a card reader attached, and I have to know my PIN (usually a simple numeric value). I must keep my PIN secret. Can a data thief steal my card? Yep, but he won't have my PIN. Can he manufacture a card? Yep, but he has to have a valid certificate from my Certificate Authority and a PIN. Can he steal my card and tamper with it to change the PIN and thus get around all these layers of security? Absolutely. But it is a lot more work than stealing or cracking my password.

This combination of something that you possess (a smart card, a PIN) and a secret we share (the private key) is known as *strong authentication*. Although a smart card solution is getting all the attention here, biometrics (the use of fingerprints, hand geometry, or retinal scans) will also work.

Smart card support (PC/SC 1.0 specification) is built in to Windows 2000. You will, of course, need to purchase card readers and cards and implement Certificate Services. Third-party products provide smart card drivers and applications for Windows NT and Windows 9x.

Smart card security is based on public key cryptography. As previously discussed, public key cryptography is used for secure channel communications over a public network, digital signatures, and authentication.

The Windows 2000 implementation of smart card services can be described by detailing

- Microsoft's design approach
- Base smart card components
- The installation process
- Smart cards and Windows 2000 logon
- Smart cards and remote access

Microsoft's Approach

Microsoft's approach to the integration of smart cards is as follows:

- Use the standard model for how readers and cards interface with the computers; thus, different cards and readers will be ipso-facto compliant.

- Use device-independent APIs for enabling smart card–aware applications to insulate developers from present and future devices and to reduce software development costs. Three mechanisms are the CryptoAPI, the Microsoft Win32 API, and SCard COM.

- Use familiar tools.

- Integrate with all Windows platforms. The smart card SDK is part of the Windows Base Services of the Platform SDK. The Platform SDK can be obtained from Microsoft at `http://msdn.microsoft.com/developers/sdk`. A developer discussion alias is found at `SmartCardSDK@DISCUSS.MICROSOFT.COM`. To join the mailing list, go to `http://www.microsoft.com/smartcard/`.

CrptoAPI can be used to isolate a developer from the intricacies of the cryptographic features of Windows 2000 while allowing her to incorporate them in applications. The CryptoAPI can be obtained from `http://www.microsoft.com/security`. For more information, see Chapter 2, "Cryptology Introduction."

Smart Card Uses

In addition to authentication, smart cards can be used to:

- Secure email

- Provide tamper-resistant storage for protecting private keys and other personal information

- Isolate security computations (authentication, digital signatures, and key exchange)

- Enable portability of credentials and other private information

Why have smart cards taken so long to be adopted? We've seen this situation before. Different formats have challenged users, led to confusion, and prevented a good idea from becoming a widespread great idea. Sometimes one particular brand will catch on (or be more heavily advertised), and a standard, such as VHS for videotapes, is born. Other times a standards organization can bring compliance by designing a standard that meets everyone's needs (IETF and Internet RFCs). Various smart card standards do exist, but with the exception of the Personal Computer/Smart Card (PC/SC) standard, the problems of interoperability and flexibility were not solved. The PC/SC standards are based on the ISO 7816 standards and therefore are compatible with the EMV and GSM specifications. The PC/SC standards have broad industry support.

Using the Win32 API to access smart cards requires a deeper understanding of the Windows OS as well as the smart cards. The demand for greater knowledge on the part of the developer is balanced by greater control.

SCard COM can be used to access generic smart card services from applications. The developer does not need to know the specifics of different smart cards. It is not a cryptographic interface.

Base Components

Microsoft Smart Card Base Components 1.0 is integrated into Windows 2000 to support public key services. They are both on the Windows 98 CD but must be installed separately. They are available for Windows NT at `http://www.microsoft.com/smartcard/`. The components are

- Service providers
- Cards
- Resource Manager
- Device drivers
- Readers

The service providers category is divided into cryptographic and noncryptographic due to import and export restrictions. Cards can have multiple service providers.

Smart Card Cryptographic (service) Providers (SCCPs) can be software based (Base Provider CSP) or hardware based (an engine on a smart card or another device attached to the computer). The SCCP performs cryptographic functions (random number generation, key generation, digital signature, key exchange, and bulk encryption) through CryptoAPI.

Smart Card Service Providers (SCSPs) present the interface to smart card services and the protocols necessary to invoke the underlying services. The ISO 7816-5 Application Identifier is similar. These services may be things such as card location, command and reply management, and card file system access.

Windows 2000 comes with service providers, resource managers, and device drivers for two brands of smart cards: Schlumberger and Gemplus. Specific cards and readers must be purchased from these companies to work with the provided drivers and SSPs. Other manufacturers provide the necessary SSPs and drivers for their own readers and smart cards.

Installing and Using Smart Cards

Smart card is a term used to identify many different devices used for different functions. Some are used as stored-value cards; some are used as integrated-circuit cards. The latter, of course, are able to perform operations such as signing and key exchange as needed in the computer industry. Cards to be used with Windows must meet ISO 7816-1, -2, and −3 standards.

Because there is no plug-and-play model for smart cards, the vendor must supply an installation program. The program should register the smart card interface with the Windows Resource Manager, which can then bind the card to the registered interfaces so that applications can access card-based services.

The Resource Manager runs as a trusted service. Smart card access requests are sent to the Resource Manager and are routed to the reader containing the card. The Resource Manager controls application access to the smart card in any reader attached to a Windows-based computer. It identifies and tracks resources, controls allocation of readers and resources across applications, and supports transaction control access of services on a specific card. (Cards require multiple commands for single functions; they need transaction services to do so without interruption to keep from corruption.)

FORTEZZA: Cards for Classified Info

FORTEZZA Crypto Cards function similarly to smart cards but have more memory and more powerful processors and implement the U.S. Government cryptographic algorithms that were chosen to secure the Department of Defense Message System (DMS). Different versions of these cards exist, from those used to protect sensitive but not classified data to those used to protect classified documents. They use special PCMCIA interfaces and are more expensive to use than smart cards and smart card readers.

FORTEZZA-based systems are not compatible with industry-standard public key information security systems. They meet the government FIPS 140-1 standard developed by the National Institute of Standards and Technology (NIST) and specifically the U.S. government requirement for design and implementation of hardware and software cryptographic modules for sensitive but unclassified information. This standard has also become a de facto standard for cryptographic care modules and has been incorporated into ISO's international standard 15408. See the NIST Web site at http://csrc.nist.gov. Microsoft provides a cryptographic service provider for FIPS 140-1 level 2 certification. For more information, see http://microsoft.com/security and http://fortezza-support.com/directiv.html.

The device driver maps the reader's features to the Windows native services and the smart card infrastructure. It tells the Resource Manager when a card has been inserted or removed. A common driver library is included with Smart Card Components 1.0 release. The device driver model varies depending on the platform. For Windows 2000, the device driver model for USB and IEEE 1394 devices is unified as the Windows Driver Model (WDM). For more info see `http://www.microsoft.com/hwdev/`.

Readers attach to RS-232, PS/2, PCMCIA, and USB interfaces. They are standard devices and have a security descriptor and a plug-and-play identifier. They can be controlled through standard Windows device drivers, and the standard Windows Hardware Wizard can be used for installation and removal.

Using Smart Cards for Windows 2000 Logon

Smart card logon requires a public key/private key pair. As previously discussed, Windows 2000 uses Kerberos, which uses symmetric keys. Although smart cards can be used with a Windows 2000 Public Key Infrastructure, they also can be integrated into the Kerberos authentication structure. To support this requirement, Windows 2000 extends the Kerberos standard. As previously stated, the private key is only known to its owner, while the public key is made available to everyone.

In fact, smart cards are integrated with Windows 2000 in three different ways:

- **Interactive logon:** AD, Kerberos, public key certificates
- **Remote logon:** Public key certificate, Extensible Authentication Protocol (EAP), and Transport Layer Security (TLS).
- **Client authentication:** Public key certificate mapped to an account stored in the AD

Look for the Logo on the Label

Readers need to meet the PC97 or PC98 hardware design requirements as well as the Microsoft implementation of the PC/SC Workgroup 1.0 specifications. Readers that meet Microsoft's standards can obtain the Windows-compatible logo. Look for it before you make a purchase.

In the normal Kerberos scheme of things, the user's password, or private key, is used during the AS Exchange to encrypt and decrypt the preauthentication data and the logon session key. To integrate a smart card logon, it is only necessary to modify the Kerberos AS Exchange. In this scenario, the KDC encrypts the user's logon session key with the public half of the user's public key/private key pair. The Kerberos client decrypts the exchange using the private key. The steps are as follows:

1. The public key/private key pair is stored on the smart card (private key and an x.509 certificate with public key).

2. The user puts the smart card into the smart card reader, which is attached to the computer.

3. The card insertion event triggers the SAS (the equivalent of Ctrl+Alt+Delete).

4. WinLogon calls MSGINA.

5. MSGINA displays a Logon Information dialog box, which requests the user's PIN.

6. User types in the PIN.

7. MSGINA sends this information to the LSA.

8. LSA uses the PIN to access the smart card and to obtain the public key certificate.

9. The Kerberos client SSP sends the certificate to the KDC as preauthentication data in KRB_AS_REQ (versus sending preauthentication as encrypted timestamp).

10. KDC validates the certificate using CryptoAPI and builds a certification path from the user's certificate to a root CA certificate in the system root store.

11. If this fails for any reason (the root certificate is not trusted, it cannot find parent certificates, revocation status cannot be determined), an error is produced.

12. KDC determines whether the issuing CA is authorized to issue the certificate for authentication within the domain. The issuing CA must be an enterprise CA published in Active Directory. (This prevents a rogue CA attack.)

13. KDC extracts the public key.

14. KDC verifies the digital signature on the Authenticator using the public key.

15. KDC Verifies the timestamp on the Authenticator (verifies that it is not a replay attack).

16. KDC Uses the User Principal Name (UPN) of the certificate to query the directory for account information such as the user SID, SIDs for domain groups, and SIDs for any universal groups (in multidomain native-mode environments). SIDs are in the TGT's authorization fields.

17. KDC Uses account information to construct the TGT.

18. KDC Generates a random session key and encrypts the TGT.

19. KDC Encrypts the logon session key with the public key from the user's certificate.

20. KDC Signs the reply with its private key (for mutual authentication).

21. KDC Signs the authorization data using the server key and then signs this with the KDC's secret key so that a rogue service cannot alter the authorization data after the TGT has been issued.

22. KDC returns the logon session key and the TGT to the client using KRB_AS_REP.

23. The client uses the private key to decrypt the session logon key.

24. The rest of the protocol is the same.

Supplemental credentials are generated so that down-level servers can be accessed.

What if the user is offline? If passwords were used, the LSA caches credentials that can be used and compared to a hash of an entered password. With smart cards, the user's private key is necessary to decrypt credentials encrypted using the public key. The private key and the certificate can be stored on the smart card.

Smart Cards and Remote Access

If the user dials in to a Windows 2000 Routing and Remote Access Service (RRAS) server, the Extensible Authentication Protocol (EAP) must be enabled on the RRAS server. EAP is enabled and then the built-in smart card support in Windows 2000 or vendor-supplied authentication modules can be used to support smart cards, one-time passwords, or biometrics.

The process includes two authentications: one to RRAS and one to the network. The process uses these steps:

1. The client authenticates to the server.

2. The connection is established.

3. RRAS policies and account attributers are applied to the client (access rights, callback options, static routes, and so on).

4. The client attempts authentication to the domain using EAP over TLS and its public key certificate. The certificate is examined for a User Principal Name (UPN). The UPN must match an account stored in AD.

Now You See It, Now...

To successfully complete a RAS logon, a dial-up connection must be made from the Logon dialog box before logging on to the local computer. If you log on to the computer and then attempt a dial-up connection to the RAS server, the connection will fail.

By using the Logon dialog box, the user gets the domain policy. If the user is logged on locally, domain logon policy is not obtained and the logon will fail.

For More Information

More information on items mentioned in this chapter can be found in the following locations in this book:

You can find information on CryptoAPI and public key/private key algorithms in Chapter 2, "Cryptology Introduction."

Chapter 5, "Kerberos in the RAW," provides a detailed description of the RFC standard and a description of the Kerberos ticket fields.

Kerberos policy for the domain and information on the KDC and its administration are provided in Chapter 11, "Securing Windows 2000 Server." Tools for modifying the policy are discussed in Chapter 9, "Security Tools."

RADIUS and other remote access authentication processes are described in Chapter 15, "Secure Remote Access Options."

Certificate authentication documentation can be found in Chapter 17, "Enterprise Public Key Infrastructure."

Interoperability issues are covered in Chapter 18, "Interoperability." Information on mapping certificates to user accounts is located in Chapter 19, "Web Security."

Summary

This chapter discussed Kerberos authentication algorithms as they are related to Windows 2000. Information was included on smart card integration, service account functionality, and NTLM use in the Windows 2000 world. Key points to remember are

- The Microsoft implementation follows the RFC implementation and extends it using extensions proposed by third parties.
- Smart card services are built in to Windows 2000 and integrated into Kerberos authentication.
- NTLM is still an integral part of authentication processes available in Windows 2000.

8

Lifecycle Choices

Anyone who has managed information systems knows that computers, operating systems, applications, and other components do not stay in one steady state. Why should a discussion on security approach these systems as if they do? Hardware is first new, then needs maintenance and repair, and then eventually gets replaced, as do operating systems. Each phase has unique security issues. The lifecycle of your Windows 2000 systems can be divided into four basic periods:

- Installation
- Maintenance
- Recovery and repair
- Death and dismemberment

Security should be a part of each of these periods. You should approach these lifecycle choices with an eye to the specific process that will not only manage security during the particular phase, but also better prepare the system for security during the next one. Finally, should recovery and repair fail (all the backups are corrupt or were washed into the Gulf courtesy of hurricane what's-its-name), do you have a plan?

Installation Do's and Don'ts for Improved Security

Any operating system has unique aspects. Properly done, you can ensure that the systems you install are reasonably secure when you put them online. The following are some do's and don'ts for improved security:

- Do plan every installation as part of your full enterprise migration or setup.
- Do install or upgrade domain controllers first and then set security policies. Use Group Policy to configure site, domain, and organizational unit (OU) security settings. Policies will propagate to computers as they are installed and join the domain.
- Do plan membership in user groups so there are as few administrators as possible.
- Do apply security templates to upgraded computers.
- Do install on NTFS partitions.
- Do test applications and replace nonconforming applications with those that do.
- If it is impossible to replace nonstandard applications and you must relax security settings on folders and registry keys, do carefully plan the installation and the gradual weakening of security so that you do the least damage possible.
- Do use a standard, unattended, silent installation to deploy Windows 2000 Professional across your enterprise. By preparing and automating the installation, you can install a uniform security model that meets your corporate policy. If the installation is silent, no one can change your settings because no one is asked, or has the opportunity, to enter information during the install. Use Microsoft's installation procedures for unattended installation.
- Do prepare security settings using templates you have customized.
- Do check servers and workstations after setup for proper configuration.
- Don't upgrade without checking the Hardware Compatibility List (HCL) and the application notes and without testing.
- Don't assume that new security holes won't appear.

Differences Between Upgrade and Clean Install

During an upgrade, the improved, more secure registry settings are not applied. (See Chapter 6, "Security from the Get–Go," to learn what these registry settings are. See the following section, "Securing Upgrade Installations," for how to apply them after installation.) An upgrade attempts to maintain the status quo when it comes to user rights and registry and file access. What effect does an upgrade have on existing system components?

- **Status of existing objects.** Existing users, settings, groups, rights, and permissions are retained.
- **System files.** System files remain in the same folder as the currently installed operating system; you have no choice to rename or move this folder.

- **User profile information location.** In fresh Windows 2000 installations and in upgrades from Windows 95 and Windows 98, ntuser.dat and ntuser.dat.log files are in %system drive%\Documents and Settings\%username% folders. Upgrades from Windows NT keep them in the %Systemroot%\Profiles\ %username% folder.

- **Special folders.** Folders, such as My Documents and My Pictures, are often redirected to network shares. If they are left on the local computer, their location will vary. In a fresh install or in an upgrade from Windows 95 or Windows 98 in which user profiles are disabled, their location will be %systemroot%\Documents and Settings. A Windows 2000 upgrade from NT 4.0 or 3.51 or an upgrade from Windows 9x with user profiles enabled will place them in %systemroot%\Profiles.

- **Application note.** See read1st.txt and the applications section of readme.doc. Also see the directory of the Windows 2000 applications Web site; many "Getting Started" topics in Windows Help are also in text files with file names of advsrv★.txt.

- **Groups.** If a Windows NT Primary Domain Controller (PDC) is upgraded to a Windows 2000 server, existing groups are converted. Windows NT local groups are converted to Windows 2000 domain local groups. Windows NT global groups are converted to Windows 2000 global groups. Unconverted NT computers that are members of the domain can continue to display and access the converted groups; they appear as Windows NT 4.0 global and local groups. However, any new group memberships in these groups that are Windows 2000–specific will not be viewed by the Windows NT computer users, and the administrators cannot modify the member properties that might impact these groups. The Windows NT client will not see groups that are members of the server global group because, in Windows NT, global groups cannot have other groups as members.

- **Distribution lists.** In Microsoft Exchange Server, distribution lists are converted to distribution groups with universal scope.

- **Down-level clients.** Non-Windows 2000 client computers that are not running the Active Directory client have a different view of Windows 2000 groups. For further discussion of down-level clients, see Chapter 13, "Securing Legacy Windows Clients."

Registry Note

Windows 2000 implements per-user class registration. Both user-specific class registration and computer-specific class registration are possible. Different users can have different sets of class registration file associations, COM components, and MIME types. In Windows NT 4.0, all users shared class registration. One user could alter the registry settings and thus affect other users. Per-user class registration isolates and allows an administrator to increase security on HKEY_LOCAL_MACHINE\Software\Classes.

Securing Upgrade Installations

Windows 2000 default file and registry Discretionary Access Control Lists (DACLs) are *not* applied during an upgrade from an earlier version of the OS to Windows 2000. To secure these installations, you can apply default settings using the command-line tool secedit. You should, of course, carefully consider the impact of making these changes. Existing applications might cease to run if applying the template restricts or removes their access to system files, folders, and registry keys. If the file system is not NTFS, the DACLs, of course, will not be applied. Therefore, thoroughly test the application of any template before applying changes to a production system.

Secedit is a command-line program that can be used to apply security templates. For more information on its use, see Chapter 9, "Security Tools." The commands to apply the default templates are as follows:

For Windows 2000 Professional:

```
Secedit /configure /cfg basicwk.inf /db basicwk.sdb /log basicwk.log
```

For Windows 2000 Server:

```
Secedit /configure /cfg basicsv.inf /db basicsv.sdb /log basicsv.log
```

Active Directory on an Upgraded Windows NT Primary Domain Controller (PDC)

When the Active Directory Wizard is activated, you must choose to join an existing domain tree or forest or to start a new tree or forest. If you join an existing domain:

- The wizard installs a directory data store and Kerberos V5 protocol authentication software. The Security Account Manager (SAM) objects are copied to a new data store. (SAM objects are security principals: users, local and global groups, and computer accounts.)

- Objects are created in the Active Directory (AD) to contain these security principals: users (users and predefined groups), computers, and built-in groups. You will find them in two folders in the Active Directory Users and Computers console. These objects are not OUs and cannot be deleted or moved. NT local groups are converted to domain local groups. NT global groups are converted to Windows 2000 global groups.

- The Kerberos Authentication and Ticket-Granting Services (TGS) are started.

- If this is a new child domain in an established forest, it establishes a transitive trust to the parent domain.

- The parent domain controller copies schema and configuration information to the new child domain controller.

- All schema and configuration information is copied to the new domain controller.

- The upgraded domain controller is a fully functioning member of the AD forest. All domain controllers receive notification of the new domain joining the forest.

When the upgrade is complete, clients can access the new domain in the following ways:

- Clients that use the AD client can perform directory queries.

- Computers running Windows NT 4.0 access the new Windows 2000 domain as if it were a Windows NT 4.0 domain. Unlike AD clients, NT clients will not be able to search the AD. NT computers can be joined to the Windows 2000 domain, but they gain no Kerberos, two-way, transitive trust relationships from their membership. Instead, the NT client thinks it is a member of an NT domain. Trust relationships between Windows NT domains and Windows 2000 domains can also be established, but the trust relationship is a one-way, Windows NT–style trust. To obtain a two-way trust, two one-way trusts must be established. There will be no transitive trust relationship with other Windows 2000 domains.

- While a domain is in mixed mode, a consistent environment is presented. The Windows 2000 domain controller uses an AD data store that is common with remaining NT 4.0 BDCs.

- A Windows 2000 domain controller can synchronize security principal changes to remaining BDCs. It is recognized as the PDC by Windows NT 4.0 Server BDCs.

- Down-level users and computers can benefit from transitive trusts and with authorization can access resources anywhere in the forest.

- Pass-through authentication provided by Windows 2000 domain controllers enables down-level clients to be authenticated by any domain in the forest.

- If the upgraded Windows 2000 domain controller goes offline and no other Windows 2000 server exists in the domain, a Windows NT 4.0 BDC can be upgraded and promoted to a Windows 2000 domain controller.

- The converted PDC supports Kerberos V5 and NT LAN Manager Challenge and Response Algorithm (NTLM). Down-level clients, including the Windows NT 4.0 BDCs, use NTLM.

Notes on Native Mode

You might be tempted to move quickly to native mode, but you should understand that Windows 2000 in native mode no longer supports many Windows NT 4.0 characteristics. Although it is true that Windows NT 4.0 computers can exist in a native-mode enterprise (they can be joined in the domain), you should make sure that all Windows NT domain controllers have been upgraded to Windows 2000.

In native mode, the Windows 2000 domain controller no longer supports NTLM replication. NTLM replication, or LMRepl, may have been used in your Windows NT 4.0 domains to replicate logon scripts and other small files to and from domain controllers and servers and to Windows NT 4.0 Workstations. Windows 2000 provides its own File Replication Service, but it is incompatible with Windows NT. Meanwhile, NTLM authentication is still supported.

Also, if a Windows 2000 domain controller had been emulating an NT 4.0 PDC to work with an NT BDC, it no longer can. In addition, an NT domain controller can't be added to the domain.

Maintenance

After you have installed the system and security policies, what then? Well, life doesn't end right after birth; there's still a lot of growing to do. Chances are you have legacy applications to support, new security holes will surface, and new requirements will be added for you and your systems. Three areas of security maintenance that will bring the most benefits are

- Picking securable applications
- Maintaining backups
- Applying and maintaining policies

Picking Securable Applications: The Windows 2000 Application Logo Standards

"Certified for xyz product" logo-standards programs are always a conundrum. The company wants the certification logo to mean something, yet it wants as many applications as possible to meet the standard so it can boast that thousands of applications run on it. If the company kept the standards high, too few applications would meet them, and few would be certified and bear the logo. What sometimes happens is that a logo program gets implemented that allows just about anyone to slap a "Certified for…" logo on the package. Some companies do a better job than others. All companies make an attempt, but they all deal with the quality issue versus the marketing issue.

Microsoft's logo program has been no different. In the past, the company has had logo programs, but purchasing an application that bore the logo did not always mean that the application was perfectly compatible. It wasn't false advertising; it was just a program with no teeth in it.

Does Your Application Meet the Security Standard?

If an application has not yet been (or never will be) submitted for logo approval, how will you know whether additional privileges are necessary? You can test the application yourself by following these steps:

1. Clean-install Windows 2000 Professional on an NTFS partition.

2. Log on as Administrator.

3. Install the application in the Program Files directory.

4. Create a test user account that is only in the Users group.

5. Logon as Test user.

6. Run the application.

7. Test every function.

However, the new Windows 2000 Application Logo Standard changes everything. Even the world-famous Gartner Group agrees that the program is stricter and more valuable to enterprises. Microsoft has changed its priorities. Microsoft wants to assure you, Mr. Enterprise CIO, that its OS is ready for mission-critical enterprise applications. The company wants you, Ms. Fortune 500 CEO, to understand that it is serious. Moreover, it wants all of us to get that nice, warm and fuzzy, safe and secure feeling as we hunker down for the long winter of our deployments.

Microsoft has changed its application certification program. There are now two challenging certifications: one for desktop applications and one for distributed applications. Enterprises that insist on logoed applications, and those that write their own to these specifications, will have better-written applications and lower operational costs (and the application will be more likely to be compatible with future OS releases). Desktop logo certifications are available for Windows 2000 Professional as well as for Windows NT and Windows 9x. Distributed applications can be certified for Windows 2000 Professional, Server, Advanced Server, and DataCenter Server. To be certified, applications must meet the standards outlined in Table 8.1.

Table 8.1   **Windows 2000 Certification**

	Profes-sional	**Server**	**Advanced Server**	**Data Center Server**
ADHERENCE TO FUNDAMENTALS				
Perform primary functionality and maintain stability.	X	X	X	X
Provide 32-bit components.	X	X	X	X
Support long filenames and UNC paths.	X	X	X	X
Support printers with long names and UNC paths.	X	X	X	X
Do not read from or write to Win.ini, System.ini, Autoexec.bat, or Config.sys on any Windows OS based on NT technology.	X	X	X	X
Ensure that unhidden files have associated file types and that all file types have associated icons, descriptions, and actions.	X	X	X	X
Perform Windows version-checking correctly.	X	X	X	X
Support AutoPlay of compact discs.	X			

continues

Table 8.1 **Continued**

	Profes-sional	Server	Advanced Server	Data Center Server
Kernel mode drivers must pass verification testing on Windows 2000.	X	X	X	X
Hardware drivers must pass WHQL testing.	X	X	X	X
INSTALL/UNINSTALL				
Install using a Windows Installer–based package that passes validation testing.	X			
Check availability and access to resources before install.		X	X	X
Observe rules in componentization.	X			
Identify shared components.	X	X	X	X
(A reference count is done on all shared application files during program installation on servers.)				
Install to Program Files by default.	X	X	X	X
Support Add/Remove Programs properly.	X	X	X	X
Ensure that your application supports advertising.	X	X	X	X
Ensure correct uninstall support.	X	X	X	X
Do not attempt to replace files that are protected by Windows File Protection.	X	X	X	X
Do not overwrite files with older versions.	X	X	X	X
Install shared files to the correct locations.	X	X	X	X
Decrement the count on shared application files during uninstall.	X	X	X	X
COMPONENT SHARING				
Do not attempt to replace files that are protected by System File Protection.	X	X	X	X
Component producers: Build side-by-side components.	X	X	X	X
Application developers: Consume and install side-by-side components.	X	X	X	X
Install any non-side-by-side shared files to the correct locations.	X	X	X	X
DATA AND SETTINGS MANAGEMENT				
Default to My Documents for storage of user-created data.	X			

	Profes-sional	Server	Advanced Server	Data Center Server
Classify and store application data correctly.	X			
Degrade gracefully on access denied.	X			
Run in a secure Windows environment.	X	X	X	X
Adhere to system-level Group Policy settings.	X	X	X	X
Applications that create ADM files must properly store their ADM file settings in the registry.	X	X	X	X
USER INTERFACE FUNDAMENTALS				
Support standard system size, color, font, and input settings.	X	X	X	X
Ensure compatibility with the High Contrast option.	X	X	X	X
Provide documented keyboard access to all features.	X	X	X	X
Expose the location of the keyboard focus.	X	X	X	X
Do not rely exclusively on sound.	X	X	X	X
Do not place shortcuts to documents, help, or uninstall in the Start menu.	X	X	X	X
Support multiple monitors.	X			
ONNOW/ACPI SUPPORT				
Indicate busy application status properly.	X			
Respond to sleep requests from the OS properly.	X			
Handle sleep notifications properly.	X			
Wake from normal sleep without losing data.	X			
Wake from critical sleep properly.	X			
APPLICATION MIGRATION				
Application must continue to function after upgrade to Windows 2000 Professional without reinstall.	X			
ACTIVE DIRECTORY (AD)				
Services publish their existence in AD.		X	X	X
Clients must query AD for services.		X	X	X

continues

Table 8.1 **Continued**

	Profes-sional	Server	Advanced Server	Data Center Server
Services must adhere to the schema extensibility rules.		X	X	X
SECURITY SERVICES				
Configure the server to run under the appropriate account.		X	X	X
Create connection authentication between client and server using the client credentials.		X	X	X
Impersonation of the client by the server.		X	X	X
CLUSTERING				
Use TCP/IP protocol.			X	X
Use virtual server IP address or virtual server network name to access cluster resources.			X	X
Clients must not crash, hang, or affect the stability of the system when the connection to the cluster node is lost.			X	X
Upon failure, clients must preserve user data.			X	X
Location of application data must be configurable.			X	X
Checkpoint either automatically or manually states information required for clean restart.			X	X
Upon failure, application can be restarted and, if applicable, recover to the last checkpoint.			X	X
Correctly handle computer name and IP address. Application should use virtual server name and IP address if necessary.			X	X
Can be installed on all nodes in the server cluster.			X	X
Can run at least one instance of an application as a cluster resource.			X	X
Can be configured at least as a generic service or application.			X	X

The following are not required but are strongly suggested:

- Installation of your application must not require a reboot on a freshly installed Windows 2000 system.

- Use `SHGetFolderPath` to determine special folder paths.

- Place files or application data in special folders such as My Documents, User Profile, Desktop, Favorites, and so on. These should be located in specific paths by referral to CISDL constants, not hard coding. Use of the `SHGetFolderPath` command and the specified CISDL constant name finds the folder path during installation. For example, use of the constant CISDL_Program_Files will locate the path and allow placement in the Program Files folder.

- Test applications with terminal services.

- AD (distributed) distributed services will advertise themselves in the AD, and clients must use the AD to query for services. In addition, the application must adhere to schema extensibility rules.

- Security (distributed) server applications must support single sign-on and not use accounts with overly elevated security.

- MSCS (distributed) for Advanced Server or DataCenter server must support clustering.

To qualify for certification, an application must comply with the Application Specification for Windows 2000 (`http://www.nsdn.Microsoft.com/certification/appspec.asp`), run on any Windows 2000 operating system, and prove it by being tested by VeriTest, an independent testing laboratory (`http://www.veritest.com/mslogos/windows2000/`).

Reduce TCO by 27 percent!

The Gartner Group recommends that developers adhere to the Application Specification for Windows 2000 even if they don't intend to be certified. The group also recommends that enterprises ask application vendors of uncertified applications to detail areas in which they do not comply and explain why. The Gartner Group claims its research shows that using complaint applications results in cost reductions in the areas of desktop support, downtime, systems research, planning, product management, and evaluation for purchase . Furthermore, these applications make it easier for companies to adopt the Zero Administration Windows (ZAW) features of Windows 2000. The sum of both steps (running compliant applications and adopting ZAW) reduces the TCO by 27%. For the scoop, see `http://www.gartner.com/webletter/microsoftwinserv/article2.html`.

Applying and Maintaining Policy

During installation, you applied a Security Policy. Even if you did not intentionally design one, you applied one. Windows 2000, as previously mentioned, uses a default template to set security settings on system files and folders, registry keys, password policies, and so on. Some settings, of course, do not meet the requirements of your organization's written Security Policy. If you carefully tested your current applications with Windows 2000 and spent time planning and studying your needs and the capability of this new OS, then you modified that default policy before installation or shortly thereafter.

During the maintenance phase, you will be tweaking that policy as new problems arise, as you implement new features, and as you add Windows 2000 services to the mix. The nice thing about policies with Windows 2000 is that you have the capability to automatically apply standard policies across multiple systems from a central location. You do not have to make multiple registry entries. You can use a GUI interface to develop, test, and deploy your policy.

You will use two major tools to implement and manage your policy: Group Policy Editor and the Security Configuration and Analysis console. Chapter 9 will guide you in their use. However, it is important to be prepared to use other tools, such as the policy interfaces of the Routing and Remote Access Service and the Internet Authentication Service, to implement policies appropriate for those services. Each new server application might add a new interface or be manageable by something with which you are already familiar.

Backup

Everyone knows the value of having a good backup of your data and system configuration. Many people have learned the hard way what is necessary to restore Windows NT. To be able to recover corrupt or missing data and/or restore a system, you must know what to back up and when. If managing security means protecting the integrity of data, then backing up the data correctly is part of that effort. Restoring from a good backup is often the only realistic response to an intrusion. (You may not be able to determine just what the intruder has done in the system.) Backups and disaster recovery may not be specifically done by a security administrator, but backup policy and disaster-recovery planning should be a part of any overall security plan. There are three areas here to understand:

- Permissions
- Backup tools and processes
- What should be backed up

The best methods and practices for repair and recovery will be discussed later in this chapter.

Permissions

Determining who can back up and restore data is not difficult. Who can do what is determined by assigned privilege, group membership, or ownership of data. To back up data, you must be at least one of the following:

- An Administrator
- A member of the local Backup Operators group (to back up data on the local machine)
- A member of the domain Backup Operators group (to back up data on any computer in the domain or in a trusted domain)
- Assigned the right to back up data
- The owner of the data you want to back up

Your right to back up or restore data may be restricted by the following:

- **Disk quota restrictions.** Because backup can now be done to a hard disk, you need to make sure backup operators required to do so have enough disk space available to back up data.
- **Dialog selection.** The Allow only the owner and Administrator access to the backup data selection can be set. (This is set in the Backup Job Information dialog box when using the Microsoft Backup program.)
- **The location of the data.** System state data cannot be backed up remotely.

The last two restrictions are important security considerations. First, if a backup operator is allowed to use backup data and restore it, the operator might gain access to data it shouldn't. Using this selection ensures that a higher level of access is necessary to manipulate the data after it is backed up. Second, because system state data includes the registry, it is important that an attacker cannot gain access to it by backup from across the network.

Tools and Processes

A solid backup program will use several tools. A new backup program and a new definition for the Emergency Repair Disk process is available with Windows 2000. Although you might choose to use a third-party product, reviewing Windows 2000 Backup will help you understand what needs to be considered and what is available at no extra charge.

In addition to backing up the contents of hard drives and system state, you should also create—and keep up to date—an Emergency Repair Disk (ERD). In preparing your backup itinerary, it is also important to note that not all tools or processes work the same way as they did in Windows NT. In addition, you have new configuration information that will be necessary should you need to recover your systems. Consider the following:

- Making an ERD does not back up the registry.
- In a Windows 2000 domain, user account information is stored in the AD, not in the registry.

- Replication of the AD is multimaster; thus, at any one time, various domain controller copies may be slightly different.
- Many components are distributed. Make sure you have proper techniques in place to capture all the necessary data or configuration information.

The tools available for your backup strategy are

- Windows 2000 Backup
- Ntbackup
- Removable storage
- ERD
- Windows 2000 boot disk

Windows 2000 Backup

Table 8.2 lists the processes in which the Windows 2000 Backup program plays an active part. It also defines associated terms.

Table 8.2   **Windows 2000 Backup Tool Functions**

Process	Notes
Archive and restore selected files and folders on the hard disk.	FAT and NTFS volumes can be backed up. Daily, Differential (files created or changed since being normal or incremental; files are not marked as being backed up), Incremental (files created or changed since the last normal backup; files are marked as being backed up), and Normal backup types can be made.
Create an Emergency Repair Disk.	The ERD can be used to help you restore damaged system files.
Copy Remote Storage data.	Remote Storage is a process in which infrequently used data is moved from storage on the local hard disk to secondary storage (disks, tapes, and so on). This frees disk space, and yet the data is available and locatable.
Copy data stored in mounted drives.	Mounted drives are those logically attached to empty folders on an NTFS volume. They are therefore labeled with and accessible from a system file path instead of a drive letter.
Copy the system state of the computer.	The system state includes the registry, AD, and configuration files. For more information, see the "System State" section later in this chapter.

Process	Notes
Back up to many storage devices.	A Windows 2000 backup can be made to a logical drive, removable media, a recordable CD-ROM, automated (robo-changer) type media pools, a hard disk, a floppy drive, and a tape.
Schedule automatic backups using the Windows 2000 Task Scheduler.	The Task Scheduler is a GUI interface to the schedule service. You must start the service before you can use the Task Scheduler to schedule and automate backup. To start the service, type `net start schedule` at the command line.

Ntbackup

Ntbackup is the command-line tool that can be used to back up Windows 2000. You can use it in scripts or at the command line. Ntbackup cannot be used to restore files and folders from the command line.

Removable Storage

Windows 2000 Backup does not manage the storage devices and media. That process is handled by the Removable Storage service. The Removable Storage service mounts and dismounts tapes and disks.

Emergency Repair Disk

The ERD is not an application; rather, it's the result of an operation. It is a tool that can be used in the recovery process. It is created from the Tools menu of the Backup program. An ERD contains the setup.log, autoexec.nt, and config.nt files. These files provide initial configuration information that can be used to repair your system, but please note that the ERD does not contain a copy of the registry; the Windows NT 4.0 ERD did. To understand how the ERD can be used, see the "System Recovery: Repair Overview" section later in this chapter.

Windows 2000 Boot Disk

To perform some repair processes, you will need a set of boot disks. Boot disks can be made by running the makeboot program from the Windows 2000 CD-ROM\bootdisk folder. Four disks are produced. Boot disks for Windows 2000 Professional are different from, and cannot be used in place of, boot disks for Windows 2000 Server. Boot disks can be used in combination with the ERD or the Recovery Console to repair Windows 2000.

You can also create a single floppy disk that may allow you to boot Windows 2000 (if the hard disk boot partition and/or related boot files are missing or damaged but the Windows 2000 system is intact). You then may be able to repair the hard disk or replace missing or damaged files. You need to create the boot disk before you can use it to repair a system. To create the disk, you must do the following:

- Format a floppy disk using Windows 2000.
- Copy relevant system files from the boot partition.

Files to copy include

- ntldr
- BOOTSECT.DOS (only necessary if you are dual booting with some earlier Windows versions or MS-DOS)
- NTDETECT.COM
- boot.ini

In Practice

To ensure that you have all the system data you need to restore a damaged system, you should have a good backup policy in place. This policy should require periodic complete backups; however, a complete restore is not always necessary or desirable. To make sure you have the tools you need, at a minimum make separate, periodic backups of your system configuration data by backing up the system state. You also should make sure to have an ERD for each system.

Running some Windows 2000 utilities, services, or applications might require special backup processes or programs if you need to restore them. Examples of applications that require special processing are Microsoft Exchange Server and Microsoft SQL Server. An example of a service that requires a special process is the Windows Media Services. If you are using these products, you should consult their documentation to develop an appropriate plan. The following lists some of these processes or paths:

- Removable Storage and Remote Storage users need to back up systemroot\System32\Ntmsdata and systemroot\System32\Remotestorage.
- If WINS is used, the WINS database can be backed up by running Backup Database from the Action menu.
- Although backing up system state backs up the Certificate Authority (CA) database, you can back up the CA and its operation data from the CA console. Here you can back up the CA public key, private key, and certificate, as well as the certificate database.
- The IIS console can be used to back up the IIS metabase. The metabase is also important to a restore of the CA.

- CMAK (Connection Manager) .CMS and .INF templates are stored in \Program Files\CMAK\Support.
- The Dynamic Host Configuration Protocol (DHCP) database can be separately backed up by copying the DHCP.mdb file.

System State

The system state is a collection of information that fully describes the current status of your system. Just as the words "red light" or "green light" capture the stop or go state of a traffic light, you can capture the state of your system. To do so takes more than a few words. When you follow the Windows 2000 Backup process to back up the system state, you are creating an archive of the following:

- System files (boot files)
- The registry
- Component services (COM+ Class Registration database)
- The AD services database (domain controllers)
- The SYSVOL directory (domain controllers)
- The File Replication Service
- The Certificate Services database (server only)

A backup of a system's system state can only be made from that system. You cannot remotely back up the system state. When you back up the system state, a copy of the registry files is saved in the %systemroot%\Repair\Regback folder.

System Recovery: Repair Overview

If your system will not start or load Windows 2000, what do you do? What features does Windows 2000 have to help you if system files become corrupted or if someone has installed device drivers that cause the system not to work correctly? Several tools and processes are available to help you. They include

- Starting in safe mode
- Using the emergency repair process
- Using the Last Known Good process
- Using the Windows 2000 Recovery Console
- Using the System File Checker

Starting in Safe Mode

Like Windows 9x, Windows 2000 can be started in safe mode. Starting in safe mode means that a minimal set of device drivers and services are started. This can be useful if you have recently installed new device drivers or software that are preventing Windows from starting or are making it unstable. You may be able to start the system in safe mode and remove the driver or other software. If your system files are missing or corrupted or if the hard disk is damaged or has failed, safe mode will not work. Additional safe mode startup options might be available if you used the Remote Installation Service to install Windows 2000. Safe mode startup options are described in Table 8.3.

Table 8.3   **Safe Mode Startup Options**

Mode	Definition	Additional Information
Safe mode	Only basic files and drivers.★	If this doesn't work, use ERD.
Safe mode with networking	Only basic files and drivers plus networking connections.★	If this doesn't work, try safe mode (without networking).
Safe mode with command prompt	Basic files and drivers. ★ Displays command prompt instead of desktop Start menu and taskbar.	If this doesn't work, use ERD.
Enable boot logging	Logs all drivers and services that are loaded or not loaded into ntbtlog.txt in the %windir% directory.	Helps you identify the drivers and services that might be causing the problem.
Enable VGA mode	Uses basic VGA driver.	Use this if you have installed a new driver for a video card and it's not working properly. Always use when safe mode, safe mode with networking, or safe mode with command prompt is used.
Last Known Good configuration	Uses registry information saved at last shutdown.	Useful in cases of incorrect configuration; does not solve problems of missing or corrupt files and drivers.
Directory Service Restore mode	Restores SYSVOL directory and Active Directory Service on domain controller.	Not applicable in Windows 2000 Professional.
Debugging mode	Sends debug information through the serial cable to another computer.	

★*Basic files and drivers: mouse (not serial mouse), monitor, keyboard, most storage, base video (basic VGA driver), default system services, no network connections*

Emergency Repair Process

You will need an ERD to assist you in repairing the
following:

- Systems files
- The startup environment (which OS to start and how) of a dual-boot machine
- The partition boot sector (contains disk file system information and a short machine language program that loads the Windows OS) on your boot volume (contains Windows 2000 OS and support files; can be, but doesn't have to be, the same as the system volume)

The ERD is made using the Backup utility from the Tools menu, but the ERD does not back up any of your data files or programs. When you update the ERD, Windows 2000 does *not* back up the files to the %systemroot%\Repair directory unless you tell it to. You are given that choice when you begin the ERD program. The first time you elect to do this, the backup program creates a new subfolder of the repair directory, called regback, and places a current copy of the registry in that folder.

During installation, a copy of the registry is placed in the repair folder for possible use in recovery. Because this is common knowledge, the possibility for attack by copying these registry files and using a password-cracking program offline exists. Deleting this copy of the registry files from the repair directory has been a popular choice for administrators wanting to reduce an attacker's opportunities. However, deleting this copy of the files prevents them from being used by a legitimate administrator attempting a repair.

To use the ERD to repair or recover a system, you must also have the Windows 2000 CD and the Windows 2000 setup disks. Note that missing or corrupt files are replaced from the Windows 2000 CD. Therefore, any files you changed using hotfixes or service packs after the original installation are lost and need to be reapplied.

To create the setup disks, you can use the Windows 2000 CD-ROM on a computer other than the installation. Run the makeboot.exe a: command from the bootdisk folder on the installation CD-ROM. You will need four formatted disks.

The repair process is started by using the setup disks, or the installation CD-ROM, as if you were going to reinstall the system. After the first reboot and at the Welcome to Setup screen, you press R to select the option to repair or recover Windows 2000. There are two choices:

- *Manual repair* enables you to choose to repair system files, the partition boot sector, or the startup environment. Manual repair does not attempt to replace the registry.
- *Fast repair* automatically attempts to repair system files, the partition boot sector, or startup environment. The registry it replaces is the original one from setup.

When the repair process is complete, the computer will restart.

Using the Last Known Good Process

The Last Known Good process can help you recover from changes made to the registry by recently added, incorrect drivers or improper changes to the HKEY_L_Machine\System\CurrentControlSet\ registry key. It will not help you recover from changes made to other registry keys. The Last Known Good process works by replacing the current copy of the CurrentControlSet key with a copy of the previous version of that key. It will not work if you have successfully booted the system before discovering you need to make the change. (A boot is considered successful if someone logs on.)

If, for example, you add a video driver that causes your system to crash or that makes it unbootable, you may be able to recover using Last Known Good. To do so, restart the system. At the Please Select the Operating System to Start message, press the F8 key, select Last Known Good Configuration, and press Enter.

However, if some change has been made that makes the system unstable but you are able to reboot the system and log on, restarting and choosing Last Known Good will not help you. This is because, after a successful boot, the previous copy is replaced with the current copy of the registry key.

Using the Windows 2000 Recovery Console

This command-line interface will help you repair system problems using command-line commands. You can use it to enable and disable services, repair a corrupted master boot record, read and write to the hard drive, or copy system files from floppy disks or CD-ROMs even if your system and boot partitions are formatted NTFS. The Recovery Console can be started from the Windows 2000 setup disks or by using the winnt32.exe command with the /cmdcons switch. If you install the Recovery Console on the computer, you can select it from the list of available operating systems. You will need to have an Administrator account and password to run the Recovery Console.

To install the Recovery Console, run \Winnt32.exe /cmdconsupgrade from the i386 directory of the installation CD-ROM.

To delete the Recovery Console if it has been installed, do the following:

- Delete the Cmdcons folder from the root folder.
- Delete the Cmldr file from the same folder.
- In the boot.ini file, delete the entry for the Recovery Console.

You do not need to install the Recovery Console to run it. If your system can start, you can run the Recovery Console by running winnt32.exe/cmdcons. If the system does not start, you must use the Windows 2000 setup disks (or boot your system from the installation CD-ROM, select the repair process, and then select Recovery Console.) Table 8.4 lists the recovery console commands; Table 8.5 defines file attributes used in the table.

Because local hard drives may be formatted as a part of recovery, make sure you have backed up your data!

Table 8.4 **Recovery Console Commands**

Command	Use	Example and/or syntax
`Attrib`	Changes file attributes	`attrib [+r][-r][+s][-s][+h][-h]`
`Batch`	Executes commands in the text file	`Batch input_file [output_file]`
		To execute do.txt and put output in done.txt, type `Batch c:\stuff\do.txt` ➥`c:\stuff\done.txt`.
`ChDir (Cd)`	Displays or changes the current directory	`ChDir [drive:][path][..]`
`Chkdsk`	Checks the disk and displays a status report	`Chkdsk [drives] [/p][/r]` where `/p` makes no changes `/r` locates bad sectors, recovers readable information, and implies `/p`
`Cls`	Clears the screen	The cleared screen shows only the command prompt.
`Copy`	Copies a single file to another location	`Copy source[destination]` A compressed file from the Windows installation CD is decompressed as it is copied.
`Delete (Del)`	Deletes one or more files	`Delete [drive:][path] filename` Only works in system directories of the current Windows installation, removable media, the root directory of the hard disk partition, or local installation sources.
`Dir`	Displays a list of files and subdirectories	`Dir [drive:][path]filename` Also lists the volume label and serial number, total files, cumulative size, and free space. For each file, lists extension, size in bytes, date and time of last modification, and file attribute. Only operates within system directories of the current installation, removable media, the root directory of the hard disk partition, and local installation sources.
`Disable`	Disables a Windows 2000 or Windows NT 4.0 system service or a device driver	`Disable {service_name ¦ device_` ➥`driver_name}` Sets startup type to SERVICE_DISABLED. Write down the startup type that appears for later reference.

continues

Table 8.4 **Continued**

Command	Use	Example and/or syntax
Diskpart	Manages partitions on the hard drive	Diskpart [/add ¦ /delete] ⇒[device_name ¦ drive_name ¦ ⇒partition_name][size]
		To delete partition 3, type Diskpart /delete ⇒\Device\HardDisk0\Partition3
		To add a 20MB partition, type Diskpart /add ⇒\Device\HardDisk0 20
Enable	Starts or enables a system service or a device driver	Enable {service_name ¦ device_ ⇒driver_name} [startup_type]
Exit	Exits the recovery console and restarts the computer	Exit
Expand	Extracts file(s) from a compressed file	Expand [/d][/y] source.cab ⇒[/F:filespec][destination]
		where
		/d lists the files contained in the cabinet file without expanding or extracting from it
		/y suppresses the overwrite prompt when expanding or extracting files
Fixboot	Writes a new partition boot sector to the system partition	Fixboot [drive]
Fixmbr	Writes a new master boot record to a hard drive	Fixmbr [device_name]
Format	Formats a disk	Format [drive:][/q][/fs:file-system]
		where
		/q is a quick format-drive not scanned for bad areas
		/fs:file-system specifies the file system such as FAT, FAT32, or NTFS
Help	Displays a list of commands	Help [commandname]
		Help /? lists the commands.
Listsvr	Lists services and drivers available on the computer	Listsvr
Logon	Logs you on to an installation of Windows 2000 or Windows NT 4.0	Logon
Map	Displays mapping of drive letters to physical device names	Map [arc]
		where
		arc displays Advanced RISC Computing device names instead of Windows 2000 device names [that is, multi(0)disk(0)rdisk(0)parti-tion(1) vs: \Device\HardDisk0\Partition1]

Command	Use	Example and/or syntax
Mkdir (Md)	Creates a directory	Mkdir [*drive:*]*path*
More	Displays contents of a text file	More [*drive:*][*path*]*filename* Use " " if NTFS and spaces in file name.
Rename (Ren)	Changes the name of a single file	Rename [*drive:*][*path*]*oldname newname*
Rmdir (Rd)	Deletes a directory	Rmdir [*drive:*][*path*] Note: The directory must be empty or the command will fail.
Set	Displays and sets system environmental variables	Set [*variable=*[*string*]]
Systemroot	Sets the current directory to the systemroot of the Windows 2000 installation to which you are logged on	systemroot
Type	Displays a text file	Type [drive:][path]filename

Table 8.5 **File Attributes**

Symbol	Attribute
D	Directory
H	Hidden file
S	System file
E	Encrypted
R	Read-only
A	File ready for archiving
C	Compressed
P	Reparse point

Understanding Startup Types

SERVICE_AUTO_START, SERVICE_DISABLED, and SERVICE_DEMAND_START correspond to Automatic, Disable, and Manual, which you set in Services in the Computer Management administration tool. SERVICE_BOOT_START and SERVICE_SYSTEM_START are used to configure the way device drivers load, either when the computer is started or when Windows 2000 starts. It's important to know the correct device driver or service startup if you are going to temporarily change this using the recovery tool. The recovery tool command disable will first display on the screen the current startup type. Write it down!

System File Checker

The System File Checker can be used to verify that all the system-protected system files are intact. If you suspect that a system file might be corrupt, run the System File Checker. If it finds a corrupt file, it will replace it from the %Systemroot%\ system32\dllcache folder. You can also use System File Checker to replace the dllcache folder contents.

System File Checker is used from the command line by entering `sfc` and one of the following parameters:

- `scannow` Scans all protected files.
- `scanonce` Scans all files one time.
- `scanboot` Scans every time the computer is booted.
- `cancel` Cancels scheduled scans.
- `quiet` Scans and replaces files without prompting for action.
- `enable` Resets status to prompt user for action.
- `purgecache` Deletes files in the dllcache folder and scans the protected files.
- `cachesize=x` Specifies how large the dllcache can be.

You can also control the System File Checker by setting policies using the Group Policy Editor. The policies are in the Computer Configuration\Administrative Templates\System\Windows File Protection folder.

Whoops!

To expand cabinet files during system recovery, use the command expand. For example, the following command expands the compressed file msgame.sys to c:\winnt\system\drivers:

```
Expand d:\i386\driver.cab \f:msgame.sys c:\winnt\system\drivers
```

You could expand all the files onto your hard disk, but I wouldn't. It'll take time and a lot of hard disk space to expand those thousands of files. In addition, the Windows File Protection Service will prevent you from replacing critical system files by simple copying. Instead, find out the name of the file you need and expand it.

Death and Dismemberment

What do you do with your computers when they no longer are useful? Many companies have programs that recycle computers by allowing employees to purchase them for home use or by donating them to charity. Others simply throw out outdated or unneeded parts. Whatever you do with equipment that you no longer need, you need to make sure there is no data on the disk drives before you recycle, discard, or abandon them.

The lengths to which you need to go will depend on the sensitivity of the data on the drives, but you should do something. Various options exist including:

- Deleting files
- Reformatting the drive
- Demagnetizing the drive
- Using a utility to overwrite the entire drive

Although any of these operations will give you some protection, you should be aware that methods exist that would enable unscrupulous people to recover data from your disk even if you have used one of these operations. The problem occurs because most operating system deletion programs do not really delete the data; they merely mark the space as available for reuse. Even if you write new data to that space, only the space you actually use is overwritten. Some data from the old file might still remain. Because operating systems manage data on a disk in a well-documented way, other programs can be written to recover the data. There are legitimate uses for such programs, including the recovery of accidentally deleted files by the owners of the files. (An example of such a tool is Undelete by Executive Software, located at `http://www.software.com`) To make sure data is actually deleted from disks, you might want to consider programs that overwrite all the data with 0s or with meaningless patterns of 1s and 0s.

A product you can examine for free is BCWipe, which is available from `http://www.bcwipe.com`. BCWipe overwrites files using random characters. The downloadable shareware version of the program enables you to do the following:

- **Wipe files and folders.** Using this feature rather than a simple Delete should enable you to make data a little bit more inaccessible.
- **Wipe free disk space.** If you deleted files using OS commands, you will need to use this process.
- **Wipe the swap file.** This will be automatically done if Wipe Free Disk Space is chosen.

Best Practices

Data backed up from a Windows 2000 NTFS volume should be restored to a Windows 2000 NTFS volume; otherwise, you might lose data or features such as permissions, encrypting file system settings, disk quota information, mounted drive info, and remote storage info.

- For a higher degree of security, grant backup rights to one group of individuals and restore rights to another.
- For the most secure site, only an Administrator should restore files.
- Secure backup devices and media.
- Back up entire volumes so you can recover from a hard disk failure and back up directory services.
- Create a backup log.
- Three copies of backup media are the recommended number; keep one copy offsite.
- Periodically, do a trial restoration to verify proper backup and to uncover any hardware issues. Hardware problems might not be found with software-verification programs.
- Schedule the use of System File Checker through Group Policy on volatile systems.
- Create ERDs when configuration changes are made and select the option to back up registry data.
- Make your own backup of registry data in the %systemroot%\repair\regbak folder before backing up new changes.
- Select applications that meet Windows 2000 application logo standards.
- Have setup disks available.
- Practice using safe mode and the Recovery Console before you need them.

For More Information

Related information on installation, maintenance, and backup can be found in chapters that deal with particular services.

To learn more about default file and registry permissions, see Chapter 6, "Security from the Get-Go."

Information on down-level clients is available in Chapter 13, "Securing Legacy Windows Clients."

Group Policy and the Security Configuration and Analysis console are covered in Chapter 9, "Security Tools," in Chapter 12, "Domain-Level Security," and in Chapter 16, "Securing the Network Using Distributed Security Services."

To learn more about policies for remote access, see Chapter 15, "Secure Remote Access Options."

Policy for Certificate Services is covered in Chapter 17, "Enterprise Public Key Infrastructure."

Summary

If security design establishes the framework on which you hang your security policies and practices, then lifecycle choices point to the three phases that the design must support. Installation, maintenance, and recovery are all important facets that should be planned for and observed. This chapter described the common security practices that should be followed for each phase and the tools available to do so. Where appropriate, these discussions are continued in future chapters.

9

Security Tools

I T SEEMS APPROPRIATE THAT AN OPERATING SYSTEM DESIGNED with security in mind would provide an array of security tools to be used with that system. Indeed, this is true. Microsoft has taken advantage of the proliferation of security tools for Windows NT to understand what information systems administrators and protectors want. In addition, Microsoft has crafted GUI tools that make it easier to manage security across the enterprise and on the local machine. The Windows 2000 Resource Kit includes a grab bag of utilities, many of them newly designed for Windows 2000. A selection called Support Tools also accompanies Windows 2000 Server and provides further resources.

This chapter will introduce two major Windows 2000 tools and a number of support and Resource Kit tools that are related to security. The tools detailed include

- The Security Configuration and Analysis tool set
- Group Policy
- Windows 2000 support tools
- Resource Kit tools

More information on Group Policy and the Security Configuration and Analysis tool set is provided in several chapters. See the "For More Information" section at the end of this chapter for specific chapter listings.

Using the Security Configuration and Analysis Tool Set

The Security Configuration and Analysis tool set includes three components:

- Security Templates
- Security Configuration and Analysis (also known as Security Configuration Editor and Security Configuration Manager)
- The secedit tool

Two of these, Security Templates and Security Configuration and Analysis, are Microsoft Management Console (MMC) snap-ins that can be used to configure, analyze, and audit Windows NT and Windows 2000 security. The third, secedit, is a command-line tool that can configure or analyze security settings.

The Security Configuration and Analysis tool set was first released with Service Pack 4 for Windows NT 4.0. It has been expanded and perfected for use with Windows 2000. Finally, you can configure access policies, local audit policy, user rights assignments, and hardware security options and can set registry, file volume, and directory security in one place. You can also compare the current settings against a stored configuration or against recommended levels of security defined in Security Templates. Thus, administrators can use the tools to fulfill Security Policy, and auditors can ensure that the policy remains in place.

In addition, the tools are extensible. Thus, as new issues are found or new applications are added, new pieces can be added to the tools. This ensures the applicability of these tools long after the initial configuration of an individual machine.

The tool set can be used to manage the policies and settings on a single computer. In distributed settings, secedit can be used to build batch files, which can be implemented across an enterprise. In a Windows 2000 domain configured with Active Directory, templates can be imported into Group Policies and therefore can automatically be implemented throughout a site, domain, or organizational unit (OU). Local settings can be overridden or set individually, and Security Policy for an OU or domain can be set, analyzed, and managed from a single location.

This makes possible a reduction in administrative cost; allows convenient, centralized configuration; suggests levels of security setting through templates; and provides an easy interface that can be used to analyze and audit security.

Security Templates

Security Templates is an MMC snap-in tool that exposes the default templates and enables you to modify them. Because each of the templates is designed for a particular version of Windows 2000, they are described in detail in chapters that discuss version-specific security. Each template includes sections as described in "Security Configuration and Analysis" later in this chapter.

Templates are .INF files and can be modified using a text editor or the Security Templates snap-in. They can be exported out of and imported into the snap-in. A good practice is to copy or export template files and develop your own templates for each computer use, then apply templates as appropriate to set a security baseline that can be returned to, analyzed, and audited.

A template can be imported into the Security Configuration and Analysis tool and be used to either configure the local computer or compare the existing settings of the computer to those in the template. The command-line tool secedit can be used in a batch file to apply the templates for configuration or analysis purposes.

Default templates are used during the Windows 2000 Professional and Windows 2000 Server installation processes and during the promotion of Windows 2000 Server to domain controller. The scesetup.log in the folder documents the template used during setup. If the computer is a domain controller, the scedcpro.log documents the template used during its promotion. Both logs (found at %systemroot%\security\logs) list the configuration specifics and note warnings and errors. The default installation templates, found at %systemroot%\inf, are

- **defltsv.inf**. The default Server setup security template
- **defltdc.inf**. The default domain controller promotion security template
- **defltwk.inf** The default Professional setup security template

Microsoft is expected to provide additional templates for other products. An additional template has already been developed for Internet Information Server (IIS) V. This template is part of the Internet Server Security Configuration Tool and is available for download from http://www.microsoft.com/technet/security/tools.asp.

Templates available to the Security Templates snap-in are stored in %systemroot%\Security\Templates. Those furnished with Windows 2000 Server and Advanced Server are in the following list. Templates ending in dc are meant to be used with domain controllers, sv with servers, and ws or wk with workstations. Exceptions to this designation are hisecws and securews, which can be used with either servers or workstations.

- Basic security templates (basicdc, basicsv, basicwk) can be applied to upgraded systems to obtain security settings, which are the equivalent of cleanly installed systems.
- The compatws template (Discretionary Access Control Lists [DACLs] are compatible with Windows NT 4.0 workstations).
- DC security template (domain controller DACLs for files and registry).
- High-security templates (hisecdc, hisecws) provide additional, network-related security settings.
- The notssid template does not use the terminal server user account SID.

- Optional components templates (ocfiless, ocfilesw) include DACLs on files for optional components such as Certificate Services and terminal services.
- Secure templates (securedc, securews) provide additional security settings as compared to basic templates.
- Setup security template matches the original settings on the computer.

Security Configuration and Analysis

Security Configuration and Analysis is a standalone snap-in tool that enables the creation and modification of text .INF files (templates) containing security configurations. These templates can be compared to the current computer policy settings and applied to change computer security settings.

Although they can be edited directly, it is recommended that you edit them (using the Security Configuration and Analysis console) to meet your specific Security Policy requirements. You can cut and paste to copy parts of the configuration from different databases and/or you can write your own.

In time, as new security flaws or recommendations surface, you can use a new, recommended configuration to analyze your system, expose its weaknesses, and determine whether making the recommended changes is right for that system. Auditors can bring in their own configurations and analyze your system against them.

To properly use this tool, you will need to

- Understand the link between the templates and the Security Policy in place on the system
- Review the practical application of the tool
- Understand each listed topic (Account Policies, Local Policies, Restricted Groups, and so on) in the policy

The Link Between Templates and Security Policy

When you import a configuration template to a computer, you create a Security Configuration and Analysis database. When a computer has a clean installation of Windows 2000, it creates the local computer policy database, which contains out-of-the-box security configuration for your system.

Each template includes prescribed security settings for areas such as account policies, local policies, restricted groups, the registry, and so on. You can use the Security Configuration and Analysis console to import these saved configurations to the security database on different computers. They can also be imported into Group Policy objects (discussed in the "Group Policy" section of this chapter) and thus be propagated automatically to the local computer policy database.

The security templates provided are based on standard and recommended configurations for typical Windows NT and Windows 2000 systems. For more information on these standard configurations, see "Securing Windows NT Installation," a white paper available from http://www.microsoft.com/security. Additional information also is provided in the chapters of this book that relate to different configurations of Windows 2000.

The local computer policy database defines security in force for the local system. It might be overridden by policies enforced elsewhere in a Windows 2000 site, domain, or OU of which the computer is a member. In either case, however, it may not define the entire security configuration. (That is, security for every file folder and path may not be defined.) This leaves room for settings to be made outside its scope. For example, users might need the capability to set security on their own files and folders. Any Windows 2000 policy (set locally or elsewhere) maintains security configurations while allowing those attributes not set to be configured elsewhere. Personal databases may be created, or settings may be changed in the normal manner using the DACL editor in Windows Explorer.

Application

To configure a computer, a template is applied to the computer. Both analysis and configuration are done from the snap-in. The process is simple, is documented, and yet may be momentarily confusing the first time it is attempted. The first time the tool is used, you must create a database by right-clicking the Security Configuration and Analysis folder and then clicking Open Database. In the File Name text box of the Open Database dialog box, you must enter the name of the database you want to create, click OK, and then select a template. Figure 9.1 is a screen shot of the dialog box.

The next time you visit this computer, you can simply open the database. After the database is open, you can change the configuration of the system by selecting Configure Computer Now from the Action menu. You analyze the system by selecting Analyze Computer Now.

An analysis produces a listing that can be viewed in the console. By navigating the listing in the Policy window, you can determine whether the computer settings match those in the template you selected. Red circles with a white X indicate areas where differences are found. The Database setting and the Computer setting are also displayed so you can see the results. White circles with a green check indicate a match. Figure 9.2 shows the results of an analysis. You can change the database settings from this policy, but changes made here will not change on the local computer unless the database is used to configure the system.

Be Safe

After an installation, your first step should be to make an Emergency Repair Disk. Your second step should be the export of the out-of-the box configuration of the computer policy database. You can use this database to restore the initial security configuration.

Figure 9.1   The Open Database dialog box.

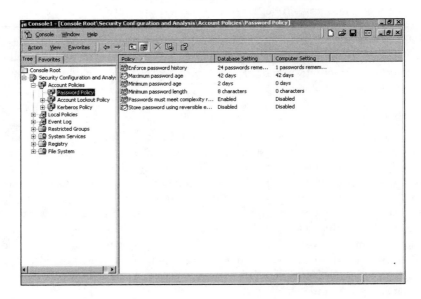

Figure 9.2   Analysis results.

The templates include various areas that either are preconfigured or may be marked as Not Defined. Any setting marked as Not Defined will not change settings on the computers already in place. Areas enabled by default for configuration and analysis are account policies, local policies, the Event Log, restricted groups, system services, the registry, and the file system.

Template Topics

Each template includes many topics, some of which have subtopics. Each topic is briefly defined in the following sections.

Account Policies

Here you will control password policy, account lockout policy, and Kerberos policies. Kerberos policy settings will only affect Windows 2000 domain controllers.

Local Policies

This area gives you access to audit policy, users rights assignment, and security options. Security options define many of the security musts that were set using a registry editor in Windows NT 4.0. Windows 2000 provides a GUI environment. Although security settings still impact the registry in Windows 2000, you now have a tool that is easy to use (you don't have to worry where to make the change or whether the documentation on the registry edit is correct) and gives you some protection (you can't make a typo and destroy your system).

Event Log

Event Log settings for system, application, and security logs are set here. You can configure the maximum log size, restrict guest access to the logs, change the log retention period or method, and implement the infamous Shut Down the Computer when the Security Audit Log is Full selection. This policy is infamous because, once set, users cannot log on if the log is full.

Restricted Groups

Restricted Groups are groups whose membership should be carefully controlled and monitored. Membership in this group restricts group membership. If a user is placed in a Restricted Group and that user is not listed in this part of the policy, he or she will be automatically removed. This is a good policy if you want to restrict the capabilities of appointed Administrators, Account Operators, and so on. If you control the security settings, you can give a user Administrator privileges but prevent the person from adding other users to security groups as listed in the Restricted Groups settings. By default, no groups are identified.

System Services

System services are listed and their startup mode (automatic, manual, disabled) can be set. Here you can set the policy for both the startup mode and DACLs on the service. Services are prelisted but not defined in the default templates. They include network services, file and print services, and telephone, fax, and Internet/intranet services. This area is designed to be extensible.

A good practice might be to disable the Telnet service. Even though the Windows 2000 telnet service is configured to use Windows authentication for access, it does open up remote control security issues.

Registry

Registry security set here instead of by using other registry editors can be refreshed. It is also a good place to review the default settings or understand how the current system is configured without traversing the registry using the registry editor, regedt32.exe. Remember that the only settings listed here are the ones set by policy. Many other DACLs exist in the registry.

File System

Permissions and Audit settings for files and folders can be configured and analyzed here.

Using the *secedit* Tool

As stated earlier, secedit is a command-line tool that can be used to analyze, configure, and audit security settings. Appropriately configured and scripted, it can be used in batch files to automatically secure and audit multiple machines on a scheduled basis. The syntax for secedit is outlined in the following tables. Where parameters are the same, they are not duplicated in the tables.

To analyze system security use the following syntax:

```
secedit/analyze[/DB filename][/CFG filename][/log logpath][/verbose][/quiet]
```

Table 9.1 defines the syntax elements.

Table 9.1 *secedit* **Parameters for Security Analysis**

Parameter	Definition
/DB filename	Path to the database that contains a stored configuration.
/CFG filename	Path to the security template you want to import into a database for analysis. Only valid with a /DB parameter. If the filename is not specified, secedit uses the configuration stored in the database.
/log logpath	Path to log file for logging the analysis or configuration process. Default: Documents and Settings*username*\\Local Settings \\Temp*filename*.log
/verbose	Give information that is more detailed during analysis.
/quiet	Suppress screen and log output. (Analysis results are viewable using the Security Configuration and Analysis snap-in.)

To configure system security, use the following:

```
secedit/analyze[/DB filename][/CFG filename][/overwrite][/areas area1 area2 …][/log
➥logpath][/verbose][/quiet]
```

Table 9.2 defines the parameters and Table 9.3 lists and defines the possible entries for the areas/parameters.

Table 9.2 *secedit* **Parameters for Security Configuration**

Parameter	Definition
/overwrite	Valid only with /CFG. The template in the /CFG argument will overwrite any template stored in the database. (The default operations would be to only overwrite those settings that conflicted and to append any new settings.)
/areas	Security areas to be applied to the system. Default: all areas. Separate areas by a space. Security areas are described in Table 9.3.

Table 9.3 *secedit* **Security Areas Mapped to Security Template Sections**

Area	Description	Mapping to Snap-in
SECURITYPOLICY	Local and domain policy for system. Includes account policies, audit policies.	Account Policies Local Policies\Audit Policy
GROUP_MGMT	Restricted group settings.	Restricted Groups
USER_RIGHTS	Logon rights and privileges.	Local Policies\User Rights Assignment
REGKEYS	Security on local registry keys.	Registry
FILESTORE	Security on local file storage.	File System
SERVICES	Security for all defined services.	System Services

To refresh security settings or to reapply the security settings to the Group Policy Object, use the secedit/refreshpolicy command. When a Group Policy object changes, the new policy is not applied immediately. To force its application, this command can be used:

```
secedit /refreshpolicy {machine_policy ¦user_policy}[/enforce]
```

Table 9.4 describes its parameters.

Table 9.4 *secedit/refreshpolicy* **Parameters**

Parameter	Definition
machine_policy	Refresh settings for local computer
user_policy	Refresh for local user account
enforce	Refresh even if no changes to Group Policy object settings

To export security settings, use the following:

```
secedit /export /mergedPolicy[/DB filename][/CFG filename][/areas area1 area2
➥…][/log logpath][/verbose][/quiet]
```

Using the mergedPolicy setting will merge and export domain and local policy. To validate a security configuration, type the following:

```
secedit /validate filename
```

filename is the name of the security template you have created. validate will ensure correct syntax before you attempt to use your template to configure a machine(s).

Using the Security Configuration Tool Set for Auditing

When you analyze the current computer system database, you are auditing the implementation of computer policy. If you use the secedit command in batch files, you can do this during times of low network use and examine the results later. You also use the tool set to set the Audit Policy for computers. Creating Audit Policies requires three steps:

1. **Enable or turn on auditing.** This is accomplished in the Audit Policy portion of the template. First determine what the policy should be on the local machine. Then configure the Audit Policy section of the Local Policies setting in the console and apply it. By defining a policy in a template and applying it, you have enabled auditing.

2. **Create the specific policy in the database.** To set a System Access Control List (SACL) on the file secret.txt, for example, you can use the File System folder in the template. After you have placed the file path in the folder, you can then double-click the file object and set the SACL. (SACLs on files also can be set using Windows Explorer.)

3. **Apply the policy.** You must then use the Security Configuration and Analysis console or the secedit command to apply the policy.

Additional auditing, such as auditing backup and restore use, can be configured using the Security Options settings of the Local Policy section.

If auditing on an object has not been set through a local policy using the Security Configuration and Analysis console, it can be set directly on the object using the proper tool (Windows Explorer for file and folder access auditing, the printer object for printer access auditing, and so on). By default, all auditing events are turned off.

The following events can be audited:

- Logon events
- Account management
- Directory service access (at domain controllers for auditing access to AD objects)
- Account logon events
- Account management
- Object access (member server or professional for access to file, registry, and printer objects)
- Policy changes
- Privilege use
- Process tracking
- System events

Group Policy

Think of Security Configuration and Analysis as the tool to configure and analyze security on one machine at a time. Yes, you can write a script that will apply a template on multiple systems across your enterprise, but Security Configuration and Analysis is most useful in its GUI form to analyze the system and immediately apply security changes or to audit Security Policy implementation. If you want a tool to globally apply preconfigured security policies across an enterprise, think Group Policy.

Group Policy is a collection of policies that address user and computer configuration as well as the security settings defined in the security templates. A Group Policy Object (GPO), a defined policy, can be written and applied to Group Policy Containers (GPCs). Group Policy Containers are Active Directory Objects to which Group Policy can be applied. Current AD GPCs are sites, domains, and organizational units. Multiple GPOs can be applied to a GPC, and Group Policies from an object higher in the domain hierarchy can be inherited. To learn how to use Group Policy, you must study six areas:

- Group Policy tools
- GPO components (what you can modify with Group Policy)
- Using Security Configuration and Analysis tools with Group Policy editors

- Default GPOs (existing GPOs):
  - Local Security Policy
  - Domain Controller Security Policy
  - Domain Security Policy
- Group Policy inheritance (how Group Policy is applied)
- Group Policy in an enterprise with Windows NT and/or Windows 9x

This section will address the first three of these. A discussion of the nuances and specifics of the Local Security Policy can be found in Chapters 10, "Securing Windows 2000 Professional." The Domain Controller Security Policy, the Domain Security Policy, Group Policy inheritance, and Group Policy in a Windows NT/Windows 9x/Windows 2000 enterprise are discussed in Chapter 16, "Securing the Network Using Distributed Security Services."

Group Policy Tools

Group Policy objects can be manipulated with two tools:

- Group Policy Editor from the properties page of the Group Policy Container (located in Active Directory Users and Computers)
- The Group Policy snap-in for the MMC

Active Directory Users and Computers

From the Active Directory Users and Computer console, you can create, link, or edit a Group Policy Object. After opening the properties page of a GPC and selecting the Group Policy tab, you do the following:

- Click Edit to edit an existing policy
- Click New to create a new policy
- Click Options to link to an existing policy

A policy can be created and then linked to multiple objects. However, because policies are applied during system startup and user logon and potentially at other times, you might want to consider the practice of linking to remote objects as being a waste of network bandwidth and user time.

Group Policy Snap-in

The Group Policy snap-in to MMC can be used to modify a particular Group Policy Object. When adding the snap-in to a console, you are asked which GPO to display. The snap-in cannot be used to create a new policy.

GPO Components: What You Can Modify with Group Policy

Each Group Policy Object can be divided into two basic areas: Computer Configuration and User Configuration. Each of these has three major subsections:

- Software Settings
- Windows Settings
- Administrative Templates

Although the subsection names of each configuration object are the same, the content of each subsection varies. Keep in mind that policies set in the computer configuration area are applied to computers; those set in the user configuration apply to users. This is the reason for the difference. The users and computers impacted by any policy are determined by where the policy is applied and where the user and computer accounts are defined.

User and computer accounts can be defined at the domain level, or organizational units (OU) can be created and user and computers nested underneath the OUs. If you define OUs, you can apply GPOs to them for granular configuration. Figure 9.3 illustrates this concept.

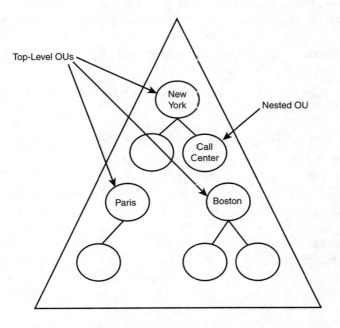

Figure 9.3 Applying a GPO at the OU level.

In the figure, the peachweaver.me domain hosts three top-level OUs: New York, Boston, and France. Each OU has other OUs nested underneath, and each OU has computer and user accounts defined beneath it. Any policy applied to the OU impacts the computers, OUs, and users nested within it. In the CallCenter OU, computers have been given the configuration Hide All Icons on Desktop. Users logging on to computers in that OU will not see any desktop icons. Computers whose accounts are in the New York OU will display desktop icons. (Further information on the impact of defining policy objects can be found in Chapter 16.)

Each section in the policy object contains several sections. The major headings are listed in the following section, with the Computer Configuration first and then the User Configuration. Details are in later chapters. (See the "For More Information" section at the end of this chapter for specific listings.)

To find out what a particular policy setting can do, double-click the setting and select the Explain tab. Information is provided to help you understand the policy.

Computer Configuration Options

Computer Configuration options are plentiful. Two important areas are

- **Windows Settings\Security Settings.** This is where specific security settings are detailed. The list matches the security template sections. Refer to the "Security Templates" section earlier in this chapter.

- **Administrative Templates\System\Group Policy.** These policies determine how Group Policy is applied.

Computer Configuration options are listed in Table 9.5, and User Configuration Options are listed in Table 9.6.

Table 9.5 **Group Policy: Computer Configuration Folder**

Configuration Item	Includes Settings For:
Software Settings	Software installation.
Windows Settings	Startup and shutdown scripts, Security Settings.
Security Settings	Categories within this area match policies listed in templates.
Administrative Templates	Windows components, System, Network, Printers.
Windows Components	Net Meeting, Internet Explorer, Task Scheduler, Windows Installer.
System	Logon, Disk Quotas, DNS Client, Group Policy, Windows File Protection.
Network	Offline files, Network and Dial-Up Connections.

Table 9.6   **Group Policy: User Computer Configuration Folder**

Configuration Item	Includes Settings For:
Software Settings	Software installation
Windows Settings	Internet Explorer Maintenance, Browser User Interface, Scripts, Security Settings, Remote Installation Service, Folder Redirection
Security Settings	Public Key Policies only
Folder Redirection	Application Data, Desktop, My Documents, Start Menu
Administrative Templates	Windows Components, Start Menu & Taskbar, Desktop, Control Panel, Network, System
Windows Components	NetMeeting, Internet Explorer, Microsoft Management Console, Task Scheduler, Windows Installer
Desktop	Active Directory, Active Desktop
Control Panel	Add/Remove Programs, Display, Printers, Regional Options
Network	Offline files and folders, Network and Dial-Up Connections
System	Logon/Logoff, Group Policy

Using Security Configuration and Analysis with Group Policy Editors

If you are editing a Group Policy Object, any changes you make will be applied. No pop-up window will ask you, "Are you sure?" No schedule has to be set; no window has to be closed. There will be a built-in delay as changes to Group Policy are applied according to a default schedule, and changes must propagate across the network. Once changed, however, policies will be applied. If you do not fully understand the impact of a proposed change, you should test its action in a test environment before implementing.

> **Note**
>
> Group Policy, unlike Systems Policy (used to enforce computer and user policies on Windows NT 4.0 and Windows 9x), does not "tattoo" the registry. If you remove the policy, the prepolicy settings will be used. Systems Policy permanently changed the registry. To recover from Systems Policy changes, you must either write a corrective policy and apply it, or visit each computer's registry and reset it.

One section of Group Policy can more easily be tested elsewhere. Use the Security Configuration and Analysis console to build and test a security template. When you are satisfied that the template is correct, use the Group Policy editor to import the security template into the Security Settings folder of the Group Policy Object. The option to import this template is available if you right-click the Security Settings folder within the Windows Settings folder of the Computer Configuration section of the GPO. Remember, if you edit the Security Settings policies directly on the GPO, each individual policy change will begin the process of propagation to the part of the enterprise defined in the Group Policy Container (GPC) immediately.

Support Tools

Windows 2000 includes some additional support tools that are not installed when you install the operating system. Some of these tools are useful in designing and managing security and can be found in the Support folder on the installation CD-ROM. Some of them also are included and/or documented in the Resource Kit. In the following list, the friendly name (where one has been given) and the associated filename are included.

- **ACL Diagnosis (acldiag.exe).** Provides information on the security attributes of Active Directory Objects.
- **Clone Principal (clonepr.dll).** Creates clones of Windows NT 4.0 users and groups and migrates them to Windows 2000.
- **dsacls.exe.** Manages access-control lists for directory services.
- **Registry Management Utility (reg.exe).** A command-line registry edit tool.
- **Security Descriptor Check Utility (sdcheck.exe).** Displays the security descriptor for an object including inherited DACLs as well as security descriptor metadata.
- **Security Administration Tools (SIDWalker).** Manages access-control policies.

Resource Kit Tools

The Windows 2000 Resource Kit is a package containing books and a CD-ROM that includes a set of tools and an online copy of the books. Most tools are also provided on the Windows 2000 installation CD-ROM, but the books are not. There is a Windows 2000 Server Resource Kit that includes several books and a Windows 2000 Professional Resource Kit that includes one book.

The collection of tools can be used for administration, diagnosis, and analysis. Some of the tools have direct security importance either because they can be used to configure security, to examine security settings, and to work with the Active Directory and registry or because they may open up security holes. Syntax and examples are included here for some of the single-purpose tools that meet these criteria. Other tools are comprehensive and would require entire chapters to describe their usage.

Documentation for the more complex tools can be found on the Resource Kit CD-ROM, often in the form of a Microsoft Word document. The tools outlined in the following sections are organized by these categories:

- Audit-related tools
- Group Policy tools
- User Management tools
- Management tools
- Registry tools
- DACLs

Audit-Related Tools

Audit-related tools can be used to modify audit policy or to examine audit logs. These tools include audit.pol, Crystal Reports, CyberSafe Log Analyst, dumpel, enumprop.exe, elogdmp.exe, and showpriv.exe.

audit.pol

audit.pol is a command-line tool that can be used to modify audit policy on the local or remote computer. Its syntax is:

```
auditpol [\\computer\[enable |
/disable\[/help/?][/category:type][/category:type]
```

where

`enable`	Enables audit
`/disable`	Disables audit
`/category`	Selects the category to audit logon, object, privilege, policy, SAM
`type`	Determines whether to audit for success, failure, all, none

To define all audit policies on a computer named *computer*, type the following:

```
auditpol \\computer /object:all
```

To display the current settings, type the following:

```
auditpol \\computer
```

Crystal Reports

Crystal Reports is a report-writer program. It can be used to extract, view, save, and publish information from Windows 2000 logs. A variety of formats are provided, and you can develop your own. Reports can be displayed and printed. Crystal Reports is installed from the Resource Kit. It can be found in the apps\crystal\disk1\ path of the CD-ROM.

CyberSafe Log Analyst

CyberSafe Log Analyst is provided as a snap-in for MMC. It can be used to assist in interpreting Windows 2000 Security Event Logs. It is located in the \apps\loganalyst directory. After installation, you must load the snap-in in the MMC. A help file is included and is readable from the snap-in.

dumpel

dumpel is a command-line utility that can be used to dump a Windows 2000 Event Log into a tab-delimited text file. You can also filter for events of a particular type. Its syntax is

```
dumpel -f file [-s server] [- log [-m source]][-e n1 n2 n3 . . . ][-r][-t][-d x]
```

where

-f	Identifies the file output file
-s	Indicates the server where the log is
-l	Indicates the log that logs system, application, security, and default applications
-m	Indicates the source with choices of rdr and serial; otherwise all are dumped
-e	Enables you to list filters n1 n2 n3 … so you can filter by event ID nn (up to 10)
-r	Is used to filter for certain records or to filter them out (if used, all except those of the type spec in -e are dumped)
-d	Includes x events for the past *x* days

To dump server puff's security log to the auditlog.out file, type the following:

```
dumpel -f auditlog.out -s puff -l security
```

enumprop.exe

enumprop.exe is a tool that dumps the directory services properties on directory service objects. This can include the security descriptor or can list only a given set of attributes. Its syntax is as follows:

```
enumprop [options] LDAP-PATH
```

The options area can be used to choose either /sec (only security descriptor) or a list of attributes (/attr:attr1, attr2.). If a list of attributes is used, only those attributed will be displayed. LDAP-PATH is the lightweight directory access protocol path for the object.

To list the properties for the Administrator of the puff.peachweaver.me computer, type the following:

```
Enumprop "LDAP://cn=administrator,cn=users,dc=puff,dc=peachweaver,dc=me"
```

elogdmp.exe

elogdmp.exe is a tool that can query the Event Log. Any user can use it to dump the application log. Only an Administrator can dump the security or systems logs. Its syntax is as follows:

```
elogdmp [-?]computername eventlogtype
```

showpriv.exe

showpriv.exe is a tool that displays users and groups that have been granted a privilege either locally or at the domain level. Its syntax is as follows:

```
showpriv privilege
```

A privilege is a right to do a system-related operation such as shutting down the system. To display who has the privilege to add a computer to the domain, type the following:

```
showpriv SeMachineAccountPrivilege
```

> **Note**
>
> By default, this privilege is given to Authenticated Users (users that have been authenticated by the system or domain). In Windows NT 4.0, this right was reserved for Administrators. In Windows 2000, Authenticated Users can add up to 10 computers to the domain.

Group Policy Tools

Group Policy tools can be used to work with Group Policy. These tools include gpolmig.exe (migrate System Policies to Group Policy), gpotool.exe (check for GPO consistency between domain controllers, and gpresult.exe (determine what GPOs have been applied).

gpolmig.exe

gpolmig.exe is a tool that can help migrate Windows NT System Policies to Windows 2000. You must realize that some registry settings differ; therefore, using gpolmig.exe might not have any effect on some applications. The migration puts the policy into Group Policy structure. You should examine it for its relevance and correctness and test before implementing. Its syntax is

```
gpolmig policyfilepath [/list][/listgpo][/migrate policytype computername GPO
⮡GPOtype]
```

where

/list	Lists policy by object type in Windows NT file.
/listgpo	Lists Group Policy Objects that are open and available to migrate to.
/migrate	Migrates the policy.
policyfilepath	Is the path and name of object in NT to use as source.
policytype	Is the NT Systems Policy type: computer, user, or group.
computername	Is the name of the computer to which to migrate the policy.
GPO	Is the name of the GPO to which to migrate. (You must have this GPO open for editing.)
GPOtype	Is the configuration type, either computer or user.

You must specify the object type (computer, user, or group) from Windows NT. To list the ntconfig.pol policy stored in the temp folder, type the following:

```
Gpolmig c:\temp\ntconfig.pol /list
```

To list the GPO group object open to use with this policy, type the following:

```
Gpolmig c:\temp\ntconfig.pol /listgpo
```

To migrate the ntconfig.pol policy to the {00000000-0000-0000=0000-000000000000} Machine policy on *computername*, type the following:

```
Gpolmig c:\temp\ntconfig.pol /migrate computer computername {00000000-0000-
➥0000=0000-000000000000} Machine
```

gpotool.exe

The gpotool.exe tool can be used to check the condition and health of the GPO on the domain controller(s). Checks are made for consistency between domain controllers, and the tool can tell you whether the GPO has been replicated to all domain controllers. Information about the GPO is displayed such as function, version, and extensions used. Policies can be checked in trusting domains. The tool's syntax is

```
[/gpo:GPO[,GPO..]][/domain:dnsname][/dc:DC[,DC..]][/checkacl][/verbose][/new:GPO[,
➥GPO…]][/del:GPO[,GOPO..]][/?][/help]
```

where

/gpo:GPO	Processes policy, GUID, and field names. (Is anything corrupt?)
/domain:dnsname	Specifies the domain to test.
/dc:DC	Finds the list of domain controllers.
/checkacl	Verifies the SYSVOL DACL.
/verbose	Gives details.
/new:GPO	Creates a new policy with a new name.
/del	Deletes a policy.

gpresult.exe

The gpresult.exe tool displays information about the results a GPO has had on the current computer and logged-on user. It gives information about the system and user including

- The OS type (Professional or Server)
- The build number, service pack, and mode
- The user information (the name and where the user account exists in the Active Directory, domain name, site, local or roaming profile, security group membership, and security privileges)
- The computer name and where it is located in the Active Directory, domain, and site

In addition, the following information is supplied:

- The last time the policy was applied
- A list of objects and details
- Registry settings that are applied
- Folder redirection
- Software management information
- Disk quota information
- IPSec settings

Its syntax is

```
gpresult [/v][/s][/c][/u][/?]
```

where

/v	Is the verbose mode
/s	Are binary values of the registry setting
/c	Is computer only
/u	Is user only

User Management Tools

User management tools are useful in scripting additions and changes to user lists and groups. Instead of using the GUI functions to make these changes one at a time, a batch file can be prepared to automate a large number of additions or changes. The user management tools include addusers, cusrmgr.exe, findgrp.exe, grpcpy.exe, local.exe, moveuser.exe, Ntrights.exe, showgrps.exe, showmbrs.exe, and usrtogrp.exe.

addusers

The addusers tool can create, edit, and delete user accounts. The easiest way to use it is with a spreadsheet, such as Excel, that can work with comma-delimited files. First you can dump an existing list to examine the headings and columns required by the tool. A minimum of headings for users, global groups, and local groups is required. Its syntax is

```
addusers [\\computername\{/c [ /p:{l ¦ c¦ e ¦d}][/d ¦/e}filename [/s:x][/?]
```

where

c	Creates the password listed
/p:	Indicates password policy (can be l, c, e, or d)
p:l	Indicates that users have to change password at next logon
p:c	Indicates that users cannot change password
p:e –	Indicates that passwords never expire
p:d –	Disables the account
/d	Dumps the current user list to the file listed in the filename parameter
/e -	Deletes the account
/s –	Changes character for delimiter field (/s:+ would make it a plus sign)

cusrmgr.exe

cusrmgr.exe is a command-line user manager. Its syntax is

```
cusrmgr -u username [-m \\computername][{-r username _ -d username}] [{-p ¦ P
➥password}][ - rlg oldgroup name newgroup name][-rgg oldgroup name newgroup name
➥][-alg localgroup name][agg global group name] [-dlg localgroup name][-dgg
➥global group][-c comment][-f fullname][-U userprofile][-n logon script][ -h
➥homedir][-H homedirdrive][{+s ¦ -s} property]
```

where

-u	Is the username
-m	Is the \\computername default local
-r	Is the username; renames user
-d	Is the username; deletes users
-p	Sets random password
-P	Sets password to Password
-rlg	Renames old to new
-rgg	Renames global group
-alg	Is the localgroup name; adds user to local cgroup
-agg	Adds user to global group

`-dlg`	Deletes user from local group
`-dgg`	Deletes users from globalgroup
`-c`	Sets comment
`-f`	Sets full name
`-U`	Sets user property in logon script
`-h`	Sets home directory
`-H`	Sets home directory c: drive
`+s`	Sets property (MustChangePassword, CanNotChangePassword, PasswordNeverExpires, AccountDisabled, AccountLockout, RASUser)
`-s`	Resets

findgrp.exe

The findgrp.exe tool can find all direct and indirect group membership for a specific user in a domain. Its syntax is

```
findgrp [yourdomain][USER_DOMAIN\username]
```

where

`yourdomain`	Is the domain from which group information is retrieved. Type localmachine to list the local groups on Windows 2000 Professional.
`USER DOMAIN`	Is the domain that contains the user account.
`username`	Is the name of the user.

To find User5 groups for longjon user5 on the domain peachweaver, type the following:

```
findgrp peachweaver longjon\User5
```

grpcpy.exe

The grpcpy.exe tool can be used to copy usernames in an existing group to another group. Users must be Account Operators or Administrators. This is a GUI tool, and the document grpcpy.doc in the Resource Kit explains its use.

local.exe

The local.exe tool displays the members of local groups on remote servers or domains. Its syntax is as follows:

```
local groupname [{domainname ¦ \\servername}]
```

moveuser.exe

The moveusers.exe tool can change the account domain and or username. Its syntax is

```
moveuser [DOMAIN/]user1 [DOMAIN/]user2 [/c:computer][/k][/y][/?]
```

where

user1	Is the user with local profile.
DOMAIN/user	For domain users, user for local domain.
user2	User will get user1 profile; user2 account must already exist.
/c:computer	Is the computer on which to make changes.
/k	If user1 is local, the user account should be kept.
/y	Overwrites the existing profile.
-?	Help.

ntrights.exe

The ntrights.exe tool can be used to grant or revoke NT or Windows 2000 rights for users or groups on local or remote computers and to place an event in the Event Log. Its syntax is

```
ntrights {-r right ¦ +r right} –u Userorgroup [ -m \\computer][-e entry]
```

where

-r	Revokes user right
+r	Grants user right
-u	Is user or group
-m \\computer	Is the computer on which to perform; default is local
-e entry	Adds a text string to the event log

To add the network logon right for the group Everyone, type the following:

```
ntrights +r SeNetworkLogonRight -u Everyone
```

To add the right to log on as a service to the account MyService001 on computer7, type the following:

```
ntrights +r SeServicesLogonRight -u MyService001 -m \\computer7
```

showgrps.exe

The showgrps.exe tool shows the groups to which a user belongs. Its syntax is as follows:

```
showgrps [/A] domain\user
```

The /A switch checks all trusted domains.

showmbrs.exe

The showmbrs.exe tool displays the members of a group. Its syntax is as follows:

```
showmbrs grouptype
```

usrtogrp.exe

The usrtogrp.exe tool adds users to a group. It will create a group if it doesn't already exist. Its syntax is

```
Usrtogrp filename
```

where *filename* is a file that has a list of users in it.

Management Tools

There are many useful management tools. The ones listed here can be used to manage security or should be restricted because their use can make the system(s) more vulnerable to attack. They include appsec.exe, associate.exe, the remote command service (rcmd.exe and rcmdsvc.exe), floplock.exe, KerbTray, klist.exe, remote console, rshsvc.exe, setx.exe, winexit.scr, and xcopy.exe.

appsec.exe

The appsec.exe GUI tool can be used to restrict the access of ordinary users to a predefined set of applications. Group Policy can be used to hide applications by removing them from the Start menu and desktop icons; appsec.exe can be used to prevent file execution. To use appsec.exe, you must list the paths and filenames of applications that users can use. Only applications whose name and path are listed can be run.

Administrators can run any application. Thus, Administrators can use the tracking feature of appsec.exe to determine which applications can be called by permitted applications. They can then list those applications as well. If Word is used as the email editor for Outlook, for example, then both Word and Outlook must be listed as permitted applications.

appsec.exe configuration is done per computer; there is not user-level capability. (That is, users cannot be restricted by security groups.) appsec.exe is typically used with terminal services, and it restricts by name of file. It has no way to check what the file is actually doing.

32-bit applications can be configured as approved for execution. If it is necessary for users to run 16-bit applications, the Administrator can enable the use of ntvdm.exe, and then all 16-bit applications (that he specifies) will be allowed to run.

associate.exe

The associate.exe tool can be used to associate (register) or unregister a file type. An associated file type is automatically run by the program associated with it. This is a good tool to use to remove file associations for known or suspected attack patterns. For example, if it had been used to unregister the association of .VBS files, the "I Love

You" virus would not have been able to execute by simply clicking on the file attachment. The associate.exe syntax is

```
associate .ext filename [/q][/d][/f][/?]
```

where

.ext	Is the extension
filename	Is the executable
/q	Is quiet; no interactive prompts
/d	Is delete (if it exists)
/f	Forces overwrite of existing file association without questions
/?	Brings up the Usage screen

Remote Command Service: rcmd.exe and rcmdsvc.exe

The remote command service consists of two programs: the client (rcmd.exe) and the server (rcmdsvc.exe). These programs can be used to remotely administer and run command-line programs on remote computers.

The server side (rcmdsvc.exe) is installed and run as a service on the server by running rcmdsvc–install. After the service is installed, it should then be started as a normal service. The client is installed on the client by running rcmd.exe.

The logged-on user must have interactive logon privileges on the remote server in order to connect. Any programs that are executed run under the context of the user's account. No elevated rights are obtained by running this program. File and registry DACLs are in effect.

floplock.exe

When floplock.exe is in place, only Administrators and Power Users can access the floppy drive on the local Professional machine. On Servers, only Administrators can use the floppy drive. floploc works by assigning a DACL to the floppy drive. floploc must be installed from the \program files\resource Kit\ path, and the service must be started.

KerbTray

KerbTray is an executable that places a ticket icon on the desktop tray. When double-clicked, it displays the Kerberos tickets from the user's ticket cache on computers running the Kerberos protocol. KerbTray can be used to view and purge the ticket cache. Ticket start, end, and renewal times as well as flags and encryption types are displayed.

klist.exe

The klist.exe tool is used to view and delete the Kerberos tickets granted to the currently logged on user. klist.exe can display the attributes, domain, encryption type, and start, end, and renewal times of the tickets. Its syntax is

```
klist [-?][tickets ¦ tgt ¦ purge]
```

where `tgt` displays the initial Kerberos Ticket-Granting Ticket and `purge` purges tickets.

Remote Console

Remote Console is a client/server application that can be used to run a remote command-line session and launch remote apps. It launches a cmd.exe process for each client connection. This is a compromise of security. Although on Windows NT you must be an Administrator to run the remote console, on Windows 2000 you can enable this to allow users to also use it. Remote console does not check to see if these users have the logon local privilege.

rshsvc.exe

The rshsvc.exe tool is the TCP/IP remote shell service. It is similar to the UNIX remote shell service. rshsvc.exe is the server side of the TCP/IP rsh.exe client command. The service is started and stopped in the usual manner:

```
net start rshvc
```

```
net stop rshsvc
```

setx.exe

Although the set command can only be used to set user-level environmental commands, setx.exe can be used to set computer environmental commands. Use the following syntax:

```
Setx variable [-m]
```

variable is the variable you want to set. -m forces the variable to be set for the computer. The default is for the user.

winexit.scr

The winexit screen saver logs the current user off after a configured time elapses. The screen saver is called the Logoff Screen Saver. You should be careful with this screen saver. If the Force Logoff box is checked, the screen saver will force application termination, and data might not be saved. The winexit screen saver is activated in the same manner as any other screen saver. You might have to copy the winexe.scr file to the %systemroot%\system32 directory.

xcopy.exe

The xcopy command is used to copy files and directories from NTFS with security intact, thus enabling backup of security-sensitive data from the hard disk without using a tape drive.

Registry Tools

There are many useful registry tools. The ones listed here can be used to back up, locate information in, dump to common file formats, and add data to the registry. They include regback.exe, regdmp.exe, regfind.exe, regini.exe, regrest.exe, and scanreg.exe.

regback.exe

The regback.exe tool is used to back up the registry. It can be used while the system is running and hives are open. Regrest.exe can be used to restore a registry backed up with regback. Its syntax is

```
regback [destination _dir][filename hivetype hivename]
```

where

`destination_dir`	Is the location of backup files
`filename`	Is the name of a backup file
`hivetype`	Is either machine or users
`hivename`	Is the name of a subtree of HKEY_LOCAL_MACHINE or HKEY_LOCAL_USERS

To back up the entire registry, type the following:

```
regback destinationfolder
```

To back up the system hive only to the system file, type the following:

```
regback c:\bacupregs\system machine system
```

regdmp.exe

The regdmp.exe tool dumps the registry to the standard output (stdout), which can be redirected to a file. Its syntax is

```
regdmp[{-m \\computername ¦ -h hivefile hiveroot ¦ -w Win95Directory}][-I n[-o
➥outputwidth] [-s] [registrypath]
```

where

`-m \\computername`	Is a remote computer
`-h`	Is a local hive to dump
`-w`	Is Win95 paths to system.data and user.data
`-I`	Is the number of characters to display indentation, default is 4
`-o`	Is output width (how wide)
`-s`	Is summary output
`[registrypath]`	Is the point in the registry to start from

To dump the listed registry key, type the following:

```
regdmp "HKEY_CURRENT_USER\Software\Microsoft Windows\CurrentVersion\Explorer\user
➥Shell folders"
```

regfind.exe

The regfind.exe can be used at the command line to search the registry for data, a key name, or a value, and as a search and replace function. Its syntax is

```
regfind [{-m\\computername ¦ -h hivefile hiveroot ¦ - w Wind95 dir}][ -I n] [ -o
➥outputwidth][ -p registrykeypath][{ -t datatype}][-n][searchstring[-r
➥replacement string]]
```

where

`-m\\computername`	Is a remote computer
`-h`	Is a local hive to dump
`-w`	Is Win95 paths to system.data and user.data
`-I`	Is the number of characters to display indentation; default is 4
`-o`	Output width (how wide, by default, to console windows if to file, otherwise 240)
`-s`	Summary output
`-p [registry path]`	Is the point in the registry to start from
`-t`	Is the data type to search for REG_SZ, REG_DWORD, and so on
`-n`	Includes key and value names in the search

To find all REG_WORD value entries under the
HKEY_CURRENT_USER\Control Panel subkey, type the following:

```
regfind -p "HKEY_CURRENT_USER\Control Panel" -t REG_DWORD
```

regini.exe

The regini.exe tool can be used in batch files to add keys to the registry using a script.
For more information, see the regini.doc file in the Resource Kit.

regrest.exe

The regrest.exe tool restores registry hive files from backups created by regback. Its
syntax is

```
regrest [newfile savefile] [hivetype hivename]
```

where

newfile	Is the backup source file name (regrest renames and uses it to replace old hivename file)
savefile	Is the filename for saving the old hivename being replaced
hivetype	Use Machine or Users
hivename	Name of the subtree of HKEY_LOCAL_MACHINE or HKEY-local users

To restore the registry key saved in savedreg.sav to the HKEY_LOCAL_MACHINE\
system hive and store the old copy of the hive to the oldreg.sav file, type the
following:

```
REGREST C:\savedreg.sav c:\oldreg.sav machine system
```

scanreg.exe

The scanreg.exe tool is a registry GREP utility. It can be used to search for any string
in key names, entry names, and values for all registry keys in the Windows 2000,
Windows NT, and Windows 9x registries. A Resource Kit document, scanreg.doc,
explains the use of this tool.

DACLs

Several tools are provided that enable you to enumerate, set, copy, and examine
DACLs. They are showacls.exe, subinacl.exe, svcalcs.exe, permcopy.exe, perms.exe,
and xcacls.exe.

showacls.exe

The showacls.exe tool will enumerate access rights for files, folders, and folder trees. It can be used to show the DACLs for a particular user. Its syntax is

```
showacls [/s][/u:domain\user][filespec]
```

where

/s	Includes subdirectory
/u	Shows DACLs for domain\user

subinacl.exe

The subinacl.exe tool gets security info (DACLs and SACLs) on files, registry keys, and/or services and transfers from user to user, from local group to local group, global group to global group, or domain to domain. It can be used to change the owner name of an object. This is a useful utility if a user moves from one domain to another domain. Its syntax is

```
subinacl [view-mode][/test_mode]object type objectname [action[=parameter]][action
↩[=parameter]][/playfile filename]
```

where

view-mode	Is No verbose, verbose, verbose=1 verbose=2.
/testmode	Changes are not actually made (test command).
object type	Is File, subdirectory, onlyfile, share cluster share keyreg, subkeyreg, service, printer, or kernelobject.
objectname	Is a valid object name.
action	Parameter /display /setowner changedomain, migratetodomain, findsid, suppress sid, confirm perm, audit, ifchange, deny, revoke, grant.
/playfile	filename

svcalcs.exe

The svcalcs.exe tool sets access control lists on service objects so you can delegate administrative control of services. You must be an Administrator to run this tool. Its syntax is

```
svcacls [\\Targetcomputer\]service [Options]]
```

where

targetcomputer	Is a UNC name for a computer
service	Is name of service

The *options* are

g	grant:trustee:permissions—Adds permission
s	set: trustee:permissions—Replaces permissions
r	revoke: trustee—Removes explicit permission
d	deny: trustee—No access

To grant the user Fred Read permission on the browser service, type the following:

```
svcacls browser g:fred:r
```

> **Tip**
>
> Don't enter svcacls with D:everyone; you can lock out the administrator.

The Permissions are

q	Query Service
s	Query Status
e	Enumerate Dependencies
c	Change Configuration
t	Start
o	Stop
p	Pause/Continue
i	Interrogate
u	User-Defined Control Command
f	Full Control
r	Read
w	Write
x	Execute

permcopy.exe

The permcopy.exe tool copies share- and file-level permissions from one share to another. Its syntax is

```
permcopy \\sourceserver sharename \\destination server sharename
```

where

sourceserver	Is where the share is to copy from
destination	Is where the share is to copy to

To copy the permission set from the share stuff on the computer named myputer to the share stuff on the computer johnsputer, type the following:

```
permcopy \\myputer stuff \\johnsputer stuff
```

perms.exe

The perms.exe tool displays user file-access permissions. Its syntax is

```
perms [domain\¦computer\]username path [/i][/s]
```

(You use either domain\username or computer\username.)
where

path	Is the path and name of the file
/I	Assumes the user is a member of an interactive group; otherwise assumes network
/s	Checks the permissions of files in subdirectory

xcacls.exe

The xcacls.exe tool sets all file system security options from the command line. Its syntax is

```
xcacls filename [/T][/E][/C][/G user:perm:spec][/R user][/P user:perm:spec […}][/D
user […]][?y]
```

where

filename	Is the filename or directory
/T	Recursively applies chosen access rights to matching files and/or directories
/E	Edits DACLs instead of replacing them
/C	Continues if the Access Denied error is received; otherwise stops
/G	Gives access to user to matching file

This is especially useful in unattended installs.

To give John Read, Write, Execute, and Delete permissions, type the following:

```
xcalcs *.* /G John:RWED:RW /E
```

These permissions are added to the existing permission sets.

Choosing the Tool to Use

To determine which tool to use, first determine whether this computer is a member of an Active Directory–based Windows infrastructure. Next, decide what it is you are going to do.

Table 9.7 lists a possible choice matrix.

Table 9.7   **Tool Choice Matrix for Group Policy, *secedit*, and Security Configuration and Analysis**

Process	Active Directory–based Windows Infrastructure?	
	Yes	**No**
Configuration	Group Policy secedit.exe SCA Console	SCA Console secedit.exe
Analysis	SCA Console secedit.exe	SCA Console secedit.exe
Auditing	SCA Console secedit.exe	SCA Console secedit.exe
Maintenance	Group Policy	secedit.exe SCA Console Local Security Policy Console
Editing Security Templates	Security Templates MMC snap-in	Security Templates MMC snap-in

When trying to decide between using Group Policy and using the SCA Console, remember that using Group Policy can ensure adherence to a set policy. Using the SCA Console does not. If the computer is not a part of an Active Directory–based infrastructure, if you are not ready to tightly integrate security with your infrastructure, if administrative duties are too distributed to fully implement this kind of security, or if you want to configure a personal security database (remember you can only set things that are not configured in the Group Policy settings), you should use the Security Configuration and Analysis snap-in. This also is especially useful in circumstances in which the infrastructure for your enterprise does not include Active Directory, yet you want to have a way to secure and maintain security on your Windows 2000 systems. Security Configuration Manager, the Windows NT version of the SCA Console, can be used to configure, analyze, and audit security settings on Windows NT 4.0 sp4 and above. The NT version has to be installed on and can only work with a local NT registry.

Information on using Group Policies is included in Chapter 16. The provided security templates can be imported into a Group Policy Object.

Best Practices

A number of recommendations can be made about these security tools:

- Import tested Security Templates into Group Policy Objects.
- Remove remote command tools. A safer alternative is to use terminal servers in administrative mode, as described in Chapter 11, "Securing Windows 2000 Server."
- Use Security Templates to develop security baselines for different computers.
- Create batch files and use secedit to audit Security Policy settings.
- Use secedit and Security Configuration and Analysis to apply security policies to Windows 2000 computers that are not joined in a domain.
- Use batch files and Resource Kit tools to speed user configuration and movement of users from one domain to another.
- Use batch files and Resource Kit tools to audit file and registry DACLs on standalone systems.
- Use Group Policy to maintain security settings including critical file system and registry DACLs and SACLs.

For More Information

This chapter introduced many concepts and techniques that are explained more thoroughly in other chapters of this book. The following list should serve as a referral source for you in locating this information.

More information on auditing and using Group Policy is presented in Chapter 16, "Securing the Network Using Distributed Security Services."

Security Policy is discussed in Chapters 10, "Securing Windows 2000 Professional."

The Domain Controller Security Policy, the Domain Security Policy, Group Policy Inheritance, and Group Policy in a Windows NT/Windows 9x/Windows 2000 enterprise also is discussed in Chapter 16.

Summary

Many tools can be used to manipulate, analyze, and audit security functions in Windows 2000. It only makes sense to investigate and use tools provided with Windows 2000 first before looking elsewhere. Tools that are natively a part of Windows 2000 and those that are available in the Windows 2000 Resource Kit were discussed here. Finally, a helpful matrix for determining when to use Group Policy or the Security Configuration and Analysis console was provided.

Securing Windows 2000 Professional

10

WINDOWS 2000 PROFESSIONAL IS THE DESKTOP VERSION of Windows 2000. It is meant to operate as a node on a network, as a standalone desktop machine, and aboard laptops. It can also be used as an administrative node by installing Domain Administration Tools.

To secure any system, you should look toward securing users and groups, data, and configuration information. Much of what you should do is determined by the use to which the system will be put. As previously discussed, Windows 2000 has a number of default security templates that can be used to help you match system use to security level.

In previous chapters, information about securing Windows 2000 was addressed in a generic way. Several security tools and areas (file systems, users, and groups) were detailed. In this chapter, these areas will be expanded to cover information specifically related to Windows 2000 Professional. Windows 2000 Professional topics that will be discussed in this chapter include

- Setting up and securing the user database
- Using Windows 2000 Professional in a Windows NT 4.0 domain
- Managing local security settings with Group Policy
- Matching security settings to the abilities of the user
- Understanding policy implementation and enforcement

- Securing wireless connections
- Understanding protocols and processes for secure data and application access
- Administering a Windows 2000 domain using Windows 2000 Professional

In future chapters, other Windows 2000 configurations will be addressed.

Setting Up and Securing the User and Group Database

You must have a user account to use Windows 2000 Professional. Although in many cases Professional will be used by one individual, it can be set up to be used by many. All users have their own account, profile, storage area for documents, and set of rights.

Unlike Windows 2000 Server, there is no way to promote Professional to a domain controller. Its use is limited to being a nonnetworked computer, a workgroup member, or a domain member computer. If the system is joined in a domain, it probably was installed as such, and no thought was given to the local database. Thus, any user wanting to use the system can log on using a domain-level account. Chapter 12, "Domain-Level Security," will discuss user issues in domain settings.

Windows 2000 Professional will often be used as a standalone system and can be accessed using the local account database even when joined in a domain. When first installed, the local account database consists of a local Administrator and local Guest account. These accounts should be secured.

By default, the Administrator account password is set during install. The local Guest account is disabled by default. Both accounts can be further secured by using Local Security Policy on standalone systems and Group Policy in domain settings. Possibilities are discussed in greater detail later in this chapter. As groundwork, you must understand the following:

- The security model
- How to manage accounts and groups in the local account database
- How to secure the local account database

Making Professional More Manageable

To make Professional more manageable, you can add Computer Management and other tools to the Start menu. To do so, right-click the taskbar and select Properties. Then, from the Advanced tab, select Display Administrative Tools. If this is not checked or is unchecked later, the tools are still available in the Control Panel. Because these tools are not automatically exposed to the casual user, they may be less vulnerable to accidental abuse. (It's not that a curious or advanced user cannot get to the tools, it's simply that many users will not be as likely to explore them because they don't appear every time users look at the Programs section of the Start menu.) In addition, the interface is less cluttered for the typical user.

Security Model

The security model of Windows 2000 is different from that of Windows NT 4.0, but the logon process contains Windows NT 4.0 components for backward compatibility. The Windows NT 4.0 and Windows 2000 security models are composed of the following parts:

- **Logon procedures.** Logon procedures accept logon requests from users and include the graphical user interface (GUI) that asks for a username and password or a smart card and PIN. The default process that does this is Microsoft Graphical Identification and Authentication (MSGINA).

- **Local Security Authority (LSA).** The LSA generates access tokens, manages Local Security Policy and interactive user-authentication services, controls audit polity, and logs audit messages.

- **Security Account Manager (SAM).** The SAM is the directory database, the main user account database. It validates to the LSA, which can be looked upon as the gatekeeper.

- **Security Reference Monitor (SRM).** The SRM checks user permissions to access an object, enforces access validation and audit polity of LSA, and services kernel and user modes. Think of the SRM as the enforcer.

Figure 10.1 displays the security model for Windows 2000. It logically relates the parts and their relationships as defined here.

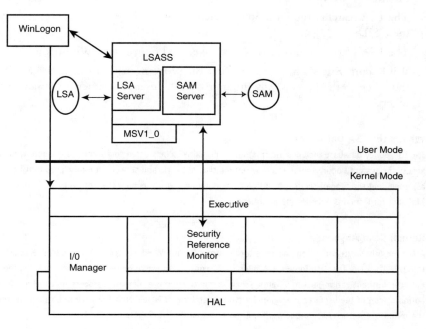

Figure 10.1   Local security model.

When Windows 2000 Professional is joined in a Windows 2000 domain, Kerberos is used for authentication during domain logons. When Windows 2000 Professional is not a member of a domain or a local account is used to log on interactively to the computer, not the domain, Kerberos is not used for authentication. Instead, the process occurs much as it did in Windows NT 4.0 for local logon. The following list details the steps involved:

1. The user logs on interactively.

2. The WinLogon service on Professional sends the cleartext user ID and password to the LSA.

3. The LSA validates the user account, encrypts the password, and calls the MSV1_0 authentication package. The MSV1_0 authentication package is the default authentication package provided with Windows 2000. For more information, see Chapter 3, "New Protocols, Products, and APIs."

4. MSV1_0 uses the SAM to compare the encrypted password passed by LSA with the one stored in the database.

5. If this were a domain logon, MSV1_0 would access domain resources to get the SIDs of global groups and the user SID. Because this is a local logon, it only obtains the user SID and local group memberships from the local database.

6. MSV1_0 returns the user account SID to the LSA.

7. The LSA searches the local policy database for local implicit groups that contain the SID of the account.

8. The LSA searches the local policy database for all user rights that contain any of these SIDs.

9. The LSA places all info in an access token and returns it to WinLogon.

10. WinLogon creates a new process, runs the program manager shell, and attaches the token to the process. Any program that the user runs inherits the same access token.

What's the LSA Database?

The LSA policy database includes information on domains to be trusted to authenticate logon, who can access the system (logon rights) and how (interactive, network, and service), the privileges that are assigned, and the type of security auditing to be done. In short, it echoes the entries made in the User Manager for Domains Account menu options.

Retinal Scan Anyone?

Are there other authentication packages for Windows NT and Windows 2000? The knowledge base article Q102716, "User Authentication with Windows NT," contains information about another package, the retinal-scan authentication package. Retinal-scan authentication is a biometric process that includes comparing a scan of the user's retina against a stored database. It is said that the pattern of blood vessels in the retina of the eye is as unique as, if not more unique than, a fingerprint.

Managing Accounts and Groups in the Local Account Database

Local accounts and groups were defined in Chapter 6, "Security from the Get-Go," but there are some points to recall and some recommended strategies for managing users and groups to make the Professional system more secure. First, you should put group membership in proper perspective:

- Default membership in the Administrators group is given to the local Administrator.

- Default membership in the Users group is given to every user.

- Local group membership is restricted to local users unless the Professional system is joined in a domain. At that time, local group membership can be granted to other domain-level groups, and Domain Admin and Domain Guest groups are given membership in local Administrators and Guests groups, respectively.

- Universal groups, some forms of group nesting, and distribution groups are not available on Professional standalone systems.

- Group nesting in Professional works as it did in Windows NT 4.0 (that is, global groups can be nested in local groups).

- The membership of Windows 2000 Professional built-in groups, as well as local groups you create, depends on whether the system is a member of a Windows 2000 domain, a Windows NT domain, or a workgroup or nonnetworked machine.

- Local groups on workgroup and nonnetworked systems can only have users in the local account database as members.

Next, consider the following recommended strategies for group management and the impact they can have on security.

Assign Resource Access via Groups

Access to resources on the local computer should be assigned to local groups of users, not to individuals. Not only is this easier to administer, it creates a standard that can be quickly adjusted to ensure that only proper access to resources is allowed.

If a user leaves the company, it is easy to disable his account. However, you also will want to remove his name from any Discretionary Access Control Lists (DACLs) on resources. If a user changes jobs, you will want to quickly remove his access to old job-related resources and grant him access to files and folders relevant to his new position. If resource access is always done via groups, it is easy to simply find the groups of which a user is a member (this information is part of the user account) and remove membership in the groups listed. If resource access is assigned via the user account, removing the access rights of a user can be an impossible job.

Deleting the account when a user leaves the company will work in most cases. (There is some risk that, because the SID of the user still exists in the DACLs, it could be used programmatically to access the resource.) However, you will not want to be constantly deleting and creating new jobs for users who merely move to other positions within the company.

Nest Global Groups in Local Groups

Local groups on systems that are members of a Windows 2000 domain can have as members global groups and domain user accounts. This is how you give domain users and the members of domain global groups access to local computer resources and privileges on the local computer.

By placing domain users in global groups and then nesting these groups in local groups, you can more easily control user access and can quickly remove that access when necessary. User membership in global groups is also listed as a property of the user account.

When a Windows 2000 Professional computer joins a Windows 2000 domain, the universal groups (in a native mode domain) and global groups of that domain can be displayed, and you can assign these groups permissions to access local resources and rights to perform functions on the local machine. Policies set at the domain or OU level can be propagated to the local computer. Local Security Policy will become some combination of local and domain, OU, or site-wide policy.

Securing the Account Database

The registry is logically divided into sections called hives and is physically divided into files. Each hive is represented by a file. The local account database is kept in the registry hive called the SAM. Every registry hive is subdivided into keys and subkeys. To secure the local account database, you need to address four areas:

- The location in the file system
- Registry files
- Permissions placed on files and folders
- Configuring security on the keys themselves

File System Location

During installation, the registry is placed in the %system root%\system32\config\ directory. A backup copy is placed in the %systemroot%\repair directory. The copy is placed in the repair directory to assist in the repair process. The copy should be protected or removed because, if it can be copied, it can be attacked with password-cracking programs.

If you delete this copy of the registry, do not delete the repair directory because it is referenced in the Emergency Repair Disk updating process. You should also be aware that you will not be able to easily repair the system.

Registry Files

Permissions on the files that make up the registry are Full Control to Administrators and the SYSTEM. Remember, each file represents a hive in the registry. Table 10.1 lists the hives and identifies for what they are used, the names of their associated files, and where they are located logically within the registry.

Hives exist within the following four major logical divisions in the registry:

- HKLM: HKEY_LOCAL_MACHINE
- HKCC: HKEY_CURRENT_CONFIG
- HKCU: HKEY_CURRENT_USER
- HKU: HKEY_USERS

For convenience, two of these divisions actually are nothing more than pointers to sections within the other two: HKCU points to the current users keys within the HKU section, and HKCC points to the SYSTEM division of the HKLM division.

Table 10.1 **Registry Hives and Files**

Logical Location of Hive	Hive	File	Contains
HKLM\SAM	SAM	SAM and sam.log	User database
HKLM\SECURITY	SECURITY	Security and security.log	User database
HKLM\SOFTWARE	SOFTWARE	Software and software.log	Settings on installed software including the OS
HKLM\SYSTEM	SYSTEM	System and system.log	Configuration settings
HKCC	SYSTEM	System and system.log	Current configuration settings
HKCU	USER	Ntuser.dat and ntuser.dat.log	Current user profile
HKU\.DEFAULT	DEFAULT USER	Default and default.log	Default profile

File and Folder Permissions

Default file and folder permissions are set on the registry. The defaults provide the required access for Windows 2000–compatible applications, but Windows NT 4.0 applications may not be usable by ordinary users because the application requires more access than is granted.

The default DACLs on the repair and configuration folder are:

- Administrators: Full Control
- Power Users: Modify
- CREATOR OWNER: Full Control Subfolders and Files Only
- SYSTEM: Full Control
- Users: Read and Execute

To accommodate legacy applications, you might have to place Users in the Power Users group. The Power Users group has access to the registry, similar to access granted Users in Windows NT 4.0. If you do not want Users to have the elevated privileges that Power Users have, you do have an alternative: You can use the compatws security template described in Chapter 9, "Security Tools." The compatws template can be applied when first migrating to Windows 2000 and then when all applications are Windows 2000 compliant. A stricter template can be used to change registry file and folder settings to be more secure.

Securing Registry Keys

Within the registry, permissions can be set on keys. Access to each hive, key, and sub-key can be restricted. Default settings are enumerated in Chapter 6 "Security from the Get-Go."

Windows 2000 Professional in a Windows NT 4.0 Domain

Windows 2000 Professional does not need to be joined in a Windows 2000 domain. As you have seen, it can be used in a workgroup or not connected to other computers. It also can be joined to a Windows NT 4.0 domain. According to Microsoft:

- A Windows 2000 Professional computer can be a member of a Windows NT domain and is compatible with Windows NT LAN Manager (NTLM)–based security.
- If RAS authentication is necessary, the Windows 2000 Professional computer can access the Windows NT 4.0 RAS server and can use the same domain-integrated logon as 4.0 users.
- Just as Windows NT Workstation 4.0 must be added to the domain by an Administrator, so must Windows 2000 Professional.
- Windows 2000 Professional is compatible with all background operations that apply security on a Windows NT user account. Exchange Server and SQL Server integrated security features are available.
- Users using Windows 2000 Professional can participate in Windows NT domain groups and can utilize user profile paths, home directories, logon and time restrictions, expiration dates, security policies, and RAS permissions.

Although local logon and local authorization remain the same, network authentication and authorization include extra steps.

Authentication in a Windows NT 4.0 Domain

Authentication in a Windows NT domain requires a few extra steps. The user enters the logon information, and the client requests logon validation from a domain controller. The domain controller gives a success or failure response. The process is described in the following list:

1. The user enters a user ID and password.
2. WinLogon calls the LSA on the local machine, specifying the authentication package to be used (typically MSV1_0).
3. If MSV1_0 is the package, LSA calls the authentication package.
4. The MSV1_0 realizes that authentication is required from a machine other than the one it is on.
5. Depending on security policies (see "Security Options" later in this chapter), a LAN Manager Challenge/Response (nonce) and/or Windows NT or a Windows NTLMv2 Challenge/Response (nonce) is computed and replaces the cleartext password in the request.
6. MSV1_0 passes the request to the NetLogon service.
7. NetLogon routes the request over the network to a domain controller.
8. The domain controller NetLogon service passes the request to MSV1_0 on its system.
9. MSV1_0 checks the One-Way Function (OWF) passwords in the SAM and computes the Challenge response.
10. The two nonces are compared.
11. The user is authenticated or rejected.
12. If the user is authenticated, the LSA recovers the user SID and the SIDs of the domain groups of which the user is a member, along with any domain-level rights or privileges.
13. An access token is built and returned to the user computer.

Authorization in a Windows NT Domain

Determining whether a user has the appropriate access permissions on a remote object is done by the SRM, the access token, and the LSA. The process is described in the following list:

1. A user attempts to access a network resource. The local token is not used for authorization.
2. Instead, the Network File Redirector system uses the SRM.

3. The Redirector uses Server Message Block (SMB) protocol and passes the request (including the user credentials) to the server. (The credentials include the user SID; a password is not sent.)

4. The server takes the credentials, contacts its LSA, and requests a token.

5. The token is built.

6. The token is returned to the server service.

7. The token is kept in the User Session list. An index to this list is the user ID (UID). It points back to the Redirector.

8. The UID is saved in the internal system list with a reference to the drive letter and/or Universal Naming Convention (UNC) share name.

9. If the user attempts to open a file on a previously opened directory, the Redirector forwards the open request using the open SMB request, drive letter, and UID to server.

10. If there is another request to a different server, the same process is followed.

11. If there is a request to the same server, the Redirector knows there is a secured user session with that server and uses that UID in SMBs to create the connection.

Managing Local Security Settings with Group Policy

When Windows 2000 Professional is joined in a domain, security settings can be controlled centrally using Group Policy. As a standalone computer, security settings are also controlled using Group Policy through the Local Security Policy console.

Local Security Policy settings can be overridden if Professional is joined in a domain. A member computer shows Local settings and Effective settings in the Local Security Policy console. The Effective settings will be followed, and they represent a combination of Site, Domain, Organizational Unit (OU), and Local settings.

In the Windows 2000 Active Directory (AD) structure, Site settings have precedence over Local settings, Domain settings have precedence over Site settings, and OU settings have precedence over Domain settings. If the computer is part of a hierarchy of OUs, the OU closest to the computer has precedence. Group Policy is discussed in greater detail in Chapter 12, "Domain-Level Security," and in Chapter 9, "Security Tools."

In an environment in which the Windows 2000 Professional computer is not a member of a domain, the effective settings are the same as the local settings.

Local Policy settings are divided into four groups:

- Account Policies
- Local Policies

- Public Key Policies
- IP Security Policies

In this chapter, the default settings will be provided for Account Policies and Local Policies. Public Key Policies are discussed in Chapter 17, "Enterprise Public Key Infrastructure," and IP Security Policies are covered in Chapter 16, "Securing the Network Using Distributed Security Services." Each section includes definitions of how its security settings might be used, and the "Policy Settings" section later in this chapter provides a general discussion.

Account Policies

Account Policies include the Password Policy and the Account Lockout Policy.
Password Policy settings and their defaults include

- **Enforce password history**: 0 passwords remembered
  A user can continue to use the same password.

- **Maximum password age**: 42 days
  A user must change a password every 42 days.

- **Minimum password age**: 0 days
  A user can change his password whenever he wants.

- **Minimum password length**: 0 characters
  A blank password is okay.

- **Passwords must meet complexity requirements**: Disabled
  Any combination, or lack thereof, of letters and numbers is okay.

- **Store passwords using reversible encryption:** Disabled
  Passwords can be decrypted.

- **User must log on to change the password**: Disabled
  Passwords can be changed before the user is authenticated on the system.

Account Lockout Policy settings and their defaults include

- **Account lockout duration:** Not defined
  If the lockout threshold is set, this says how long the lockout is for.

- **Account lockout threshold:** 0 invalid logon attempts
  A user can have as many guesses at his password as he wants.

- **Reset account lockout after**: Not defined
  If lockout is defined, this specifies the number of minutes between invalid attempts at which point the counter restarts.

Local Policies

Local Policies include the Audit Policy, User Rights, and Security Options.

Audit Policy

No Audit Policy is set by default.

User Rights

User Rights apply to user accounts. Permissions apply to objects. Basic rights for users were outlined in Chapter 6. The Local Security Policy console can be used to assign additional rights to groups and individual users. As you examine them, keep in mind that these are initial settings and can be overwritten when the computer joins a domain, by Local Administrators, by Domain or Enterprise Administrators, or by Global Policy settings.

The important distinction to remember when considering user rights on Professional is that Account Operator, Server Operator, and Print Operator groups do not exist as local groups on the Professional system. In addition, the Power Users group is not a domain-level group. The Power Users group has roughly the combined rights of the Account Operator, Server Operator, and Print Operator groups.

Some user rights have no meaning on a standalone Professional system. They are

- Add workstations to the domain. (This is not relevant on a workstation.)
- Enable computer and user accounts to be trusted for delegation.
- Log on as a service. (A user account can be used by a service to establish a security context for that service.)
- Synchronize directory service data.

User rights should be assigned to groups, not to users. This way, any user assigned membership in a group gets the permission designated for that group. Administration of user rights is eased. New to Windows 2000 is the right to deny specifically any type of file access. Also new are more specific deny rights.

Security Options

The Security Options section will look familiar to people with experience in securing Windows NT 4.0. It enables users of Windows 2000 to make well-known, security-related registry settings without editing the registry. Security options available for setting on Windows 2000 Professional and their defaults are listed in Table 10.2.

Table 10.2 **Windows 2000 Default Security Options**

Option	Local Default Setting
Additional restrictions for anonymous connections	None, rely on default permissions
Allow system to be shut down without having to log on	Enabled
Allow to eject removable NTFS media	Administrators
Amount of idle time required before disconnecting sessions	15 minutes
Audit the access of global system objects	Disabled
Audit the use of Backup and Restore privileges	Disabled
Automatically log off users when logon time expires (local)	Enabled
Clear virtual memory pagefile when system shuts down	Disabled
Digitally sign client communication (always)	Disabled
Digitally sign client communication (when possible)	Enabled
Digitally sign server communication (always)	Disabled
Digitally sign server communication (when possible)	Disabled
Disable Ctrl+Alt+Delete requirement for logon	Not defined
Do not display last username in logon screen	Disabled
LAN Manager Authentication Level	Send LM and NTLM responses
Message text for users attempting to log on	
Message title for users attempting to log on	
Number of previous logons to cache (in case domain controller is not available)	10 logons
Prevent system maintenance of computer account password	Disabled
Prevent users from installing printer drivers	Disabled
Prompt user to change password before expiration	14 days
Recovery Console: Allow automatic administrative logon	Disabled
Recovery Console: Allow floppy copy and access to all drives and all folders	Disabled
Rename Administrator account	Not defined
Rename Guest account	Not defined
Restrict CD-ROM access to locally logged-on user only	Disabled
Restrict floppy access to locally logged-on user only	Disabled
Secure channel: Digitally encrypt or sign secure channel data (always)	Disabled

continues

Table 10.2 **Continued**

Option	Local Default Setting
Secure channel: Digitally encrypt or sign secure channel data (when possible)	Enabled
Secure channel: Digitally sign secure channel data (when possible)	Disabled
Secure channel: Require strong (Windows 2000 or later) session key	Disabled
Send unencrypted password to connect to third-party SMB servers	Disabled
Shut down system immediately if unable to log security audits	Disabled
Smart card removal behavior	No action
Strengthen default permissions of global system objects (for example, symbolic links)	Enabled
Unsigned driver installation behavior (Silently succeed, Warn but allow installation, Do not allow installation)	Not defined
Unsigned nondriver installation behavior (Silently succeed, Warn but allow installation, Do not allow installation)	Not defined

Many of these settings are recognizable from suggested security modifications to the Windows NT registry, and the results of their settings are obvious from their titles. Others are not. Here is a listing of the more frequently confused settings along with descriptions and suggestions for Windows 2000 Professional.

Additional Restrictions for Anonymous Connections

Anonymous connections are used to list accounts and groups. This option can be used by the Administrator of a domain to add users in a trusted domain to resources in his. It also can be abused to gain information about a domain by individuals who should not have that access.

Allow System to be Shut Down Without Having to Log On

When enabled, a shut down button on the logon screen is available to enable a system to be shut down without having to log on first. This is convenient for users of Windows 2000 Professional. It is a policy choice, as you would not want a casual user or a person walking by to shut down a Web, file, or application server during business hours unless the person has that right. To determine whether the person has the right to shut down the server, it should be possible to make him log on first. Although a malicious or unthinking user could flip a power switch if it is not disabled or could unplug the machine, the "casual" user will not, but he might be tempted to or might accidentally click the shut down button.

Allow to Eject Removable NTFS Media

This keeps just anyone from removing a drive by normal, automated means and from being able to walk away with it. I will discuss removable drives in more detail later in this chapter.

Audit the Access of Global System Objects

Auditing global system objects is not necessary to track normal user and services access to the system. Global system object audit is useful to software and device driver developers. Examples of global system objects are threads, symbolic links, and processes. Typically, in a nondevelopment environment, you do not want this option turned on due to the unnecessary overhead on the processor and the large number of entries to the Security Event file.

Audit the Use of Backup and Restore Privileges

Auditing the use of Backup and Restore privileges generates a large number of entries in the Security Log. Each file and folder that is backed up or restored creates entries. Therefore, object access of this type is not usually audited. You can, however, enable it.

Automatically Log off Users When Logon Time Expires

If a user's logon time is set, this feature will log him off. Two uses of this facility are:

- Temporary workers, contract workers, and so on can be assigned logon hours appropriate to the hours of the day and days of the week they work. This prevents the possibility of their logon being used from a remote site or locally during nonbusiness hours.

- The policy can set logon hours for most users that do not extend past normal working hours so that utilities such as backup can be run with no files open.

In both cases, logoff will occur.

Clear Virtual Memory Pagefile When System Shuts Down

When Windows 2000 is shut down, data may remain in the paging file, pagefile.sys. This file is used to temporarily hold data when the existing physical memory is not sufficient. There is always the chance that there might be data in the file that could be used to compromise the system. While the system is up, the pagefile is protected, but when it is shut down, it might be vulnerable to attack. To prevent this type of attack, clear the file when the system shuts down.

> **To Buy or Not to Buy**
>
> Just when you thought Windows 2000 had everything and you didn't need a third-party product, you learn that the on-board defrag doesn't defragment the pagefile. Although you can enable the Clear Virtual Memory Pagefile when System Shuts Down security option, this makes Windows 2000 create a new pagefile on boot. The problem with this is that you shouldn't have to reboot so frequently, so a third-party product may not be a bad idea.

Digital Signing of Client and/or Server Communications

Digital signing refers to SMB signing, and it is not normally set because it slows performance. It can, however, make communication more secure. If it is set to always be enabled, the computer will not be able to connect to a computer that cannot digitally sign SMB packets. If it is set to be used when possible, some communication will be signed, but communication with other systems that cannot sign SMB packets can occur without it.

> **Note**
>
> SMB is the method of file sharing used in Windows systems. It is now considered part of Common Internet File Systems, a RFC-proposed standard.

More information can be found in Chapter 13, "Securing Legacy Windows Clients."

Disable Ctrl+Alt+Delete Requirement for Logon

Before a user logs on, he normally must use the key combination Ctrl+Alt+Delete to obtain the logon screen. Using these keystrokes is a precaution against a Trojan Horse program that might seek to capture passwords on entry. The Ctrl+Alt+Delete key combination stops such a running process if it is present and therefore protects against such an attack. Disabling this option leaves the user ID and password entry screen available and negates this valuable protection.

Do Not Display Last Username in Logon Screen

When the logon screen is present, it conveniently displays the user ID of the last person to log on. Although this is useful to that person (because it requires less typing), it does give an interloper a valid logon name. If our interloper knows that the person holds an administrative account, then the information is valuable indeed; it's information he needs to break in to the system with permission to do anything. Although many people claim this does not matter because they think a logon can be guessed, many others believe in the principal of layered security, which states that every deterrence helps.

LAN Manager Authentication Level

LAN Manager, or LM NTLM and NTLMv2, are the names of network authentication protocols used in the old LAN Manager OS and Windows NT. All of them are deemed less secure than Kerberos, but NTLM is less vulnerable than LM, and NTLMv2 is less susceptible to attack than NTLM. If all the computers in your Windows network can speak Kerberos, then this setting can be changed to eliminate any possible LAN Manager authentication. Conversely, you can allow only certain computers to connect and enforce this by varying the settings here. Your job is to make sure that all the computers you want to allow to communicate can do so in the most secure fashion. For more information see Chapter 13.

Message Text for Users Attempting to Log On

Warning criminals not to enter your house will not necessarily prevent them from doing so. Neither will setting a stern message here prevent unauthorized people from attempting to log on. The real benefit is to legally show that you do not welcome this type of advance. Many a case against a digital intruder has failed when the attorney for the hacker pointed out that the logon screen said "Welcome." Make sure yours doesn't. As an additional precaution, the warning should be repeated in every major language spoken by users of the computer.

Message Title for Users Attempting to Log on

Here's where to enter a statement for the title bar of the message window that includes the logon message discussed in the preceding section.

Number of Previous Logons to Cache (In Case Domain Controller is Not Available)

When users log on to a domain, their authentication information is approved by a domain controller. If approved, they are logged on and can access the system. If the domain controller is not available, they are still able to log on. How can this be? Their information is cached and can be used. They might not be able to reach some resources, but they can still get some work done. Although this logon information is well protected, you might want to disable or limit the storage of this information on the local computer. You can also set the cache higher to assist in cases in which multiple people use the same computer.

Of course, if you set the cache to 0, the user cannot log on unless his system can contact the domain controller for authentication. In some cases this might be what you want, and you might be willing to deal with the occasional interruptions of service that this might entail.

Prevent System Maintenance of Computer Account Password

In NT 4.0 domains, trust relationships are formed between domains by initially setting a password. After the trust is established, the password is periodically reset by the system. This can cause problems in cases in which slow communication links exist between domain controllers. This security option prevents that computer password from being changed periodically by the system. When a computer is joined in a domain, an implicit trust exists between the computer and the domain. A computer account and password exist in the domain for each computer joined in the domain, and the password is changed periodically by the system. Windows 2000 Professional systems, like Windows NT 4.0 domain controllers in trusts, can have the same issues with slow links. If this occurs, you can use this setting to prevent the password from changing.

Prevent Users from Installing Printer Drivers

How much management control needs to be placed on a Windows 2000 Professional computer? Should users be prevented from adding printers to their systems? Perhaps traveling laptops need this requirement because people need to make arrangements for printing outside the corporate enclave. Perhaps this is a good thing to control in just such an environment. However, two dangers exist. First, an unauthorized printer driver might not be certified for Windows 2000. It might overwrite system files and interfere with the operation of the computer. Second, drivers might operate within the kernel, and any program that can do this should be controlled by someone who understands the possibility that the new driver found on xyz Web site might not be what it seems; it might be a malicious program masquerading as a great printer driver.

Prompt User to Change Password Before Expiration

Set a number of days here. Windows 2000 will prompt the user. Be sure to coordinate this with the length of time a password is valid.

Recovery Console: Allow Automatic Administrative Logon

The Recovery Console (discussed in Chapter 8, "Lifecycle Choices") provides utilities to mend an ailing system. It also enables access from a floppy boot to NTFS folders and drives. To protect your system, require an Administrator account and password. (This is the default.) However, to simplify its use for mere mortals, set this option.

Rename Administrator Account

Everyone knows that the name of the Administrator account is Administrator. Changing this name to something else might deter a few curious hackers. Because the SID of the Administrator is well known, renaming the account is considered by many to not help much security-wise. However, security composed of many layers is always wise. Should I leave my door unlocked just because it's an easy lock to break?

Locking down anonymous access removes the possibility that nonauthenticated network users can use applications that identify the Administrator by the well-known SID. Using this option to rename the account helps prevent anonymous users from learning the name of the Administrator account.

Rename Guest Account

Although some people might question how useful this option is, I've seen many an improper entry into resources when someone was able to enter "Guest" when presented with a blank logon pop-up. A simple renaming would have prevented the attempt. Although the Guest account is disabled by default, that status can be changed. It is always helpful if multiple ways of securing the system are used.

Restrict CD-ROM Access to Locally Logged-On User Only

Because the CD-ROM drive is given an administrative share at bootup, it makes sense to provide some way to restrict network access to the drive. Whether this policy should be enforced depends on the nature of the data on the CD-ROM. It might be that you want to share its contents with others. It might be that it is confidential data that should not be exposed. In general, unless this system is seen as a sharepoint for CD-ROM data, this would be a good choice.

Restrict Floppy Access to Locally Logged-On User Only

The reasons for using this setting are identical to those for the CD-ROM access just mentioned.

Secure Channel: Digitally Encrypt or Sign Secure Channel Data (Always)

Domain controllers and their clients and domain controllers in a trust relationship might need to communicate for purposes of authenticating computer accounts, user accounts, and trusts. The name for this logical connection is "secure channel." Four secure channel settings allow for backward compatibility or Windows 2000–only security. If this setting is enabled and the client and server cannot negotiate encryption level, no secure channel can be established and communication will fail. (The client cannot log on, for example.) However, communication that does take place will be more secure from attack.

Secure Channel: Digitally Encrypt Secure Channel Data (When Possible)

If data-encryption-level negotiation fails, communication can still take place, but data is less secure.

Secure Channel: Digitally Sign Secure Channel Data (When Possible)

If signing cannot take place, communication still can.

Secure Channel: Require Strong (Windows 2000 or Later) Session Key

In a native mode Windows 2000 domain (no NT 4.0 domain controllers) with no down-level clients, enable this to use the strongest encryption. the secure channel (SChannel) is used for authentication and data integrity. It can be configured in various ways. SChannel enables you to control whether data is encrypted or signed. For the tightest security, enable the Always policy. Keep in mind, however, that communication with some resources and clients using this protocol will not be possible.

Send Unencrypted Password to Connect to Third-Party SMB Servers

Samba is a product that simulates an NT domain controller on a UNIX system. The advantage, of course, is interoperability with UNIX systems in a mixed-OS environment. The downside is a dependency on unencrypted passwords. If this characteristic is necessary in your network, the option is here to choose.

Strengthen Default Permissions of Global System Objects (For Example, Symbolic Links)

Symbolic links and other system objects such as threads and processes must also operate under a system of permissions. (Symbolic links are simply the OS's way of managing "other names" for objects). You and I use the drive letter C to refer to a disk drive; that object name is mapped to a more complex but accurate device identification. The object manager, as a component of the OS, manages its namespaces by using many symbolic links. Strengthening the default set of permissions for access makes good sense in some environments.

Unsigned Driver Installation Behavior

Poorly written and untested drivers can cause a system to be unstable at best. At worst, a rogue program could be introduced into the system masquerading as a new and better device driver. With Windows 2000, drivers for all devices will be signed by Microsoft if approved for use within Windows 2000. By changing the setting on this option, a Windows 2000 administrator can control the device driver process much more closely. The three possible settings are Silently Succeed, Warn but Allow Installation, and Do Not Allow Installation. Setting to Do Not Allow Installation will prevent any but those signed from being installed. Alternatively, you can just ask to be warned, or you can ignore the issue entirely. What you do will depend on the level of security you need. If you insist on not allowing installation, you might find there are some systems and devices you cannot use because you cannot load the proper drivers to make them functional. If you require a very secure system, however, then you will use a different system or device instead. The reasonable path to adopt is to set Warn but Allow Installation on most systems. If you do this, you might find yourself increasing the number of help desk calls as users load incompatible drivers and make their machines inoperable. However, many perfectly usable drivers that will not cause any problems, but that have not yet been approved and digitally signed by Microsoft, will exist. You might have to stick to the Warn option, test drivers, and train users (if possible) to forgo downloading unknown drivers. At some point, as more device manufacturers learn how to write proper drivers and/or get their drivers approved, you might be able to insist on a stronger stance.

Unsigned Nondriver Installation Behavior

If you want Windows 2000 to check all applications that you install for possible digital signatures, you can do so here. The options work like those in the preceding section.

Policy Settings

So how should you set your policies for your Windows 2000 Professional system(s)? That depends on the risk to which you feel your system will be exposed and the corporate Security Policy. If there is no corporate Security Policy or if this is a personal system, then a policy needs to be developed in some form.

A true policy considers security needs and requirements and then approaches the potential for settings within the operating system. You can set a Security Policy based on what is available, however, therefore obtaining some degree of security while working on the ideal policy. After you have your written policy, you can determine whether changes in settings are necessary.

An initial policy is set and can be changed in the Local Security Policy console. In a domain system, policies are set at the domain or OU level and propagate to the member workstations and servers.

For standalone or personal laptop system environments, there are three security templates you can use to begin implementing stronger security. You can apply them, analyze your current settings against them, or mix and match parts of them to get the level of security you feel you need. You can add to these templates later or can develop your own to get the policy that works best for you. To learn more about the templates for Windows 2000 Professional, see Chapter 9, "Security Tools." To see how the differences between various templates designed for Windows 2000 Professional, see the "Policy Implementation and Enforcement" section later in this chapter.

Matching Security Settings to the Abilities of the User

One policy does not always fit all. When a system is a member of a domain and groups of users receive privileges and access rights to resources, there is a tendency to treat all users the same when it comes to their capability to access features of their desktop machines. This, of course, is much easier to administer and is very necessary in larger environments. Any activity that freezes user choices seems to be a good way to go.

There are many reasons, however, for making policy more personalized. Users might have backgrounds and training in operating systems and programming. Rather than frustrate them with settings meant for users whose only choice is to answer customer-service calls or prepare reports, more responsibility in the care of data and system access can be allowed. In a domain system, there is the capability to fine-tune group policies to provide a hierarchical approach to policy settings (see Chapter 12, "Domain-Level Security").

On a Windows 2000 Professional system that is not part of a domain, it often is the primary user who becomes responsible for the care and feeding of the machine. Depending on the ability, nature, and training of the user, this might prove frustrating and time consuming. This user might have been given access to display features and so on and might have been trusted to make reasonable choices and have responsibility for system maintenance, backup, coordination with main offices, and many other tasks—without proper training. Is it a wonder when this system becomes compromised?

You need to decide which, if any, users should be Power Users or Administrators on their own systems. The question that needs to be answered is what level of authority they need to do their job.

One reason for granting users Power User status is that not all applications they might need to run have been developed with Windows 2000 in mind. Many of the enhanced security features and default settings are provided and expected to work with applications that are built to respect the requirements of Windows 2000. Unfortunately, there will be lots of legacy software to deal with. You might need to add users to the Power Users group or temporarily include the INTERACTIVE group in the Power Users group until this situation is resolved. By putting interactive users in the Power Users group, you ensure that only locally logged-on users gain increased privileges on that particular machine. Before giving blanket membership to the Power Users group, however, you need to determine if it is warranted.

Policy Implementation and Enforcement

Setting policies on multiple Windows 2000 Professional machines will not be a challenge if these systems are part of a Windows 2000 domain. Policies can be established at the domain and OU level.

Setting policies in the Local Security Policy console on one machine at a time is tedious at best. To make your job easier, Windows 2000 provides sample security templates and a Security Configuration and Analysis toolset. The toolset consists of two MMC snap-ins (Security Configuration and Analysis and Security Templates) and a command-line tool (secedit). You can use provided sample templates or create your own. Four templates (hisecws, basicwk, securews, compatws) are designed for setting Windows 2000 Professional security. If you compare their settings, you get an idea of where they might be used to set and maintain security levels. The areas to examine include

- Password Policy
- Account Lockout
- Audit Policy
- User Rights
- Security Options
- Event Log Settings

> **Note**
>
> See Chapter 12 for more information on the implementation and use of the Security Configuration and Analysis tool in a domain setting.

Password Policy

Only securewk and hisecwk enforce password history, setting it to 24 passwords remembered. A user would have to wait two years before he could reuse a password. This is indeed a useful policy because the compromise of a password will not gain an intruder access in a short period of time. It is unlikely that a password will be remembered long enough for it to be reused. Both of these templates also enhance security by setting the minimum password age to two days and its length to eight characters. Not allowing users to reset their passwords immediately can thwart some attacks. Having a minimum password length of eight characters presents the possibility of a good compromise between a password that is too long to remember and one that is harder to crack.

Complexity requirements for passwords are enabled, too. This means passwords need to have combinations of letters and numbers, uppercase and lowercase, or special case characters combined. No part of the username can be in the password. If you examine how many password-cracking utilities work, you will find that complex passwords take longer to crack. But a complex password policy is hard to enforce. This policy does the work for you by rejecting passwords that are improperly formulated. It's similar to the passfilt DLL that could be implemented in Windows NT 4.0.

The compatws template shows everything as Not defined. This is because this template is used to reset registry and file settings back to Windows NT compatibility mode. It does not impact the policy settings that might have been made before it was applied. It is meant to provide an environment that might be necessary when running legacy applications.

Account Lockout

The Account Lockout policy is also set in securews and hisecws. Securews sets the lockout duration to 30 minutes, the lockout threshold to five invalid attempts, and the reset count to 30 minutes. Hisecwk also uses five invalid attempts and a 30-minute reset wait. However, it also puts the account lock out duration to 0, which means that, once locked out, the user needs to have an administrator reset the account.

Seven, Eight, or Nine Characters: Which is More Secure?

A number of theorists have proposed that there is a magic number for Windows passwords. Although in general it is usually true that the longer a password is the harder it is to crack, the Windows LAN Manager (LM) passwords algorithm for encryption gave no more security when passwords were more than seven characters in length. Here's why.

Instead of encrypting a 14-character password, the LM algorithm divided the password into two separate seven-character words and encrypted them separately. Then the halves were combined. This made it easier for the password to be broken because a seven-character password is easier to crack than a 14-character one.

Audit Policy

Audit Policy is also set in securewk and hisecwk.

Table 10.3 **Audit Policy Comparison**

Audit Policy	Securews	Hisecws
Audit account logon events	Success, Failure	Success, Failure
Audit account management	Success, Failure	Success, Failure
Audit directory service access	Not defined	Not defined
Audit logon events	Failure	Success, Failure
Audit object access	No auditing	Success, Failure
Audit policy change	Success, Failure	Success, Failure
Audit privilege use	Failure	Success, Failure
Audit process tracking	No auditing	No auditing
Audit system events	No auditing	Success, Failure

Both securews and hisecws require logging of failure events; hisecws even logs some successes.

User Rights

All user rights for the hisecws and securews templates are not defined. The rationale is that they don't want to update or change rights that might have been developed over time to make installed programs work.

Security Options

Security options represent registry changes that can be made to enable various security settings. They are as follows:

- **Additional Restrictions on Anonymous Connections.** Securews prevents the enumeration of SAM accounts and shares; hisecws prevents any access to this information without explicit permissions.
- **Clear Virtual Memory Pagefile when System Shuts Down.** This is enabled only in hisecws.
- **Digitally Sign Client Communication (always).** This is enabled in hisecws, as is Digitally Sign Server Communications (when possible).
- **Digitally Sign Server Communications (when necessary).** This is enabled in both securews and hisecws.
- **Disable Ctrl+Alt+Delete Requirement for Logon.** This is disabled in both securews and hisecws.

- **Do Not Display Last Username in Logon Screen.** This is enabled in hisecws.

- **LAN Manager Authentication Level.** This is Send NTLM Response Only for securews and Send NTLMv2 Response Only\Refuse LM & NTLM for hisecws.

- **Prevent Users from Installing Printer Drivers.** This is enabled in both securews and hisecws.

- **Secure Channel: Digitally Encrypt or Sign Secure Channel Data (Always).** This is enabled for hisecws.

- **Secure Channel: Digitally Encrypt Secure Channel Data (When Possible).** This is enabled for both securews and hisecws.

- **Secure Channel: Digitally Sign Secure Channel Data (When Possible).** This is enabled for both hisecws and securews.

- **Secure Channel: Require Strong (Windows 2000 or Later) Session Key.** This is enabled only for hisecws.

- **Smart Card Removal Behavior.** This is Lock Workstation for both securews and hisecws.

- **Unsigned Driver Installation Behavior.** This is Warn but Allow Installation for securews and Do Not Allow Installation for hisecws.

- **Unsigned Nondriver Installation Behavior.** This is Silently Succeed for both securews and hisecws.

Event Log Settings

Securews does not define the maximum application log size but does set a size on the security log of 5,120 kilobytes. Guest access to all logs is restricted. The entries in the log are not aged out of existence but removed as needed.

The only difference between the securews template and the hisecws template is the change in the size of the security log. Hisecws defines the maximum size of the security log to be 10,240 kilobytes. Neither template requires the system to be shut down if the audit log is full.

Securing Wireless Connections

You watch a demo of infrared connectivity in Windows 2000. The speaker moves two systems close together and—blip, blap, bloop—they start talking. She can easily copy a file from one computer to another. Boy, you're thinking, don't that just beat all. Now we can copy files without a floppy drive. Now traveling folks won't have to rely on having a floppy or run into disaster because the file is too big for one.

Think again. What is to protect your system from *unauthorized* file copying? The following sections discuss how wireless file copy works.

Wireless Connectivity: Computer to Computer

Wireless connectivity is available in all versions of Windows 2000. Infrared light is used to transmit data from one system to another. Files and digital images can be transferred from computer to computer and from devices such as digital cameras to computers.

Windows 2000 supports Infrared Data Association (IrDA) protocols for data transfer. If the computer has compatible hardware, plug and play automatically detects and installs the IrDA drivers and *enables file transfer!* Management of the device is through the Wireless Link applet in Control Panel. If you move your infrared ready system near another one, an icon appears on your desktop and taskbar, as shown in Figure 10.2. If you have sound enabled, a "boing" sound will notify you as well.

Figure 10.2   This wireless icon appears when another IrDA device is within range.

The service can be used to do the following:

- Use the Wireless Link dialog box to specify files to transfer.
- Drag and drop files on the Wireless Link icon.
- Right-click files and use Send To Infrared Recipient.
- Send jobs to an infrared-enabled printer.
- Use the connection to map shared drives as if you had a traditional network connection.
- Install other third-party software that provides additional methods or uses for infrared connectivity.

The default location for file transfer is the desktop. If you have installed Windows Professional on an NTFS volume, the permissions on this folder by default are restricted to the user, the SYSTEM, and Administrators.

This would seem to say that you can control infrared access by setting NTFS permissions on the folder configured to receive transferred files. This is not true. Imagine, if you will, Alice and Bob sitting down on opposite sides of a table. They place their laptops in front of them, which means the IrDA port on the back of each faces the other. For our purposes, Alice will attempt to transfer a file; she is the sending user of IrDA. She will attempt to send it to Bob, the receiving user. When she attempts a wireless transfer, she must have Read access to the files to be sent. She does. On the receiving side, Bob, the logged on user, needs no access rights to Alice's file; he only needs Write access to the selected receiving folder (by default, his desktop).

Let's presume that Alice does have Read permissions on the file she wants to send and that only Bob (not Alice *and* Bob) has Write permissions to his desktop. Alice has no rights or permissions anywhere on Bob's laptop. Alice starts the transfer. Bob is given a pop-up window asking if the file should be saved. He clicks OK and the file is saved. Remember, Alice does not have any permissions or rights on Bob's system. A malicious user might try to trick a user into saving a Trojan or virus onto his machine. The user *is* asked whether he wants the file; however, I wonder how many users, given no training in wireless technology and conditioned to just hit Enter when given a message box, will blindly say okay.

Part of your Security Policy should be to clear the check box "Allow others to transfer files to your computer using infrared communications" if wireless file transfer is desired. A knowledgeable user can be given permission to reset it.

Wireless Connectivity: The Infrared Network Connection

Setting up an infrared network connection is accomplished by using the Make New Connections Wizard from the Network and Dial-Up Connections window. A connection can be established by selecting "host" or "guest" roles on the appropriate computers. You can restrict connectivity to the "host" role by selecting users allowed to use the connection.

If the server is a member of an AD domain, you will need to set and manage infrared network connections via the Routing and Remote Access console. (See Chapter 15, "Secure Remote Access Options.")

Protocols and Processes for Secure Data and Application Access

Windows 2000 Professional can participate in secure communications with other Windows 2000 computers and other systems. Three common scenarios are

- The use of IPSec for network communications
- A virtual private network (VPN) connection
- Participation in a Public Key Infrastructure (PKI)

IPSec is covered in Chapter 16, "Securing the Network Using Distributed Security Services." VPN connectivity is covered in Chapter 15, "Secure Remote Access Options." PKI is covered in Chapter 17, "Enterprise Public Key Infrastructure."

Administering a Windows 2000 Domain Using Windows 2000 Professional

You can use Administrative Tools from the Windows 2000 Advanced Server CD-ROM to administer a Windows 2000 enterprise. Administrative Tools are a number of Microsoft Management Console snap-ins and other tools that enable you to manage your Windows 2000 enterprise from your Windows 2000 Professional system. Available tools and how to obtain them are discussed in the following section.

Available Tools

Some management tools are available on both Windows 2000 Server and Windows 2000 Professional; others must be loaded. You should be aware of how each of these tools can be used to remotely administer other Windows 2000 computers, either so you can use them to your advantage to secure remote systems or so you can protect against them being used by rogue users. Native Windows 2000 Administrative Tools are

- Component Services
- Computer Management
- Data Sources (ODBC)
- Event Viewer
- Performance
- Services

Although the use of these tools on Windows 2000 Professional is meant for managing the local computer, any that have the capability of managing other computers can be used for that purpose, too. Thus, if you have appropriate permission to monitor other computers, you can use Event Viewer. Other tools are not present on Professional but can be installed. These tools are

- Active Directory Domains and Trusts
- Active Directory Schema
- Active Directory Sites and Services
- Active Directory Users and Computers
- Certification Authority
- Cluster Administrator
- Connection Manager Administration Kit

- DHCP
- Distributed File System
- DNS
- Internet Authentication Service
- Internet Services Manager
- QoS Admission Control
- Remote Boot Disk Generator
- Routing and Remote Access
- Telephony
- Terminal Services Manager
- Licensing and Client Connection Manager
- WINS

The tools are located in the I386 directory of the Windows 2000 Server and the Windows 2000 Advanced Server installation CD-ROMs. To install them on Professional, click the Adminpak.msi file. A Setup Wizard will help you install the tools to your Administrative Tools folder.

Alternatively, the Windows 2000 Server Software Installation snap-in can be used to deploy the tools. You can use the snap-in to assign the Administration Tools to other computers, and they will be automatically installed. If you prefer, publish the tools in Active Directory. Then Administrators can use their local computer Control Panel Add/Remove Programs to install the tools.

Best Practices

To secure Windows 2000 Professional, you should observe the following best practices:

- Place users in groups and assign groups permissions on files and folders.
- Use EFS to protect files.
- Encrypt folders, not files.
- Disable wireless connections and enable them only when ready to use.
- Use care when writing a Security Policy for the enterprise. Consider all classes of workstation machines as well as servers. Implement on a test system and test. Use Security Configuration and Analysis or Group Policy to apply the policy and Security Configuration and Analysis to ensure that the policy has not changed.
- Use prepared security templates and modify for your own use.
- Develop an IPSec policy for the network and implement it at the workstation level for more secure communications where necessary.

- Protect remote storage by setting permissions so that users who need access to manipulate data in libraries are placed in a group for this purpose. There is no need, for example, to give the entire Users group access to the backup library.

For More Information

This chapter discussed services for which complementary information exists in other chapters of this book.

An introduction to encryption can be found in Chapter 2, "Cryptology Introduction."

For help with Group Policy, see Chapter 9, "Security Tools," Chapter 12, "Domain-Level Security," and Chapter 15, "Secure Remote Access Options."

Summary

Windows 2000 Professional is an advanced, multifaceted operating system. To secure it, you need to understand how security is applied, how it's going to be used, and how to match security features to use and perceived risks.

Many things are the same in Windows 2000 Professional and Server File system access (for example, the availability of NTLM and LM for backwards compatibility as well as user rights). There are also many things that are different. This chapter discussed these differences. In the next chapter, the server side of the security picture will be discussed.

11

Securing Windows 2000 Server

Windows 2000 Server can be used as a file and print server or to host applications and network services. It can be used as a standalone product, be integrated into non-Microsoft networks, or perform as a member server in a Microsoft Windows NT domain. Server also can be promoted and become a domain controller. The security features available to be implemented, and how you choose to use them, depend on how the server is used.

This chapter begins by discussing server roles followed by a description of the default security setup for Windows 2000 Server. It also will discuss security settings including Local Security Policy. Information is also included on Security Templates and the local user database where they differ from Professional.

The use of Server as a standalone or member server will also be explored. In this role Server performs as an application, file, and/or service server. Several roles will be described, and references will be made to other chapters where roles such as Certificate Server and Routing and Remote Access Server are detailed. The following specific topics will be discussed:

- Server roles
- Installation security defaults
- Policy settings
- Server security templates

- Using and securing terminal services
- Securing interoperability services

Server Roles

Windows 2000 Server has many roles. Roles are actually of two types: how the server relates to other Windows computers and for what it is used.

Server Relationships

Roles define how Server relates to other servers. Such roles include Server being:

- A standalone server in a workgroup setting
- Joined in a domain
- A domain controller

Standalone Server

A standalone server is not part of a Windows domain. It is installed as a member of a workgroup. Although the workgroup is given a name and the Windows 2000 browser service will list the servers underneath that name, the name of the workgroup has no administrative meaning. Each standalone server must be administered and secured as a separate entity. A standalone server can be used as a remote access server, an Internet Authentication Server, a tunnel server, a file server, or an application server.

Because a standalone server is not joined in a domain, it will rely on its local user and group database for authentication. This database is kept in the registry. Authentication will take place via LM, NTLM, or NTLMv2, depending on the client operating system and the requirements set in Security Options. All security is controlled locally and can be configured through the Local Security Policy.

Joined in a Domain

Server, like Professional, can be joined in a domain. Another name for this type of server is *member server*. There are significant security benefits if Server is joined in a domain:

- Central administration is possible.
- Authority can be delegated.
- The domain user and group database can be used in granting user rights and resource access.
- Kerberos can become the default network authentication protocol for all Windows 2000 computers (only available in a Windows 2000 domain).
- Certificates, as part of an enterprise-wide Public Key Infrastructure, can be used to grant authority and access.

Server is joined to the domain by using the Network Identification tab of the System Properties pages.

Domain Controller

Server can also be promoted to become a domain controller. When this is done, the Active Directory (AD) service is installed and the AD database, including domain-level user and computer accounts, is created, or if previous domain controllers exist, a copy is replicated to the new domain controller.

Server Uses

Server can also run many applications and services. Many services, such as Certificate Services and Internet Authentication Services, are not installed by default but come with the base system. Others, such as Services for UNIX, must be purchased separately, while applications such as SQL Server or Exchange Server are separate products. Each role can offer special security benefits or present new security challenges. Some of the roles that Server can play are as follows:

- As an application server:
  - Proxy Server
  - Messaging server (Exchange Server)
  - Database server (SQL Server)
  - Host Integration Server (SNA Server)
  - Systems Management Server (SMS)
- As a services server:
  - Certificate Services Server
  - Routing and Remote Access Server (RRAS)
  - Terminal Services Server
  - Internet Authentication Server (IAS)
  - Tunnel Server (VPN endpoint)
  - Smart card enrollment station
  - Encrypting File System (EFS) recovery station
  - Domain Name Server (DNS)
  - Dynamic Host Control Protocol (DHCP) Server
  - Windows Internet Naming Services (WINS) server
  - Web server (Internet Information Server[IIS])
  - File and Print Server

Application Server Role

Microsoft BackOffice products such as Exchange Server, SQL Server, SNA Server, SMS Server, and Proxy Server will eventually be rewritten and integrated with the AD. Securing these products will then be a process of securing the underlying operating system as part of a domain, applying any specialized security that is part of the product, and if the server is joined in a domain, using the security features of Windows 2000. As you learn more about these features, think how they would benefit and protect these systems.

Of course, many other third-party applications will be rewritten to run in the new environment as well. One of your challenges will be to determine how to best secure these systems, and the first step will be to determine whether they can utilize the extra security provided by Windows 2000. If they can, your job will be easier.

To determine any application's capability to operate in the new environment, you can check its compliance with the Microsoft logo program. As discussed in Chapter 6, "Security from the Get-Go," the new Windows 2000 logo program is comprehensive and has different levels of compliance, one for each version of the operating system. Applications are tested by an independent organization, Veritest (`http://www.veritest.com`). To be certified, applications must pass rigorous tests. Evidence of certification can be an indication of the following:

- A server application supports the global infrastructure.
- A server application supports distributed security structures.
- Server components of distributed applications:
    - Use the Active Directory
    - Document storage and replications
    - Document use of objects and attributes
    - Document services that require more than user-level privileges to run
    - Support single sign on for win32 clients running in a trusted domain.
    - Run servers in appropriate security context
    - Provide connection authentication between client and server
- A server application uses standard security credentials and security descriptors to validate access to resources and data

In addition, evidence of certification can be an indication that scope of damage due to a compromised service or compromised service account password is limited to the capability of the account under which the service is running. (In other words, service accounts run with the least privileges necessary to perform their functions.)

If you are developing commercial or in-house client/server or N-tier applications, you should visit Veritest's Web site and download the document, "The Windows 2000 Application Specifications for Desktop and Server Applications." This document, written by Microsoft, specifies for the developer what the application must do to be certified. This document is also helpful to administrators and security officers because it provides test scenarios that can be used to pretest applications that do not have a logo to see how they will operate in the Windows 2000 environment.

As an example, I have paraphrased the recommended steps to test whether an application can participate in single sign-on (SSO):

1. On the server: Select the option for authenticated logon, if one is provided.

2. Use an anonymous, unauthenticated client to try to access the server. You should be prompted for user logon or denied access.

3. Use an authenticated trusted domain account. Access to expected resources should be provided without logon prompting.

4. On a server that allows anonymous, unauthenticated logon only (there is no option for authentication), the application will not be certified (it will not work).

Logo certification test results for applications submitted for testing are posted in summary form on the Veritest Web site. Results include a list of all the elements complied with as well as any variations, notes, or waivers that might exist. Systems used in the testing are documented as well.

Services Server Role

As a standalone or member server, Windows 2000 Server can be used to provide services to the network. The range of services is determined by the domain role that the server plays. For example, a standalone Windows 2000 Server cannot be an Enterprise Certification Authority (CA) in your Public Key Infrastructure. It can, however, still be a standalone CA. This is because some services, including Enterprise CA, require participation in the AD, and a standalone server, by definition, does not participate in the AD.

Services are further defined and references are provided in the "For More Information" section at the end of this chapter.

Installation Security Defaults

Installing Windows NT 4.0 involves choosing the primary server role: domain controller or standard server. The selection is a major one. There is no going back. If you install NT as a server and decide at a later time that you would like it to be a domain controller, you will be forced to reinstall the operating system. This is not true for Windows 2000 Server. Windows 2000 can be installed as a server and later be promoted to domain controller. Demotion is also possible.

Installation security defaults are set for users and groups, file and registry Discretionary Access Control Lists (DACLs), and Security Policy. Initial settings come from the application of the defltsv.inf template. This file, along with the installation template for Professional and the template applied when a server is promoted to domain controller, can be found in %systemroot%\system32\inf. (For a review of file and registry DACLs, refer to Chapter 6.)

Users and Groups

User and groups on the newly installed Server are the same as those for Professional. All user and group accounts are kept in the local account database, or Security Account Manager (SAM), in the registry. If the server joins a domain, the local account database remains. A Windows 2000 server joined in a domain can be accessed using a domain account or can be logged on to interactively using a local account. If the server is promoted to domain controller, however, the local account database is unavailable. Instead, the domain database must be used to administer the system or to access domain controller resources.

Local Security Policy

When Windows 2000 Server is used as a standalone server (a server not joined in a domain), security settings are controlled through the Local Security Policy console. Member servers and domain controllers also have a Local Security Policy; however, any settings made there can be overridden by site, domain, or organizational unit (OU) settings.

The range and initial values of most of the items for Server are the same as for Professional. The major differences are with file and registry permissions and in how some of the security options are used. You will see these settings when you open the Local Security Policy console.

Local policy settings are divided into four major headings:

- Account Policies
- Local Policies
- Public Key Policies
- IP Security Policies

Public Key Policies are discussed in Chapter 17, "Enterprise Public Key Infrastructure." IP Security Policies are discussed in Chapter 16, "Securing the Network Using Distributed Security Services." Information on Account Policies and Local Policies can be found in the following sections.

Account Policies

Account Policies include

- The Password Policy
- The Account Lockout Policy
- The Kerberos Policy

Account policies set in the Local Security Policy console affect only the local account database. If the server is joined in a domain, the domain-wide policies apply to all domain-level accounts used. The local account policies will only come into play if a user logs on using a local account database account. If the server is promoted to domain controller, the local account database is not accessible, and these settings have no meaning.

The Password Policy is set as:

- Enforce password history: 0 passwords remembered
  A user can continue to use the same password.

- Maximum password age: 42 days
  A user must change his password every 42 days.

- Minimum password age: 0 days
  A user can change his password whenever he wants.

- Minimum password length: 0 characters
  A blank password is okay.

- Passwords must meet complexity requirements: Disabled
  Any combination, or lack thereof, of letters and numbers is okay.

- Store passwords using reversible encryption: Disabled
  Passwords cannot be decrypted.

The Account Lockout Policy is as follows:

- Account lockout duration: Not Defined
  If the lockout threshold is set, this says how long the lockout will last.

- Account lockout threshold: 0 invalid logon attempts
  Users can have an infinite number of guesses at their passwords.

- Reset account lockout after: Not Defined
  If lockout has been defined, this specifies the number of minutes between invalid attempts at which point the counter restarts.

Kerberos Policy is established at the domain level. The server template includes the policy parameters but does not define them. The Local Policy for Professional, of course, does not include them.

Local Policies

Local Policies include

- Audit Policy
- User rights
- Security options

No Audit Policy is set by default.

User rights apply to user accounts. The basic rights for users were outlined in Chapter 6. User rights for server systems that have not been promoted to domain controller are the same as those for Professional. Account Operator, Server Operator, and Print Operator groups do not exist as local groups on the nondomain controller server; the Power Users group does exist.

When you examine the rights set in the console, keep in mind that these are initial settings that can be overwritten when the computer joins a domain. Local administrators, Domain Admins, Enterprise Admins, or Group Policy settings can make changes. When a computer joins a domain, the local policy settings are only effective if different settings are not made at the domain level or OU level. To determine effective rights, simply view the Effective Rights column within the Local Security Policy console.

Some user rights have no meaning on a standalone or member server but become meaningful when that server is promoted to domain controller. These user rights are

- Add workstations to domain.
- Enable computer and user accounts to be trusted for delegation.
- Synchronize directory service data.

The Security options available on Windows 2000 Server and their defaults are shown in Table 11.1. I have noted where Professional default settings are different from Server with an asterisk (*). Settings that change when a server is promoted to domain controller are in brackets [].

Table 11.1 **Windows 2000 Default Security Options**

Option	Local Default Setting
Additional restrictions for anonymous connections	None, rely on default permissions
Allow system to be shut down without having to log on	Disabled
	*Professional: Enabled
Allow to eject removable NTFS media	Administrators
Amount of idle time required before disconnecting sessions	15 minutes
Audit the access of global system objects	Disabled
Audit use of Backup and Restore privilege	Disabled
Automatically log off users when logon time expires (local)	Enabled [Disabled]
Clear virtual memory pagefile when system shuts down	Disabled
Digitally sign client communication (always)	Disabled
Digitally sign client communication (when possible)	Enabled [Disabled]
Digitally sign server communication (always)	Disabled
Digitally sign server communication (when possible)	Disabled [Enabled]
Disable Ctrl+Alt+Delete requirement for logon	Disabled

Option	Local Default Setting
Do not display last username in logon screen	Disabled
	★Professional: Not Defined
LAN Manager Authentication Level	Send LM & NTLM responses
Message text for users attempting to log on	
Message title for users attempting to log on	
Number of previous logons to cache (in case domain controller is not available)	10 logons
Prevent system maintenance of computer account password	Disabled
Prevent users from installing printer drivers	Enabled
	★Professional: Disabled
Prompt user to change password before expiration	14 days
Recovery console: Allow automatic administrative logon	Disabled
Recovery console: Allow floppy copy and access to all drives and all folders	Disabled
Rename Administrator account	Not Defined
Rename Guest account	Not Defined
Restrict CD-ROM access to locally logged-on user only	Disabled
Restrict floppy access to locally logged-on user only	Disabled
Secure channel: Digitally encrypt or sign secure channel data (always)	Disabled
Secure channel: Digitally encrypt secure channel data (when possible)	Enabled
Secure channel: Digitally sign secure channel data (when possible)	Enabled
Secure channel: Require strong (Windows 2000 or later) session key	Disabled
Send unencrypted password to connect to t hird-party SMB servers	Disabled
Shut down system immediately if unable to log security audits	Disabled
Smart card removal behavior	No Action
Strengthen default permissions of global system objects (for example, symbolic links)	Enabled
Unsigned driver installation behavior (Silently succeed, Warn but allow installation, Do not allow installation)	Not Defined
Unsigned nondriver installation behavior (Silently succeed, Warn but allow installation, Do not allow installation)	Not Defined

If you modify these settings, you are making changes to the registry. It's a lot easier to make changes and determine current settings in the console than it is to use a registry editor.

As stated, many of these options have the same definition for Server as for Professional (as described in Chapter 10 "Securing Windows 2000 Professional"). The following options are those that are *different* or that now have more significance because they are applied to Server.

Additional Restrictions for Anonymous Connections

Anonymous connections are used to list accounts and groups from the SAM. The Administrator of an NT 4.0 domain might use this list to give users in a trusting domain access to resources in the trusted domain. Individuals who should not have that access can abuse it to gain information about a domain. Because Windows 2000 Server and Professional systems have a local account database, you might want to close this hole by changing this setting to No Access Without Explicit Anonymous Permission or Do Not Allow Enumeration of SAM Accounts and Shares.

If you require explicit anonymous permissions, then you must also edit the registry to provide these permissions or include this information in the Registry Settings portion of the Security Policy or template. This is done by granting permission to appropriate users on the following key:

HKEY_LOCAL_MACHINE\SYSTEM\CurrentControlSet\Services\Control\ LSA\RestrictdAnonymous

Be very careful here. Many Windows 2000 services and third-party programs rely on anonymous access in order to work. If you change this policy in Security Options to Do Not Allow Enumeration of SAM Accounts and Shares or No Access Without Explicit Anonymous Permission (and do not provide access for users), the following problems may occur:

- Down-level member workstations or servers as well as down-level domain controllers cannot set up a NetLogon secure channel.
- NT users cannot change expired passwords.
- Macintosh users cannot change passwords.
- The browser service will not be able to obtain domain or server lists from master browsers on these systems.

Warning

The hisec templates change this setting to Do Not Allow Enumeration of SAM Accounts and Shares. Before applying these templates, you should carefully examine the repercussions and test in your lab to make sure your production systems do not break.

I recommend that you not use the setting Do Not Allow Enumeration of SAM Accounts and Shares if you have any down-level systems. Only apply No Access Without Explicit Anonymous Permission if you are willing to carefully test and provide permission for all necessary accounts. As in any configuration change, you must not apply to production systems unless you have thoroughly tested the results.

Allow System to Be Shut Down Without Having to Log on

This setting is disabled by default for servers to prevent accidental shutdown. Servers must remain available to users connecting across the network and are usually left up but with no session active. This setting is enabled by default for Professional. Users might appreciate the convenience of having the Shut Down button on the logon screen so they do not have to log on to shut down a system.

Digital Signing of Client and/or Server Communications (Four Settings)

Server Message Block (SMB) is the method of file sharing used in Windows systems. (It is now considered part of Common Internet File Systems.) Digital signing refers to SMB signing, although it is not normally set because it slows performance. It does, however, make communication more secure. If it is set to always be enabled, the computer will not be able to connect to a computer that cannot digitally sign SMB packets. That is why the Security Option that indicates signing will be set for clients when possible. If a client attempts a connection with a server that is asking for digital signing, the client can respond.

SMB signing settings are primarily provided to assist in securing communications from down-level clients. Windows 2000 systems can be configured to use the IP Security (IPSec) protocol.

Disable Ctrl+Alt+Delete Requirement for Logon

As mentioned in the preceding chapter, this policy can be an end-run around smart card logon requirements. When smart card logon has been configured and smart cards and readers have been provided for all users, your policy might be to insist that smart cards always be used. When smart card authentication is installed, the GINA is modified to allow either the traditional Ctrl+Alt+Delete leading to a request for user ID and password, or the insertion of a smart card into a smart card reader, which then prompts for a PIN.

You might want to remove the option to use Ctrl+Alt+Delete on all workstations. You can use this policy to do so. Be very careful to apply this policy to workstation systems, not to domain controllers. (Some operations require administrators to log on and provide a password.)

Do Not Display Last User Name in Logon Screen

This option has been discussed in the Chapter 10; however, it is interesting to note that the default for Server is Disabled, while for Professional it is Not Defined.

Prevent System Maintenance of Computer Account Password

Every Windows NT Workstation and Server and every Windows 2000 Professional and Server that are joined in a domain have a secure communications channel with their domain controller. The password for this channel is stored with the computer account by the domain controller (NT: SAM; 2000: AD) and in the local computer Local Security Authority (LSA) secret account for the local system. This password is frequently changed (every 7 days in NT; every 30 days in Windows 2000) and then replicated with other data. In a large enterprise with large numbers of workstations, these frequent password changes can cause network congestion and communication problems if passwords are out of synch.

Selecting this option in Local Security Policy on a Windows 2000 system will prevent password changes. Selecting this option in Domain Controllers Policy will enable the domain controller to refuse the password change.

Prevent Users from Installing Printer Drivers

Although the Local Security Policy of the Professional system disables this option and thus allows users to install printer drivers, Server installs with this option enabled, thus preventing the ordinary user from installing a printer driver. Domain Admins, Server Operators, Administrators, and Printer Operators will still be able to install printer drivers. For more information see this section in the preceding chapter.

Secure Channel: Digitally Encrypt or Sign Secure Channel Data (Always)

Domain controllers and their clients, and domain controllers in a trust relationship, need to communicate for the purpose of authenticating computer accounts, user accounts, and trusts. These communications might cross routers, leased lines, and public networks. Rather than describe the real path that these communications take, we simply speak of the logical connection as if it were between two servers connected by the same cable. The name for this logical connection is *secure channel*. Figure 11.1 illustrates the logical connection. Four secure channel settings allow for backward compatibility or Windows 2000–only security.

If this setting is enabled and client and server cannot negotiate an encryption level, no secure channel can be established and communication will fail. (A client cannot log on, for example). However, communication that does take place will be more secure from attack.

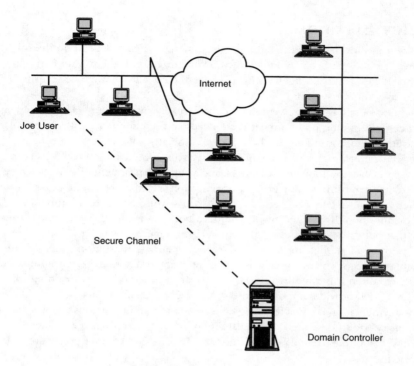

Figure 11.1 The secure channel.

Secure Channel: Digitally Encrypt Secure Channel Data (When Possible)

If data–encryption–level negotiation fails, communication can still take place, but data is less secure.

Secure Channel: Digitally Sign Secure Channel Data (When Possible)

If signing cannot take place, communication still can.

Secure Channel: Require Strong (Windows 2000 or Later) Session Key

In a native-mode Windows 2000 domain (no NT 4.0 domain controllers) with no down-level clients, enable this setting to use the strongest encryption.

Policy Settings

Policy settings for Servers, like those for Professional systems, depend on the role the system plays and the Security Policy of your organization. If there is no corporate Security Policy, you still might want to change the defaults to improve security on a particular system or systems.

The best policy is always written by considering security needs and requirements and then determining how to meet these needs and requirements with a particular operating system. You might not have a written Security Policy, nor the time or authority to prepare one. You can, however, set your OS security policies based on the settings available, the provided templates, and your understanding of good security as tempered by your knowledge of your organization's needs and requirements. In this manner you can obtain a degree of security while working on the ideal policy with your organization. If you do obtain an official policy at a later date, you then need to apply that policy where it differs from the existing one.

Windows NT 4.0 left most security settings open. Administrators could ignore security settings or create a policy as best as they could. Those experienced in security issues were often frustrated by the lack of a clear-cut methodology for doing so. Windows 2000 provides a more secure system right out of the box and provides for easy implementation of policies using consoles described in previous chapters. Chapter 9, "Security Tools," described the availability of security templates for different Windows 2000 roles. Templates available for Windows 2000 Server policy are described next.

Server Security Templates

The Security Configuration and Analysis tool can be used, as described in Chapter 9, to analyze the server's security settings against other preconfigured templates or against one you create. There are two categories of preconfigured templates available for Server: One set of templates can be used against a standalone or member server; another can be used to analyze and configure a domain controller. Each category has basic, secure, and high-security templates. In addition, there is one server Optional Component File Security template (ocfiless.inf) and one compatibility template (compatws.inf).

As previously discussed, you can examine the default settings for all available templates by creating an MMC and opening the Security Templates snap-in. You can also modify these templates. To analyze existing settings against a template or to apply a new template, you open the Security Configuration and Analysis snap-in. You also can restore default security (that is, return the server to its "just-installed" status) by applying the basic templates.

There are a number of templates provided for use with Server. In addition, two templates provided for use with Professional (securews.inf and hisecws.inf) can also be used with Server. Preconfigured templates for Server are as follows:

- **Basic templates** hold settings like those made during server install (basicsv.inf) or during promotion to domain controller (basicdc.inf).

- **Secure templates** (securedc.inf and securews.inf) apply settings that make the system more secure. Password policy, account lockout, and audit policies are set. Some security options are changed.

- **High-security templates** (hisecdc.inf and hisecws.inf) apply settings that impact network security; for example, they set LM authentication to accept only NTLMv2.

- **The Optional Component File Security template** (ocfiless.inf) sets file and registry settings to those that would be set during the installation of these optional components during setup. (Optional components are programs like Terminal Services and Web Services.)

- **The compatibility template** (compatws.inf) can be used to change registry and file settings to those used in Windows NT 4.0. This provides greater access to the registry and file system and can be used to allow legacy applications to run.

Tip

Use the compatibility template if you need to use legacy applications that will not run under the default settings on Server or Professional systems. This does reduce security, but it allows the applications to run, and you will not have to make users members of Power Users to do so. In addition, once the application has been replaced or upgraded so that it meets compatibility standards for Windows 2000, you can apply a template to return a higher level of security. You do not, therefore, have to remember which users are Power Users, or should be, or worry that you have changed users' rights. The change should be transparent to users.

If you need to reset a system to virgin configuration, remember that templates apply security incrementally. That is, they do not include settings that might have been made in previous templates. For example, the hisecdc template does not include settings that might have been made in the securedc template. You cannot obtain the cumulative settings produced by applying the default settings and then basicdc, securedc, and hisecdc by simply applying hisecdc. You can recreate the settings mix by applying all templates in order.

To apply a higher security level, you can create your own templates, modify existing ones, or use the additional templates provided.

Using and Securing Terminal Services

Terminal Services is an optional service that can be installed on Server or Advanced Server. Terminal services has two modes: Application Server mode and Remote Administration mode. The Application Server mode of Terminal Services allows non-Windows (using third-party products) and Windows clients to access centrally operated and administered applications in a multiuser environment. The applications run on the server; only keystrokes, mouse clicks, and display screens cross the network. Remote administration of any Windows 2000 Server can be provided by enabling the Terminal Services Administrative mode.

Tip

Terminal Services can be enabled on Windows 2000 servers that play any role, but you should not enable application sharing on Windows 2000 domain controllers. To allow access to applications running on Terminal Servers, users must have the right to log on locally, even though they are accessing the server across the network. The right to log on locally, though given for accessing Terminal Server–hosted applications, does give them the capability to sit at the Terminal Server and log on interactively. Don't give them the right to log on locally to your domain controller!

Terminal Server clients can access the server over a wide range of connections including the Internet, dial-up remote access, wireless, WAN, and VPN. If the service must be accessed across firewalls and routers, be sure to allow communications across port 3389, the Remote Desktop Protocol port. (If you are restricting client access to particular subnets, be sure this port remains closed on routers that connect to other networks.)

Clients are available for CE devices, MS-DOS, Windows for Workgroups and better Windows systems, UNIX, and Macintosh.

To secure Terminal Services, you will use many of the same functions used to secure Server. These standard functions are

- User profiles
- Group Policy
- NTFS
- User rights
- Guest access
- Data encryption

These functions are described elsewhere (see the "For More Information" section later in this chapter). There are, however, some unique security tasks and tips of which you should be aware. They include the following:

- Logon rights
- Application issues

- The Terminal Services Configuration Tool
- Data encryption

Logon Rights

If Terminal Services is installed on a standalone server, mandatory user profiles can be used to restrict user access to applications. If Terminal Services is installed on a member server, separate domain profiles and mandatory Terminal Services profiles can be used. When the user is connected to the Terminal Server, the mandatory Terminal Server profile will be used. When he accesses domain resources, his domain profile will be used.

Administrators will use Group Policy to control registry settings and folder settings, specifically for Terminal Services computers. All partitions should be NTFS. User areas can be protected from other users, and applications can be protected from modification.

When Terminal Services is enabled, user rights are changed. If the mode enabled is Application Sharing, all members of the Users group are granted logon local rights. You should change this default by doing the following:

1. Create a group called TerminalUsers.

2. Give this group the logon local right.

3. Remove the logon local right from the Users group.

4. Place only those who need to access the applications into the TerminalUsers group.

Terminal Services in Remote Administration mode does not grant local logon rights to Users. Only Administrators need to be able to log on locally to use it, and they already have that right.

Note
Smart cards cannot be used to authenticate Terminal Server access.

Application Issues

When enabling Terminal Services in Application Sharing mode, you will be asked to select a permission level for users of Terminal Services. If you select Permissions Compatible with Windows 2000 Users, you will have the most secure settings, but some legacy applications will not run. These legacy applications might need access to registry and file locations to which Windows 2000 users do not have access. If you need to ensure the capability to use legacy applications, choose Permissions Compatible with Terminal Server 4.0 Users.

Users logged on using the RDP client are automatically members of the implicit Terminal Services Users local group. To control Terminal Services users, control this group. This group is already restricted. They cannot install applications or invoke the Windows installer. The Windows installer is sometimes used to install missing parts of applications. Because the Terminal Services Users local group cannot invoke the Windows installer, users cannot install missing parts of applications. Terminal Services users, therefore, unlike normal Windows users, cannot install any kind of application on the Terminal Server.

Terminal Services Configuration Tool

A Terminal Services–specific tool, the Terminal Services Configuration Tool, is used to assign user permissions and to disconnect sessions.

> **Tip**
> Configure guest access in the Client Connection Manager so no user can connect without entering a username and password. If you leave Guest access enabled, any user with an RDP client can connect to the Terminal Server.

Data Encryption

Encrypt data transfer. Choose from three levels:

- **Low.** RC4, 56-bit key. Encryption is client to server.
- **Medium.** Traffic in both directions is encrypted.
- **High.** RC4 with a 128-bit key.

You can protect data further by setting up VPN tunnels between clients and servers or router to router using PPTP or L2TP tunnels with encryption. For a discussion of the increased protection added via tunnels, see Chapter 15, "Secure Remote Access Options."

Securing Interoperability Services

Several services are available for Windows 2000 that enable you to have various levels of compatibility with other operating systems. Services for Macintosh allows Macintosh users to authenticate in a Windows 2000 domain and access files and printers. These services are provided with Windows 2000. Services for UNIX must be purchased separately.

Services for Macintosh

Shared files and printers are made available to Macintosh users by installing and configuring File Services for Macintosh and Print Services for Macintosh. There are several "gotchas" that can cause problems in setting this up and issues that make your system more vulnerable.

If your requirements are simply to provide Macintosh users with access to resources, configuration is simple, but you must follow a few rules:

- Macintosh clients and the Windows 2000 system must both use TCP/IP or both use AppleTalk. Macintosh systems need Ethernet connectivity, or your server needs a LocalTalk card. (Token Ring on both systems also can be used.) You must establish network connectivity.
- At least one NTFS partition must be available. This was recently changed.
- Macintosh users must have a User Authentication Module (UAM) installed. Microsoft and Apple provide UAMs. The UAM is used to interface with the Windows 2000 authentication system.
- Macintosh users must have a valid Windows user ID and password.

To make your Macintosh/Windows 2000 connectivity secure, you must also take into account normal security configuration (folder and file permissions) and consider special Macintosh issues. Macintosh issues include

- File and folder permission differences between the OSs
- The need for reversibly encrypted passwords to be stored for Macintosh users
- The difference between the Apple UAM and the Microsoft UAM
- Difficulties in restricting print services for Macintosh users

Permission Differences

It is the permission differences and file-handling processes that require the designation of a volume for use by Macintosh users. When File Services for Macintosh is installed, this volume is prepared to interpret the permission differences. Once established, Macintosh and Windows users can store, access, edit, and delete files and folders if permissions are established for their user or group accounts. Both types of users can share files as well. Macintosh users will not be able to access volumes that have not been designated for use by Macintosh systems. This enables you to restrict their access. Setting permissions on folders further restricts access. You also can set a password on the volume. This password is not restricted to a particular user, but you can limit the Macintosh users who can access this volume by controlling the distribution of the password.

File permissions on Macintosh systems prior to OS 8.5 are

- See Files (see and read files in a folder)
- See Folders (see folders within a folder)
- Make Changes (modify file content; rename, move, create, and delete files)

If the Macintosh OS is 8.5 or above, it supports Windows-like privileges:

- Read-only
- Write-only (add files or folders)
- Read and Write (add, delete, change)
- None (prevents access)

Macintosh groups are Owners, User/Group, and Everyone. A file or folder is either private (only the owner needs to see and use it), available for a group, or public property. Folder-level permissions, but not file permissions, are supported. It is possible to inadvertently lock Macintosh users out of files if Windows users set permissions on the files that are different than those on the folders.

Reversibly Encrypted Passwords

Macintosh users must have Windows 2000 user IDs and passwords. If they already have accounts that can be used from their Macintosh systems, there is no need to give them a new account. Authentication choices are

- Allow guest access
- Allow cleartext passwords
- Use Apple Standard Encryption (the Apple UAM), up to 8 character passwords
- Use the Microsoft User Authentication Method (UAM), up to 14 character passwords

Encrypted options (all except cleartext) do not send the password over the network. The server provides a random number that the Macintosh client encrypts using the user-entered password. This response, or nonce, is returned to the server, which can compare it to its own user-password encrypted challenge. If the results match, the client is authenticated.

Normal Windows authentication does not require the server to store the password in reversibly encrypted form. A one-way encrypted password (OWF) is stored. Because Windows clients can use the same algorithm to encrypt the user-provided password, an algorithm based on using the OWF password can be used. One-way encryption is considered to be more secure than reversibly encrypted.

For Macintosh users to log on to Windows 2000 systems, however, their passwords must be stored in reversibly encrypted form. This can be done in the Default Domain Policy console in the Password Policy container.

Tip

There is no way to provide reversibly encrypted passwords for Macintosh users only. Once you take this step, you are making all passwords more vulnerable to attack. Therefore, if a more secure environment is necessary, isolate the Macintosh users to a single domain or standalone server. The other domains can keep the default OWF password form.

You should also take care to identify the Primary group for each Macintosh user in the user's property pages. The Primary group setting has no real meaning in general, but for Macintosh users, it designates the group that should have ownership of a folder that a Macintosh user creates. You will want to make this the group that the Macintosh user, or the group of Macintosh users for which he is creating folders, uses most frequently.

UAMs

For Macintosh users to log on using their Windows user accounts, they will need to load a UAM. Macintosh provides a module, but the Microsoft UAM will provide you with a higher level of security. The Microsoft UAM allows longer passwords (14 characters versus 8) and always encrypts the password. The Apple UAM can use cleartext or encrypted passwords.

Printer Permissions

If a Macintosh user can connect to a Windows 2000–managed printer across the network, the Mac user can print to it. There is no native Macintosh printer authentication. You cannot restrict Macintosh user access to printers in the normal Windows 2000 way (by setting DACLs for any user or group in printer properties). If Peter is a Macintosh user with an account ID of PeterP and you set the DACL on the printer to deny him print privileges, he will still be able to print.

Instead, to restrict all Macintosh users, you configure the MacPrint service. This service is installed as part of the installation process when you install Services for Macintosh. It is configured to run under the Local System Account. Configure it to run under a Windows 2000 user account that you provide for this purpose. You can then restrict this account's use of each printer in the normal manner. If you want all Macintosh users to print, do nothing. Because the user account will be a member of the Users group, which by default can print, all Macintosh users will be able to print. If you want to keep Macintosh users from printing to a printer, you must create a group of users that can print (don't include the MacPrinter user) or specifically deny the MacPrinter user account.

Services for UNIX

Services for UNIX provides password synchronization, a Telnet server, a scripting tool, the Korn shell, numerous utilities, and the capability to share files and printers with UNIX systems.

UNIX systems often use the Network File System (NFS) to share files among UNIX systems. NFS uses the same logical concept with which Windows users are familiar. NFS allows a file system to be logically *mounted* on a client system. To the client, the data seems to be on a local drive. This is similar to the share mapping used in the Windows world. In both systems, users read and write files without caring where the data actually resides.

NFS is based on the Open Network Computing Remote Procedure Call (ONC-RPC). Remote Procedure Calls (RPCs) are described in RFCs 1831, 1050, and 1057. NFS data transfer uses Open Network Computing External Data Representation (XDR), described in RFC 1832 and 1014.

The XDR data transfer protocol is not used by Windows 2000, but Services for UNIX implements NFS on Windows 2000. Users using a UNIX client must have a Windows 2000 account and be permitted access to the shared volume. Because UNIX users are identified by user ID (UID) and group ID (GID) and Windows users are identified by SID and group SID, you must map UNIX users to Windows 2000 users. You also need to map UNIX groups to Windows groups. This is done in a configuration utility on the Windows 2000 systems that have had Services for UNIX installed. Figure 11.2 shows UNIX user peterp mapped to Windows user PeterP, and the UNIX group Staff mapped to the Windows Users group. If a folder is provided and the Users group is given Full Control, Windows user PeterP can create a file called secret, grant Full Control to himself and the staff group, and grant other permissions as well. If he then logs on to his UNIX system and mounts the volume, the file will appear listed as:

```
rwxrwxr_x 1 peterp staff 2347 March 5 12.59 secret
```

The first nine characters identify who has what kind of access on the file. The first three characters represent the permissions for the owner, the second three for the group, and the third three for others.

To secure access for UNIX clients, set original permissions on the mountable volumes to provide the access desired and nothing more. Place UNIX users in appropriate UNIX groups and, on Windows 2000, in complementary groups. Map UNIX users and groups to Windows 2000 users and groups. Cooperation between Windows 2000 and UNIX administrators is of paramount importance if secure access is to be achieved.

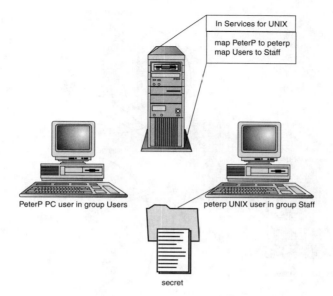

Figure 11.2 Mapping users and groups.

Password synchronization can be accomplished between Windows and UNIX clients for those UNIX clients mapped to Windows 2000 user accounts. Synchronization is one-way. Users must change their passwords on the Windows 2000 side, and the information is propagated to UNIX systems. The data can be encrypted if a ssod (single sign on daemon) is loaded on the UNIX systems or in cleartext if it is not. A ssod is available for some UNIX systems, and sample source code is provided by Microsoft with the product should you want to write your own for other UNIX systems. The ssod uses 3DES for encryption. Ssod can interoperate with NIS (a network management system for UNIX). In this case, the ssod is only placed on the NIS management system UNIX server. Passwords are delivered to the NIS system, and then it propagates changes to the other UNIX servers that it controls.

Figure 11.3 shows password synchronization to different UNIX systems. Password synchronization is controlled by defining PODs in Services for UNIX. A POD represents a group of UNIX systems. If there are differences in synchronization (for example, the difference when NIS is used on the UNIX side), then servers must be in a different POD. In the figure, the Windows 2000 Server is running Services for UNIX and can synchronize passwords with two PODs (in this example, only two pods are being synchronized, more pods could be managed). POD 1 consists of three UNIX systems. When Joe User changes his password from his Windows client, the change is passed on to each server in POD 1. POD2 is managed by an NIS Domain Master. Joe User's password change is passed to the NIS Domain Master, which passes it on to the two UNIX hosts it controls.

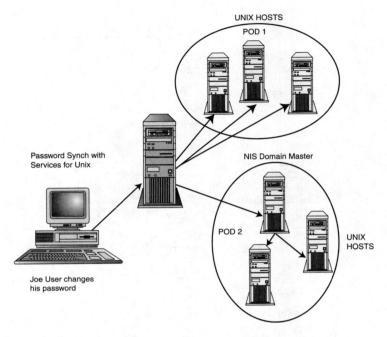

Figure 11.3 Windows 2000 and UNIX password synch.

Print services for UNIX is provided with Windows 2000. It does not give UNIX users administrative privileges over Windows 2000 printers. It does run a lpdsvc (line printer daemon service) service that will respond to UNIX client lpr (line printer) commands.

Best Practices

To secure Windows 2000 Server, you should observe the following best practices:

- Install Terminal Services on member servers or standalone servers, not as domain controllers.
- Install Terminal Services on NTFS partitions.
- Use the command-line tsshutdn command to shut down Terminal Server. Using the shutdown Start menu option does not notify users. Users might have files open and data loss can occur.
- Place users in Terminal Service user groups and use Terminal Server–specific, mandatory profiles.
- Use the Terminal Services starting program option. This will restrict users to this program.

- Create preconfigured client connections for groups of users. Use these to restrict clients.

- Install the Microsoft UAM on all Macintosh systems that will be accessing files, folders, or printers in the Windows 2000 network.

- Restrict Macintosh users to one domain or to a standalone server and restrict their access by only creating Macintosh-accessible volumes on as few file servers as possible.

- Carefully investigate any changes to security options.

- Test changes in a lab before deploying.

- Determine which provided template to use as a base for configuring security. Then add any changes you want. Save as custom templates and apply across all like systems via scripting or Group Policy.

- Use Group Policy to the fullest in your domains to make and maintain security configurations.

For More Information

This chapter discussed services for which complementary information exists in other chapters of this book. The following should serve as a referral source for you in locating this information.

An introduction to asymmetric encryption can be found in Chapter 2, "Cryptology Introduction."

A discussion of LM, NTLM, and NTLMv2 authentication protocols can be found in Chapter 3, "New Protocols, Products, and APIs."

A generic Public Key Infrastructure was described in Chapter 4, "Public Key Infrastructure (PKI)."

In-depth information on Kerberos and the Windows 2000 implementation can be found in Chapter 5, "Kerberos in the RAW," and Chapter 6, "Security from the Get-Go."

For a discussion of Distributed Security Services, see Chapter 16, "Securing the Network Using Distributed Security Services."

For a discussion on domain security issues, see Chapter 12, "Domain-Level Security." A discussion on securing Windows NT and Windows 9x clients can be found in Chapter 13, "Securing Legacy Windows Clients."

In addition, several services were introduced in the "Server Roles" section in this chapter. More information on these services can be found in chapters shown in Table 11.2.

Table 11.2 **Windows 2000 Server as a Services Server**

Service	Description	Chapter Reference
Routing and Remote Access Services	A collection of services that allow a server to be a router, demand–dial router, or remote access server.	15
Demand-Dial Routing	Allows the connection of networks across a demand–dial infrastructure such as POTS.	15
NAT	Stands for Network Address Translation. Allows the use of one Internet IP address by many computers.	15
Remote Access Service	Allows dial-in access to organization's network.	15
Tunnel Services	Combines remote access services and security protocols to create virtual private networks.	15
Internet Authentication Services	Microsoft RADIUS server/ authentication, authorization and accounting for remote access clients.	15
Certificate Services	Establishes Public certificates for authentication, smart cards; controls EFS Recovery Agent keys.	17
Web Services	Internet Information Server 5.0.	19
Terminal Services	Administrative or Application mode. Supports multiuser operations.	11
DHCP	Dynamic Host Configuration Protocol (dynamic assignment of IP address).	12
Domain Name Server	DNS server/Dynamic DNS.	12
Services for Macintosh	File and print services for Macintosh users.	11
Services for UNIX	An add-on product.	11

Summary

This chapter explored default security settings for Windows 2000 Server. It also introduced issues in securing the operating system by using Local Security Policies and by securing services that you install.

In the past, you were often given similar explicit instructions for securing a single NT server. The tools to do so were different, but many of the instructions were the same. When you asked how to translate those settings to multiple computers or attempted to address issues beyond these functional methods, you often received a Script It response. If you worked really hard and talked to lots of people, you might have eventually, system by system, patched together the best way to secure your network.

Security for Windows 2000 should not be approached in a piecemeal fashion. The holistic approach should be used and used from the beginning. The tools are available to do this. You can finally cross the boundary from thinking about a local system to thinking about the global system of which it is a part. To begin, you must understand the Windows 2000 domain structure and the AD. These issues will be discussed in the following chapters.

III

Securing the Local Area, Microsoft Network

Domain-Level Security

ALTHOUGH THE BASIC OPERATING SYSTEM PROVIDES SOUND security and a range of methods to harden the system, the Windows 2000 domain provides substantial benefits and opportunities to excel in security management and policy enforcement. The Windows 2000 domain, which logically groups multiple Windows 2000 and Windows NT 4.0 computers and provides for centralized control, can be initialized by promoting a Windows 2000 Server or Advanced Server to a domain controller. Next, other Windows 2000 Servers, Windows 2000 Professional systems, Windows NT 4.0 servers, and NT 4.0 workstations can be joined to the domain and can benefit from increased, distributed security operations as well as centralized administration and control. Distributed security services such as Single Sign-On, EFS recovery management, Public Key Infrastructure (PKI), Kerberos authentication, and comprehensive access control become possible, centrally manageable, or truly operational at the domain level.

To harness the power of these distributed security services and to be able to implement them, you must

- Understand the Active Directory (AD)
- Learn how to secure dynamic DNS
- Investigate domain policies such as Kerberos, IPSec, and Public Key
- Compare network authentication methods

This chapter will cover these topics.

Introduction to Active Directory (AD) Concepts

Active Directory (AD) is the directory service included with Windows 2000. Information about network objects and services is stored in the AD and is thus available to users, applications, and computers. Its organization is based on the Domain Name Service (DNS) hierarchical naming system, and although it is not an RFC standard X.500 directory, its structure is similar. Like a telephone book, which has white pages for alphabetical lookup by name and yellow pages for lookup by service, the AD can be referenced in more than one way. To understand AD, you will need to learn its hierarchical structure and be familiar with DNS. DNS and AD are interlinked in several ways:

- Before the AD can be installed, DNS must be available on the network.
- DNS hierarchical naming is used for AD domain names.
- The location of AD services is determined via DNS query.

AD does not require Windows 2000 DNS; however, the DNS used must support the IETF RFC 2052, "A DNS RR for Specifying the Location of Services (DNS SRV)," which specifies the use of *resource records*. Resource records are records that can be used to locate network services. Windows 2000, Windows NT 4.0 (SP4), BIND 8.2, BIND 8.1.2, and BIND 4.9.7 support these features. Windows 2000 DNS, however, provides some features that BIND, or some versions of BIND, does not. Specifically:

- Windows 2000, BIND 8.2, and BIND 8.1.2 support dynamic update.
- Only Windows 2000 uses the secure dynamic update based on GSS-TSIG.
- Windows 2000 and Windows NT 4.0 support WINS and WINS-R records.
- Windows 2000 and BIND 8.2 support incremental zone transfer.

Service Records

AD servers publish their addresses using Service Resource Records (SRV RRs). SRV RRs map a service to a server that provides that service. This makes it easier for clients to find a required service. Service records include information about the service, the protocol, and the fully qualified domain name (FQDN). If the DNS server supports dynamic updates, the SRV RRs for a server are dynamically published during installation. Dynamic DNS allows automatic name registration by approved servers. AD servers use TCP for Lightweight Directory Access Protocol (LDAP), a directory search protocol. As per the standard, a SRV RR has the format:

Service.protocol.name TTL Class SRV Priority Weight Port Target

Service is the service offered such as Kerberos or LDAP. Protocol can be either TCP or UDP. Name is the name of the domain. TTL stands for Time To Live, and the class is SRV, or service. Priority can be used to specify a particular order for clients to access one of multiple hosts. If there are several with the same priority, weight can be used to assist in load balancing. Port is the port on the target host of this service. Target is the domain name of the target host.

The general format for an LDAP service record, then, would be ldap.tcp.domainname. The service record for the peachweaver domain is ldap.tcp.peachweaver.com.

The Windows 2000 dcpromo program is used to promote a Windows 2000 Server to be a domain controller. It can be entered from a command line or chosen from the Configure Your Server applet available from Administrative Tools in the Start menu. AD is created as part of this promotion. If a DNS server is not available in the network, Microsoft DNS can be installed at this time, too.

In Windows 2000 a domain identifies the objects (computers, printers, users, services) that can be centrally administered and also provides a security boundary. Objects can thus be managed by appointed administrators. These administrators have no privileges outside their domain boundary. Meanwhile, privileges they might exercise within the domain cannot be applied in other domains, and security policies instituted within the domain do not extend to other domains.

Active Directory Hierarchy

The AD hierarchy is composed of sites, trees, forests, domains, and organizational units (OUs). The basic unit upon which the hierarchy is built is the domain. Domains are logically collected into the hierarchical structures called trees and forests, physically subnetted into sites, and themselves composed of inner groupings of users and computers called organizational units.

Trees and Forests

Each domain can have a parent, or a domain that exists above it, in the hierarchy. Each domain also can have one or many child domains, which exist below the domain in the hierarchy. The hierarchy allows easy search and retrieval of information about the location of resources within it. It does not, however, imply control of resources within domains that are lower in the hierarchy by those higher in the hierarchy.

Instead of inventing some new naming standard to indicate the hierarchical relationship, Windows 2000 domains use DNS naming conventions. Domains that share the same DNS namespace are said to be in the same tree. A diagram of the tree looks like an inverse tree with the root domain at the top of the structure. Figure 12.1 provides an illustration of a single AD tree that shows parent and child domains. The root domain peachweaver.com has the children alberta.peachweaver.com and missouri.peachweaver.com.

If different namespaces exist, domains still can be part of the same hierarchical structure. In this case, they each will reside in their own tree with their own root but will be combined together into a forest. Figure 12.2 illustrates this point by joining the peachweaver.com tree to the colorgrinder.com tree. The lines between the domains indicate trust relationships. The two trees are joined by a trust relationship. This particular situation might arise when one company acquires another.

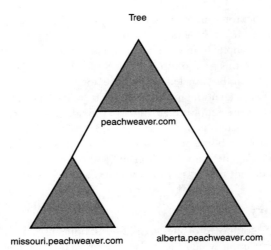

Figure 12.1   An Active Directory tree.

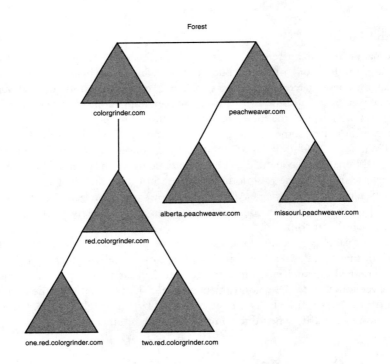

Figure 12.2   An Active Directory forest.

Organizational Units (OUs)

Each domain can be subdivided into internal groups of computers and users. These groups, or organizational units (OUs), contain subsections of the domain's computers, users, or both. Wise distribution of users and computers into OUs can allow the delegation of administrative chores to nonadministrative personnel and can ease in the application of security and control.

Sites

Just as forests, trees, OUs, and domains model a logical network, *sites* model a physical network. Although computers in a domain might exist entirely at one physical location, they do not have to. Each domain's domain controllers, member servers, and Windows 2000 Professional systems can be present at many locations.

Because each location will have its own set of subnetworks, a site is defined by this collection of subnetworks. If a Windows 2000 computer has an address in one of the subnetworks for a defined site, the Windows 2000 computer is said to be part of that site.

The definition of sites does more than give you another way to define a group of computers; it allows Windows 2000 to more efficiently manage the replication of AD information between physical locations. It also allows the dissemination of administrative and security controls, which impact computer systems in several domains. For information on how this dissemination can be accomplished and the issues it entails, see Chapter 16, "Securing the Network Using Distributed Security Services."

Schema

Domains, OUs, computers, users—these are just a few of the objects in the AD. To track these objects and define their properties, the AD uses a *schema*. The schema is composed of classes and attributes. A class is merely a description of what attributes an object might have, what attributes it must have, and what relationship the object has to other objects. Attributes are the properties that can be used by a class. The user class has attributes such as name, email address, password, and so on. When a new object (the physical implementation of a class) is created, its attributes are given specific meaning. User, then, describes a class; the user Nancy Smith concretely defines a specific user that has specific attributes defined. (Her name is Nancy Smith, her email address is Nsmith@anydomain.com, her password is ******, and so on.)

Global Catalog

Complete domain data is stored on every domain controller and is replicated between all domain controllers in the domain. Domain data is also replicated between domains in a multiple-domain forest. But, although every object in the domain's directory is replicated between domains, not all of the attributes of the object are replicated, and not all domain controllers store the information from other domains. The interdomain replicated information is stored in the *Global Catalog*. Domain controllers within the domain are designated as *Global Catalog servers*.

Trust Relationships

Windows NT 4.0 domains allow resource access across domain boundaries if the domains are participating in a trust relationship. NT 4.0 trust relationships have to be specifically arranged, can be difficult to maintain, are one-way, and are not transitive.

Figure 12.3 displays three domains: A, B, and C. Domain A trusts Domain B, and Domain B trusts Domain C. Because trust is nontransitive, however, Domain C does not trust Domain A. Furthermore, because the trust is one-way, Domain C does not trust Domain B, and Domain B does not trust Domain A. In a large environment, this imposes a significant administrative burden. Before Compaq Computer Corporation changed over to Windows 2000, for example, one system administrator's entire job was to manage these trusts.

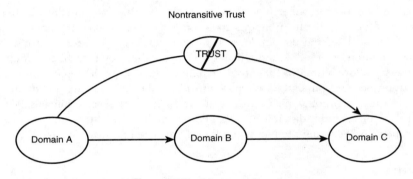

Figure 12.3 Nontransitive trust.

Windows 2000 trusts are automatically defined when

- A server is promoted to domain controller and is joined to an existing domain
- The first domain controller in a new domain elects a parent domain

In addition, Windows 2000 trusts are transitive and two-way. Figure 12.4 shows three domains: A, B, and C. Domain A trusts Domain B, and Domain B trusts Domain C. Transitive trust means that trust relationships do not have to be explicitly defined for all domains. Therefore, Domain C trusts Domain A. Because trusts are two-way, Domain A trusts Domain C, Domain B trusts Domain A, and so on. Trust relationships are maintained as part of the AD structure.

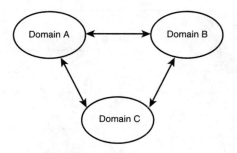

Figure 12.4 Transitive trust.

Trust relationships can also be manually defined. This is the case when

- Two or more trees are joined to create a forest
- You want to create a trust between NT 4.0 domains and Windows 2000 domains
- You want to create a trust between a Windows 2000 domain and a Kerberos realm
- Shortcut trusts are defined to improve hierarchical searches

The beauty of AD lies in its capability to provide an enterprise-wide service. Search utilities can travel up and down the hierarchy to find the location of a required resource or service. Unfortunately, as the AD grows, so does the time required to do the search. For important connections between objects spaced far from each other, it might be necessary to create shortcut trust to facilitate the search.

Figure 12.5 shows a shortcut trust between missouri.peachweaver.com and counter.acme.colorgrinder.com. A server in counter.acme.colorgrinder.com is an enterprise Certificate Authority (CA). As such, it must make available a list of revoked (not to be trusted) certificates. It does so by publishing a Certificate Revocation List (CRL). The shortcut trust allows a quicker response (because the Kerberos trust path is shorter) to the missouri.peachweaver.com domain when access to the CRL for this CA is needed. As described in Chapter 5, "Kerberos in the RAW," Kerberos tickets must be obtained between Kerberos trust paths in a hierarchical trust. The diagram shows, using plain arrows, the ordinary path taken to obtain the ticket and the shortcut path (the bold arrow) between the two domains.

Trust relationships assist hierarchical searches and can provide a way to extend resource access across domain boundaries. They do *not* automatically extend authority or resource access privileges to nondomain members. An administrator in one domain has no privileges in another. As a user in one domain, I have no access rights to files or printers in another domain. All access and privileges must be explicitly granted. The trust relationship merely exposes the list of users and computers in one domain to another domain's administrators so they can assign privileges and access as appropriate.

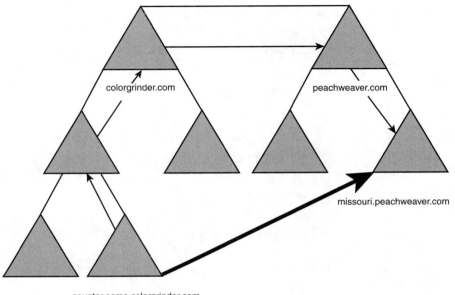

Figure 12.5 Shortcut trust.

Data Storage and Replication

The Windows 2000 AD stores data for an entire forest. The AD directory tree is parti-tioned into logical segments. Some of these segments contain forest-wide information such as schema (data about data) or configuration data; others store only information about a single domain (that is, user and group information). Each partition is replicated so that data is available as needed. Replication is multimaster, which means changes can be made at any domain controller and will be replicated to all domain controllers. Although data is *physically* distributed, it is *logically* centralized.

Every domain stores forest-wide schema and configuration information, so every domain can reference every other domain. Each distinct item in the directory is called an object, and every object is defined by its attributes. With the exception of the initial domain creation, only changes to attributes and the creation and deletion of objects are replicated.

Mixed Mode, Native Mode

Windows 2000 domains are said to be in either mixed mode or native mode. When a server is promoted to domain controller, it is placed by default into mixed mode. Mixed mode means that Windows NT 4.0 domain controllers can function as members of the domain. This facility is provided to ease migration from Windows NT 4.0 to Windows 2000. When all Windows NT domain controllers have been retired or upgraded to Windows 2000 domain controllers, you can change the mode to native.

Native mode domains can have the following as members:

- Windows 2000 domain controllers
- Windows 2000 member servers
- Windows 2000 Professional
- Windows NT 4.0 member servers
- Windows NT 4.0 workstations

Windows 9x computers can be clients in a Windows 2000 native mode or mixed mode domain. The only Windows 9x and above computer that a Windows 2000 native mode domain *cannot* have is a Windows NT 4.0 domain controller.

To change a domain to native mode, you use the AD Domains and Trusts console and change the mode on the General Properties page.

Note

After a domain mode has been changed to native mode, it cannot be changed back to mixed mode!

Many things change when a domain is put into native mode including its group scope, group membership, group nesting options, the scalability of the AD, and its logon behavior.

Group Scope

When a domain is changed from mixed mode to native mode, a new type of group, the *universal group*, becomes available. This group allows an enterprise composed of many domains to group users from every domain into one group. The scope of the universal group is the entire forest. It can have as its members users or computers and global groups. Universal groups can be members of local groups in any domain in the forest. Because local groups are given resource access and rights at the local level, this strategy simplifies the administration of access control.

Group Membership

In a mixed-member domain, the Enterprise Admins and Schema Admins groups are domain global groups. When the domain is changed to native mode, these two groups become universal groups. Both groups, by default, include one member: the Enterprise Administrator.

Group Nesting

In a mixed-mode domain, users can be members of local groups and global groups. Global groups can be nested within local groups. The recommended strategy for giving users access to resources is to place users into global groups, nest global groups in local groups, and give the local group resource permissions. Groups in native domains have more flexible nesting rules, and thus there is a different recommended strategy for granting resource access. The rules of group nesting in a native mode domain are as follows:

- Universal groups can have accounts, other universal groups, and global groups from any domain as members.
- Global groups can have accounts from the same domain and other global groups from the same domain as members.
- Local groups can have accounts, groups with universal scope, global groups from any domain, and other domain local groups from the same domain as members.

The recommended strategy for providing resource access is as follows:

- Place users in domain global groups.
- Place domain global groups in universal groups.
- Place universal groups in domain local groups.
- Give local groups permissions to access resources.

Although this adds an organizational step to the design and implementation of access control, it provides simplification in implementation at the local resource level. If these steps are followed, only a small number of universal groups need to be added to each local resource rather than a large number of global groups.

Universal group membership is stored in the Global Catalog. Because the Global Catalog is available forest wide, membership can be determined from any domain.

Group Changes

Universal groups cannot exist in a mixed mode domain. Therefore, there are no default universal groups upon domain creation. When a domain is changed from mixed to native mode, the two mixed mode global groups, Enterprise Admins and Schema Admins, are changed to become universal groups.

Logon Behavior

Group membership must be determined during logon. To determine membership in a universal group, the Global Catalog must be available. This is because only the Global Catalog will have all the members of the universal group. If the Global Catalog is not available, cached credentials can be used.

LDAP

Active Directory is an LDAP-compatible directory. This means that LDAP can be used in a Windows 2000 domain to search for and update objects within the AD. LDAP is defined by RFC 2251, "Lightweight Directory Access Protocol." AD supports both LDAP Version 2 and Version 3.

In most cases, administrators use LDAP to add, modify, and delete objects, while users use it to search and view. If a user wants to find the phone number of an employee or the closest printer that can print color, he uses the graphical user interface (GUI) search tools
provided. The underlying protocol that the search tools will use is LDAP.

Dynamic DNS

Windows 2000 domains use DNS for name resolution and to build their hierarchical structure. Windows 2000 domains map to the DNS namespace in a network. As previously mentioned, the DNS server used does not have to be a Windows 2000 DNS server. The DNS server should, however, support dynamic DNS (see RFC 2136, "Dynamic Updates in the Domain Name System") and must support the use of SRV records (see RFC 2052, "A DNS RR for Specifying the Location of Services [DNS SRV]").

If the DNS server supports dynamic updating, additional risks to network security exist. If the capability to update DNS records is not controlled, rogue DHCP servers and users might change IP addresses or add unauthorized computers and services to your DNS server. A corrupted DNS database is at best a disruption for your network and can be the source of numerous attacks.

Windows 2000 supports service records and dynamic DNS. In traditional DNS, a zone file represents the sum total of resolvable addresses for a DNS namespace. Windows 2000 also supports AD-integrated zones. The zones place the DNS namespace information within the AD. When AD-integrated zones are used, secure dynamic update zones can be configured.

To secure Windows 2000 dynamic DNS, you must know how it works. The following section begins with a discussion of how dynamically and statically assigned IP addresses are dynamically added to DNS and ends with a discussion on how dynamic updating can be secured.

How Dynamic DNS Works

In a traditional DNS environment, administrators manually post records to DNS databases. Thus, every change or addition offers the possibility for accidental error. Many organizations use the Dynamic Host Control Protocol (DHCP) to dynamically assign IP addresses and TCP/IP configuration information to computers. If they use a traditional DNS server, these dynamic address changes must be manually updated or left out of the server. In a Windows NT 4.0 or Windows 2000 environment, the Windows

Internet Name Service (WINS) is dynamically updated and can be used to provide name resolution for computers that receive dynamic IP addressing.

A dynamic DNS server provides facilities for the automatic addition and updating of IP addresses. Computers and DHCP servers that are configured to do so can add and edit their own IP addresses on the server.

This is how it works in Windows 2000:

1. A Windows 2000 DNS server is installed, and addresses and service records for domain controllers and DHCP servers are statically assigned.

2. When servers are promoted to domain controllers, they automatically update DNS with their IP address and appropriate service records.

3. The Windows 2000 DHCP service does the same for Windows 2000 Server and Professional whether their addresses are dynamically or statically assigned.

In standard DNS, two records are written to the DNS server database for every host. One of these is the host record. It can be used for name resolution; the friendly computer name is resolved to an IP address that can be used by TCP/IP to find the desired computer. The other record is the PTR record. It can be used to find the computer name if the IP address is known. This is often used to determine the location of the computer. By resolving IP addresses to FQDN, a link with the domain and thus a registered address can be found.

By default, Windows 2000 computers that use the DHCP server to obtain their IP addresses post their own IP addresses to the DNS server. The DHCP server posts the PTR record. When the DHCP server changes their addresses, an edit occurs.

Finally, by default, Windows 2000 computers that do not use DHCP (they have addresses manually assigned and configured) post both host and PTR records to DNS. Even though these computers are not using DHCP, it is the DHCP client on board their system that does the posting. If the IP address is changed, the changed information is used to edit the DNS record. If non-Windows 2000 computers don't use DHCP for IP address assignment, they will not post any part of their address to the dynamic DNS. Their records must be manually posted to the dynamic DNS.

Figure 12.6 shows a dynamic DNS and DHCP server and clients of both types. The sources for updates to the DNS server are indicated.

If the client is getting an address from the DHCP server, you can change who posts which part of the address. By default, the DHCP server updates DNS according to the request made by the client. By default, the client asks DHCP to update the PTR record and not to update the host record.

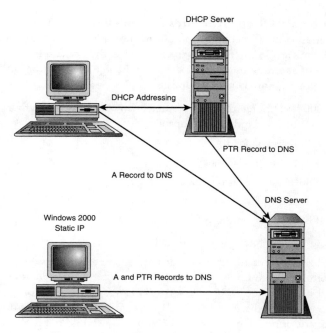

Figure 12.6   Dynamic updating of DNS records.

DNS options to set on the DHCP server are made in the DNS tab of the DHCP Server Scope property pages. The choices are

- **Do not update DNS records**. DHCP never updates the record. (Make sure boxes are cleared on the DNS tab.)

- **Automatically update DHCP—if client requests**. Allow clients to request posting preferences. (Check the box Automatically Update DHCP Client Information in DNS, then check the radio button Update DNS Only if DNS Client Requests.)

- **Automatically update DHCP—Always.** DHCP always updates both the A and the PTR record. DHCP uses the FQDN included in the DHCPRE-QUEST message to determine the domain name and updates the DNS server. (Check the box Automatically Update DHCP Client Information in DNS, then check the radio button Always Update DNS.)

- **Stop forwarding lookups if the lease expires.** (Check the box Discard Forward [Name-to-Address] Lookups when Lease Expires.)

- **Update both PTR and A records for non-Windows 2000 computers.** Non-Windows 2000 computers do not include a FQDN with their DHCPRE-QUEST message, so the DHCP server must use the domain name defined for the scope of addresses used. (Check the box Enable Updates for DNS Clients that Do Not Support Dynamic Update.)

On Windows 2000 computers, DHCP adapters, static adapters, and remote access adapters can post updates. Updates will occur

- When TCP/IP is changed
- When a DHCP address is renewed
- When a DHCP address is obtained
- When a plug-and-play event occurs
- When IP is added or removed for a static adapter
- Every 24 hours

Multihomed clients with static addresses for both adapters will register the first address for each adapter. If you are using DHCP to obtain addresses for a multihomed client, be aware that, by default, the DHCP server will change the address for every host record for a computer to the new IP address it has given out. It cannot distinguish the fact that it is overwriting a legal address. Therefore, you should never allow DHCP to post A and PTR records for multihomed computers.

To keep a Windows 2000 computer from updating its DNS record, edit the DNS tab on the Advanced property pages of TCP/IP. Clear the Register This Connection's Address in DNS check box.

Securing Dynamic DNS

To secure dynamic DNS, you must secure DHCP and dynamic DNS services.

Securing DHCP Services

A network that is victim to a rogue DHCP server is not a pretty sight. In a non-dynamic DNS environment, it does damage by handing out unauthorized IP addresses to unsuspecting clients and interferes with communications. In a dynamic DNS environment, problems are multiplied as requests for name resolution receive incorrect addresses.

Limited protection can be provided against rogue Windows 2000 DHCP servers because Windows 2000 DHCP servers must be authorized to be useful on a Windows 2000 network. DHCP services installed on other operating systems are not affected by this policy. A Windows 2000 DHCP server installed on the root domain controller will be authorized by default, but a DHCP server installed on a member server, and one installed on the domain controller of a child domain, must be authorized after installation by selecting Authorize from the Action menu of the DHCP console. You must be a member of the Enterprise Admins group to authorize the DHCP server.

You cannot prevent administrators from installing Windows 2000 DHCP servers on the network. You can, however, prevent those Windows 2000 DHCP servers from assigning addresses. When a Windows 2000 DHCP server comes online, it checks to see whether it is authorized in the AD. If it is not, it will not start its service. A Windows 2000 DHCP server also periodically checks to see whether it remains authorized in the AD.

You can find a list of authorized DHCP servers in the NetServices node of the Services container in the AD Sites and Services console. If you must delegate authority to authorize DHCP servers (for example, to an administrator at another location), you can do so in this node. This will allow the remote administrator to get the job done without making him a member of the Enterprise Admins group.

Securing Dynamic DNS Services

Until you secure dynamic DNS services, your DNS server is vulnerable to several types of attacks and accidental damages. Rogue DHCP servers could change host records, redirect data, and prevent name resolution. Clients that are accidentally configured incorrectly or that are modified by malicious users can replace correct DNS records. Attempts at direct manipulation (direct modification of DNS records) of DNS files might succeed.

> **Tip**
>
> The Windows 2000 TCP/IP client accepts responses to its DNS queries from any DNS server that responds. It does not check, by default, to see whether the DNS server was the one it queried. This might be a security risk. If the client's query is captured and the incorrect response given by a rogue DNS server is received first, then the client might not find its destination or might find itself redirected to a rogue server. To ensure that clients only accept responses from DNS servers they know, add the registry value QueryIPMatching with a value of 1. This REG_DWORD value needs to be placed at HKEY_LOCAL_MACHINE\SYSTEM\CurrentControlSet\Services\DNSCache\Parameters.

To make sure that only authorized, valid records are in your zone files, you must secure the dynamic DNS service. Securing dynamic DNS is accomplished by configuring Microsoft dynamic DNS for secure update. To do this:

- The DNS zone for the domain must be an AD-integrated zone.
- Change the Zone General Property Page setting from Allow Dynamic Updates to Only Secure Updates.
- Specify which users and groups can modify zones and resource records using ACLs.

When the zone is configured, the following protection is available:

- Only computers with domain accounts can create DNS records.
- The only computer that can update a record is the owner of the record. The computer that creates the record owns it.
- The authoritative DNS server for the zone only accepts updates from computers that you authorize to send dynamic updates.
- You specify which groups, users, and computers can modify zones and records.
- Make appropriate changes at the client level.

Tip
You do have an alternative to configuring for secure update: You can prevent dynamic updating of the zone files. To do this, you must open DNS property pages from the DNS console. On the general page, change Allow Dynamic Updates? to No.

You create an AD-integrated zone file by modifying a standard primary zone file. When you create the integrated zone file, the secondary zone file that matched that primary is deleted. It is your choice as to which type of zone file to use, but remember that, although both traditional and AD-integrated zone files can be updated dynamically, only AD-integrated zone files can be securely updated.

After you have converted your zone file to AD integrated, you can control who can make changes to it. By default, authenticated computers (computers with domain accounts) and users (users who have authenticated with the domain controller) can add records to the zone file. You use the Security tab of the object to further control who can make changes to it. It is important to do this for servers and resource records to keep them safe from unauthorized modification.

By default, clients will attempt dynamic update, and if you have properly protected your zone files, they will fail. If they do, they will attempt to negotiate secure dynamic update. To insist that the client always tries secure dynamic update, change the value UpdateSecurityLevel to 256. The value can be found at HKEY_LOCAL_MACHINE\SYSTEM\CurrentControlSet\Services]\Tcpip\Parameters.

Resetting the value to 0 will put it back to the default. Setting it to 16 will always use insecure update.

Warning
An unsecured DNS server will allow a client to overwrite the IP address record of a currently registered computer. An attacker can effectively spoof a legitimate machine by changing the name of his computer to that of another system and entering his own IP address. The Windows 2000 computer will attempt to register this name and address with the dynamic DNS and, if the dynamic DNS has not been secured, will be successful. This can also happen accidentally. In addition to providing a security hole from which an attack can occur, this opens up an annoyance hole, one from which users of client computers can no longer communicate on the network. This denial of service is just as effective whether it's accidental or planned.

To secure your dynamic DNS server against such a problem, you should configure the DNS zone for secure update. If this cannot be done, you can configure Windows 2000 computers under your control with the following registry entry. Navigate to

HKEY_Local_MACHINE\SYSTEM\CurrentControlSet\Services\Tcpip\Parameters

Add the DWORD DisableReplaceADdressInConflicts value and set it to 1. This prevents the client from overwriting a host record if there is a conflict.

The secure update process itself is defined in RFC 2078, "The Generic Security Service Application Program Interface (GSS-API)," and in the draft "GSS Algorithm for TSIG (GSS-TSIG)." Other RFCs on secure updating of DNS include RFC 2535, "Domain Name System Security Extensions," and RFC 2137, "Secure Domain Name System Dynamic Update," but they are not supported by Microsoft dynamic DNS.

GSS-API uses a token model to pass a security context from the client to the server. Kerberos is used to negotiate a security context that is only used for this process. The resource records TSIG and TKEY are used. TKEY transfers security tokens from the client to the server and back and is used during the establishment of secret keys. TSIG sends and verifies digitally signed messages.

If you have modified the default action to prevent attempts at unsecure updates, the process of securing the update goes like this:

1. The client queries the local name server and finds the authoritative server for the zone where the name resides.

2. TKEY negotiation ensues to determine which security the client and server should use.

3. TKEY tells the client to use Kerberos.

4. Mutual authentication occurs.

5. A security context is established that includes a TSIG key.

6. The client attempts to update the zone file using TSIG.

7. The server uses the security context and TSIG to verify that the update is ok.

8. The server attempts to add, delete, or modify the resource record in AD.

9. The server is successful if the client has permission.

10. The server tells the client whether the operation was a success or a failure.

Non–Windows 2000 computers cannot update the zone files. If they are DHCP clients, however, their records can be updated by the DHCP server. These records also can be secured. The DHCP server that adds the record owns it and therefore protects it.

You will want to protect yourself from a situation in which this DHCP server becomes unavailable. In that case, the record could not be changed by another DHCP server. To counter this effect, add all DHCP servers to the DNSUpdateproxy computer group. This group does not allow the record creator to maintain ownership. Make sure

you modify the ACL of the IP address of the DHCP server so that only it can change
its own record. Adding DHCP servers to the DNSUpdateproxy group will not impact
Windows 2000 computers that use DHCP for IP address assignment. They will maintain ownership of records they register by default.

> **Warning**
>
> Do not make a DHCP server a member of the DNSUpdate group if the DHCP server is installed on a
> domain controller. If you do so, the DHCP server has control over all DNS objects in the AD. This is
> because the DHCP server runs in the context of the computer account. A domain controller computer
> account has access to all DNS objects in the AD. It could take ownership of any DNS record, even those
> in zones configured for secure update.

Introduction to Distributed Security Services

Distributed security services operate across the enterprise, not just within the boundaries of a single computer. Just as distributed applications have parts that run on
different systems, distributed security services use the multicomputer collections of
domains, trees, forests, and sites for security operations. Distributed security services
include

- **Single Sign-On (SSO).** Provides the capability to log on once and access
  resources throughout the enterprise.
- **Kerberos for network authentication.** Authentication with the Kerberos
  Key Distribution Center (KDC) provides the client with a Ticket-Granting
  Ticket to be used throughout the logon session to obtain service tickets to other
  computers.
- **Secure resource access using a Security Access Token.** The Kerberos
  ticket contains a field that can be used for authorization information. Windows
  2000 uses this field to contain a list of user and group SIDS that can then be
  used by resource services to authorize access to resources. The SIDs are matches
  against resource ACLs.
- **Centralized administration.** A large number of administrative tools based on
  the Microsoft Management Console (MMC) are available to manage computers
  from a central administration station. Other management snap-ins can be added
  to MMCs and customized administration consoles developed.
- **Group Policy security settings.** Local Security Policy is used to configure
  and maintain Security Policy on standalone systems or to participate in hierarchical computer and user management. Group Policy is used to implement centralized administration and maintenance of computers and users. Group Policy
  includes a security settings component. Group Policy can be implemented at the
  local computer and also at the site, domain, and OU level. The final result can be

controlled by making appropriate settings at the right level. One can almost hear Windows administrators whispering, "I have the power," as they gleefully configure their settings to match policy, watch as they are applied across the enterprise, and snicker when someone tries to change things at the local level to no avail.

- **Certificate Services.** A CA is installed as part of the development of a company's Public Key Infrastructure (PKI). This PKI can be created and used for several reasons including authentication and/or email using smart cards, EFS Recovery Management, authentication of trading partners, authentication by Web services, and IPSec authentication. Policy settings can be made for the organization by using the Public Key Policies container in Group Policy.

- **EFS Recovery Management.** On standalone systems, a certificate is created that enables local users to encrypt and decrypt their own files. Recovery is by recovery agent; the default Administrator account is given that role. In a Windows 2000 domain with a CA present, recovery can be managed on a domain-wide basis. Recovery certificates can be created for specially assigned *Recovery Agents*, user accounts created or designated for this purpose. Administrator account recovery agent certificates can be deleted.

- **IPSec Policy Management.** Any Windows 2000 computer can participate in an IPSec encrypted communication with another IPSec-enabled Windows 2000 computer. IPSec Policy Management allows the central management of IPSec communications using the IPSec Policy container within Group Policy.

Distributed security services are not available in exactly the same way outside of a domain. The key thoughts here are centralized management, enforcement, and maintenance of security policies and practices.

Several of these services are fully explained in future chapters. (See the "For more Information" section later in this chapter for specific references.) IPSec policies and Kerberos policies are examined here.

IPSec Policies

IPSec is a standard network protocol that can be used to secure communications between two computers on a network. It is used to encrypt tunneled data in an L2TP VPN (This usage is described in Chapter 15, "Secure Remote Access Options".) It can also be used, however, to negotiate a secure connection and encrypt data traveling between two computers without the benefit of tunneling or special remote access servers.

Specifications and requirements are configured in IPSec Policy. IPSec Policy can be implemented via Group Policy at the local, domain, or OU level and therefore can be distributed across the domain. Although Group Policy is discussed more thoroughly in Chapter 16, this section covers the basics of the IPSec Policy available at the domain level.

Although IPSec Policy can be defined at a very granular level, there are three default policies. None of the policies are assigned (enabled) by default. To use them, you determine which computers need more secure communications and then enable the appropriate policy on servers and clients. Table 12.1 defines the policies and has suggestions for their use.

Table 12.1 **IPSec Policies**

Policy	Explanation	Recommendation
Client (Respond Only)	A computer with this policy set will never insist on negotiated or encrypted communications. Instead, if it is asked to participate, it will.	This is a good choice for clients that either might need to occasionally communicate with a secure server or need to make sure that communications with Secure Server (Require Security) policies are always encrypted.
Secure Server (Require Security)	This policy insists on secure, encrypted communications. It will not participate in any communications that are not encrypted.	If you want to ensure that all communication with this server is encrypted, pick this policy. If a client cannot respond in kind, there will be no communications.
Server (Request Security)	This server will request encrypted communications but will not refuse a connection from a client that cannot participate in them.	If only certain clients need to establish a secure path, this policy is correct. This policy sounds strange: Why ask for security but then give in if a client can't participate? It makes more sense, however, if you remember that sensitive data is protected on the server by strict access controls. Less sensitive data may be available to more users. If those users who might be editing and transferring sensitive data are required to only pass encrypted data— their clients are configured with the Client (Respond Only) policy—then these communications are correctly protected by this server-side policy.

Kerberos Policy

Kerberos Policy is established at the domain level. The server template includes the policy parameters but does not define them. Table 12.2 lists the policies. The default domain controller settings are included in the second column. Kerberos policies are set only at the domain level.

Table 12.2 **Kerberos Policy**

Policy	Default	Explanation
Enforce user logon restrictions	Enabled	Session ticket requests are validated by checking the user rights policy on the destination computer. The user must have Log on Locally or Access This Computer From Network rights before a session ticket is granted. This can put additional load on the network and reduce response time. A valid session ticket is not going to get a user access to a system to which he has been denied access.
Maximum lifetime for service ticket	600 minutes	The session ticket = service ticket. The range is 10 minutes to less than "Maximum lifetime for user ticket."
Maximum lifetime for user ticket	10 hours	The user ticket = TGT. The default presumes that most users will be logged on for a maximum of 10 hours. This setting then makes sure their TGT is valid for the length of their logon.
Maximum lifetime for user ticket renewal	7 days	TGT tickets can be renewed. If you are working late and the "Maximum lifetime for user ticket" expires, you will not see a request for a user ID and password. Your ticket will be renewed. However, if you exceed this setting—say you leave your system constantly logged on—you will eventually run out of renewals and will need to obtain a new ticket.
Maximum tolerance for computer clock synchronization	5 minutes	Many Kerberos processes are time sensitive. Computer clock times are included in messages and are checked against the current time on the server to assist in the prevention of replay attacks. Replay attacks use captured information in an attempt to fool servers that a real and trusted client is asking for access. The

continues

Table 12.2 **Continued**

Policy	Default	Explanation
		time difference between the client and the server is important because it can cause otherwise-legitimate requests to fail. Setting this setting too large might allow a replay attack to succeed. Setting it too small might not allow enough time if the network is congested.

Comparing Network Authentication Services: Kerberos and NTLM

On standalone machines that are logged on to interactively (the user is sitting at the console), neither NTLM nor Kerberos is used. The cleartext password is hashed using the same one-way function (OWF) used to store the user password in the local database (registry). This OWF can be compared to the one stored and logon can be granted or denied.

Logon to domains from across the network involves the use of LM, NTLM, NTLM v2, or Kerberos. Windows 2000 computers are configured to use all these methods to ensure backwards compatibility. Table 12.3 is an authentication grid that shows the possible authentication processes that might take place between the operating systems. You can restrict the use of these protocols depending on the OS of the clients for which you need to provide service and the availability and use of AD client software provided for down-level clients. Why might you want to?

The LM, NTLM, and NTLMv2 protocols are considered less secure than Kerberos. Within the LM series of authentication protocols, the level of security from least to best is LM, NTLM, and then NTLMv2. Because it is your job to provide the most secure environment practical and necessary for your organization, you should seek to always ensure the use of the most secure protocol. Understand that you must configure clients and servers to ensure the best level of security. To determine what authentication protocol is used between two Windows OSs, consult Table 12.3.

Table 12.3 **Authentication Grid**

	Windows 95	Windows 98	Windows 98	Windows NT	Windows 2000
Windows 95	LM	LM	LM	LM	LM
Windows 98	LM	LM	LM	LM	LM
Windows 98 with AD Client or Second Edition	LM	LM	LM or NTLMv2	LM or NTLMv2	LM or NTLMv2

	Windows 95	Windows 98	Windows 98	Windows NT	Windows 2000
Windows NT	LM	LM	LM or NTLMv2	NTLM or NTLMv2	NTLM or NTLMv2
Windows 2000	LM	LM	LM or NTLMv2	NTLM or NTLMv2	Kerberos, NTLM, or NLLM v2

As you will recall, NTLM/NTLM v2 is a very different protocol than Kerberos. There are some differences that should be highlighted.

In neither of these authentication methods does the user password cross the network at all. A hash of the password is used to encrypt a random challenge and to return a response. Because the domain controller, or the resource server in the case of a standalone server, has the OWF, a comparison with the response and confirmation or rejection of the attempt is possible. The difference lies in the number of times this challenge and response occurs.

In the LM/NTLM world, each time you access a resource, the resource calls on the domain controller for authentication, after which a new, local access token is built. It's like we are the children and these parental authorities must chatter amongst themselves before allowing us to come over and play with their toys.

Kerberos, on the other hand, makes the client responsible for its own authentication with resources. The client receives a ticket that enables her to access a particular resource or one that enables her to come back to the KDC and ask for such a service ticket. Both of these types of tickets can be reused. The presentation of the service ticket to the resource is used in place of an authentication conversation between the resource server and the domain controller. This reduces network activity and the exposure of password information on an open network.

Second, Kerberos further protects authentication information with the usage of session keys, timestamps, authenticators, and other checks and balances.

Best Practices

To ensure the security of DNS records and servers as well as DHCP services, follow the information provided in this chapter. Specifically, the following recommendations should be incorporated in your practices:

- Use AD-integrated DNS zones and secure them for updating.
- Secure all server records—both resource and service records—to keep them from erroneously being updated by other computers.
- Take special care in securing DHCP servers.
- Use ACLs to secure Professional systems used in sensitive areas.

- Evaluate security policies and develop templates based on the level of security required. This can be determined by evaluating for what the computer is used.

- Thoroughly test any policy changes including those that would be made using Microsoft-provided templates.

For More Information

This chapter discussed services for which complementary information exists in other chapters of this book. The following should serve as a referral source for you in locating this information.

IPSec RFCs and the protocol in general are described in Chapter 3, "New Protocols, Products, and APIs."

Public Key Policies are delineated in Chapter 4, "Public Key Infrastructure (PKI)"

Group Policy is first defined in Chapter 9, "Security Tools," and is further explained in Chapter 16, "Securing the Network Using Distributed Security Services."

Summary

Without the Active Directory and DNS, there can be no Windows 2000 domains. In this chapter, the concept of Active Directory was introduced. Dynamic DNS also was explored along with the integration of DHCP in the Windows 2000 network. An introduction to distributed security, a look back at NTLM authentication, and the description of domain-wide policies (IPSec Policies and Kerberos Policies) completed this section.

13

Securing Legacy Windows Clients

I T'S EXCITING TO IMAGINE HOW THE NEW SECURITY FEATURES of Windows 2000 can be used to help secure the enterprise. However, not every organization will be able to immediately upgrade all its systems. It is important to consider how legacy systems will be secured. This chapter provides information essential to this process.

Microsoft refers to legacy Windows systems (Windows 95, Windows 98, and Windows NT) as down-level clients. Whether you choose to use this politically correct term or not, you can benefit from the instructions provided for securing these systems. Although these systems cannot take advantage of many security features inherent to Windows 2000, the security on these legacy systems can be improved. This chapter will show you how you accomplish this by

- Improving authentication practices
- Securing network communications
- Improving basic systems security

Instructions in the basics of securing down-level systems can be found through the Appendix, "Resources," at the end of this book.

Improving Authentication Practices

Previous editions of Windows use LM, NTLM, or NTLMv2 for authentication. Which protocol these editions use depends on the operating system, the service pack level, registry configuration, and the way in which Windows 2000 system security has been configured. Because down-level clients cannot use Kerberos for authentication, NTLMv2 is recommended. To use NTLMv2, however, you must do more than just require it on the server side. To implement NTLMv2, you must:

- Understand user logon from a legacy client to a Windows 2000 domain
- Configure each down-level client so that it can use NTLMv2
- Configure Windows 2000 domain controllers to require NTLMv2 authentication from down-level clients

Understanding Down-Level Client Logon

The logon process for LAN Manager Authentication (LM, NTLM, and NTLMv2) was detailed in Chapter 3, "New Protocols, Products, and APIs." When down-level clients log on to a Windows 2000 domain, they use their default authentication protocol. Windows 95 and Windows 98 use LM, and Windows NT uses NTLM. However, this might not always be the most secure choice. To make sure that these clients have available and always use the most secure choice, you might need to add additional client software or service packs, and you will need to configure the client and server to use the newer protocol.

In cases in which multiple protocols for authentication are available, the choice is made according to registry entries at both the client and the server. You can apply these settings directly to the registry or, in some cases, through special tools. Before you can determine the best authentication protocol choices for your network, you should

- Review the protocol descriptions in Chapter 3
- Examine some authentication processing differences between Windows 9x, Windows NT, and Windows 2000
- Examine the Active Directory client
- Review the Active Directory client–managed Windows logon process

Down-Level Client Authentication and Account Processing Issues

Although the use of a less secure authentication protocol is the largest down-level client authentication issue, there are other difference in how these clients handle authentication and how their accounts are managed.

Windows 95 and Windows 98 computers, for example, cannot be assigned computer accounts in the Active Directory (AD). Users, of course, can have domain-level user accounts in the AD. Authentication from down-level Windows clients can be handled by any Windows 2000 domain controller in their domain. However, when users of down-level clients (that do not have the AD client installed) change their Windows 2000 password, the operation actually will occur at the Windows 2000 domain controller designated as the Primary Domain Controller (PDC) emulator. The PDC emulator is one of the operations masters, and it acts as a Windows NT PDC for down-level Windows clients that do not have an AD client installed.

If users of down-level clients have local accounts on a Windows 2000 system, the account is stored in the local Windows 2000 SAM. The local SAM can perform authentication between a Windows 2000 AD account and a down-level client. In both cases (domain and local logon), the down-level client thinks it is talking to a Windows NT system. To the user, everything looks like it normally does.

Processing between the AD database and store (the AD information located on the hard disk) is also different. The Directory Service Agent (DSA) is part of the Local Security Authority (LSA) on the Windows 2000 system. It is the DSA that accesses the AD store. Windows 9x clients cannot query the store because they do not understand how to communicate with the DSA. If the AD client (described in the next section) is installed, Windows 9x clients can use the LDAP protocol to connect to the DSA.

Windows NT 4.0 (Service Pack 4 and above) clients connect to the DSA using a Security Account Manager (SAM) API interface. The SAM API is the interface between the client, which wants to authenticate with information stored in a Windows NT registry, and the very different structure of the AD. The Windows NT 4.0 system does not have to be modified to allow authentication with the AD.

The Active Directory Client

The Active Directory (AD) client was developed to give down-level clients access to some of the technology incorporated in Windows 2000. The AD client for Windows 9x computers is provided on the Windows 2000 Installation CD-ROM at client\Windows9x\dsclient.exe. The AD client for Windows NT will be part of Service Pack 7 for Windows NT.

By adding this client to a Windows 9x system, you add several features. The client

- Adds LDAP search capabilities. Users can search the AD for printers, shares, and so on. Browsing is not needed to find these resources.
- Adds the capability to log on to the Windows 2000 domain controller closest to it in the network.
- Allows Active Directory Services Interface (ADSI) scripting to AD.
- Provides access to Windows 2000 Distributed File System fault tolerant and fail-over file shares in the AD.
- Enables the use of NTLMv2 authentication.

The AD client does *not* add

- Kerberos support
- Group Policy or Intellimirror (a collection of new Windows 2000 technologies used to support ease of configuration and fault tolerance) support
- IPSec or L2TP support
- Service Principal Name (computer account in the AD) or mutual authentication

AD Client Authentication for Windows 9x

Windows 2000 computers in a Windows 2000 domain can be accessed by an Lightweight Directory Access Protocol Version 3 (LDAPv3) client. The LDAP client can negotiate with the server to find the best possible authentication process. LDAPv3 uses the Simple Authentication and Security Layer (SASL) model, which uses a layered architecture and describes the use of multiple security providers. Windows 2000 implements three authentication types for LDAP clients on the local network:

- Plaintext password
- NTLM or NTLMv2
- Kerberos v5

Other authentication methods are used for Internet and dial-up access.

The AD client for Windows 9x systems includes a limited LDAP client. The client can only choose between versions of LAN Manager; it cannot participate in Kerberos authentication, nor can a plaintext password be used for network logon.

The following steps outline the AD client logon process. To show the LDAP statements, we assume an account in the peachweaver.com domain.

1. The user attempts to log on to the domain by entering his user ID and password and pressing Enter.

2. The LSA performs a one-way encryption on his password and stores it in its cache.

3. The AD client locates an AD domain controller for its domain by sending a DNS name query to its DNS server.
   Query name: *ldap*.tcp.peachweaver.com
   Query type: SRV (service locator resource record)

4. The DNS server responds with the DNS names and IP addresses of the domain controllers for the peachweaver.com domain. If there is more than one site, the domain controller in the local site is given priority.

5. The system attempts to contact a domain controller from the list. It will continue to attempt contact using all names on the list until it gets a response. The first server to respond is the one used for logon.

6. Because this is a local LAN logon and the client is not a Windows 2000 client, the domain controller checks to see what types of LAN Manager authentication can be used.

7. The domain controller begins the negotiation by offering the most secure protocol first.

8. The client checks to see what type of authentication challenge it can and should respond to.

9. The process continues if there are multiple possibilities. If no common authentication process is found, the logon is rejected.

10. The server issues a challenge, and the client responds. The nature of the response depends on the authentication choice agreed upon. If the client information is correct, the client is authenticated.

Implementing NTLMv2: Step One—Down-Level Clients

Windows 2000 is configured by default to enable Windows clients to use the authentication protocol they prefer. Legacy Windows clients will use their default LAN Manager protocol regardless of whether a service pack or AD client has been loaded. You see, adding additional software just makes the version of LAN Manager they use configurable; it doesn't configure it. It's up to you to configure the clients for the most secure protocol they are capable of using. Windows NT 4.0 clients can be configured to use NTLMv2. Windows 9x clients with the AD client installed can also use NTLMv2. In both cases, extra configuration is necessary.

To make down-level clients use NTLMv2 for authentication, you must make changes in each down-level client's registry. To make Windows 2000 require a minimum of NTLMv2 authentication from down-level clients, you must make changes at every domain controller.

Changes for the following down-level systems are listed in the next sections. Changes necessary for Windows 2000 domain controllers (DCs) are outlined later in this chapter.

Windows NT

Windows NT 4.0 (Service Pack 4 and above) has the capability of using NTLMv2. While you are waiting for the AD client, you can still take steps to secure your Windows NT 4.0 clients. You need to make settings at the following registry location:

HKEY_LOCAL_MACHINE\SYSTEM\CurrentControlSet\Control\LSA

If the value is not present, add the following:

```
Value: LMCompatibilityLevel
Type, REG_DWORD
Range: 0-5
```

The default value is 0, which means there is no restriction. To restrict authentication, enter one of the values described in Table 13.1. In the table, all NT systems are assumed to be version 4.0, SP4 or above. Windows 9x systems do not have the AD client installed.

Table 13.1 **LM Compatibility Level**

Level	Result	Notes
0	Use LM response and NTLM response; never use NTLMv2.	NT servers and workstations will negotiate either LM or NTLM. They will not respond to NTLMv2. This provides backward compatibility with previous versions of Windows. An NT DC will accept NTLM, NTLMv2, or LM.
1	Use NTLMv2 session security if negotiated. Can also use NTLM or LM authentication.	NT servers and workstations can still communicate with previous versions of Windows but will choose NTLMv2 if available. A DC accepts LM, NTLM, NTLMV2.
2	Send NTLM authentication only. Use NTLMv2 session security if the server supports it.	NT servers and workstations cannot connect to Windows 9x and below. They will not use LM. The DC accepts LM, NTLM, and NTLMV2 authentication.
3	Send NTLMv2 authentication only. Will use NTLMV2 session security if the server supports it.	NT servers and workstations cannot communicate to Windows 9x, NT pre-SP4, or nonconfigured NT SP4 systems. They will not include the LM password hash in their communications with the DC. The DC accepts LM, NTLM and NTLMv2.
4	If this is an NT 4.0 DC, it refuses LM authentication. Client uses NTLMv2 for authentication and uses NTLMv2 session security if negotiated.	Windows 9x clients can't connect. DC accepts NTLM and NTLMv2.
5	DC refuses LM and NTLM authentication; it accepts only NTLMv2. Client uses NTLMv2 for authentication and uses NTLMv2 session security if supported.	Windows 9x clients can't connect. Pre-SP4 NT and nonconfigured clients can't connect. DC rejects NTLM and LM.

To secure your Windows NT 4.0 SP4 and above Workstation and Server clients, change the value to 3. Before configuring your domain controllers, you need to make sure you have configured all clients.

Windows 98/95

Windows 9x systems cannot be configured for NTLMv2 until you have installed the AD client for Windows 9x. The AD client is located on the Windows 2000 Server or Advanced Server installation CD-ROM in the Client\Windows9x\ folder. The file is dsclient.exe. The client uses 56-bit encryption by default. Because 128-bit encryption is regulated by import and export laws, if you are not located in the United States or Canada, you might need to ignore the first two items in the following list.

1. Make sure you have Internet Explorer version 4.1 or above.
2. Install the 128-bit connection support for Internet Explorer.
3. Run dsclient.exe.
4. Run regedt32.exe.
5. Navigate to HKEY_LOCAL_MACHINE\SYSTEM\CurrentControlSet\Control\LSA.
6. Add the value `LMCompatibilityLevel` with a value of 3.

The possible settings and their meanings are the same as in Table 13.1, except that client actions refer to Windows 9x rather than Windows NT server or workstation, and of course, there are no Windows 9x domain controllers.

The following files are installed when you install the client:

- secur32.dll
- msnp32.dll
- vredir.vxd
- vnetsup.vxd

If you want to verify which strength of encryption will be used, check the version of secur32.dll you are using. To do so:

1. Use Windows Explorer to locate the file at %systemroot%\system.
2. Right-click and choose Properties to view the version.
3. The 56-bit version will say Microsoft Win32 Security Services (Export Version).
4. The 128-bit version will say Microsoft Win32 Security Services (US and Canada only).

Implementing NTLMv2: Step Two—Requiring NTLMv2 on Windows 2000 Domain Controllers

To make NTLMv2 the only LAN Manager authentication protocol used by down-level clients in a domain, you need to make changes on every client and every domain controller. Fortunately, this is easy. To change the policy on domain controllers, you can use Group Policy. To do so, visit the Domain Controller Security Policy console and define the Security Option policy setting LAN Manager Authentication Level. Set it to Send NTLMv2 Response Only\Refuse LM.

Be sure to test this configuration before deploying it across the enterprise.

Securing Network Communications

Now that you have tightened your authentication policy, its time to think about network communications. With down-level clients, you do have choices.

Session security is decided when the client requests one of the following:

- Message integrity
- Message confidentiality
- NTLMv2 session security
- 128-bit or 56-bit encryption

The server will respond, indicating whether it supports the request, and the session is considered negotiated. You can require a particular type of session security, but you should be aware that requiring this security will prevent connections if the server cannot provide it. This, of course, is what you indicate that you want when you make these settings. Just make sure you know what you want.

Two possibilities for session security with down-level clients are

- Server Message Block (SMB) signing
- NTLMv2 negotiated session security

SMB Signing

SMB is the method used for file sharing in Windows networks. Windows NT 4.0 SP3 provides an enhanced version of SMB that includes the capability to do SMB packet signing. SP3 and above SMB follows the standard Common Internet File System (CIFS). (Microsoft has only recently been calling SMB by the CIFS name, and most documentation still speaks of SMB.)

To secure file access, creation, and download between Windows 2000 servers and down-level clients, implement SMB signing. Doing so provides mutual authentication and message integrity for these operations.

Mutual Authentication

Mutual authentication can prevent "man-in-the-middle" attacks. In such attacks, the attacker masquerades as the other side of the conversation. To the client, he pretends to be the server. To the server, he pretends to be the client. This enables him to listen in on conversations, pass along erroneous information, or block communication in one direction.

When mutual authentication is used, the attacker cannot prove to the server that he is the client, nor can he prove to the client that he is a server. He cannot "sign" the packets as either one. The man-in the-middle attack is thus thwarted.

Message Integrity

SMB signing also can be used to determine whether the data in the packets has been altered in any way. A packet that has been modified can be rejected.

Implementation

To implement message signing, understand that you have a choice. Message signing can be simply enabled—it will occur if the other side requests it—but if both sides do not have SMB signing enabled, it will not be used. Message signing can also be required. If you require message signing and the other side does not have it enabled, no communication will take place.

Windows 98 and Windows NT 4.0 SP3 and above need two registry modifications to implement this. If Windows NT 4.0 servers are part of your enterprise, secure them as well.

Windows 2000 can participate in this process to secure communications with down-level clients. The registry modifications can be made using Group Policy.

To enable message signing on down-level clients, run `regedit` (Windows 98) or `regedt32` (Windows NT 4.0) and add the following value to the registry key indicated in Table 13.2:

```
Value: EnableSecuritySignature
Data type: REG_DWORD
```

A value of 0 disables the feature; a value of 1 enables it. When you have completed your registry entry, close `regedit` or `regedt32` and reboot the system.

SMB Signing Does Have a Cost

The process of SMB signing does have an impact on CPU performance. Some tests have shown up to 15 percent degradation at both the client and the server. For this reason, it is not something to implement on a whim. In certain cases in which sensitive files are being accessed, you might want to implement SMB signing between the server and the clients that access it. You might consider the degradation a small price to pay for the security it offers.

Table 13.2 **Enable SMB Signing**

OS	KEY
Windows NT 4.0 Server	HKEY_LOCAL_MACHINE\SYSTEM\CurrentControlSet \Services\LanManServer\Parameters
Windows NT 4.0	HKEY_LOCAL_MACHINE\SYSTEM\CurrentControlSet \Services\Rdr\Parameters
Windows 98 (includes updated SMB, 95 does not)	HKEY_LOCAL_MACHINE\SYSTEM\ CurrentControlSet\Services\VxD\Vnetsup

To require message signing, run `regedit` (Windows 98) or `regedt32` (Windows NT 4.0) and add the following value to the registry key indicated in Table 13.3. You must also be sure to add the preceding key, `EnableSecuritySignature`, and set it to 1 as well. If you do not, communication will fail.

```
Value: RequireSecuritySignature
Data type: REG_DWORD
```

A value of 0 disables the feature; a value of 1 enables it. When you have completed your registry entry, close `regedit` or `regedt32` and reboot the system.

Table 13.3 **Require SMB Signing**

OS	KEY
Windows NT 4.0 Server	HKEY_LOCAL_MACHINE\SYSTEM\CurrentControlSet \Services\LanManServer\Parameters
Windows NT 4.0 Workstation	HKEY_LOCAL_MACHINE\SYSTEM\CurrentControlSet \Services\Rdr\Parameters
Windows 98 (includes updated SMB, 95 does not)	HKEY_LOCAL_MACHINE\SYSTEM\CurrentControlSet \Services\VxD\Vnetsup

To enable or require message signing with Windows 2000 systems, you can modify the registry with `regedt32`, but the preferred method is to use Group Policy. The security options involved are:

- Digitally sign client communication (always)
- Digitally sign client communication (when possible)
- Digitally sign server communication (always)
- Digitally sign server communication (when possible)

Always, then, means required; *when possible* means enabled.

Using NTLMv2 Negotiated Session Security

Using NTLMv2 negotiated session security is not possible for every communication because not every network communication uses NTLM. If a program uses NTLM to negotiate session security, then it can require NTLMv2 session security. An example of this type of program is any program that uses Secure RPC.

To restrict sessions security, you will need to either use Windows NT 4.0 SP3 or above or use Windows 9x with the AD client installed. Then use `regedt32` (Windows NT) or `regedit` (Windows 9x) and make the following change:

1. Locate the key HKEY_LOCAL_MACHINE\System\CurrentControlSet \Control\LSA\MSV1_0.

2. Add the REG_WORD value `NtlmMinClientSec`.

3. Enter the value you require from Table 13.4.

The values listed in Table 13.4 can be used to require session security.

Table 13.4 **Require Session Security Level**

Value	Required	Note
0x00000010	Message integrity	If message integrity is not negotiated, connection fails.
0x00000020	Message confidentiality	If message confidentiality is not negotiated, connection fails.
0x00080000	NTLMv2 session security	If NTLMv2 is not negotiated, connection fails.
0x20000000	128-bit encryption	If 128-bit encryption fails, connection fails.
0x80000000	56-bit encryption	If 56-bit encryption fails, connection fails.

Improving Basic Systems Security

Windows 2000 has Group Policy to help configure security and control clients. Unfortunately, it can only be interpreted by Windows 2000 computers. It cannot be applied to down-level clients.

Although the Windows 2000 Group Policy and Security Configuration and Analysis tools cannot be used to manage Windows 9x or Windows NT, native NT and Windows 9x tools can be used instead.

Windows NT and Windows 9x System Policy Editors can be used to create policy files. These files—ntconfig.pol for NT clients and config.pol for Windows 9x clients—can be placed on domain controllers in the NetLogon share. When clients log on, the part of policy that applies to them is written to their registries and affects what they can and cannot do as well as how their systems are configured.

Windows NT 4.0 Service Pack 4 introduced another tool, the Systems Configuration Manager. This tool is similar to the Windows 2000 Systems Configuration and Analysis tool. In fact, it was backported from the Windows 2000 developing product.

System Policy Editor

The first thing to remember about System Policy is that policies created on one Windows OS do not always work on other Windows OSs. You must use the correct tool, and you must run it on the OS for which it was developed. Table 13.5 lists which files can be used to control which OSs.

Table 13.5 **System Policy/OS Compatibility**

OS Created in	OS Can Run in			
	Win 95	**Win 98**	**Win NT 4.0**	**Win 2000**
Win 95	X	X		
Win 98	X	X		
Win NT 4.0			X	
Win 2000				X

System Policy is created by changing settings provided in template .ADM files. A policy can include separate settings for users, groups, and computers. Changes made in the GUI are reflected in the registry. Figure 13.1 shows an expansion of the Default User System Policy Editor policy. As you can see, it looks similar to sections within Group Policy.

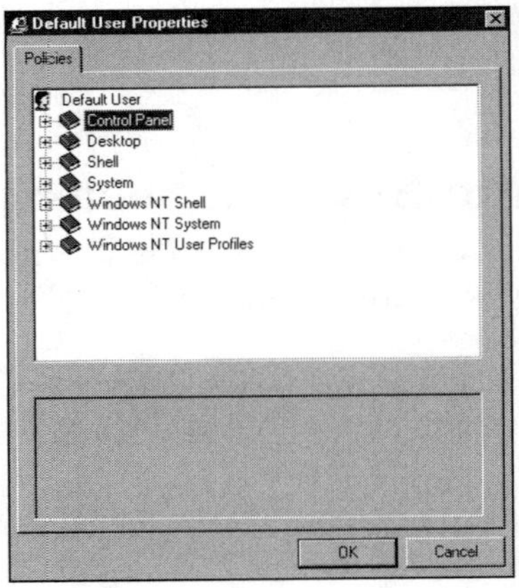

Figure 13.1 System Policy Editor.

The settings control a collection of items for users or computers. Each collection is related to an area of configuration within the OS. Table 13.6 lists the categories that can be configured.

Table 13.6 **System Policy Setting Categories**

Users/Group	Computers
Control Panel	Network
Desktop	System
Shell	Windows NT Network
System	Windows NT Printers
Windows NT Shell	Windows NT Remote Access
Windows NT User Profiles	Windows NT Shell
	Windows NT System
	Windows NT User Profiles

Each category contains a number of settings that can be enabled, disabled, or not defined by manipulating check boxes. Figure 13.2 shows this. These settings change registry settings when applied during logon.

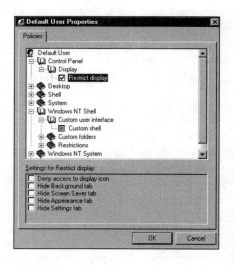

Figure 13.2   Changing settings in System Policy Editor.

Some of the things you can do with System Policy are

- **System policy update.** Set mode to Manual or Automatic and change the policy location to check.
- **System startup.** Record and set items to run at startup.
- **Logon banner.** Create and display a logon banner.
- **Do not display last logged-on user.** Display a blank instead of the name of the last logged-on user.
- **Automatically detect slow network connections.** Detect slow network connections.
- **Slow network default profile operation.** Set to download profile or use local profile when a slow network connection is detected.
- **Restrict Display.** Restrict the Display applet in Control Panel (that is, deny access to it; hide the Background, Screen Saver, Appearance, and/or Settings tabs; and so on).
- **Screen color scheme.** Preset the color scheme.
- **Change shell restrictions.** Remove the Run button from the Start menu, hide Network Neighborhood, and so on.
- **Change system restrictions.** Disable registry editing tools, run only allowed Windows applications, and so on.
- **Change other restrictions.** Remove Map Network Drives and remove View/Options menu from Explorer.
- **Affect Windows NT System.** Disable logoff and Task Manager.

The available items to set depend on the contents of the .ADM files loaded in System Policy Editor. Each OS provides standard .ADM files that can be used to configure policy. Additional .ADM files are provided for other Microsoft products. You can also create your own .ADM files or add settings to the provided ones.

The .ADM files are standard text files. You can use them to manipulate any registry entry. You must, of course, know the entry precisely, and enter the information correctly in the .ADM file.

Good, Bad, Ugly!

The wonderful thing about System Policy files is that once they are loaded on the domain controller, they are applied to all computers and users that you designate within the file. Each time the user logs on, appropriate settings are made.

The bad thing about System Policy files is that once they are loaded on the domain controller, they are applied to all computers and users that you designate within the file. You see, System Policy files "tattoo," or make permanent changes to, the registry. If you remove a System Policy file from the domain controller, you will not return the registry to its prepolicy state. There is no way to remove a bad policy. You have to either create a good one and apply it or directly modify the registry and replace the poor choices with good ones.

A detractor for System Policy files is that there is no central clearinghouse of information on exactly what the settings will be doing. There is no listing of registry entries. In many cases, this is easy to figure out. In others, it is quite difficult.

You should plan and test your implementation of system policies for down-level clients before deployment. To create the files, you must use the appropriate System Policy Editor and use it on a system type on which it will run. So for Windows NT 4.0 systems policies, create an ntconfig.pol file on a Windows NT 4.0 system. For a Windows 98/95 System Policy, create a config.pol file on a Windows 98/95 system. The files are created by the tool and should be placed on every domain controller NetLogon share. The NetLogon share for Windows NT is at %systemroot%\ system32\repl\import\scripts. For Windows 2000, it is at %systemroot%\SYSVOL\ sysvol*name of the domain*\SCRIPTS.

Security Configuration Manager

To install Security Configuration Manager (SCM), you need to do the following:

1. Make sure you have installed NT 4.0 SP4 and have rebooted your system.
2. Run the installation program, mssce.exe. The Security Configuration Manager executable, mssce.exe, is in the mssce\i386 folder on the Service Pak 4 CD-ROM. It is also downloadable from Microsoft.
3. Install the MMC. (When asked whether you want to install the Microsoft Management Console, select Yes.)

To use the program, add the SCM snap-in to an MMC console. The snap-in has two containers: one for the current configuration (the database) and one for "Configurations" or templates. To manage security, you can load the current database and

- Adjust settings manually and then apply them
- Import a configuration and analyze the current database against it
- Import a configuration and apply it to the current computer
- Create your own configurations and export them to a file to be used on other systems

You can also use the command-line tool `secedit` to apply or analyze security settings, just as you can in Windows 2000.

The SCM database holds entries in many of the same categories as that of Group Policy Security Settings, as shown in Table 13.7.

Table 13.7 **SCM to Security Settings Comparison**

Category	SCM	Group Policy Security Settings
Account Policies	Password Policy	Password Policy
	Lockout Policy	Lockout Policy
		Kerberos Policy
Local Policies	Audit Policy	Audit Policy
	User Rights Assignment	User Rights Assignment
	Security Options	Security Options
EventLog	Settings for Event Log	Settings for Event Log
Restricted Groups	(holds restricted groups)	(holds restricted groups)
Systems Services	(holds systems services)	(Yes on Domain Controller Policy and Domain Policy, No on Local Policy)
Registry	MACHINE	(Yes on Domain Controller Policy and Domain Policy, No on Local Policy)
File System	(installation volume settings)	(Yes on Domain Controller Policy and Domain Policy, No on Local Policy)
Public Key Policies	(not present)	(contains policies)
IP Security Policies	(not present)	(contains policies)

You can use the `secedit` tool in a batch file to collect analysis information on multiple systems. Like Security Configuration and Analysis in Windows 2000, you will have to view the results in the GUI, or write your own scripts to interpret the data.

Unlike Windows 2000, security settings are not applied automatically across computers and users using Group Policy. Security Configuration Manager has no way to easily do this. It also cannot automatically reapply your configuration. You can, of course, schedule such a refresh, but if you do not, nothing will happen. You will have to schedule periodic analysis to determine whether the settings are remaining set and then reapply the settings if necessary.

Best Practices

To secure down-level clients:

- Install AD client.

- Require NTLMv2 for authentication.

- Consider SMB message signing.

- Learn to use Security Configuration Manager and System Policy Editor to secure clients.

- Thoroughly test all new security configurations.

For More Information

This chapter discussed services for which complementary information exists in other chapters of this book. The following should serve as a referral source for you in locating this information.

LAN Manager protocols are defined in Chapter 3, "New Protocols, Products, and APIs."

Information on Group Policy is provided in Chapter 9, "Security Tools," Chapter 12, "Domain-Level Security," and Chapter 16, "Securing the Network Using Distributed Security Services."

Security Configuration and Analysis is also discussed in Chapter 9, "Security Tools."

Summary

Securing down-level clients is not an easy task. It's also one that gets neglected in the rush to integrate new operating systems and practices. Working on Windows 9x and Windows NT issues is not sexy or glamorous, but learning to do so can better prepare you to configure Windows 2000 domains.

The processes you use have counterparts on Windows 2000 systems: Group Policy to System Policy Editor, Security Configuration Manager to Security Configuration and Analysis, SMB signing to IPSec. It's not that the tools and processes are the same; it's that they have similar goals and can have similar results.

Remember, security is only as good as its weakest link. Find those links and secure them. This chapter presented a number of ways in which to secure down-level clients. The next chapter will return to a discussion of Windows 2000–specific security.

14

Securing the Distributed File System

THE WINDOWS 2000 DISTRIBUTED FILE SYSTEM (Dfs) does not provide any exotic new security features, but careful attention still has to be paid to properly setting file and folder Discretionary Access Control Lists (DACLs). Dfs does, however, introduce potential vulnerabilities. As files are distributed across multiple systems, there is a potential risk that file access control might not be properly managed across all systems. To secure Dfs, then, you must first thoroughly understand it. Dfs provides administrators with a tool to more easily manage and present file locations, and coupled with the File Replication Service (FRS), it can provide data redundancy.

Understanding Dfs from a security perspective requires:

- Knowledge of what it is and why it will be used
- An understanding of the FRS and how it is used with Dfs
- An understanding of how to securely plan, implement, maintain, and audit Dfs across the enterprise

Understanding Dfs

An earlier version of Dfs was introduced in Windows NT 4.0 Service Pack (SP) 3. Its purpose was to enable administrators to create a cohesive namespace for shared files across the enterprise. Windows 2000 has extended this to include capabilities for managing file replication for fault tolerance and availability.

The issue with securing Dfs is that its data can reside on multiple types of partitions. FAT, NTFS, and even Novel can host shared data that can become accessible through Dfs. To understand the issues and to create a reasonable strategy for securing Dfs, you must first learn something about

- Common Dfs definitions, components, and concepts
- How Dfs works
- The uses of Dfs
- Dfs clients

Definitions, Components, and Concepts

Dfs is not difficult to understand, but it does present a number of new words and basic concepts. The following list should help you become comfortable with the basics:

- **Dfs root.** The first share in a Dfs hierarchical structure. The root can reside on Windows 2000 domain controllers, member servers, and standalone servers. If a Dfs root is hosted by a domain, it is known as a domain-based Dfs root. When a standalone server (one not joined in a domain) hosts the root, it is known as a standalone root.

- **Namespace.** A logical view of an area, such as computer memory, storage, or distributed computing architecture. A namespace often takes a complicated physical structure and presents an understandable one. A company's registered DNS domain name names the Internet namespace for that company. A Dfs namespace begins at the Dfs root. A namespace is addressed by the incorporation of the base name in all components.

- **Name transparency.** Knowledge of the location of an element is not necessary. In Dfs, a user does not need to know on which server a file is located; the user only needs to know the Dfs server name in a server-based Dfs topology or the domain name in a domain-based Dfs topology and the name of the Dfs root.

- **Dfs Link.** A logical connection or mapping between the Dfs root and one or more shared folders or another root. The connection is implemented using standard Universal Naming Conventions (UNC).

- **Dfs server.** A server that hosts a Dfs root. Only Windows 2000 Server, Windows 2000 Advanced Server, and Windows NT 4.0 SP3 can host Dfs roots.

- **Dfs client.** A system that can access shares and files using Dfs. Various Windows operating systems have different levels of interoperability with Dfs. Dfs clients are often specified by giving a revision level that indicates the level of compatibility with Windows 2000 Dfs. A discussion of Dfs clients can be found in the "Dfs Clients" section later in this chapter.

- **Replica.** A duplication of a Dfs root or existing Dfs links. A Dfs root replica is a server that provides redundancy and availability. Replicas of links provide these features for files. Dfs replicas will be discussed in the section "Understanding the File Replication Service (FRS)" later in this chapter.

- **Replica set.** A set of file shares that provides access to copies of subfolders and files.

- **Dfs topology.** The entire logical structure of Dfs. On any given domain or standalone Dfs server, the topology can be viewed from the administrative console. Topology includes roots, links, replica sets, and shared folders.

- **Partition Knowledge Table (PKT).** This table maps the Dfs root and its replicas to referrals (physical servers and shares). A domain-based Dfs PKT is stored in the Active Directory (AD); a standalone Dfs is stored in the registry of the server that hosts the Dfs root. Each referral is given a Time-To-Live (TTL), which specifies how long a Dfs client can cache the referral(s).

How Dfs Works

Prior to Dfs, shared folders on Windows servers could be accessed by using either the UNC name or the drive-mapping graphical user interface (GUI). They still can be; however, you need to know the name of the server and the share. The client Redirector (workstation service in Windows NT and Windows 2000) locates the server and negotiates a connection at the share-point. Locally defined permissions at the share level determine whether the connection can be successful and whether the share can be used as the client requested. A UNC representation including the server name, share name, and file path can be used to directly access a file. Again, locally defined permissions on the share and file determine whether access is granted or denied. Administrators determine which folders to share and set access permissions at the shared folder, its subfolders, and files.

This process works reasonably well on a single file server but does not scale well. To access or provide access across multiple servers and share-points, you must be knowledgeable of the location of the files (on which share) and of each share (on which server in what domain or workgroup) or be willing and able to browse every server to find it. Because each mapped connection needs to use a drive letter for identification, you also can run out of drive letters—only 26 are allowed, and a minimum of three will already be reserved (drives A, B, and C).

In the Dfs, shared folders are collected underneath a central root or roots. To find your files, you just need to know the name of the Dfs root server or Dfs domain and the name of the Dfs root. To access another set of files, you revisit the root. Of course, in a larger system there might be multiple roots, but by using Dfs, you can reduce the complexity of location.

Figure 14.1 displays the traditional folder-sharing environment. Three servers are represented. Each server has shares. The shares that exist on each server are enumerated inside the box. Underneath each server are the net use commands necessary to access the shares across the network.

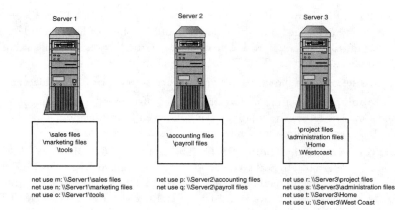

Figure 14.1 Traditional folder share access.

Figure 14.2 illustrates the same collection of shared folders incorporated into a single Dfs namespace. The Dfs root resides on the peachweaver.me domain controller, and all shared folders are physically located as they were in Figure 14.1. Below the domain controller and Dfs root name is the net use statement that will provide access to the share-points. Users can also browse to the Dfs root using Windows Explorer or any other application that provides this capability.

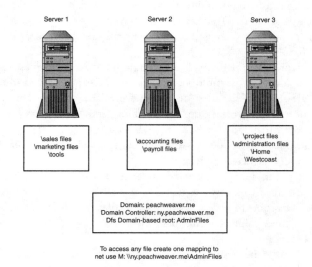

Figure 14.2 Accessing folders in a Distributed File System.

Dfs seeks to make it easier for users to locate the files they need and for administrators to manage the copious files and folders spread across their distributed systems. Before you look at the structures involved in its administration, consider the steps that occur during the process of user access in a domain-based Dfs:

1. A user desires access to a particular folder and selects, or enters, a command that includes the folder's logical address (the domain name where the Dfs root resides and the Dfs root name).

2. If there are multiple possible locations of the root, the IP address of the client is used to determine the client's Windows 2000 site.

3. A Dfs-aware Redirector, the Server Message Block (SMB) Service, and a Dfs driver work together to determine the list of Partition Knowledge Table (PKT) referrals available for the desired link. (There might, of course, be only one referral for the request.)

4. The list is ordered first by client site and then by other sites. Order within each portion of this list is random. The list includes the server, share name, and TTL for each location of the data.

5. The list is passed to the client and is cached. The cached list is known as the client portion of the PKT. TTL information is passed with the list and determines how long the information is cached.

6. The client selects a referral.

7. An attempt at session setup is made. This includes passing the credentials of the client to the server.

8. If a failure occurs (the server is not on the network for some reason, the particular disk is not available, the client's credentials are refused by the server, and so on), a fail-over process begins. This process gets another referral from the client-cached PKT and tries again.

9. The DACLs on the share and on the shared folder determine access to the server file system.

10. Access to the folders and files is determined by their DACLs.

After step 1, the process is transparent to the user. As in traditional shared folder access, the user makes a selection using Window Explorer or any application and then either gets the requested data or is denied.

The components involved are shown in Figure 14.3. The application uses the Dfs client to connect to the Dfs service, which uses information from the PKT. The PKT is stored either in the AD or in the registry. The Dfs console is used to administer the service.

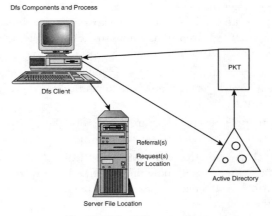

Figure 14.3   Dfs processing.

Uses of Dfs

Dfs can be used in Windows 2000 to

- Alleviate the confusion surrounding accessing files in a large infrastructure
- Provide load balancing for multiple share-points of duplicated data
- Provide fault-tolerance
- Organize and provide a single point of access to all network shares
- Increase availability
- Provide easier Internet and intranet publishing
- Maintain a single point of entry for Windows, UNIX, and Netware shares
- Improve performance

Note that Dfs is not envisioned as a method to provide additional security or to ease the burden of providing file security. In fact, because it promotes and makes easy the proliferation of duplicate files and file systems, it can make the securing of these files more difficult. However, the very process usually used to ease the administrative burden of creating and maintaining multiple copies of files, the FRS, can be used to enforce consistent application of file- and folder-level security. To understand how this is possible, see the sections "Understanding the File Replication Service (FRS)" and "Securing Dfs" later in this chapter.

Dfs Clients

Dfs client software is provided for Windows 95, Windows 98, Windows NT 4.0 SP3, and Windows 2000 (all versions). To use the fault-tolerant features of Windows 2000 Dfs from a Windows 9x client, you must install the Directory Services client provided on the Windows 2000 CD-ROM. Microsoft has indicated that a Directory Services client for Windows NT will be provided by Microsoft with SP7.

If you want to access Dfs links on UNIX or Netware servers, you must be using Windows NT 4.0 SP3 or above or Windows 2000.

Understanding the File Replication Service (FRS)

The Windows 2000 FRS is automatically used to replicate system policies and logon scripts stored in the system volume (SYSVOL) located at %system root%\. SYSVOL contains the Active Directory database and other data that will be replicated. FRS replaces the LMRepl service that was used in Microsoft Windows NT. It can be used to replicate files and folders in a replica set defined in Dfs.

Defining FRS Capabilities

The LMRepl service is not implemented by default in Windows NT. It can be configured to replicate files between domain controllers and servers. Windows NT Workstation can be configured as a destination, but not as a source of replicated files. Replication in LMRepl is not multimaster; it's one-way. A server is configured as the exporting server and pushes data to import servers. If data on the import server is changed, it is overwritten on the import server the next time it is changed on the export server. This service is not suitable for the replication of large amounts of data; it is most suitable for the replication of logon scripts.

FRS provides this service for the SYSVOL folder. In addition, it

- Provides automatic, multimaster replication of SYSVOL data. Changes made on any Windows 2000 domain controller are replicated to any other domain controller in the same domain.
- Can be used to provide multimaster replication of Dfs data.
- Provides configurable scheduling for the replication of Dfs data through directory management of replication for remote sites.
- Starts automatically on domain controllers.
- Can be configured to start automatically on servers.
- Can replicate file and folder properties (including DACLs).

The replication of file and folder DACLs provides the only additional security feature of FRS.

Files and folders in Dfs links on volumes that are not Windows 2000 NTFS cannot be replicated.

Using FRS with Dfs

You must configure and implement FRS for Dfs. It is not automatically turned on. To do so requires the following:

- Dfs must be configured.

- A replica set must be established.

- A replication policy must be established for the replica set.

Files and folders that can be reached through a Dfs link but cannot be replicated are:

- Shared folders and files that are not on a Windows 2000 NTFS volume

- Shared folders and files on a standalone server (the server is not joined in a Windows 2000 domain)

- Files and folders encrypted with the Encrypting File System (EFS)

Creating a replica set allows increased availability of data and provides fault tolerance. An example of a replica set is shown in Figure 14.4. The top large box is an example of a Dfs topology. At the top of the hierarchy is the Dfs root, 'sales files'. Underneath the root are the links (Boston, New York, Chicago). Replica sets are created by using the Add a New Replica Wizard selected by right-clicking a link. In the Dfs administration console, you can display replicas by selecting the link and viewing the Replica pane. In the figure, the peachweaver.me Dfs root 'salesfiles' contains three links: New York, Boston, and Chicago. New York has a replica set that includes three replicas: Brooklyn, Queens, and Manhattan. Boston and Chicago do not have any replicas, just one location. The data folders and files available at each link are listed within the link/share box displayed below the Dfs topology. Notice that the folders and files in each link share box in the New York link are exactly the same. This is because each server hosts a copy of the replica set.

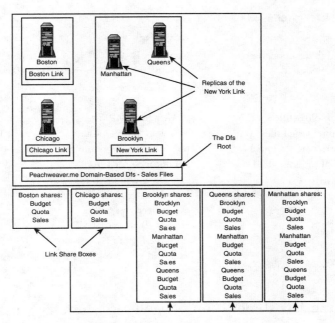

Figure 14.4 Replica sets.

There are several advantages and disadvantages to using FRS with Dfs. Table 14.1 presents a list of these issues.

Table 14.1 **Advantages and Disadvantages of Using FRS with Dfs**

Feature	Advantage	Disadvantage
Data changed on one server is replicated to all other servers in the set.	No master/slave relationship. It doesn't matter where the file is modified.	Conflicts and latency might exist.
Conflict resolution is last writer wins.	No complicated resolution procedure.	Data integrity cannot be guaranteed especially for high-volume changes.
Replication is via the File Replication Service at scheduled intervals.	Replication can be configured to limit bandwidth usage to off-hours.	Replication latency means file content might vary between locations in a replication set.

continues

Table 14.1 **Continued**

Feature	Advantage	Disadvantage
File and folder properties are also replicated.	Can push DACLs consistently across the enterprise.	Because changes can be made anywhere, DACLs cannot be guaranteed to remain consistent.
File and folder filters determine which files and folders are excluded from replication.	.BAK and .TMP files, as well as NTFS mount points and reparse points, are not replicated. You can add additional file extensions to create your own filters. You can remove .BAK and .TMP from the list of files excluded.	Filters must be managed for each Dfs link on a link-by-link basis.

Managing Dfs Replication Schedules

You can create schedules for the replication of replica set data. This is accomplished in two places: the connection objects used by Active Directory Replication (connection objects are defined in Active Directory Sites and Services and represent the preferred replication points between sites) and the replica set itself. Although replication schedules configured via connection objects will override replications set at the replica set level, it might be easier to set replication once for a large replica set versus setting it multiple times for multiple connection objects.

Scheduling for replication is set either on or off for a period of time. Replication is not always occurring; it is triggered by changes to files and folders in a replica set. Once triggered, it will occur during the time set for replication in the replication schedule.

If replication is being used to transfer the change of DACLs on a file, then the replication schedule may be an important part of securing Dfs.

Securing Dfs

There are three elements to secure in the Windows 2000 Dfs:

- The Dfs topology
- File and folder DACLs
- The File Replication Policy

Securing the Dfs Topology

To secure the Dfs topology, first set permissions on the Dfs root. By controlling who can access and modify the Dfs structure, you are preventing accidental or purposeful changes that could destroy the topology or otherwise reduce availability of Dfs links. Securing the topology is managed by changing permissions on the Dfs objects in the AD and in the Windows NT and Windows 2000 registry. AD objects can be manipulated in the Dfs Administration console. Registry objects can be manipulated via regedt32. The location of registry objects is HKEY_LOCAL_MACHINE \CurrentControlSet\Services\DFSDriver\LocalVolumes and HKEY_LOCAL_MACHINE\SOFTWARE\Microsoft\DFSHost.

Windows 2000 registry permissions, of course, can be set in Group Policy.

By default, you must be a member of the Domain Administrator group to create a Dfs domain-based root. You must be a member of the local server's Administrators group to create a Dfs standalone-based Dfs root. After the root is created, changes can be made and information read by various groups. Table 14.2 lists these permissions.

Table 14.2 **Permissions at the Dfs Domain-Based Root**

Group	Permissions
Administrators	Read, Write
Authenticated Users	Read
Domain Admins	Full Control
Enterprise Admins	Full Control
System	Full Control

You might want to restrict the rights to change data or permissions to a subgroup of administrators.

Securing Files and Folders

Dfs does not create any new security functions that would allow the centralized control of file and folder permissions. Rather, it integrates with the existing security function set through DACLs directly on the folders and files in the normal manner. In other words, Dfs plays by the rules. Although Dfs makes it easier to find out the path to folders and files, permissions set on shares, folders, and files control the access. A user might be able to access Dfs and find all the locations for the salesfigures.doc file, but if this user does not have permission to access the file, he will not gain any new permission to the file by using Dfs. If he has permission to read the file, he will still only have permission to read the file should he access it through Dfs, through a normally mapped share, through the net use command, or if he can log on locally to the file server, through directly accessing the file.

File, folder, and share permissions should be set and maintained in the normal manner. The largest issue comes from the existence of multiple copies of folders and files. Files in replica sets must have consistent access permissions set. If DACLs are not consistent across the replica set, authorized users might not be able to do their jobs, and unauthorized users might gain access or additional permissions where they should not.

To set and maintain DACLs, you do have choices. You can

- Visit each server to set and maintain DACLs at each location

- Set DACLs on original copies of files and implement the FRS for the replica set. FRS replication will replicate the file and folder permissions when replicating the files and folders. If you restrict Full Control privileges, you can control irresponsible or malicious changes.

- Set DACLs through Group Policy if files and folders on servers follow the same naming conventions. You do this by creating an organizational unit (OU) for servers in a replica set and using the File System folder within the Security Settings division of the Group Policy object for the OU.

Securing the File Replication Policy

The File Replication Policy is set through the property pages for each link. The capability to set the policy is controlled by permissions set at the Dfs root. To determine who can manage replica sets, you must visit the Active Directory Users and Computers console and navigate to the System\File Replication Service\Dfs Volumes\dfsroot\dfsreplicaset object. To further protect the replication process, maintain control over the files and folders where the replication database is stored. Permissions are set on the FRS, the Dfs volume container, and each Dfs root and replica set. Table 14.3 displays the initial permission set.

Table 14.3 **Dfs Replication DACLs**

Container	Administrators	Authenticated Admins	Domain Admins	Enterprise Users
File Replication Service	Read, Write, Create All Child Objects	Read	Read, Write, Create All Child Objects, Delete all Child Objects	Full Control
Dfs volume	Read, Write, Create All Child Objects	Read	Full Control	Full Control
Dfs root	Read, Write, Create All Child Objects	Read	Full Control	Full Control
Replica set	Read, Write, Create All Child Objects	Read	Full Control	Full Control

The SYSTEM, of course, has Full Control. The replication database is stored at systemroot\ntfrs\Jet\Ntfrs.jdb.

Initial permissions set during a clean install of Windows 2000 are Administrators and SYSTEM: Full Control.

Planning a Secure Dfs Architecture

You should plan your Dfs architecture and its security when planning your Windows 2000 implementation or migration. One way to do this is to create a logical naming standard and structure for files, folders, and Dfs roots. You also can duplicate file folders and names to separate servers that will be used in replica sets. By doing so, you have made file access and maintenance easier. You can add permissions to paths you establish in Group Policy Object Security Settings. Even if you cannot do this, it is much easier to remember and maintain consistent DACLs on folders and files with the same names.

Second, you can plan usage of the FRS to automatically replicate initial file DACLs to all copies in the replica set and/or for maintenance of changes.

Third, you can test replication latency to determine the best replication schedule. If permissions on NTFS-stored Dfs folders are changed, you will want to make sure the changes are replicated as quickly as possible to other locations.

Finally, you can provide a select group of administrators to manage Dfs and to modify default permissions before any Dfs roots are implemented.

If you need to migrate an existing Dfs topology from Windows NT 4.0 to Windows 2000, you still have an advantage if you carefully plan the process. You might be restricted by previously established naming conventions and administrative policy.

If you already have Dfs in place or are layering Dfs over an existing file storage system, you will have to do what you can to implement the secure practices previously listed.

Implementation and Maintenance

To maintain security during implementation, you should restrict the administrators allowed to implement Dfs roots, links, and replica sets. A good practice to follow is to designate one individual as the implementation leader. It is ideal for all activity to be developed by one person, but at least have one person in charge of the process.

Maintaining security on Dfs involves following the previously outlined practices and making sure to implement a backup and disaster recovery plan. By creating root replicas, you can probably prevent the loss of your Dfs topology at the cost of using additional servers. By creating replica sets, you can create fault-tolerant Dfs because folders and files are maintained at additional server locations.

None of this, however, is a replacement for good backups. Because the topology is expressed in the registry for standalone based Dfs and in the registry and AD for domain-based Dfs, backing up the registry and the AD will allow restoration of the topology. At least one copy of the data, including one copy of data in replica sets, should always be made.

Data restoration of typical links, or of replica sets whose data is manually replicated, is the same as any data restore. Restoring data in replica sets is a little more complicated.

If data is restored from a backup that is older than some other copy of the replica set, there is potential for overwriting newer data. Of course, corrupt data or data lost during a hard drive crash can be restored by removing corrupt data or by replacing a crashed hard drive, creating the share and Dfs link, and allowing normal replication to restore the data as changes are made to the intact copies. This process could take a long time, however, and could unnecessarily tie up network bandwidth if the replica set is large.

A special type of restoration, the nonauthoritative restore, can be used to replace data and still ensure that old data will not overwrite new data at other locations. This process is the same process used to restore a copy of the AD to domain controllers without causing damage to existing domain controller copies of the AD. Authoritative and nonauthoritative restores are further explained in Chapter 16, "Securing the Network Using Distributed Security Services."

Auditing Dfs Security

Auditing Dfs security requires you to be able to check DACLs on Dfs objects (roots, links, and replica sets) and on the files and folders referenced by these objects. Although viewing the DACLs through the Windows 2000 interface might be tedious, two other choices are available.

First, the Security Configuration and Analysis Tool can be used to compare ideal DACLs that are defined by policy to those that are currently set. The use of this tool is described in Chapter 9, "Security Tools."

Second, batch scripts can be written using command-line tools found in the Windows 2000 Support Tools folder and in the Windows 2000 Server Resource Kit. In particular, the following Resource Kit tools can be used:

- **enumprop.exe**. Dumps all properties (including security descriptors) set on any directory service object
- **showacls.exe**. Enumerates access rights placed on files and folders
- **subinacl.exe**. Enumerates security information on files, registry keys, and services
- **xcacls.exe**. Sets file-system security
- **srvcheck.exe**. Lists shares on a computer and enumerates users on the DACLs for each share

Support tools, some of them former Resource Kit tools, are provided in the support Tools folder on the Windows 2000 Server CD-ROM. Support tools must be installed separately from the operating system. A description of these tools is available in the current Resource Kit help system. Relevant security tools are:

- **acldiag.exe**. Lists security attributes on Active Directory objects
- **dsacls.exe**. Manages access-control lists for directory services
- **windiff.exe**. Displays differences between two text files or two folders
- **sdcheck.exe**. Displaces the security descriptor for an object including inherited access control lists (ACLs)

Best Practices

Microsoft recommends the following best practices related to securing Dfs:

- Set permissions by groups, not individual users, to secure Dfs root, Replication Policy, shares, folders, and files.
- Because replica sets require the same DACLs for folders and files, use FRS to synchronize.
- FRS transactions are stored in jet database to protect the database.
- If a user has no permissions on a folder, the folder appears empty. He can still traverse the folder hierarchy to reach folders and files on which he does have permission. Protect sensitive files by maintaining strict control of permissions. If you don't need access to files in a folder, you don't need the List Files and Subfolders permission for that folder.

Summary

This chapter investigated the functions of, uses of, and security issues related to the Dfs. Although Dfs does not provide any additional security features, it does present a new wrinkle to the establishment of security on files and folders that are part of Dfs replica sets.

Replica sets that have FRS replication configured will automatically replicate file and folder changes including changes to DACLs. Proper control of permission changes allows control of initial configuration and maintenance. Setting DACLs on one object sets those DACLs on all copies of the object. Adjustments must be made for replication latency. Group Policy can also be used to maintain DACLs on file sets with the same exact names and paths.

Dfs also provides an environment that must itself be secured because unauthorized access to this rich environment could cripple a business reliant on its design.

IV

Securing Real-World Networks

15

Secure Remote Access Options

Windows 2000 provides many secure remote access options. If you need to offer employees, business partners, customers, or the public access to your resources, there are services, features, and utilities that can be used to do so securely. This chapter will specifically address three tools that can be used to accomplish this:

- Routing and Remote Access Service (RRAS)
- Internet Authentication Service
- Terminal Services

I will also discuss securing remote administrative access.

Routing and Remote Access Service (RRAS)

Routing and Remote Access Service (RRAS) is installed by default but is not started. This service provides routing as well as remote access choices. Remote access can be configured using the following four elements of RRAS:

- Network Address Translation (NAT)
- Internet Connection Sharing (ICS)
- Remote Access Policies
- Virtual Private Networking

Configuring remote access requires the selection of a computer or computers to act as remote access servers. Windows 2000 Server or Advanced Server can be used to host this service. These servers can be either standalone servers or servers joined in a domain. Servers joined in a domain can use the domain account list (available through the Active Directory) for authentication.

The server used for remote access can be configured to use dial-up hardware or network-based connections. The physical process of connectivity is not discussed in this chapter, unless it has bearing on your choices. For example, to use Remote Access Services over the Internet, an Internet connection must be available to the client and server. How you obtain that connection is not important; how you secure it is.

A server, or a hardware device used to connect a network to a public network, is often referred to as a *network access server*, or NAS. This might be a modem bank, a Windows 2000 server using Remote Access Services and its associated hardware, or some other operating system–based remote access service. You will often see the initials NAS loosely used. In this chapter, NAS will always mean a Windows 2000 RRAS unless specifically defined otherwise. In any network, you must question the use of the term NAS to determine what kind of hardware and software it represents.

Network Address Translation (NAT) and Internet Connection Sharing (ICS)

Network Address Translation (NAT) is a process performed to assist IP communications between two networks. When packets cross from one network into the other, the IP address contained in the address header is changed or translated. Internet Connection Sharing (ICS) also performs this translation, but although it is similar in concept, it has less functionality than the NAT service.

NAT is not a new function, and many routers, firewalls, and remote access servers have their own flavor of NAT. Informational RFC 2663, "NAT Terminology and Considerations," explains the general definitions and compares different models of NAT. In this chapter, of course, all discussion is about NAT as implemented by Microsoft in Windows 2000.

Process and Configuration Requirements

The process used to perform NAT is illustrated in Figure 15.1. In the drawing, the NAT server has two addresses: 192.168.2.25 on the internal network and 208.168.156.3 on the external network. This simplified network consists of internal addresses on the 192.168.2.0 network and external addresses on the Internet. Routers are not shown for convenience. The numbered steps in the figure are defined in the following list.

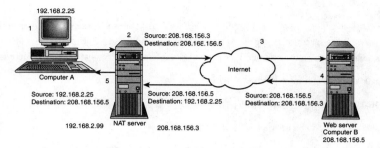

Figure 15.1   The NAT process.

1. Computer A on Network A wants to read a Web page on Web server Computer B on the external network.

2. Because Computer A exists on the internal network without connection to the outside world and with only an internal address, it sends its request packets through the NAT server.

3. The NAT server replaces the source IP address of Computer A (192.168.2.25) with a valid Network B address (208.168.156.3) and sends it on to Computer B. (The NAT server has been configured with one or several valid addresses it can use.)

4. Computer B receives the packet and prepares a response. This packet will have the valid destination address of 208.168.156.3.

5. The NAT server replaces the destination address with Computer A's valid IP address (192.168.2.25) and sends the packet on to Computer A.

As you know, to communicate on the Internet, each computer must be assigned a valid Internet IP address. You cannot simply use any IP address as the IP address of the computer you are using on the Internet. If you use a NAT service, you do not have to have a valid address for every computer in your network that needs to be connected to the Internet. You do, however, need to have at least one valid IP address. The valid address will be used on the NAT server's external network interface. When your internal systems need to access the Internet, the NAT server will replace the internal address with the public, or external, address or addresses it has been given.

Your internal network can use a private address range. This range can be from the three private address ranges identified as not being valid Internet address ranges. If internal computers use these addressing schemes, they will not be able to directly access other computers on the Internet.

> **Note**
>
> Three network address ranges are identified by RFC 1631 as IP networks that are not valid for Internet use. They are not specifically assigned to any organization and thus cannot conflict with any organization's address range on the Internet. They can be used internally on a private network. These ranges are
>
> 10.0.0.0 with a subnet mask of 255.0.0.0
>
> 172.16.0.0 with a subnet mast of 255.240.0.0
>
> 192.168.0.0 with a subnet mask of 255.255.255.0
>
> If you are using NAT to provide access for your internal network, you can use one of these address ranges for all computers on the internal network and the internal adapter of the NAT server. The NAT server will also require a valid Internet address for its external adapter. It might also require a range of valid Internet addresses if it is to be configured to provide a range of addresses for NAT services.

Other important security advantages of NAT might have suggested themselves to you and are listed here:

- No knowledge of the actual IP address of Computer A is made available to any computer on Network B. In fact, no knowledge of any internal network address is made available to external computers. This capability, the hiding of internal network addresses, is a valuable aid to securing your network.

- The NAT server manages incoming packets by matching them with prior outgoing requests. Alternatively, you can preconfigure a route for an incoming request. In this manner, a request to access a Web server on the internal network can be granted. If, however, no request or route exists, an incoming packet has nowhere to go and is dropped. An attacker seeking to penetrate your network will have a harder job doing so.

- If internal addresses are from the private IP address ranges (addresses that are not valid Internet addresses), attackers will not be able to use them even if they somehow are obtained. The IP address, because it is not valid on the Internet, will not be routed to the server, and the server, by default, will not route external packets with internal destination addresses.

To configure NAT, you must do the following:

- Configure the IP address of the internal network adapter.
- Enable and configure RRAS.

- If a dial-up connection is used:
  - Enable routing on the dial-up port.
  - Create a demand-dial interface to connect to the ISP.
  - Create a default static route that uses the Internet interface.
- Add the NAT routing protocol.
- Add Internet and internal network interfaces to the NAT routing protocol.
- Enable the network address and name resolution.
- If desired, add special ports for computers (such as a Web server) on the internal network that need to be accessed from the external network, and map these ports to the internal computers address.

NAT Editors and Proxy Requirements

Additional services must be added or configurations made for some types of connections over NAT. This includes the configuration of NAT editors or proxies.

NAT enables translation of IP addresses in the IP header, TCP port numbers in the TCP header, and UDP port numbers in the UDP header. This is sufficient for many connections. Many applications and protocols, however, might require changes in additional information or require that IP address and TCP/UDP port information stored in the payload be translated. If these applications or protocols will be used over a NAT connection, then special processing can be provided by NAT editors or proxy software.

Applications that require NAT editors and for which Windows 2000 provides one are

- File Transfer Protocol (FTP)
- Internet Connection Message Protocol (ICMP)
- Point-to-Point Tunneling Protocol (PPTP)
- NetBIOS over TCP/IP

NAT proxy software is required for

- H.323 (standard streaming multimedia applications)
- Direct Play
- LDAP-based Internet Locator Service (ILS) registration
- Remote Procedure Call (RPC)

Tip

IPSec cannot do NAT! If you are using NAT, you cannot establish a virtual private network (VPN) using Layer 2 Tunneling Protocol (L2TP) of IPSec. Instead, use PPTP with MPPE. See the section "Virtual Private Networking" later in this chapter.

Allowing Inbound Connections

When an internal computer initiates a connection to a host on the external network, the NAT server will return a response from the external host to the internal computer. Internet users, however, cannot access your internal resources through the NAT computer unless you take special action. If you want to allow inbound communication initiated by Internet users, you must configure this access. To do so:

- In the NAT interface, reserve, or configure, a static, external address that can be used specifically to represent the resource computer on the internal network. The resource computer will not be assigned this address. This address should include the NAT server external address as the gateway and the address of the DNS server.

- If the address is not reserved in the NAT list of external addresses, make sure this address is not one allocated by the NAT computer (if the NAT computer allocates multiple external addresses for the internal network).

- Configure a special port or static mapping from this public address and port number to a private address and port number. If you want to provide access to an internal Web server, for example, you would configure a specific mapping using port 80.

- Figure 15.2 illustrates this arrangement. The internal Web server has an internal address of 192.168.5.4 and is listening on port 80. On the NAT server, one of a range of valid IP addresses, 208.64.88.145, and the NAT server's port 80 is mapped to the internal web server's IP address and port 80. Internet users (1) entering www.peachweaver.com in their Web browser can access the internal server. Their browsers use DNS (2) to obtain the 208.64.88.145 address and to reach the (3) NAT server. The NAT server will then translate the address to 192.168.5.4, and (4) the Web server will get the connection request. Outbound responses from the Web server (5) will be re-sent to the requesting (6) browser's computer.

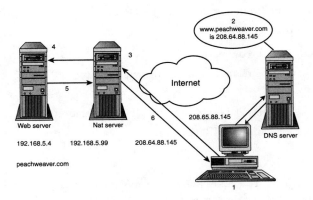

Figure 15.2 Inbound connections.

Internet Connection Sharing

Internet Connection Sharing (ICS) is NAT for the small-office or home-office network. Like NAT, ICS provides network address translation, but unlike NAT, ICS can be implemented on a Windows 2000 Professional system.

ICS does not provide the full features that implementing NAT on a RRAS does. A summary of differences between NAT and ICS is listed in Table 15.1.

Table 15.1 **Difference Between NAT and ICS**

Feature	NAT	ICS
Method of connection	Dial-up; network.	Dial-up.
DHCP	Can use DHCP to supply outbound addresses. Can coexist with internal DHCP servers.	Provides DHCP addressing for the entire network. Cannot coexist with statically configured computers or other DHCP servers.
Server addressing	You configure static addresses for internal and external adapters.	Reconfigures the internal network adapter and provides another IP address.
Modifications	Modify settings as necessary when things change. You configure the addressing parameters for your internal network.	Cannot modify the default. Cannot disable the DHCP allocator or the range of private IP addresses, or disable DNS proxy or inbound mappings.

ICS is enabled on the computer that has a physical modem connection to the Internet and has been configured for dial-up access. For other computers to use this service, they must have the TCP/IP protocol configured and be configured to use ICS by connecting to the shared connection.

> **Warning**
>
> ICS should not be configured on a network that has or will have other Windows 2000 domain controllers, DNS servers, gateways, DHCP servers, or statically configured IP addresses. If you do configure it on a network with any of these services, you will have to use NAT to use these services.

To configure ICS, you must configure both the computer that will do the network address translation (the NAT computer) and the clients. To configure the NAT computer, you must

- Configure an Internet connection.
- Test the connection from this computer.

- Enable Internet connection sharing on this interface by completing the following:

    - From the Sharing properties page of the connection, check Enable Internet Connection Sharing for this Connection.
    - If the connection should automatically dial when another internal computer attempts to access external resources (the Internet, for example), check Enable On-Demand Dialing.

To configure clients:

- Add, if necessary, TCP/IP.
- Configure TCP/IP to obtain an address automatically.

Remote Access Service

Remote access is configured using the Routing and Remote Access console. To establish routing and remote access, you must

- Enable remote access
- Accept the default policy, configure the default policy, and/or create policies
- Set an authentication method for Remote Access Services
- Enable dial-up access at the user level on the server

Authentication Methods

The Windows 2000 Routing and Remote Access Server can be configured to use either of two authentication methods: Windows Authentication or Remote Authentication Dial-In User Service (RADIUS). This choice determines whether the RemoteAccess Policies are determined by the local server or are centrally managed by a RADIUS server. Windows 2000 implements RADIUS in its Internet Authentication Service (IAS). IAS is described in the section "Internet Authentication Service (IAS)" later in this chapter.

> **Tip**
>
> If you need to use a Windows NT 4.0 RAS server in a Windows 2000 network, you must make sure the Windows NT 4.0 system has had Service Pack 4 or above applied. You must also make sure the Windows 2000 domain is configured to allow pre-Windows 2000 servers to access Active Directory. This can be done by placing the Everyone group in the Pre-Windows 2000 Compatible Access group. If, when the domain was established, you selected the option to Allow Pre-Windows 2000 Servers to Access Active Directory, then this is done for you. If you did not make this selection, it can be configured by adding the group in Active Directory Users and Computers or by using the following command:
>
> ```
> net localgroup "Pre-Windows 2000 Compatible Access" "Everyone" /add
> ```
>
> When the Windows NT 4.0 RAS server is upgraded or replaced by a Windows 2000 RAS server, be sure to remove this group. Placing groups or users in the Pre-Windows 2000 Compatible Access group is a security risk. This group allows anonymous users to access information about your network.

The default authentication method for RRAS is Windows Authentication. This means that remote access requires the RRAS server to use the domain-level user IDs if the server is joined in a domain or the local Security Account Manager (SAM) accounts if the RRAS server is a standalone server. Remote access policies created on the remote access server are used.

The RADIUS authentication method requires that the RRAS server act as a RADIUS client and contact the RADIUS server prior to establishing any session. The RADIUS server still uses Windows 2000 accounts to authenticate the connection; however, it participates in this process, and policies written on the RADIUS server are the ones that apply.

Figure 15.3 shows the authentication process for both Windows Authentication and RADIUS. In the upper-right part of the diagram, User A attempts a connection to the office network. User A's system dials in to the RRAS server on the office network. RRAS1, the RRAS server whose authentication method is Windows Authentication, checks its policies to see if one applies to User A. One does, so RRAS1 checks the Active Directory of its domain for the user's credentials. When the credentials and all aspects of the policy coincide, User A gets a session to the office network.

In the lower part of the figure, User B dials in to RRAS2. RRAS2 has authentication method RADIUS, so it contacts the RADIUS server. The RADIUS server checks its defined policies and, when appropriate, the Active Directory of the office network. In this example, the user is authenticated and allowed to begin a session.

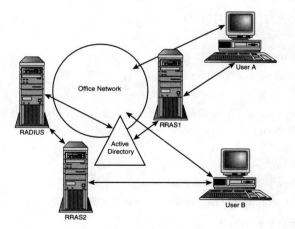

Figure 15.3 Windows Authentication and RADIUS methods.

Policies

To control remote access using RRAS, you create policies on the server. These policies are used to control and restrict remote access when Windows Authentication is chosen as the RRAS authentication method. Windows 2000 provides a large array of choices in configuring policies. You can restrict users, groups of users, and protocols; change authentication and encryption methods; configure the type of connection request that triggers the policy; define a dial-up profile for the policy; and determine access by creating permissions on the policy. A default policy is set when remote access is enabled.

Default Policy

The default Remote Access Policy is written to allow access if dial-in permission is enabled for the user account. If access is not enabled at the user level, remote access through this server is denied. This policy ensures that easy, complete, dial-in access can be easily configured in a manner similar to Windows NT 4.0. The default settings can be edited to make the following changes:

- Additional conditions can be added, and the original default condition of allowing access 24×7 can be removed.
- Remote access can be denied instead of allowed if the user meets the conditions.
- The profile can be edited. Default settings are
    - MS-CHAPv2 or MS-CHAP for authentication
    - Any level of encryption including none
    - PPP
    - No dial-in constraints
    - Multilink as per server settings
    - IP policies as per server settings
- User accounts can be modified to specify the use of policy on the remote access server, to configure callback options, or to deny access.

Creating Policies

To create a policy, you must do the following:

- Specify the conditions that will trigger the policy
- Assign permissions to use the policy
- Configure a dial-in Profile

When a policy is configured, the conditions must be specified that trigger this policy. Conditions consist of attributes. For example, if you want to create a condition that operates depending on the protocol used, the condition would consist of the attribute "The protocol to be used" and the name of the protocol (for example, PPP). In many cases, the attribute can be defined by a range or a list. Some attributes require that a corresponding service be available. For example, to configure a policy based on the attribute "Phone number from which the call originated," the phone line must provide the Caller ID feature. Another external service requirement is for Dialed Number Identification Service (DNIS) or "Phone number dialed by user."

Attributes include

- Phone number dialed by user
- Phone number from which the call originated
- Friendly name for the RADIUS client (IAS only)
- IP address of RADIUS client (IAS only)
- Manufacturer of RADIUS proxy of NAS (IAS only)
- Time periods and days of week during which user is allowed to connect
- The protocol to be used
- String identifying the NAS originating the request
- IP address of the NAS originating the request (IAS only)
- Type of physical port used by the NAS originating the request
- Type of service user has requested
- Tunneling protocol to be used
- Windows group that the user belongs to

Each policy must have permissions assigned. It must identify which groups or users are granted or denied remote access privileges when their requests for remote access trigger the condition. You might want, for example, to create a group called Remote Access Users and grant that group the right to remotely access the network. You could use that group name as the specific qualifier for the attribute "Windows group that the user belongs to." However, other groups can be designated as the ones that can use a particular protocol or attribute.

A user or group can further be restricted or configured by completing a Dial-in Profile. This profile includes several levels. Each level and a description or a pointer to a table that further describes it (if applicable) is given in the following list:

- **Encryption levels**. See Table 15.2.

- **Authentication methods.** This affects the client's method of authentication. If the policy is to control settings via policy, you expand or limit the options for client authentication here. User connection configuration also can set authentication methods, but server-side configuration determines which of these can be used. If the Extensible Authentication Protocol (possibly for smart card authentication) is desired, it must be enabled on the client and server side. Table 15.3 lists the client authentication methods.

- **Dial-in constraints.** See Table 15.4.

- **IP address assignment policy.** See Table 15.5.

- **Multilink.** Determines whether this client can use multiple ports and, if so, to what degree.

- **Advanced.** Configures additional information for use with RADIUS, with specific modems, or with routers.

Table 15.2 **Encryption Levels**

Level	Definition
No Encryption	No encryption is used
Basic	40-bit DES
Strong	56-bit DES

Table 15.3 **Authentication Methods for Clients**

Method	Notes
EAP	Smart card or MD5 challenge can be configured. EAP must be used if clients will use smart cards.
MS-CHAPv2	Recommended for most secure access if EAP is not enabled.
MS-CHAP	An improvement over CHAP.
CHAP	Encrypted authentication.
PAP, SPAP	Unencrypted authentication.
Unauthenticated access	PPP clients can connect; no authentication method is used.

Table 15.4 **Dial-In Constraints**

Constraint	Notes
Disconnect if idle for	Enters the number of minutes. This is an important security consideration because you should not allow endless idle connections. These connections tie up resources and can become a security liability on an unattended computer.
Restrict maximum session to	Restricts the length of a connection in minutes.
Restrict access to the following days and times	Restricts users to times when access can be monitored or to times when they are expected to work. You might want to restrict contract or other temporary workers, for example, to normal work hours. Attempts at penetrating the network may be more likely to occur during off hours.
Restrict dial-in to this number only	Enters a phone number. A particular group of users can be restricted to a single dial-in number. Access to particularly sensitive networks might be more easily blocked by ensuring that certain remote access users enter the system far from these areas. Other users might require special access and can be given a particular number.
Restrict dial-in media	Access for this group or connection can be restricted to a particular media, such as DSL, ISDN, VPN, or another. If some remote access must always be via VPN, this is the way to restrict it.

Table 15.5 **IP Address Assignment Policy and Filters**

Policy	Notes
IP address assignment	Selects one: server must supply, client may request, or server settings define policy.
Define IP packet filters	IP packet filtering can be configured on packets sent by the client or to the client.

If the RRAS connection is the only thing between your network and the outside world, you might want to configure filters so that only the protocols required for the type of connections this group of users need are allowed.

Account Lockout

An additional feature of the Remote Access Service is the capability to lock out a user account after a number of unsuccessful authentication attempts. If an unauthorized user is attempting to guess the password of a known account, if an attacker is using a dictionary attack (a computer-directed attack in which all possible words of a provided dictionary are tried against the logon account), or if a valid user enters his password incorrectly, this feature will lock out the account after the number of attempts configured. A successful connection will reset the failed attempts count. This is a feature separate from the Account Lockout policy set for all accounts and all connections within a Windows 2000 domain and is only applicable to remote access connections.

To configure the feature, you must edit the registry of the server that provides the authentication. If the remote access server authentication method is Windows Authentication, edit the registry on the remote access server. If the authentication method is RADIUS, edit the registry on the IAS server.

To enable lockout, set MaxDenials (the number of failed attempts before account lockout) to 1 or greater. MaxDenials is set in HKEY_LOCAL_MACHINE\SYSTEM\CurrentControlSet\Services\RemoteAccess\Parameters\AccountLockout.

To disable account lockout, reset MaxDenials to 0.

Modify the time period after which the number of failed attempts is reset by setting ResetTime value in minutes.

The account of the user that is locked out will be reset after the expiration of ResetTime. You can manually unlock the user account by editing the Account Lockout subkey named after the user account.

Note
Although setting MaxDenials seems like a good idea, you should be aware that a malicious user could launch a denial-of-service attack by repeatedly attempting to log on to user accounts. The attacker will not gain entry; however, the account will be locked out, and the legitimate user will be denied access.

Data Encryption

Remote access via the Routing and Remote Access Server can also be further protected by requiring a connection to use a virtual private network (VPN). Either PPTP with MPPE encryption or L2TP with IPSec encryption can be used. You configure the VPN in Routing and Remote Access, and then you can require that it be used via policy.

Virtual Private Networking

The ultimate in securing communications between two pieces of a network is to secure the link. In the past, this was accomplished by leasing the communication line between two points. Later, sharing semiprivate communications links between well-trafficked points was the accepted modus operandi. Today, we create VPNs to carry our data across public networks.

As previously discussed, in the common definition of this scenario, encrypted data is tunneled between two endpoints across a public network. Although all data on a public network is subject to interception, data traveling through a VPN is thought to be safe because it's encrypted and because additional secure practices usually are implemented both to protect data transport and to evaluate the data received at the other end. The tunnel functions to make the communication path, which traverses multiple routing points, look as if it's a point-to-point connection. A VPN is given the "virtual" moniker because the connection and the tunnel are usually created only when there is a need to send data. It's as if a completely enclosed walkway is built over the Los Angeles expressway every time someone needs to walk across.

Commercial products and services exist with which you can create your own private network over the Internet. Windows 2000 provides native VPN constructs and protocols that enable you to create a VPN without purchasing special software. You can even create tunnels across your LAN to provide secure transport of sensitive data.

To learn about the capabilities of these tools, you must first ground yourself in knowledge of the components and then evaluate when to choose one protocol over the other, how to maximize your use of them, and where to place the components.

General Considerations

VPNs are created to operate from endpoint to endpoint. The endpoint can be a Windows 2000 Professional, Server, or Advanced Server. Windows 2000 Professional is used in a client-to-server arrangement. In this scenario, a business traveler with Windows 2000 Professional on her laptop can dial in to an Internet connection, access a Windows 2000 RRAS, make a connection to the VPN endpoint (which can reside on the RRAS server or another Windows 2000 server), and create a tunnel. Data is encrypted and remains so from the laptop to the VPN server. In a server-to-server construct, two Windows 2000 servers form the endpoints of the tunnel, one on each side of the Internet. Any data that passes between them can be securely tunneled. Data traveling to the destination computer from the tunnel endpoint, or from source systems to the endpoints, is not protected by the tunnel. It can be secured with other means.

For the actual tunnel to be used, the endpoints must be configured. Four components must be in place:

- A physical connection to the Internet including any hardware that must be configured
- VPN software (this must be added or enabled and configured)
- Remote access policies (these must be established)
- Domain groups (these must be configured so they can be used in allowing VPN access)

Internet Connections

You must first establish a connection to the Internet. This connection can be direct, as in a T1, T3, or other communications line that is designed to be always "up," or it can be a dial-up connection using a modem and standard phone lines. The capability to make an Internet connection is assumed and is not described further in this book.

VPN Software

Establishing endpoints that can be used to create the tunnel on demand requires the configuration of VPN software. On the server, you must

- Enable the RRAS
- Configure a static address pool
- Establish appropriate connection authentication methods
- Configure static routes to reach intranet and Internet locations (including routes to branch offices)
- Increase the number of PPTP or L2TP ports
- Configure PPTP or L2TP packet filters
- Set the ISP phone number for each PPTP or L2TP device

You also must complete additional VPN security configuration as necessary. If L2TP over IP Security (IPSec) is used or if smart cards are used for authentication, Certificate Services are required. To allow the use of smart cards, the Extensible Authentication Protocol (EAP) must be enabled.

> **Note**
>
> PPTP uses port 1723 for control and protocol number 47 for data. Protocol number 47 is the General Routing and Encapsulation (GRE) protocol. PPTP uses this for data. L2TP uses port 1701 (UDP). If IPSec is used, additional protocol IDs come into play: number 50 for the Encapsulation Security Payload (ESP) and number 51 for the Authentication Header. A full listing of protocol IDs and ports used by Windows 2000 can be found in the appendix of the Server Resource Kit book, TCP/IP Core Networking Guide. A listing is also kept up to date at http://windows.microsoft.com/windows2000/reskit/webresources.

The tunnel can be configured to be mandatory (when a connection is made from point A to point B, a tunnel is automatically used) or voluntary (when a connection is established, a tunnel is requested).

To configure a Windows 2000 Professional system as an endpoint (to create a client-to-server tunnel connection), you must first create a connection. You can use the Make New Connection Wizard from the Network and Dial-Up Connections Window to do the following:

- Select the type of connection to be Connect to a Private Network Through the Internet.

- Determine whether the initial connection should be dialed or the user must first make the physical connection.

- Set the hostname or IP address of the VPN server.

- Limit access to the connection to a single user or make it available to all users of the computer.

- Adjust the authentication method the client will use.

- Select the type of connection: Automatic, L2TP over IPSec, or PPTP. A selection of Automatic will attempt an L2TP connection first and then a PPTP connection.

Like the client-to-server VPN connection, the router-to-router connection requires configuration of both endpoints of the tunnel. To configure these connections:

- Create a demand-dial connection between the two routers. (The demand-dial interface can be configured to disconnect after idle time or to remain persistent.)

- Create user accounts for each router to use.

- Set the connection to be one-way initiated (branch office to home office) or two-way demand-dial; either router can start the connection.

- Create a static route for each router that points to the other router's internal network with a gateway address of the other router's external interface address. For example, if David and Brendan are the names of the interfaces at each endpoint, a David account is created on the server with the Brendan interface, and a Brendan account is created on the server with the David interface. The Brendan account is used to call the Brendan interface and vice versa.

Remote Access Policies

You might recall that Remote Access Policies can be created that affect the use of VPN connections and can enforce their use. By setting all user accounts to be controlled through Remote Access Policy and deleting the default Remote Access Policy on the RRAS, you establish the appropriate use of the tunnel.

To establish appropriate connections from the Internet, the port type is set to VPN, and the Called-Station-ID is set to the IP address of the Internet interface of the VPN server. By making this IP address the required interface, use of the tunnel can only be initiated from outside the company.

Domain Groups

Different VPN settings and usage can also be controlled through policy. Access to and use of these can be controlled though setting permissions. To effectively manage their use, create groups of appropriate users. For example, you might want to create one group for employees and another for business partners. If you need to establish tunnels between routers, you can create a third group to hold these computer accounts.

Tunnel Choices

If the decision is made to implement a VPN, several tunnel-related choices have to be made:

- The network configuration (where to place the VPN server)
- The type of tunnel (either mandatory or voluntary)
- The tunneling protocol (either L2TP over IPSec or PPTP)

Placement and Type

The VPN router should be placed on the border or periphery of the network with one interface to the Internet and one to the internal network. The VPN router can be protected by a firewall, and the firewall must be configured to allow the appropriate protocols to pass. Protocol numbers and ports are listed in the information provided about them. A composite list can be found at http://windows.microsoft.com/windows2000/reskit/webresources.

Figure 15.4 shows the arrangement for client-to-server remote access through a VPN. Access to the internal network can be reached through the VPN. The VPN router has a connection to an ISP and therefore can be accessed across the Internet. The Windows 2000 Professional laptop initiates the connection by first dialing in to an ISP and then, through the ISP, connecting to the VPN server. After this initial connection, the client attempts a VPN connection. The server authenticates the client via the Active Directory, authorizes the connection via Remote Access Policy, and the tunnel is established.

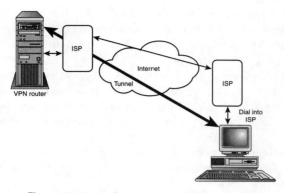

Figure 15.4   A client-to-router VPN tunnel.

A client-to-router connection type is a good choice if you need to provide access to traveling users, telecommuting users, or small branch offices with one or two primary users.

Router-to-router connections allow the creation of VPN connections without the configuration of client-side software. The connection is configured to automatically dial (if necessary) the connection if users attempt to connect to resources on the other network. The connection can be configured to maintain a persistent connection. Figure 15.5 illustrates a router-to-router VPN. When User A on Network A attempts to access a resource on Network B, the router establishes a VPN tunnel between the two networks over the Internet. Data is encrypted and tunneled between the two routers. Data from User A to the router, and from the Network B router to the user's desired resource, are not tunneled or encrypted.

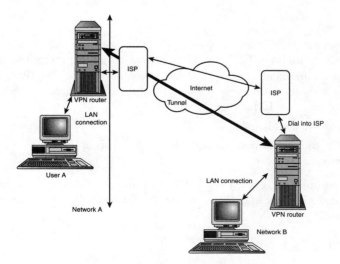

Figure 15.5   A router-to-router VPN.

Router-to-router connections are a good choice when many users need to access resources on another network from a common point. This type of connection, however, does not provide end-to-end security. (Security from the first contact with the network to the final destination.)

A client-to-router connection likewise does not create perfect end-to-end security, but it does provide a VPN tunnel and encryption from the client on the less-trusted network (the Internet) to the VPN router on the border between the Internet and the trusted network. Table 15.6 summarizes the choices and security reasons for making them.

You can determine whether client-to-router, router-to-router, or both types of connection are allowed through configuration and Remote Access Policy.

Table 15.6 **Choosing a Connection Type**

Need	Client-to-Router	Router-to-Router
Traveling users	Provides security across the Internet from client to router	N/A
Telecommuters	Provides security via dial-up access to the Internet	N/A
Branch office connection	Many clients to configure, does not provide end-to-end security	One server to configure, centralized client access control

Protocols

Two choices are available for VPN protocols when you create a VPN tunnel with Windows 2000: PPTP or L2TP over IPSec. Both protocols provide the basic services of authentication, tunnel creation, and data encryption. L2TP over IPSec is generally considered to be the more secure choice, but there are two situations in which you absolutely cannot use L2TP over IPSec:

- When you are using NAT
- When you do not have, do not want to purchase, or do not want to implement Certificate Services

A discussion of PPTP, IPSec, and L2TP can be found in Chapter 3, "New Protocols, Products, and APIs." Table 15.7 summarizes the features of the protocols as they exist in Windows 2000.

Table 15.7 **Protocol Choices**

Feature	PPTP	L2TP Over IPSec
Data encryption	Uses MPPE	Uses IPSec
Remote policies	Can govern the use of the tunnel and the protocol	Can govern the use of the tunnel and the protocol
Client configuration and connection	Available	Available
NAT	Yes	No
NT 4.0 and Windows 98 clients	Yes	No
Authentication of user via Kerberos	Yes	Yes
Authentication of machine via Public Key certificate	No	Yes
PKI	No	Required
40-bit encryption	Yes	Yes
56-bit encryption	Yes	Yes
128-bit encryption	Subject to export and import laws	No
Triple DES	No	Yes
Multiprotocol support	Yes	Yes

Internet Authentication Service (IAS)

When you need multiple remote access servers, or some combination of VPN tunnel servers and remote access dial-up servers, it is easier to manage Remote Access Policies if you provide centralized control. Centralized control of remote access servers can be established with a RADIUS server. Windows 2000 comes with an implementation of the RADIUS service, the IAS. IAS can provide:

- Centralized authentication (IAS uses the Active Directory.)
- Auditing (IAS can centrally log activity.)
- Authorization (Remote access policies on the IAS server are used for all remote access authorization.)

Although IAS is represented as a service that runs on a Windows 2000 Server, the concept of centralized remote access authentication, authorization, and audit has its own complement of players. Before continuing, make sure you understand the following definitions:

- **NAS.** The server that provides access to a network. In a Windows 2000 IAS design, the NAS is represented by a Routing and Remote Access Server.

- **IAS or RADIUS client.** The service that provides an interface between the dial-up or other remote client and the IAS server.

- **Dial-up client.** The computer system that accesses the RRAS server via a dial-up line.

- **Other remote access clients.** Clients that access a network from outside the network, such as users of a VPN.

- **IAS or RADIUS server.** The Windows 2000 server that has IAS installed.

To implement IAS to provide these services, you must do the following:

- Consider the placement and configuration of the IAS server.
- Write IAS Remote Access Policies.
- Consider where a VPN might be applicable for use with IAS.
- Determine when you should use IAS and when you should use RRAS alone.

Errors in Understanding

When first introduced to RADIUS or IAS, most people get confused by two terms: RADIUS client and NAS. Remember that in our IAS design, the NAS is simply a Windows 2000 RRAS server. The RRAS server acts as the RADIUS client. Another design could use another type of NAS, but this would then require an IAS proxy. A Windows 2000 IAS proxy does not exist—yet. Do not confuse this with a dial-up client. Dial-up clients have no direct contact with the IAS server.

IAS Configuration and Placement

To force Routing and Remote Access Servers to operate under the control of an IAS, the RRAS authentication method is changed to RADIUS. When this is done, any policies that reside on the RRAS server are no longer used. When a request for access to the network is received by the RRAS server, a new authentication process takes place as diagramed in Figure 15.6. Numbers on the figure match those in the following numbered list:

1. A dial-up client wants to access the network.

2. RRAS acts as a RADIUS client and relays this request to the IAS server.

3. The IAS server requests authentication of the user from Active Directory.

4. The IAS server is informed of the results. In the drawing, the client is authenticated.

5. The IAS server checks its Remote Access Policies; if one of the IAS Remote Access Policies is triggered, it is applied.

6. If the user is granted access, this information is relayed to the RRAS server.

7. The RRAS server relays a positive response to the client, and a connection can be made. (The actual connection and results will depend on the server that the client wishes to access. That authorization process is not completed by IAS or RRAS but by the destination server in the usual manner.)

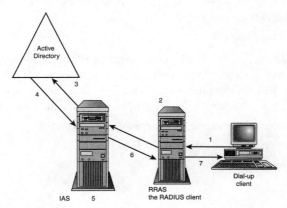

Figure 15.6   Authentication and authorization with IAS.

Configuration

Configuration of IAS depends on whether you will need to support dial-up access, extranet, Internet, outsourced dial-in, or VPN access.

General configuration consists of the following:

- Installing the IAS service
- Configuring IAS ports
- Configuring event logging
- Configuring interaction with realms
- Adding NASs and (if required) PPTP servers as clients on the IAS server
- Setting NAS authentication to RADIUS
- Configuring NAS as dial-up or VPN servers
- Creating Remote Access Policies on IAS
- Configuring authentication and accounting logs
- Copying configuration to any backup IAS server
- Registering IAS servers in the RAS and IAS Servers group in Active Directory

To copy an IAS configuration to a secondary or backup IAS server, use the `netsh` command. First, obtain the configuration `netsh aaa show config ,<path>\file.txt`, which places all configuration information (Remote Access Policies, registry, logging) in the file.txt file. Next copy this file to the new IAS server computer. Then use `netsh` to apply the following configuration:

```
netsh exe <path>\file.txt
```

Several scenarios exist that describe the placement of the IAS server. In each of these scenarios, the idea is to provide centralized control. Wherever the IAS server might need to be reached via the Internet, it should be placed behind the firewall. The firewall needs to be configured to allow access to packets, which are all of the following:

- The destination or source IP address of the IAS server
- The destination or source port for RADIUS
- Those using UDP

Note

Two radius ports exist: For authentication, port 1645 or port 1812 can be used. For accounting, port 146 or 1813 is used.

You can also restrict access to the IP address used by the client if this is known.

Centralized Control of Multiple RRAS Servers

In the simplest arrangement, the centralized control of a number of RRAS servers at one location is required. The process here is simple. All remote access servers, whether they are dial-up servers or VPN routers, can be pointed toward the IAS server by simply changing their authentication method. The IAS server has to be reachable from the RRAS servers and able to reach the Active Directory. All servers are joined in the domain. Figure 15.7 shows the IAS server, multiple RRAS servers, and a VPN router. Dial-up clients and an Internet client connect to the RRAS servers and the VPN router, respectively. Each client is eventually authenticated by having credentials passed to the IAS server and to the Active Directory.

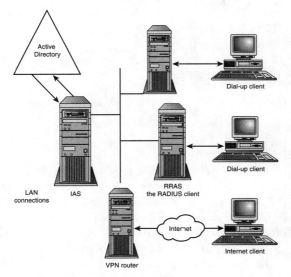

Figure 15.7   Multiple RRAS servers: one location.

Centralized Control of Remote Access at Several Locations

IAS can also control the Remote Access Policies of RRAS servers at multiple locations. Figure 15.8 shows an implementation of IAS in which the IAS server resides at corporate headquarters in New York, while RRAS servers are placed in division offices in Boston, Bar Harbor, and Brattleboro. Telecommuters dial in to their local division offices. Only the initial logon authentication and authorization to remotely access resources are funneled through the corporate IAS server. Although initial connection times are slower than local processing, daily phone charges are reduced. For this company, the advantages of central control of remote access outweigh the slight delay at the beginning of a workday.

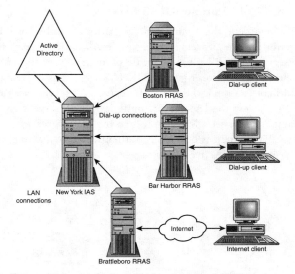

Figure 15.8 Multiple RRAS servers: multiple locations.

Control for Traveling Employees

If a company has traveling employees, the desire to reduce long-distance charges and to centrally control remote access can be accomplished by subcontracting the remote access servers to an ISP. In Figure 15.9, several ISP locations are using remote access servers to receive calls from traveling corporate employees. The ISP's remote access servers then channel requests to the corporation's IAS server. Once authenticated and authorized, the remote user is able to access company resources via the ISP's communication lines. This arrangement can make access widely available at a reduced cost. A VPN tunnel can be set up between the ISP and corporate headquarters for further security. The ISP's RRAS servers and VPN tunnel servers must be configured as clients on the IAS server.

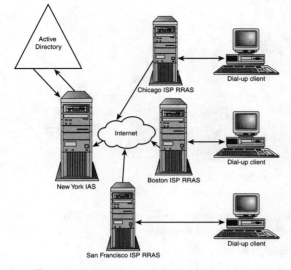

Figure 15.9   ISP RRAS/IAS corporate partnership.

Access for Business Partners

If business partners require access to corporate assets, you can control that access using IAS and RRAS. A VPN connection to the corporate assets from any number of business-partner locations can be configured. A smart card solution here would also be useful. The corporation could issue authorized business-partner employees a smart card and reader. The VPN tunnel server can be configured to request authentication via an IAS server. Certificate services must be configured, and the EAP protocol must be enabled as an authentication method on the VPN server and IAS server. Figure 15.10 displays the steps and configuration used by Peachweaver to provide access to its business partner, Cote. The steps are repeated in the following list.

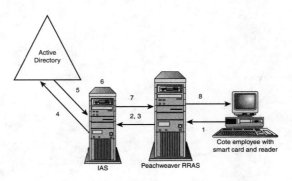

Figure 15.10   Extranet access and IAS.

1. A Cote employee inserts a smart card into the reader and selects the dial-up connection configured for Peachweaver.

2. The Peachweaver RRAS server answers the call.

3. The RRAS server (the IAS client) contacts IAS for authentication and authorization.

4. The IAS server accesses the Active Directory.

5. Because the user certificate is mapped to the user's account in the Active Directory, the validity of the user request can be verified and a positive reply made to the IAS server

6. The IAS server checks its policies for this user's requirements for authorization to access corporate resources.

7. A response is returned to the RRAS server.

8. The RRAS server allows the connection if the response is positive.

ISP Remote Access Management

An ISP can use RADIUS (IAS) to control, authorize, and audit multiple users of multiple services. The IAS hosts multiple IAS servers (at least one backup IAS is required) and multiple RRAS servers. Subscribers dial in to the RRAS servers to access the Internet. Because the RRAS servers are IAS clients, the authentication of users and their authorization to use the service requested (perhaps a special number for special services) can be authorized, and accounting information can be recorded for billing purposes. Extensive IAS policies can determine who gets to do what and when. Figure 15.11 details this arrangement.

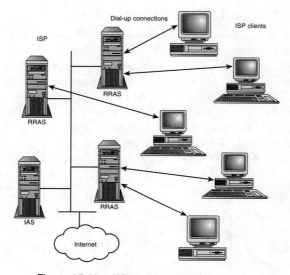

Figure 15.11 ISP remote access management.

IAS Policies

IAS policies are configured on the IAS server. They can be copied to back up IAS servers using the `netsh` command previously discussed. (For a general discussion of how to set policies and the types of policies that can be designed, refer to the section "Remote Access Policies" earlier in this chapter.)

The important thing to remember is that, once an RRAS server is modified to use RADIUS authentication, any policies configured on the server are ignored. You must configure all Remote Access Policies on the IAS server. You can configure specific policies for a particular RRAS server, but you must do it by modifying the attributes of the Remote Access Policy on the IAS server.

Using a VPN with IAS

If a VPN is established using a Windows 2000 RRAS, the Remote Access Policies for this server can be centrally controlled by making the VPN server a RADIUS client of an IAS server. (Figure 15.7 shows this arrangement.) The VPN server must be configured separately and tested. Then, switch its authentication method to RADIUS to centralize policies.

When to Use IAS and When to Use RRAS

Several factors will decide whether it is advantageous for you to use IAS over RRAS. The first decision is easy. If you have one location and few remote access clients, IAS provides no advantage: Set up a single RRAS server. If you have a large number of remote access users at a single location and you must configure multiple RRAS servers, then IAS provides the benefit of being able to centrally implement policies, modify policies, audit and control remote access. If your needs for Remote Access Services are at multiple locations, then the advantage or need to use IAS might depend on whether your IT management is centralized or decentralized and whether the delay provided by the WAN authentication is justified and maintainable.

Terminal Services

Terminal Services provides user access to server-run applications. Its use on the local network was discussed in Chapter 11, "Securing Windows 2000 Server." Terminal Services can be made available, however, over a dial-up connection and over the Internet. Both user application access and remote administration can be used if some configuration changes are made. There are also some additional security issues to consider. We will discuss these issues in the following sections.

Providing Remote Access for Users

If a user can remotely access a network on which a terminal server resides, then access can be provided to the terminal server.

Remote Access Configuration

First, appropriate remote access, either dial-up or Internet must be configured. Remote access configuration and policies must be determined and implemented. If the user has dial-up access configured and the Terminal Services client installed on his computer, then access to the terminal server is the same as if the user was on the local network.

It would be a good practice to remove any unnecessary network services from the terminal server system and to remove the OS2 and POSIX subsystems. Anytime you offer remote access to internal services, it is a good idea to limit the possibilities for attack.

Administrative Practices

Administrators might want to modify user configuration so that users can reconnect to a session if the dial-up connection is broken. Dial-up access to the network is controlled through Remote Access Policies on the remote access server, not on the terminal server. Access to the terminal server can be controlled at the terminal server.

You might want to modify the encryption level if users are remotely accessing the terminal server. Remember that medium- and high-level encryption encrypts data traveling in both directions. Low-level encryption only encrypts the data from the client to the server. Screen shots of sensitive data would not be encrypted if the low-level encryption strength was used.

Additional security can be provided by requiring a VPN tunnel for all remote terminal service access or for a select group of users. Smart card access can also be configured.

Providing Remote Access for Administrators

Terminal Services can also be run in Remote Administration mode. This gives only members of the Administrators group access to the server and provides a secure way to remotely manage these systems because encryption of data traveling to and from the server is built in to the server and its client.

If you allow remote access to the network for Administrator accounts, you should protect them via a VPN connection.

Securing Remote Administrative Access

An argument can be made that no remote administrative access should be allowed. People who make this argument perceive that the risk is too great. They say that if an administrator is allowed to remotely access a server, then all one has to do is hack the administrator's account to gain control of the system. If an administrator has to sit at the console to administer the system, then two things are needed: a hacked Administrator account and physical access to the server. However secure this policy might be, in most environments, it is not practical. Instead, attention should be paid to securing the administrator's account and the communications between the administrator and the server. To do so, you must first be aware of the methods that can be used to administer the server across the network.

Several possibilities exist for providing remote administrative access:

- Users with Administrator accounts can be permitted to use dial-up access with no additional security.
- Users with Administrator accounts can be given smart cards, readers, and accounts configured to provide access via smart cards.
- Users with Administrator accounts can be required to use a VPN tunnel when they access the network using this account.
- Telnet can be used to access and control servers.
- On the local network, IPSec policies on the server and client can insist on IPSec encryption of administrative access to servers for administration purposes.

Controlling Access Using Policy

On the remote access server, special policies can be written to insist on the security requirements you require. If the tightest security is not required for all remote access, at least provide for administrative access that meets as many of the following requirements as possible:

- Only the strongest authentication methods—MS-CHAPv2, or smart cards using EAP/TLS—should be used.
- If using L2TP over IPSec VPN, insist on the strongest authentication encryption algorithms (triple DES in the United States and Canada).
- If a certificate structure is not available, use MPPE encryption over PPTP for the VPN tunnel protocol.
- Do not use telnet!
- Configure policies to restrict their use to as few administrators as possible.
- Audit access.

Using Telnet

If telnet must be used, understand the difference between the telnet service provided with Windows 2000 and the one provided with Services for UNIX and configure appropriately.

Native Windows 2000 telnet services allow two telnet connections. By default, the service is required to use NTLM authentication. Although this is not the securest protocol, standard telnet might not require any authentication other than cleartext. Make sure the telnet services have not been configured to allow cleartext authentication.

Microsoft Services for UNIX provides for 63 telnet connections. The Windows 2000 command or the KORN shell may be used. Windows Scripting Host or KORN shell scripts can be written and used to administer Windows 2000 using these services over a telnet connection. Anytime you add additional services to Windows 2000, you are opening the server up to additional possible attacks.

Best Practices

Decisions on the best way to provide remote access will vary depending on the tools you have chosen. Here are some thoughts:

- Install and test RRAS servers before making them IAS clients.
- Immediately after installation, back up the IAS database file ias.mdb from the %systemroot%\system32\ias folder.
- Back up the ias.mdb file whenever changes to the IAS configuration are made.

- The IAS and RRAS servers should be dedicated servers. This will help eliminate the possibility that unauthorized users will gain access and weaken the security configuration.
- Physically secure IAS, VPN, and RRAS servers.
- Protect IAS and VPN routers behind a firewall.
- Turn on the account lockout feature.
- Disable authentication protocols you do not use. Do not use PAP unless you must support legacy systems.
- Determine desired logging for audit purposes and back up IAS logs.
- Do not use telnet.
- Secure remote administrative sessions with IPSec or with VPNs if these sessions are being initiated externally to your network.
- Increase encryption levels on Terminal Services when providing remote access.

For More Information

This chapter discussed services for which complementary information exists in other chapters of this book. The following should serve as a referral source for you in locating this information.

Information on the local use of Terminal Services is provided in Chapter 11, "Securing Windows 2000 Server."

IPSec and RADIUS are discussed in general in Chapter 3, "New Protocols, Products, and APIs."

The Windows 2000 implementation of IPSec is covered in Chapter 16, "Securing the Network Using Distributed Security Services."

Access to resources over the Internet is explored in Chapter 19, "Web Security."

Information on public key/private key encryption and Public Key Infrastructure can be found in Chapter 17, "Enterprise Public Key Infrastructure," Chapter 4, "Public Key Infrastructure (PKI)," and Chapter 2, "Cryptology Introduction."

Interoperability issues are explored further in Chapter 18, "Interoperability," and Chapter 20, "Case Study in Interbusiness Access: Distributed Partners."

Summary

Remote access is not a luxury for privileged administrators or technologically savvy sales departments. Remote access is used to provide access for telecommuters, business partners, and traveling employees of all levels. Remote access is not difficult to configure; the real issue is secure remote access. In this chapter, tools to provide remote access—and how to secure them—have been explored. Centralized security through IAS servers and their Remote Access Policies was presented as well as the configuration of Remote Access Policies and dial-up access of terminal servers. Finally, reasons for not using the Windows 2000 telnet service, and how to lock it down a little better, were discussed.

16

Securing the Network Using Distributed Security Services

Windows 2000 has many new tools and processes that enable the knowledgeable administrator to protect resources and configure and analyze security. Previous chapters discussed user accounts, file and registry access, and how to set policies to control a single machine as well as the possibilities inherent when using the Security Configuration and Analysis and Group Policy tools. Chapter 12, "Domain-Level Security," described the Active Directory and how centralized control of users, computers, and other resources could be managed. Although this chapter laid the foundations, it did not provide the details that show the full potential of this utility.

Managing distributed security without taking the time to understand its processes is like flying a stealth bomber without any lessons. If you know a great deal about flying a small plane, you might get the bomber up in the air, you might stay aloft for some time, and you might even get someone to talk you through a landing. But while you're aloft, if something goes wrong or the enemy attacks, you're history. And something will go wrong. The enemy will attack.

If you are going to distribute Security Policy across your Windows 2000 network, you will need to know:

- How Active Directory (AD) information is distributed across the enterprise
- How to protect and recover the AD
- How Group Policy inheritance works

- The range of computer configurations and installation items that can be controlled via Group Policy
- What happens to policies when Windows 2000 computers and Windows NT 4.0 computers exist in the same infrastructure

This chapter will discuss these items.

Active Directory Operations

Knowledge of AD operations is important in order to understand how security information is distributed across the enterprise and how best to protect the AD. To update and maintain the AD, data is constantly moving between domains, from domain controller (DC) to domain controller, and from domain controller to member computers. From a security perspective, there are several important elements of this process:

- What information is replicated and when
- How Group Policy is propagated to objects within the AD
- Where the data is physically stored
- How to protect the replication process
- How to protect the data
- How to protect the schema

As you will recall, information that describes the AD configuration and the AD objects is stored on each domain controller in a domain. Most domain-specific data can be changed on any domain controller of the domain. Changes to AD data, configuration information, and the schema must therefore be communicated between domains. In a multiple-domain forest, data from each domain must be shared with every other domain. To accomplish this, AD replication takes place at regular intervals. Replication is primarily multimaster; that is, all domain controllers can participate in the changing of data. Some types of data, however, are controlled by, changed at, and replicated from specific domain controllers. These domain controllers take on this role in addition to their normal role and serve as operations masters (also known as flexible single master operations, or FSMOs).

AD Replication

AD replication is the process by which changes to data in AD partitions or segments are synchronized to corresponding partitions on other domain controllers. To understand the data movement, you must know

- What the partitions contain and where they reside
- The replication operations that take place
- The roles that DCs can play

AD Data Partitions and the AD Database

The AD data is all contained in one database, the ntds.dit. Each domain controller in a domain has its own copy of ntds.dit. Within the database, data is segmented into three different areas. These areas or logical partitions are called domain, schema, and configuration partitions.

Forest-wide data is stored in the schema and configuration partitions, while domain data is stored in the domain partition. All domain controllers throughout the domain have these three partitions. The data in the partitions might vary due to replication latency and due to any extra roles the domain controller plays. An exact copy of any partition that exists on a domain controller is called a replica. The partitions, however, are all stored in the single ntds.dit database. The database itself is not physically partitioned (or spread across multiple servers).

> **Note**
>
> Typically, if you speak of a partitioned database, you are speaking of a database in which the data is distributed across multiple physical platforms. Each physical partition contains different data. The sum of these different partitions defines the database. The AD is not a partitioned database by this definition. Although its data is divided into different segments called partitions, the data has the potential for remaining the same from DC to DC.

If you search for the ntds.dit file, you will find two versions on the domain controller. Only one is actively being used and updated. The other existed prior to the server's promotion to domain controller and was used in that operation. The copies can be found at their default locations:

%SystemRoot%\NTDS\ntds.dit. This is the database in use

%SystemRoot%\System32\ntds.dit. This is the distribution copy of the default directory used when a Windows 2000–based computer is promoted to a domain controller.

Replication Operations

Replication operations are performed periodically across the forest. The following information defines the replication components of the Windows 2000 replication process, or *replication model*.

- Replication operations are either single master (changes take place at one domain controller only) or multimaster (changes can take place at any domain controller). All changes are replicated to all domain controllers in the domain. Figure 16.1 shows two domains in a forest. Each domain has two domain controllers. The three partitions exist on each domain controller, but one domain controller in each domain is shown to have a Global Catalog. Single-master and multimaster replication operations are illustrated.

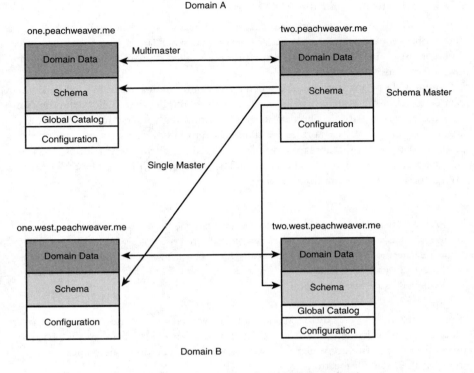

Figure 16.1 Single master and multimaster replication.

- Replication follows the loose consistency with convergence model. This means that a partition can have many writable replicas (copies), but each copy is not guaranteed to be consistent at a precise moment in time. Eventually, the system will reach a steady state, or converge. In this state, all replicas are exactly the same.

- Movement of data is store-and-forward. Changes are not replicated to every domain controller at the same time. Initially, a change is sent to only a few domain controllers. Each one of these then passes, or forwards, the changes on to another set of domain controllers. Figure 16.2 illustrates this point. It shows that Joe User has been added to the peachweaver.me domain on the boston domain controller on the right. The change first propagates to domain controllers newyork, houston, and sanfran. Finally, the change is delivered to rochester, dc, dallas, ftworth, oakland, and segunda.

It is possible that replication cycles (in which data in domain A is replicated to B, is seen as changes that need to be replicated to C, and then C replicates to A) can occur because multiple connections can reduce latency and tolerate a single failure. Propagation dampening, however, or the automatic reduction in repetitive replication, is used to eliminate redundant replication.

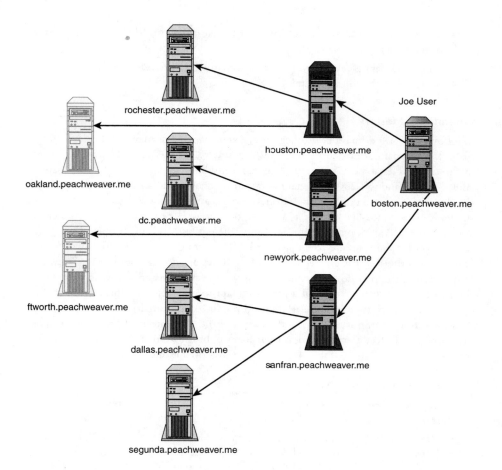

rochester.peachweaver.me

houston.peachweaver.me

Joe User

oakland.peachweaver.me

dc.peachweaver.me

boston.peachweaver.me

ftworth.peachweaver.me

newyork.peachweaver.me

dallas.peachweaver.me

sanfran.peachweaver.me

segunda.peachweaver.me

Figure 16.2 Store-and-forward replication.

- The method of replication used is pull-replication. Replication partners pull changes from domain controllers where changes have been made. The domain controller with the change does not "push" the change on to other domain controllers.

- Replication is state based. Replicas store per-object and per-attribute change information; they do not use a change log. Because each change received includes an update sequence number (USN), the replica can determine whether to apply the change. By using a sequence number instead of a time stamp, the replica will always have the latest update even if clocks are not synchronized.

- Replication between sites is under administrative control. Administrators can select replication bridgeheads (preferred replication partners between sites) and schedule replication.

- The topology is managed automatically. (You do not need to determine replication partners.)
- Some AD data is replicated between domains. As previously described, this data is placed in the Global Catalog.

Operations Masters

Windows NT 4.0 domain controllers are either primary domain controllers (PDCs) or backup domain controllers (BDCs). Windows NT 4.0 BDCs are read-only copies of the domain database. Changes to data can only be made at the PDC. There are no BDCs with Windows 2000. Domain data can be changed at all domain controllers in the domain. To avoid conflicts, however, the replication of some data is controlled by a single domain controller known as an operations master, or flexible single master operation (FSMO). Any domain controller can manage these additional operations master roles. Two of these roles are forest-level roles. They are created when the first domain controller in the forest is created. Three of the roles are domain-level roles. They are created when the first domain controller in the forest is created and when a new domain is added to the forest. In a three-domain forest, therefore, there will be 11 operations masters: two for the forest and three for each domain. Knowledge of these additional roles is important if you are to secure the AD. You must know what operations masters do to determine what their loss might mean. You should learn how to recover from their failure. Table 16.1 defines these operations master roles.

Table 16.1 **Operations Masters**

Role/Operations Master	Definition	Number
Relative ID (RID) Pool Allocation	Each security object in a domain is provided with a security identifier (SID). The SID is a combination of a domain number and a unique portion called the relative ID (RID). Thus, each SID is unique. Within a domain, the RID identifies the object uniquely. The RID Pool Allocation master ensures that RIDs are not duplicated within a domain by allocating a unique pool of RIDs to each domain controller.	Each domain has a single RID Pool Allocation master.
Schema Modification	The schema of a forest must remain consistent. If changes were allowed to be made to the same schema object at different domain controllers at the same time, replication might cause corruption. Therefore, changes to the schema must occur at a single domain controller.	One in the entire forest.

Role/Operations Master	Definition	Number
Primary Domain Controller (PDC) Emulator	To remain backward compatible with Windows NT 4.0, a PDC Emulator master must be provided. Windows NT backup domain controllers that are joined to this domain will see this Windows 2000 domain controller as if it were a Windows NT PDC. In a mixed mode Windows 2000 domain, this master will replicate account database changes to the Windows NT BDCs.	One in every domain.
Infrastructure Operations	Moved and deleted objects need to be handled in a special way. This operations master manages the changes necessary (including updates to the SID) to all references to these objects throughout the domain.	One in every domain.
Domain Naming	Domain names need to be unique in the forest. This operations master makes sure that this happens.	One in the forest.

Transfers and Seizures

The information provided in Table 16.1 should give you some idea of the problems that would occur if one of the operations masters were lost. If an operations master needs to be taken off the network for brief periods of time, this might not create a serious problem. If you need to, however, you can transfer control from one domain controller to another, or if the operations master cannot be accessed to do this, you might seize control of the role and give it to another domain controller.

A *transfer* is an orderly change with both domain controllers participating in the change. The data is synchronized with the data managed by the role owner going to the server receiving the role before the role itself is transferred. In a *seizure*, the role is grabbed or seized from the current operations master. The recommended action depends on the operations master and the length of time it will be off the network. Specifically:

- If the primary domain controller emulator is lost, a user of a Windows 3.51 or 4.0 system that does not have the AD client cannot change his password. Users cannot log on if their passwords expire. If you need to take this operations master off the network for maintenance, you should transfer the role to another domain controller. The total loss of this operations master should be recovered quickly by seizing control of the role and moving the role to another domain controller.

- The temporary loss of the infrastructure master might not be worth fixing. It probably will not be immediately noticed unless you have recently moved or renamed a large number of items. If it is necessary to seize control of this operations master, select a domain controller that is not a Global Catalog server. (If the Global Catalog server is also the infrastructure operations master, cross-domain object references in the domain will not be updated because, by definition, the Global Catalog server already has information on the other domain.)

- If the schema master, domain-naming master, or RID master will be temporarily down, it is not necessary to transfer or seize control of their roles. If one of these operations masters is destroyed, then the role should be seized.

To transfer or seize a role, you must have the appropriate Change role permission as listed in Table 16.2. By default, these permissions are granted as shown in the table.

Table 16.2 **Change Role Object Permissions**

Permission	Granted To
Change Schema Master	Schema Admins
Change Domain Master	Enterprise Admins
Change RID Master	Domain Admins
Change PDC Emulator	Domain Admins
Change Infrastructure Master	Domain Admins

To seize control, use the Sites and Services console, use the ntdsutil tool, or script the seizure using a Visual Basic Script.

Each domain controller stores a full copy of the AD information relevant to its domain. Global Catalog servers store the full copy of their own domain's AD database and the partial replica of information from all other domains in the forest.

Global Catalog

The Global Catalog data represents all the data in the forest. It is due to the Global Catalog that objects in any domain in the forest can be queried from any other domain in the forest. To make its size manageable, only a limited set of attributes for each object is contained in the Global Catalog. The object attributes that should be replicated to the Global Catalog are marked for replication in the schema. Although Microsoft defines a base list, Domain Admins can add other attributes to the replication process. The process of replication produces the catalog. Objects represented here are not modified directly, but changes that occur at the domain level are replicated to the Global Catalog.

Global Catalog data does not reside in its own database; rather, it is part of the configuration partition of the ntds.dit database on the server that hosts it.

The role of the Global Catalog becomes even more important in a native-mode domain. The Global Catalog must be available so that users can log on. (If it is not, users can log on with cached information; a Domain Admins member can log on without the Global Catalog server or cached information.) The reason a Global Catalog server must be available is because Universal Group membership is not stored on all domain controllers; instead, it's only stored in the Global Catalog. As previously discussed, a list of a user's group membership SIDs is compiled at logon for use during his request for object access. If a user is allowed to log on without this membership information, she might be denied access to objects to which she should be given access (or be given access to objects to which she should be denied).

Replication Topology

A *replication topology* defines the set of connections used by the domain controllers in a forest to synchronize their common partitions. The Knowledge Consistency Checker (KCC), a built-in process, automatically creates the replication topology. The KCC collects all the object attributes marked for replication and places them in each Global Catalog server's database. As each new domain is added to the forest or as additional domain controllers are designated as Global Catalog servers, they are added to the topology. It works like this:

- The KCC runs on each domain controller.
- It generates a topology every 15 minutes based on information in the AD.
- It creates the most effective connections it can at that time.
- Links and connections between domain controllers in a domain are automatically created. If you have multiple sites, you define the links between the sites using the AD Sites and Services console; the KCC creates the connections between them.
- Replication within a site occurs by default every hour. This can be changed to none, once per hour, twice per hour, or four times per hour.
- Replication between sites is by default set to every three hours. This also can be modified.
- Replication occurs using the Remote Procedure Call (RPC) port mapper at port 135 on the server. The RPC port mapper assigns dynamic port mappings.

> **Tip**
>
> If you need to define port filters to secure entrance points into your network, you can specify a fixed port for RPC. To do so, you will need to make a registry change. The value to change is HKEY_LOCAL_MACHINE\SYSTEM\CurrentControlSet\Services\NTDS\Parameters\TCP/IP Port entry.
>
> Be sure to assign this value a valid port number that is not in use elsewhere.

Protecting the Active Directory

Protecting the AD consists of three parts:

- Protecting the replication process
- Protecting the data in the AD
- Protecting the configuration and schema of the AD

Protecting the Replication Process

Securing the replication process is important for two reasons: First, a rogue source could pretend to be a replication partner and make unauthorized directory changes. Second, replication partners share secrets. If a rouge source can become a replication partner, that secret is compromised.

Security is accomplished by mutual authentication of replication partners and by access control at the replication source. The specifics are transport-dependent. Transport between sites can be either RPC over IP or Simple Mail Transport Protocol (SMTP).

Intrasite replication of AD data always occurs using RPC over IP and is not compressed. Replication between sites uses RPC over IP or SMTP over IP. It can be scheduled and utilizes data compression.

Data Integrity During Replication

Data integrity is maintained in three ways:

- Changes are tracked on every domain controller.
- Updating is done in a systematic way.
- Replication is based on the object GUID (a globally unique ID).

RPC Transport Security

Mutual authentication is via Kerberos if both domain controllers are Windows 2000 domain controllers. If one of the domain controllers is a Windows NT 4.0 BDC, then NTLM is used. Authorization at the replication source is controlled by Discretionary Access Control Lists (DACLs) on the topmost object in the directory partition. The right set is the DS-Replication-Get-Changes control access right. Domain Admins and Enterprise Admins are given this right during dcpromo.

SMTP Security

Replication transport between sites can use the SMTP protocol. When SMTP is used, mail messaging or the Intersite Messaging Service (ISM) is used. ISM can use SMTP servers other than Exchange Server. ISM uses a certificate-based authentication and encryption mechanism similar to the Internet standard Secure/Multipurpose Internet

Mail Extensions (S/MIME). The receiving domain controller verifies the certificate and then uses data within it to help it determine that the sending server is an authorized AD domain controller.

Active Directory Data Protection

Each object in the AD has a security descriptcr, which is defined in the schema. Default settings are applied when the AD is installed and the schema is created. New objects are given default security settings when they are created (with a few exceptions; see `http://windows.microsoft.com/windows2000/reskit/webresources`).

Permissions on the partitions consist of

- Full Control—All permissions.
- Read—Read information.
- Write—Add information.
- Replicating Directory Changes—Manually trigger replication.
- Replication Synchronize—Synchronize replication.
- Manage Replication Topology—Change directory replication topology.
- Inheritable Full Control—Full Control on objects added below this one.
- Inheritable List Contents—List contents on objects below this one.
- Inheritable Read—Read information on objects below this one.
- Inheritable Auditing—Set auditing on objects below this one.
- Enable Inheritable Full Control—Enable the inheritance of the Full Control permission.
- Enable Inheritable Auditing—Enable the inheritance of the Full Control permission.
- Change Schema Master—Change schema data.
- Audit Successful/Failed—Turn on auditing for this object.

Table 16.3 lists default permissions on directory partitions with the exception of the permission given to the Everyone and Pre-Windows 2000 Compatible groups, which are explained directly following the table. Rights are inherited by the attributes and classes in the AD from the DACLs and SACLs on the schema container.

Table 16.3 **Default Security on Active Directory Partitions**

Partition/Permission	Domain Admins	System	Authenticated Users	Built-in Administrators	Enterprise Admins	Schema Admins
DOMAIN						
Full Control	X	X				
Read			X			
Replicating Directory Changes				X	X	
Replication Synchronize				X	X	
Manage Replication Topology				X	X	
Inheritable Full Control					X	
CONFIGURATION PARTITION						
Full Control	X	X				
Read			X			
Replicating Directory Changes				X	X	
Replication Synchronize				X	X	
Manage Replication Topology				X	X	
Enable Inheritable Full Control					X	
SCHEMA						
Write on fSMORole-Owner attribute						X
Change Schema Master						X

Partition/ Permission	Domain Admins	System	Authenti- cated Users	Built-in Adminis- trators	Enterprise Admins	Schema Admins
Inheritable Full Control						X
Replication Directory Changes				X	X	
Replication Synchronize				X	X	
Manage Replication Topology				X	X	
Read				X		

Although Replication permissions given to Enterprise Admins give them the capability to manage replication throughout the forest, the Built-in Administrators group can use these permissions to troubleshoot replication problems on a single domain controller.

The Pre-Windows 2000 Compatible Group has a special collection of permissions on domain partition objects only. These permissions are

- Inheritable Read on RAS Information
- General Information
- Membership
- User
- Account Restrictions
- User Logon on all User Objects

Inheritable Auditing successful/failed Writes in the domain partition is a permission automatically given to the group Everyone. If an audit policy is activated within a domain, then any writes to the directory will trigger an audit event. This occurs without further configuration of AD objects. Enable Inheritable Auditing to Writes by the Everyone Group is applied to the configuration directory partition. Audit successful/failed Writes on the schema directory partitions is set for the group Everyone.

Protecting the Schema

The schema is protected in three ways:

- Membership in the Schema Admins group is required to change the schema. By default, the Enterprise Administrator is the only member, although other members can be added.
- The schema must be changed at one location, the schema operations master.

- By default, read-only access is provided to the schema. Without a registry modification, the schema cannot be changed. To modify the schema, a registry entry has to be made.

Three additional issues might arise when the schema is changed:

- Replication conflicts are not an issue due to the designation of a schema operations master. Schema changes can only be made at one location and then must be replicated from there to all domains. Latency, however, can cause copies of the AD schema to be inconsistent. This can cause problems if a new object is created and replicated before the schema definition reaches the domain. This can happen if a new schema class, for example the "shuttle" class, is defined on server D, and an object of this type, "belt-shuttle," is immediately created on that server. If the "belt-shuttle" object replicates to server E before the schema definition of its class, "shuttle" replication of this valid object will fail. If the replication of an object fails, the AD will immediately trigger a schema update on server E and rereplicate "belt-shuttle."

- A conflicting AD schema change, for example the adding and deleting of the same attribute to the definition of a class, cannot occur. Any change to the class is protected by the addition of the change attribute to the class during the transaction. The first program thread (path of execution) writes the attribute; another thread will respect that attribute by not attempting to make its own change. Although this guarantees the consistency of the schema, it does not guarantee which changes out of a batch change operation will succeed. It also does not prevent an addition and then a deletion; they just cannot happen at the same time.

- Invalid object instances can occur if the class of the object is modified. As an example, consider the class "belt" and the object instance "belt-shuttle." If "shuttle" has the attribute "edge degree" as a mayContain (an attribute may be defined for this object) and the object instance "belt-shuttle" is created to include that attribute, if you modify the class "shuttle" to deactivate the attribute "edge degree," the object "belt-shuttle" is now invalid. Nonvalid objects will remain in the AD and are prevented from causing problems to the rest of the schema. Nonvalid objects are not automatically removed.

Modifying the Schema

To even look at the schema, you have to do the following:

Register the schema tool by using the `regsvr32 schmmgmt.dll` command or by adding, or removing and adding back in, the administration tools. The adminpak.msc from the i386 folder of the installation CD-ROM can be used to add Administration Tools to a Windows 2000 Professional system.

Then, create a console by adding the snap-in Active Directory Schema.

Before you can modify the schema, you must add a new value, Schema Update Allowed, to the following registry key on the schema FSMO:

HKEY_LOCAL_MACHINE\system\CurrentControlSet\Services\NTDS\Parameters

Set the value to 1. A value of 0 will disable schema updates on this domain controller.

> **Tip**
>
> Do not install two Active Directory[nd]aware programs (programs that will modify the Active Directory)
> at the same time. If you do, you might find that the preceding situation causes one of the installs
> to fail. Because the install might have effected some changes, it might be difficult to start the install
> program over again. Instead, install one, make sure the schema changes have replicated, and then
> install the other.

When changes are made, checks are applied to help prevent accidental corruption of the schema. These checks are either consistency checks or safety checks.

Consistency Checks

Consistency checks are listed in general terms here. (For specifics, field names, and syntax, refer to the Windows 2000 Distributed Systems Guide, which is part of the Windows 2000 Server Resource Kit.)

- The display name and schema GUID of an attribute are unique.
- The display name and schema GUID of a class are unique.
- The class-schema addition and modification extensions pass tests to ensure the following:
    - *governs*ID must be unique.
    - Attributes defined as contained must already be in existence.
    - Classes defined as subclasses, auxiliary classes (classes from which this class can be derived), and superior classes must already exist.
    - Several classes listed as system auxiliary (or auxiliary, superior) have specific requirements such as being members of certain classes, following X.500 specifications, or being a Unicode-string.
    - The attribute ID must be unique.
    - If ranges are specified, then the lower end of the range must be lower than the higher end of the range.
    - Other specific attribute fields must follow specifications for uniqueness, matching, or membership.

Safety Checks

Safety checks are used to prevent schema updates from breaking a currently installed program. Schema changes can be made by members of the Schema Admins group and by programs installed by them. Because the possibility exists that applications might be incompatible with each other because of schema changes they must have, this type of check is extremely valuable. The kind of safety checks that apply depend on whether the schema object being changed is part of the original schema (Category 1) or has been added after the first domain in the forest was installed (Category 2).

There are three types of checks:

1. **Check one:** A `mustContain` attribute (the object must have this attribute defined) cannot be added to a schema class (category 1 or category 2 schema object) either directly or through inheritance. It also cannot be added by adding an auxiliary class.

2. **Check two:** You cannot change the following Category 1 schema objects:

   - `rangeLower` and `rangeUpper` of an attribute

   - `objectClassCategory` of a class

   - `defaultObjectCategory` of an instance of a class

   - `attributeSecurityGUID` of an attribute

   - `lDAPDisplayName` of class or attribute

   - The name of the object

3. **Check three:** You cannot deactivate a Category 1 class or attribute.

You can deactivate (make defunct) a Category 2 class or attribute by modifying the isDefunct attribute of the class or attribute. The definition for defunct classes and attributes remains in the AD schema, but they cannot be used. You cannot create new instances of objects of a defunct class, and you cannot use a defunct attribute to define an object or new class.

The reason you cannot delete classes or attributes is due to the difficulty in determining whether other classes refer to this class or use this attribute and the long time it might take to do a system-wide check.

Recovering the Active Directory

The backup of the AD is discussed in Chapter 8, "Lifecycle Choices." Options for restoring the AD are detailed here.

Restoring replicated data requires special techniques due to the problems that might occur if old data from a backup replicates and therefore eliminates current information. A local Administrator is given the Restore privilege for AD data. Two techniques exist:

- Reinstall Windows 2000, dcpromo the domain controller, and make other configuration changes. Let normal replication update the AD and bring it up-to-date.

- Don't reinstall the OS; instead, restore replicated data.

If data is to be restored, a decision has to be made as to whether the restore is nonauthoritative or authoritative.

A nonauthoritative restore restores the distributed services on a domain controller. The data is updated through replication. This is a good technique to use when a domain controller fails due to hardware or software problems.

In an authoritative restore, first the Backup tool is used to do a nonauthoritative restore. This is done to restore distributed services. Next, the ntdsutil tool is used to select the domain controller's directory, subtree, or objects and to designate them as taking precedence over any other instance on any domain controller in the domain. The directory, its subtree, or objects that are so designated are replicated as necessary to the other domain controllers. The restored domain controller becomes known as authoritative; it has the final say over other domain controllers in its domain. This method can be used to return to a known state, such as before objects were deleted. (Objects added to the AD after the backup will remain in the AD).

Restoring with the Backup tool is a nonauthoritative restore. The ntdsutil command-line tool can be used to authoritatively restore AD data. For specific instructions on how to do this, refer to online help or the Windows NT Server Resource Kit.

Trust Issues

Trusts between domains are secured by passwords, as are computer accounts. If these passwords have been renegotiated after the backup, when you restore, you might find these trust relationships to be invalid. Invalid trust relationships can prevent communications with other domains or between member servers and domain controllers until passwords can be reset using the AD Domains and Trusts console. Trust relationship passwords are automatically reset at seven-day intervals.

Checking the Success of Active Directory Restore

Other distributed data are interrelated with the AD. When backing up or restoring the AD, you should make sure these other services still work. If the AD is restored, you should check to make sure other distributed data (File Replication Service [FRS], Certificate Services, registry, and so on) are operational. You can verify the AD restore immediately after restoring the domain controller by following these steps:

1. Restart the system in Directory Services Restore mode.
2. Check the NTDS subkey at HKEY_LOCAL_MACHINE\SYSTEM\CurrentControlSet\Services. At the end of a successful restore, the RestoreInProgress entry is deleted. If it still remains, the restore might not have been successful. Do not manually delete this key.
3. Close the Registry Editor and Run ntdsutil tool and type **Files** to display the Files menu. Type **Info** to display the Information menu. If AD has been successfully restored, ntdsutil will display that.
4. Restart in the normal mode.

Controlling Computers and Users with Group Policy Objects

Chapter 9, "Security Tools," introduces the Group Policy Editor and the concept of centrally managing security settings. Chapter 12, "Domain-Level Security," highlights the Group Policy security settings and their usage in domain and domain controller OUs. In this section, I will

- Explain the Group Policy process
- Explain Group Policy inheritance
- Introduce other elements that can be managed via Group Policy and their relationship to securing the enterprise
- Explain how Group Policy objects are replicated

Group Policy Processing

Group Policy on a single machine presents a useful management tool. The Local Computer Security Policy (the Group Policy Object for the local system) enables the Administrator of the local machine to set security for that system without having to make registry edits. Group Policy used correctly in a domain is impressive.

Group Policy is created at a central location and then is inherited by groups of computers and users. If you understand how policies are inherited and which policy takes precedence, you can create a Group Policy design that assists you in managing your enterprise. First, however, you must understand how Group Policy works. The next sections will describe the rules.

Group Policy Only Affects Windows 2000 User and Computer Accounts

Computer-related Group Policy settings only affect Windows 2000 computers. User-related Group Policy settings only affect users who are logged in to the domain. To secure down-level clients, use System Policy.

Group Policy Has Nothing to Do With and no Impact on Security Groups

The name Group Policy sometimes interferes with the understanding of its impact. Group Policy applies to groups of computers and users but not to a formal "group," as traditionally defined by Windows and other operating systems. In the traditional group context, a group is defined as a collection of users, and the group is assigned access rights and privileges. Membership in the group means the right to any right or privilege held by the group. This context still exists in Windows 2000 as a security group. However, Group Policy is not another way of creating a security group. It cannot be assigned (linked) to a security group. Group Policy is linked to a Group Policy Container (GPC) in the AD.

Figure 16.3 shows two GPCs and the users and computer accounts that exist at each GPC. The triangle represents the domain Group Policy Object (GPO). The circle within it represents the NewYork organizational unit (OU) GPO. Boxes within the triangle represent lists of domain users and domain groups. OU users are listed within the OU circle. The Accountants group exists at the domain level with members Alice and Bob. As you can see, Bob's account exists at the domain level, and Alice's account is in the NewYork OU. A GPO linked at the domain level will affect both Bob and Alice but not because of their membership in the Accountants group. The GPO affects Bob because his account is at that level, and it affects Alice due to inheritance. A GPO linked to the NewYork OU will only affect Alice, not Bob.

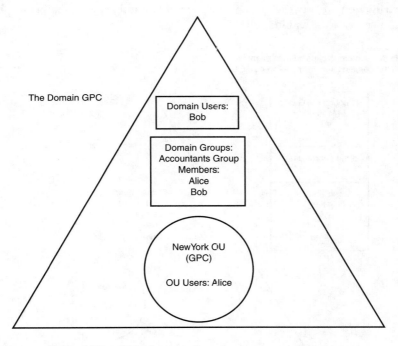

Figure 16.3 GPOs have no direct impact on security groups.

A Group Policy Object Can Be Linked to a Site, a Domain, or an OU

GPOs are linked to GPCs in the AD. Currently, GPCs are sites, domains, and OUs. A GPO can be linked to multiple GPCs.

Group Policy Affects Groups of Computers or Users

A user or computer account can be created or moved to an OU. If a GPO is linked at the domain level, it will impact directly any computers and users whose accounts exist at this level. It will affect user and computer accounts that exist within an OU of this domain via inheritance. If a GPO is linked to an OU, it will directly affect users and computers whose accounts exist in this OU. If any OUs are nested within the OU, the policy will affect any users or computers within that OU.

Figure 16.4 expands Figure 16.3 by adding another OU and more user accounts. The listing of groups and their members is moved to boxes next to the domain for clarity, but the groups exist at the domain level. Although the traditional complement of security groups exists, the "group" meaning in Group Policy is simply the collection of accounts that exist within the GPC.

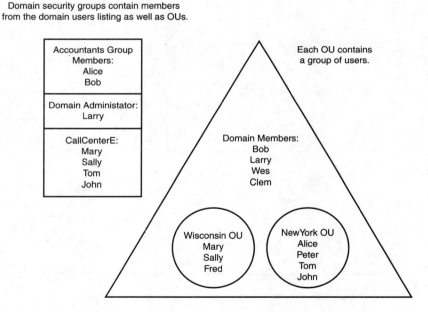

Figure 16.4 The meaning of "group" in Group Policy.

GPOs Linked to a Domain Object Have No Affect on Computers or Users in Another Domain

Due to the hierarchical structure of the forest, you might expect to find policies created at domains that reside higher in the hierarchy to have an impact on domains lower in the hierarchy. This is not the case. Domains are security boundaries. A GPO linked to the domain GPC in domain A will have no impact on users and computers with accounts in domain B. A site-level policy can have affect on multiple domains but only on the domains that exist within its site.

Domain Group Policy Object Versus Domain Controller Group Policy Object

Within the domain, two default OUs exist: domain computers and domain controllers. As you would expect, you set policies that apply to domain controllers in the Domain Controllers OU (use the Domain Controller Security Policy console) and policies that apply to domain computers in the Domain Computer OU (use the Domain Security Policy). There are some exceptions, however, or special cases.

Account policy can only be set at the domain level. There is only one Kerberos Policy, one Password Policy, and one Account Lockout Policy for the entire domain. If users are logging on to the domain, they will be affected by the policy set in the Domain GPO. Local Policies, such as User Rights Assignment, are set in the Domain Controller GPO. Any policy settings in the Domain Computer OU will only affect users logging on locally to a member computer.

> **Note**
>
> The concept of setting account policies in the Domain GPO is extremely important. Any account policies set here will override account policies set in GPOs at other OUs. Users logging in to the domain will be affected by the policies set in the Domain GPO. Users logging in locally to a server in another OU will be affected by the GPO for that OU.

A Group Policy's Impact Can Be Filtered By Security Groups

Although you cannot apply a GPO to a security group, the impact of a GPO on a GPC can be filtered by security group. This is done by setting permissions on the GPO. It is possible to arrange these permissions so that the policy has no affect on security group members (or to give them the right to manage the policy, but so that it will have not impact on their membership). The permission that can be set are

- Full Control—All permissions.
- Read—Read the policy.
- Write—Edit the policy.
- Create All Child Objects—Add new items.
- Delete All Child Objects—Delete items.
- Apply Group Policy—The policy will be applied.

For a GPO to have an impact on a user or computer within the GPC, the security group of which user or computer is a member must have the Read and Apply Group Policy permissions. To prevent the policy from applying to a group, add that group to the list and deny those permissions (or remove the Authenticated Users group, add all groups that should be affected, and allow those permissions).

To manage the OU, a security group is usually given Read, Write, Create All Child Objects, and Delete All Child Objects permissions. By default, these permissions are given to Domain Admins. Note that the permission Apply Group Policy is not given to Domain Admins. Because Domain Admins are members of the Authenticated Users group, however, the policy will apply to any Domain Admins whose account is within the GPC. If the Authenticated Users group is removed from the GPO, then the Domain Admins group will not have the policy applied.

Group Policy Inheritance

Group Policy inheritance is the process that describes how Group Policy settings trickle down to objects in OUs. It explains the order of policy application and which setting wins if there is a conflict. There are several policy inheritance rules, which will be discussed in the following sections.

GPOs Are Inherited From the Site, Domain, OU, and Parent OUs of the OU of which a Computer Or User Is a Member

To determine which GPO has an impact on a particular user or computer, you can simply make a list of the GPOs that follow the hierarchical line from the site down to the OU where the account exists. Figure 16.5 illustrates the GPOs that will affect the Call Center OU. In the figure, circles represent OUs and rectangles represent GPOs. Each GPO is shown near its GPC. For example: The domain controllers GPO and the domain computers GPO are listed next to the triangle, while the newyorkb and nyconfig GPOs are listed above the New York OU. The GPOs that will impact the Call Center OU are listed in the rectangle to the left of and outside the triangle.

The Local Group Policy Object (Local Computer Security Policy) Is Applied First, Then the Inheritance Follows the Active Directory Hierarchy

The order of the application of Group Policy is important because it specifies which policy wins if there is a conflict. Local Computer Security Policy is applied first, then site policy, then Domain, then OUs starting with the first or top-level OU, and continuing with each nested OU until the OU of which the computer or user is a member is reached. If there are policies nested within this OU, their policies are not applied.

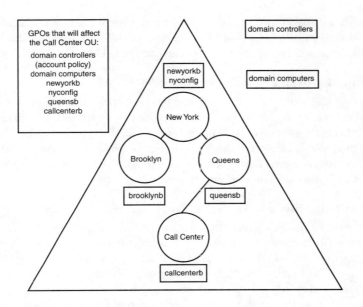

Figure 16.5   Inherited GPOs.

If Multiple Policies Exist at a Certain GPC, the Order of the Policy in the List of Links on the GPC Determines the Order of Policy Application

For example, three GPOs (A, B, C) are linked to the Accounting OU, and the Accounting OU is a first-level OU in the peachweaver.me domain. In the Group Policy property page for the Accounting OU, the policies have been listed in alphabetical order. There is no site policy. Alice's account is in the Accounting OU. Policy is applied in the following order:

1. Local Security Policy
2. Peachweaver.me domain policy
3. Accounting A policy
4. Accounting B policy
5. Accounting C policy

Policy Application Is Cumulative Unless There Is a Conflict

Every policy may configure a large number of items, so there are many opportunities for conflicts. In reality, many policies will not conflict with each other because different object settings are set within each policy. For example, the local policy might specify that the system can be shut down without logging on. The domain policy might specify a password policy, and the OU for the computer might indicate that anonymous users cannot list account information. There is no policy conflict here, so all policy settings will be applied to a computer in the OU.

If a Conflict Exists, the Last Policy Applied Wins

Because Local Computer Security is applied first, any conflicting policy anywhere that affects this computer or users of this computer will be overridden. If there are conflicts between other GPOs applied, the last one applied will be the winner. You can determine which elements are overridden by opening the Local Computer Security Policy console. Two columns exist in the Policy window: Local Setting and Effective Setting. The Effective Setting column displays the policy in effect.

Exceptions Exist: Block Policy Inheritance and No Override

Two exceptions to this rule exist: Block Policy Inheritance and No Override. The use of Block Policy Inheritance will prevent policies higher in the hierarchy from having any affect on the GPC to which it is applied. No Override is applied to a GPO and will prevent a local Block Policy Inheritance from preventing the higher-level GPO from being applied.

The flow chart in Figure 16.6 can be used to trace the flow of Group Policy inheritance and to determine the impact of Blocking Inheritance and No Override.

Figure 16.7 shows an example of the use of Blocking Inheritance. In the Lucky Town domain, a single Group Policy exists at the domain level, and a single GPO exists in the NewYork OU. In the domain-level policy, the security option Allow System to Be Shut Down Without Logging On is disabled. In the NewYork GPO, this option is not defined. At the local level, it is enabled. In the figure, GPOs are OU represented as rectangles and are labeled. Also, the security option Allow System to be Shut Down is not listed in the figure, just whether it is not defined or enabled. In the normal Group Policy Inheritance model, the domain policy would be applied at the NewYork OU level. Computers in the NewYork OU would not be able to be shut down from the logon prompt. A user would have to log on to shut the system down. Because this option is usually enabled in the Local Security Policy object, the Local Security Policy console would show the local setting as Enabled and the effective setting as Disabled.

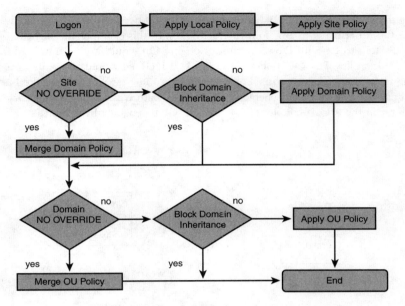

Figure 16.6 Group Policy inheritance.

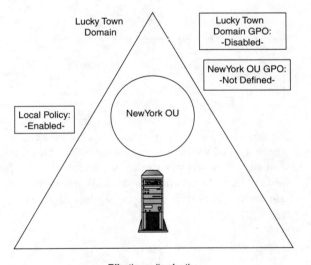

Lucky Town
Domain

Lucky Town
Domain GPO:
-Disabled-

NewYork OU GPO:
-Not Defined-

Local Policy:
-Enabled-

NewYork OU

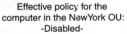

Effective policy for the
computer in the NewYork OU:
-Disabled-

Figure 16.7 Normal inheritance.

In Figure 16.8, however, the Blocking Inheritance has been applied. This effectively blocks the Inheritance of any domain-level policy. In this example, the security option Allow System to Be Shut Down Without Logging On would not be inherited from the domain policy. The OU policy setting of Not Defined would allow the local setting to be the effective setting. For computers in the New York OU of the Lucky Town domain, the choice to enable or disable this feature can be set locally for each computer in the OU. If left alone, of course, it will be enabled by default.

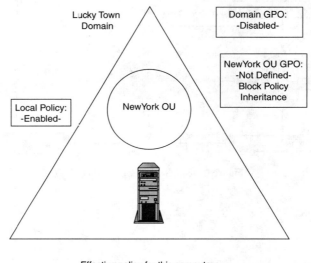

Figure 16.8   Blocking Inheritance.

The same domain structure is displayed in Figure 16.9. In this case, however, the No Override rule has been applied to the domain Group Policy. This time, the New York attempt to block domain policy will not work. All computers in the New York OU (as well as any outside the OU but within the domain) will have the policy disabled. The computers must be logged onto before they can be shut down.

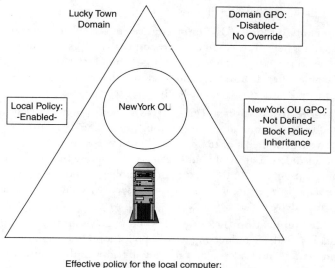

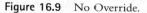

Figure 16.9 No Override.

Other Items to Manage with Group Policy

Group Policy is not just for managing the security-related settings in the Security Settings folder. This is only a small part of Group Policy. For both computers and users, major areas are available to manage software installation and to manage computers across the enterprise. This section will not detail every aspect of computer management; rather, it will take a look at how some of these settings can be used to enforce security policies or to assist in protecting systems.

Computer and User Management

Two folders are available to help administrators manage computers and users: Windows Settings and Administrative Templates.

Windows Settings is the folder within which the Security Settings folder resides. Additionally, logon scripts (User Configuration) and startup and shutdown scripts (Computer Configuration) are assigned here. Using your knowledge of Group Policy inheritance, you can create a granular arrangement of appropriate scripts throughout your domain.

Within the User Configuration section only, Windows settings includes policies for:

- **Internet Explorer (IE) maintenance.** This is where a policy can be set regarding how IE is configured. To ensure that users use the appropriate proxy server to reach the Internet and not go around it, to be able to update user machines after deployment, and to ensure that users use the security settings for Security Zones and Content Ratings, set the policy here.

- **Remote Installation Services (RIS).** User options available when RIS is used to install computers are controlled here. The type of setup and tools allowed, even denial of the use of RIS can be set. Because policy can be different for different areas of your organization, the use of RIS can be controlled by these settings and by the linking of the policy at the appropriate OUs or domains. In a setting in which extreme security policies are in affect, you might want to deny the use of RIS.

- **Folder replication.** Here is where you might want to set the policy for where data is stored. By redirecting users' Application Data, Desktop, My Documents, and Start Menu folders, you can centrally control them and can avoid the problems of backing up local storage.

Administrative templates, on the other hand, list a wide range of settings, many of which have to do with simple computer configuration. Others can be used to enhance security. They also can be extended to provide additional security settings. Some of the Computer Configuration settings that can be used (and how) are listed in Table 16.4. User Configuration Settings are listed in Table 16.5. When policies are similar for Users and Computers, information is not repeated in Table 16.5. An explanation of each setting with some security commentary is available from the Explain tab of the policy itself. Settings that apply to Group Policy are detailed later in the chapter.

Table 16.4 **Some Computer Configuration Administrative Templates Security-Related Settings**

Folder	Policy	Use
NetMeeting	Disable Remote Desktop Sharing	Prevent the attacker from having access to items on the user's desktop.
Internet Explorer	Security Zones: Do not allow users to change settings	Configure Internet Explorer with appropriate capabilities for trusted and untrusted sites (such as when to allow Active X scripts to run); apply this setting to keep users from changing.
Internet Explorer	Authenticode	Designate software publishers and credentials as trustworthy. You can predetermine which software, such as Active X controls, a user can install by setting approval here by publisher.

Folder	Policy	Use
Internet Explorer	Disable periodic check for Internet Explorer software updates	Keep Internet Explorer updates under administrative control.
Internet Explorer	Disable automatic install of Internet Explorer components	Keep Internet Explorer updates under administrative control.
Task Scheduler	Prevent Task Run or End	Prevent attackers from installing and running malicious programs.
Task Scheduler	Disable New Task Creation	Prevent users and abusers from creating tasks. Keep task creation under the control of administrators.
Windows Installer	Disable Windows Installer	Prevent programs from being installed using this technique. Use the For Nonmanaged Apps Only option to permit only the installation of programs that a system administrator assigns or publishes. (This does not prevent users from using other methods to install programs.)
Windows Installer	Always install with elevated privileges	This is a dangerous option. If enabled, a user is given elevated privileges when using the Windows Installer to install a program. If it is not enabled or is disabled, the user's privileges are used to install programs. An advanced user could figure out a way to use this privilege (if enabled) to gain access to restricted files and folders. Recommendation: Disable this setting.
Windows Installer	Cache transforms in secure location on workstation Properties	Transforms are the special instructions to modify or customize programs during installation. They usually are stored as part of the user's profile and could be tampered with. Transforms are used whenever a user reinstalls, repairs, or deletes a program. Setting this option will store the transforms securely on the user's computer.
Offline Files	Enabled	Offline files allow the storing of copies of files on a user's local system. This is important if a user needs to be able to work offline if the system fails or if he is traveling with the computer. In some scenarios, however, there are strict policies that are meant to keep users from placing copies of

continues

Table 16.4 **Continued**

Folder	Policy	Use
		sensitive files on local computers. Use this policy setting to prevent the capability to automatically download files to the local system. It will not prevent the copying of files.
Offline Files	Files not cached Properties	Prevent files with listed extensions from being cached for offline storage. You enter the file extensions.
Network and Dial-up Connections	Allow configuration of connection sharing properties	Internet connection sharing enables a user to share an Internet connection with other users. Doing so, however, changes IP settings in the network; therefore, to protect addressing integrity, this policy should be disabled. By default, it is not available on dial-up connections; however, an administrator can enable it and then users could use it.
Printing	Web-based printing	Enable or disable Internet printing support on servers. If enabled, printers can be displayed on Web pages and viewed, managed, and used across the Internet or intranet. Enabling this policy can open network printers to denial-of-service or other attacks across the Internet.

Table 16.5 **Some User Configuration Administrative Templates Security-Related Settings**

Folder	Policy	Use
Netmeeting	Prevent Sharing	Prevent users from sharing desktop, applications, and so on.
Internet Explorer	Administrator Approved Controls	Control which controls can be used (Media Player, Shockwave Flash, Carpoint, MSNBC, and so on) in security zones. The combination of setting and configuring security zones in the Security Zones policy and enabling or disabling controls in this section will only allow users to use approved controls. Thus, you have prevented an exposure to buggy and/or malicious controls masquerading as media controls.

Folder	Policy	Use
Windows Explorer	Removes the Folder Options menu item from the Tools menu	Folder Options enables users to change settings (for example, allowing them to display hidden files). Disabling this policy prevents changes made through Explorer.
Windows Explorer	Multiple hide and remove policies	Prevent users from accessing things such as drives, menu items, hardware information, and so on in applets that are part of the Explorer shell, such as Control Panel. These policies can be used effectively to maintain the integrity of the computer configuration because users cannot use the tools to install or change settings.
Microsoft Management Console	Restricted/Permitted snap-ins	Prevent users from adding snap-ins or allow them to add only specific ones. Because snap-ins can allow management of specific components, restricting their availability is one step in controlling their use.
Microsoft Management Console	Restrict the user from entering author mode	Author mode enables users to create console files or to add or remove snap-ins. You can control exactly what they have the capability to manage via the MMC.
Start Menu & Taskbar	Various remove and disable policies that prevent users from using specific features	Items such as disabling links to Windows Update, removing program groups from the Start menu, and others can restrict and prevent some users. If the feature can be used in another way, multiple settings might need to be combined to make this work.
Control Panel	Disable Control Panel	Many applets in Control Panel enable users to make configuration changes and add drivers. Disabling Control Panel prevents many of these possibilities. A sophisticated user, however, might find another way to do this. Combinations of policy settings will help to lock down the desktop.

Software Settings

Software settings manage the software-installation policies in place for the GPC. Administrators can determine the software that can be installed on a user or computer basis. Packages can be published and installed either automatically or when first run. A user's capability to install and use software will depend on where his account resides, not at which computer he is sitting. If OUs and their membership have been carefully designed, you have only to place the correct information here to control use of centrally available software.

Replication and Management of Group Policy Objects

GPOs are changed by default on only the first domain controller in the domain. Group Policy information is replicated when AD replicates. Replication is only in one direction—to all the other domain controllers. Each policy is given a GUID, and this is used to keep them synchronized. Group Policy is not backed up separately from the AD.

GPOs are local and nonlocal. The Local Computer Security Policy object is stored locally on each Windows 2000 computer. Nonlocal policies are stored in the AD. Within the AD, Group Policy is stored in two locations:

- **GPC.** As you have seen, the GPCs are sites, domains, OUs, and objects within the AD. GPO properties are stored for both computer and user Group Policy information. For example, the settings for what is available for software installation and the status of the software are included here. The actual software files are in the template.

- **Group Policy Template.** Templates are stored in the sysvol folder of the domain controller (sysvol*domain name*\Policies*GUID*). Within each Group Policy are Adm, MACHINE, AND USER folders. Group Policy information stored here includes

    - .ADM text files (administration settings).

    - The registry.pol files—one for users and one for computers. These are policy settings that affect the registry. They are different than the .POL files produced to administer Windows NT 4.0 or Windows 9x. A .POL file created on one Windows operating system cannot be used by another Windows operating system.

    - Script files.

    - Applications available for installation.

    - Gpt.ini, a file that stores information on client-side extensions, whether user or computer configuration is disabled, and the version number of the snap-in extension that created the GPO.

Policy Application

Group Policy is applied at system startup, user logon, and periodically throughout the day. The following list summarizes when, by default, policy is applied.

- Computer settings are applied at startup.

- User settings are applied when the user logs on.

- Group Policy is also processed periodically (by default, every 90 minutes for all computers except domain controllers).

- Group Policy is refreshed every five minutes on domain controllers.
- Default settings can be changed by modifying settings that affect Group Policy.
- Group Policy can be refreshed immediately by using the `secedit refreshpolicy` command.

Periodic Group Policy processing kicks off at the preceding time settings. Policy is only applied, however, if the policy has changed. By using Group Policy settings, you can force its application at every automatic processing time. Group Policy settings are

- **Disable background refresh of Group Policy.** Group Policy is only applied during startup and logon.
- **Apply Group Policy for a computer asynchronously during startup.** Policy is usually applied synchronously, and a user cannot log on before computer policy application is complete. To shorten policy application time, however, you can change this. (The logon prompt is available before policy is complete.) It is not advisable if it might compromise security.
- **Apply Group Policy for a user asynchronously during logon.** Similar to the preceding item, this is not advisable if it might give users access or privileges that would be restricted were policy complete before the user's desktop was available.
- **Group Policy refresh interval for computers.** Change the default refresh interval (0 to 45 days in minutes)
- **Group Policy refresh interval for domain controllers.** Ditto but for DCs.
- **User Group Policy loopback processing mode.** Alternate user policies (set administratively) when a user logs on. This ensures that a user's GPC membership does not influence the policy in place on this system. Often used for kiosks.
- **Group Policy slow link detection.** Defines the speed that will be considered a slow link. The default value is 500 kilobits per second.
- **Slow Link and apply Policy.** Even if they haven't changed granularity, similar policies exist for several categories: Override customized settings put into place by applications. Can be allowed to be applied even over a slow link and if the policy hasn't changed. These types of policies are available for:
  - IE Maintenance policy processing
  - Software Installation policy processing
  - Folder Redirection policy processing
  - Scripts policy processing
  - Security policy processing
  - IP Security policy processing
  - EFS Recovery policy processing
  - Disk Quota policy processing

Policy in Mixed Windows OS Networks

Group Policy cannot be used by down-level clients. You can create System Policies for down-level clients and store them on the domain controllers that these clients will use. The ntconfig.pol and config.pol files should be placed in the Netlogon share:

%systemroot%\SYSVOL\sysvol\<domain name>\SCRIPTS   Windows 2000

%systemroot%\winnt\system32\Repl\Import\Scripts   Windows NT 4.0

To create System Policies, you must use the operating system–specific version of the System Policy Editor, and you must use it on that particular operating system. To create a system policy for all NT computers in a domain, run the System Policy Editor provided with Windows NT on an NT domain controller. Run it on a domain controller instead of a workstation so you can create policies for domain groups and for computers in the domain. To create a System Policy for Windows 9x clients, you must create the policy on a Windows 9x computer using the `poledit` program. The files can be stored on an NT domain controller or a Windows 2000 domain controller, but they must be created in the operating system that will be applying the policy.

These policies will then be applied to users of these down-level (Windows NT or Windows 9x) systems. Remember, only Windows 2000 computers will have Group Policy applied. If the systems are Windows 2000 but they are joined in a Windows NT 4.0 domain, or if they are joined in a Windows 2000 domain but the user logging on has an account in a Windows NT domain, different combinations of System Policy and Group Policy will occur. In the following list, which shows what happens for different user and computer account locations, all computers have Windows 2000 installed.

- **Computer and User account on Windows NT Domain Controller.** Local Group Policy is applied at startup. When the user logs on, Windows NT 4.0 System Policy for the computer is applied. Windows NT 4.0 System Policy for the user is applied. If Local Group Policy changes, first Local Group Policy is applied and then System Policy for the user.

- **Computer and User accounts Both on Windows 2000 Domain Controllers.** Group Policy for the computer is applied at boot. Group Policy for the user is applied at logon.

- **Computer has a Windows NT 4.0 account; User has a Windows 2000 account.** Local Group Policy is applied at boot. Because the user does not log on to the Windows NT 4.0 domain, the computer System Policy will not be applied. At logon, the Group Policy for the user is applied.

- **Computer has a Windows 2000 account, user logs on to Windows NT 4.0.** All Group Policy for the computer is applied at system startup. At logon, System Policy for the user is applied.

> **Tip**
>
> When upgrading Windows NT 4.0 computers to Windows 2000, there might be problems if Windows NT 4.0 System Policy was used. System Policy tattoos or permanently changes the registry. Group Policy does not. Before upgrading, you might want to apply a System Policy that reverses registry settings, or you might need to make registry changes after upgrading.

Delegation of Authority for GPOs

As discussed in Chapter 12, administrative control can be delegated to nonadministrative users. This is a good way to offload administrative tasks to appropriate user groups without giving them full administrative privileges on your network.

Likewise, management of Group Policy can be delegated in Windows 2000. Although by default you must be an administrator to manage, link, and edit Group Policy, an administrator can delegate certain tasks to other nonadministrative users. Delegation is done at the OU level. The following Group Policy tasks can be delegated:

- Managing Group Policy Links
- Creating GPOs
- Editing GPOs

Of course, other permissions and rights, such as the capability to log on to a local or remote domain controller and the permission to use MMC consoles, will also affect whether the user or group to which you want to delegate authority can use the right. Delegation is accomplished by running the Delegation of Authority Wizard from the Task menu of the OU.

For More Information

This chapter discusses services for which complementary information exists in other chapters of this book. The following should serve as a referral source for you in locating this information.

For more information on Local Computer Policy settings, see Chapter 6, "Security from the Get-Go," Chapter 10, "Securing Windows 2000 Professional," Chapter 11, "Securing Windows 2000 Server," and Chapter 12, "Domain-Level Security."

Introductory information about AD can be found in Chapter 12, as can information on specific policies for services. Chapter 17, "Enterprise Public Key Infrastructure," covers public key policies, and Chapter 15, "Secure Remote Access Options," covers remote access and RADIUS policies.

Summary

Understanding the foundations for distributed services in Windows 2000 will enable you to design, implement, and manage distributed security within your organization. This chapter provided information about the foundation for distributed services, the AD, and the use of a primary distributed security function—Group Policy processing. This information, combined with information presented earlier on its structure, the implications of trust relationships between domains, and security structures within a domain, will enable you to more easily assimilate information provided in future chapters.

The next chapter, "Enterprise Public Key Infrastructure", examines a service that can be used to distribute security within a domain, within a forest, and with external business partners, customers, and the larger public. Although the chapter discusses Windows 2000 Certificate Services, later chapters will examine its interoperability with other Certificate Services providers, its use by Web services, and its function in business relationships.

Enterprise Public Key Infrastructure

WINDOWS 2000 INCLUDES A CERTIFICATE SERVICE. It is not installed by default; it is available with Windows 2000 Server and Advanced Server. If this certificate service is properly installed, configured, managed, and protected, it can provide support for a wide range of certificate-aware applications. These applications can be used to create an enterprise-wide Public Key Infrastructure (PKI). The PKI can be enforced via Group Policy and used in all domains in the forest. Chapter 4, "Public Key Infrastructure (PKI)," discussed PKI by providing information on the standards and different types of implementations and concepts. This chapter only covers Windows 2000 PKI. Windows 2000 specifics will be detailed. Wherever possible, only brief definitions will accompany concepts that already have been discussed.

Windows 2000 Certificate Services has many functions. It can be used as follows:

- To centrally control the Encrypting File System (EFS)
- To provide authentication services for use with smart cards, Web services, and IPSec
- To support digitally signed and sealed email
- To provide code signing

Before you can implement these applications, you need to understand how Certificate Services in Windows 2000 are structured and what it takes to prepare the infrastructure that will support them.

This chapter will detail the following five components of an enterprise Public Key Infrastructure:

- The structure of Windows 2000 Certificate Services (the tools available and necessary to establish a Public Key Infrastructure)
- The certificate lifecycle (how the tools are used together to provide expected services)
- Group Policies for Public Key Infrastructure (items that can be configured in a GPO and propagated across the enterprise)
- Additional Certificate Services security practices (any configuration that is not a part of PKI Group Policy)
- Certificate/PKI-aware applications (the applications that can use certificates and those that require certificates to function)

Windows 2000 Certificate Services Structure

To establish Certificate Services, you must first establish a Certificate Authority (CA). The CA is responsible for managing the certificates used in the PKI. Although you can use third-party certificates with many PKI-aware applications, you should first consider the free services provided with the Windows 2000 servers. The components that make up this service are

- Certificate Authorities
- A certificate hierarchy
- Keys
- Certificates and certificate templates
- A Certificate Revocation List
- A public key policy
- Certificate stores
- Cryptographic Service Provider
- A Certificate Trust List

Certificate Authorities

The Certificate Authority is responsible for managing the certificate lifecycle; this lifecycle includes creating, assigning, revoking, and managing certificates. To establish a

Windows 2000 CA, you install Certificate Services. The process you use depends on the type of CA you want to install and the protective mechanisms you will be using. Windows 2000 has four different CAs:

- Enterprise root CA
- Enterprise subordinate CA
- Standalone root CA
- Standalone subordinate CA

Root CAs

The root CA is the first CA in any PKI and is the source from which all trust flows. Although all CAs have a special CA certificate, the root CA creates its own root certificate while a subordinate CA gets its authority via a certificate provided by the root.

The root CA can create certificates for other CAs as well as for other computers, users, and services, but its most important role is to be the root, or the point from which all trust flows. It's the keystone, the linchpin, the "buck stops here" focus of your entire Certificate Services enterprise. For any certificate-aware application to function, it must use certificates whose authority can be traced back to the root. Because of its central role, the root CA needs the ultimate in protection. Its compromise would destroy any security that relies on Certificate Services in your enterprise. If someone wants to penetrate your organization, and has access to the root CA, he could simply

1. Use the root CA to produce a subordinate CA certificate
2. Build his own CA
3. Produce as many certificates as he needed or desired to access any of your resources

Many companies establish their root CA and then take it offline and store it in a locked vault. To understand how this might work, see the "Certificate Hierarchy" section later in this chapter.

Windows 2000 is capable of hosting two types of CAs: an enterprise root CA or a standalone root CA. The enterprise root CA requires the Active Directory (AD) and therefore is installed on a domain controller (DC) or member server. The standalone root CA, as the name implies, is installed on a standalone server. By default, only a member of the Enterprise Admins group can install an enterprise root CA.

Subordinate CAs

A subordinate CA must have a certificate from a root CA or from a subordinate CA that has been given (by a root CA) the authority to issue subordinate CA certificates. Subordinate CAs are used to issue certificates for any number of Certificate Services. A CA does not have to be dedicated to one kind of certificate; however, it is often relegated to issuing a few types of certificates in the large enterprise. The workload can then be distributed.

Two types of Windows 2000 subordinate CAs exist: the enterprise subordinate CA and the standalone subordinate CA.

Differences between Enterprise and Standalone CAs

Many differences between enterprise CAs and standalone CAs exist. Table 17.1 lists and defines the differences.

Table 17.1   **Enterprise and Standalone CA Differences**

Feature	Enterprise CA	Standalone CA
Require the AD.	Yes	No
Publish certificates in the AD.	Yes	No
Use the AD to validate a certificate request. The user or computer account requesting the certificate can be queried to determine whether it has the rights necessary to receive a certificate.	Yes	No
Use local directory.	No	Yes
Can be taken offline.	No	Yes
Is usually configured to automatically issue certificates.	Yes	No
Waits for administrator approval of certificate requests.	No	Yes
Uses certificate templates.	Yes	No

Installation Issues

Installation is straightforward and simple if you have done it before. Here are the "gotchas":

- You cannot change the computer name after installation.
- The name of the CA does not have to be the computer's name; in fact, for the sake of convenience, name it something different.
- DNS must be available.
- To install an enterprise CA, you must be an Enterprise Admin.
- If you are installing a subordinate CA, you must obtain a CA certificate from a root CA or from a subordinate CA that has been given this right. An enterprise subordinate CA can obtain this certificate online (if the enterprise root CA is online). To install a standalone CA, you must provide the certificate in a file that can be created by the enterprise CA.
- If you are not using one of the provided Cryptographic Service Providers (CSPs), you must have the CSP drivers available.

- If you are planning to use smart cards, you will need to obtain hardware (a reader and cards) from third-party sources. If the smart cards are not one of the two whose drivers are provided with Windows 2000, you will need drivers as well. Check the compatibility list before you buy.

- Have the CA certificate ready if you are installing a subordinate CA or understand the process for obtaining one and realize that your CA will not be operational until your provide it with a certificate.

Certificate Hierarchy

In a PKI, CAs are arranged in a certificate hierarchy with the root CA at the top and various layers of subordinate CAs underneath. The hierarchy can provide both depth and breadth for your Certificate Services. Current Microsoft recommendations are not to exceed a depth of three or four levels of CAs.

Figure 17.1 illustrates a CA hierarchy in which there are three levels of CAs. The first level is a standalone root CA. The second level is composed of enterprise subordinate CAs. Each CA represents a geographic area for the company. In the third level, composed of additional enterprise subordinate CAs, each geographical area has task-based CAs. A CA is provided for smart card operations, IPSec operations, and EFS operations.

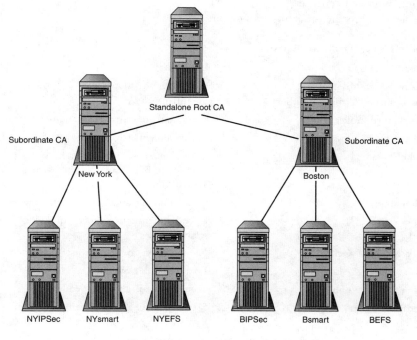

Figure 17.1 Certificate hierarchy.

Keys

A public key/private key pair and a certificate are generated and provided by the CA. The key pair is necessary for the activities of Certificate Services; the keys are used by certificate-aware applications. The public key is available to the public, and the private key is kept secret by its owner. Public, as used here, can mean different things. In a closed environment such as your LAN or WAN, public might mean only your authorized users. In an open environment such as the Internet, it can mean anyone who has the appropriate certificate-aware application (a browser or an email program perhaps) loaded.

Certificates and Certificate Templates

In Chapter 4, certificates were examined and their contents listed. Windows 2000 certificates are x.509 v3 standard. The certificate carries information that enables it to be identified. In addition, the certificate contains a copy of the CA's public key; finally, it is signed by the CA that issued it. If this CA is not the root CA, then enough information is provided so that a path or trust list can be traced back to the root CA. The certificate, then, is the public compendium of information that can be used to encrypt messages being sent to its owner, to prove the identity of its owner, and so on. The EFS uses the public key to encrypt the symmetric key used to encrypt the file.

Enterprise CAs have access to multiple certificate templates that ease the process of creating requested certificates.

Table 17.2 lists the different types of certificates.

Table 17.2 **Certificate Types**

Certificate	Used For
Root CA certificate	Identifying the root CA
Subordinate Certificate Authority	Identifying a CA
Domain controller	Client authentication, server authentication
Web server	Server authentication
Administrator	Code signing, Microsoft trust list signing, Encrypting File System, secure email, client authentication
Computer	Client authentication, Server authentication
User	Client authentication, Encrypting File System, secure email
EFS recovery agent	File recovery; can decrypt user-encrypted files
Basic EFS	Encrypting File System
User signature only	Securing email, client authentication
Smart card user	Securing email, client authentication, smart card logon

Certificate	Used For
Authenticated session	Client authentication
Smart card logon	Client authentication, smart card logon
Code signing	Code-signing certificates are used to provide the user with the capability to tell if code really comes from who it says it's from. Code signing is used to identify drivers that have been certified by Microsoft and system files that have been produced by Microsoft. The code is signed by a private key belonging to Microsoft; Windows 2000 has the public key and can therefore determine whether the file was actually signed by Microsoft.
Trust list signing	Microsoft trust list signing
Enrollment agent	Certificate request agent (user)
Enrollment agent	Certificate request agent (computer)
Exchange enrollment agent	Certificate request agent
IPSec	Authentication
Router	Client authentication
CEP encryption	Certificate request agent
Exchange user	Securing email, client authentication
Exchange user only	Securing email, client authentication

Certificate Revocation List

In the normal course of events, a certificate is issued with an expiration date and is either renewed or expires. An expired certificate cannot be used. A certificate-aware application will check the expiration date of any certificate presented to it.

Public Key Policy

If the certificates are issued and stored within the AD, they come under the jurisdiction of public key policy. Like all Group Policy components, public key policy can be set as part of multiple Group Policy Objects, and it follows the normal rules for distribution and conflict resolution. More information on this component is available in the "Group Policy for Public Key Infrastructure" section later in this chapter.

Certificate Stores

Certificates are stored in certificate stores. Windows 2000 certificate stores are either physical or logical. Physical stores represent the actual location: the registry, the Active

Directory, or for increased security, on a smart card. The logical store is simply the pre-sentation of the certificate information for ease of administration. The logical store contains pointers to the physical locations of the certificates it displays.

The Windows 2000 logical certificate store can be viewed by opening the Certificates console. The Certificates console can be created by adding its snap-in to an MMC. When adding the snap-in, you must choose to view certificates for yourself (current user) or for the computer. This distinction is important because many opera-tions than can be done in the console depend on locating the proper certificate. The store is divided into seven sections:

- **Active Directory User Object.** Only shown in the user console. Contains certificates published in the Active Directory for this user.
- **Enterprise Trust.** Contains the Certificate Trust List (CTL).
- **Intermediate Certificate Authority**. Contains certificates for subordinate CAs.
- **Personal.** Contains user certificates.
- **Request.** Contains pending or rejected requests.
- **SPC.** Contains certificates of software publishers trusted by this computer.
- **Trusted Root Authorities.** Contains certificates for root CAs.

Cryptographic Service Provider

The Cryptographic Service Provider (CSP) is the body of code that does the actual encrypting and decrypting. A CSP may provide a choice of algorithms. The applica-tion can use the CSP and therefore does not have to include complex cryptographic code. This enables the application to be more easily written and avoids the weakening of the cryptography that might result due to improper coding. The cryptographic code can be written once and then implemented uniformly across all applications. If an error is later found, it can be corrected in one place. Conversely, if an error is found, all applications that use the CSP are compromised; however, if another compatible CSP is available, all applications can be quickly fixed. A CA requires a CSP in order to operate.

Windows 2000 has native CSPs and more can be added. A certificate-aware appli-cation might demand a particular CSP, or the CSP might be selected during installa-tion and maintenance. For example, if you are going to implement a smart card solution using Schlumberger or Gemplus smart cards on Windows 2000, you must chose the CSP they have provided when installing the smart card services and creating certificates. The provided CSP generates the public key/private key pair. You cannot use the Schlumberger CSP with Gemplus cards and vice versa.

CSPs provided with Windows 2000 are defined in Table 17.3.

Table 17.3 **Windows 2000 CSPs**

CSP	Definition	Notes
Microsoft Base Cryptographic Provider v. 1.0	Broad set of cryptographic functions. Uses RSA technology. Often referred to as the Microsoft RSA Base Cryptographic Service.	Can use MD4, MD5, SHA-1 hash algorithms. Not subject to U.S. government export restrictions. Should be used by third-party CAs to issue certificates for use by EFS.
Microsoft Base DSS Cryptograhic Provider	Data signing and signature verification .	Uses the SHA-1 hash algorithm (DSA). Uses the Digital Signature Algorithm (DSA). Not subject to U.S. government export . restrictions
Microsoft Base DSS and Diffie-Hellman Crytographic Provider	DSS plus Diffie-Hellman key exchange, hashing, data signing, signature verification.	Subject to government-imposed export restrictions.
Microsoft Enhanced Cryptographic Provider	Supports algorithms and key lengths supported by the Base provider. In addition, supports DES, Triple DES, and longer key lengths.	Subject to government-imposed export restrictions.
Schlumberger Cryptographic Service Provider	Provided for use with Schlumberger smart cards.	Uses MD4, MD5, SHA-1, or SSL3 SHAMD5 hash algorithms.
Gemplus GemSAFE Card CSP v. 1.0	Provided for use with Gemplus smart cards.	Uses MD4, MD5, SHA-1, or SSL3 SHAMD5 hash algorithms.

Encryption and hashing algorithm strengths of Microsoft-based and enhanced CSPs are compared in Table 17.4. In some cases, there is a default and a maximum key length; in other cases, one key length is provided and listed under the default column. All key lengths are expressed in bits.

Table 17.4 **Base Versus Enhanced CSP Algorithms**

Algorithm	Base Default	Base Max	Enhanced Default	Enhanced Max
RC2 Block Encryption	40	X	128	X
RC4 Stream Encryption	40	X	128	X
DES	X	X	56	X
Triple DES (2-key)	X	X	112	X
Triple DES (3-key)	X	X	168	X
RSA Public Key Signature	512	16384	1024	16384
RSA Public Key Encryption and Exchange	512	1024	1024	16384

In general, the longer the key, the stronger the encryption. It is also generally true, however, that the longer the key, the more performance suffers, especially in software-based encryption. Hardware-based encryption is usually so fast that speed is not an issue.

Note

It is important to note that FIPS 140-1 Level 1 Certification has been received by the Microsoft CSPs. This is a National Institute of Standards and Technology (NIST) certification required by many government operations.

Certificate Trust List

A Certificate Trust List (CTL) is used to establish trust between your organization and another organization. You use the list to identify which certificates granted by another root CA can be used in your organization. This is an invaluable tool.

If your CA and the other organization's CA were granted CA certificates from the same CA root, then establishing trust between your organizations might not be necessary. Because they share the same root, certificates granted by either organization's subordinate CAs can trace their trust back to the same root and therefore establish trust between them. Many organizations, however, will want to establish their own root CA. By doing so, they can control the CAs and thus the certificate issuers that they want to trust. If a third-party CA is used as the root, they will not have this control but must trust the third party to exercise diligence in granting trust.

This presents another dilemma. How can trust be established between different organizations? The answer is that each organization must provide a mechanism for doing so. A Windows 2000 CA can use its CTL to do this.

Certificate Lifecycle

When you establish the CA hierarchy, you issue CA certificates. These certificates are not valid forever: They can be revoked, and they will eventually expire. This is also true of every type of certificate issued by the CA. The certificate passes through stages that are documented as parts of the certificate lifecycle. Understanding this process will allow you to design, administer, and troubleshoot Certificate Services.

Because every component of Certificate Services uses certificates, the stages of the lifecycle document the entire Certificate Services process. Stages of the lifecycle are not simply progressive: Many of them are iterative, or cyclical. The stages are described in the following sections.

When the Root CA Is Installed, a Root CA Certificate is Issued

This certificate is self-signed.

The Root CA Can Issue Certificates for Subordinate CAs if Requested

In a very small organization, one that has chosen to only use Certificate Services internally, there might only be one CA provided the root CA. To operate a PKI securely, however, most organizations will have one or multiple CAs, and the root CA will be kept offline and only be used to issue subordinate CA certificates. The certificate is placed in a file that can be copied to a floppy disk for use in installing and activating the subordinate CA.

Subordinate CAs Can Issue Certificates for Other Subordinate CAs

Subordinate CAs can be used to issue certificates for other subordinate CAs; in fact, this is how a certificate hierarchy is created. In a larger organization, there might be one or more levels of subordinate CAs that are only used to issued CA certificates for other subordinate CAs. These subordinate CAs might also be kept offline and be distributed to different geographic locations so that local divisions of a company can create and renew their subordinate certificate hierarchy.

A Certificate Revocation List Is Published Periodically

A CRL is published to locations where any PKI-aware applications can access it. This location might be the Active Directory, a file share, or a Web site location. The CRL must be available to these PKI-aware applications for them to determine whether a certificate is valid. If, for example, smart cards are used for authentication and a valid CRL is not available, user logon will fail. CRLs have expiration dates, but they can be scheduled to publish automatically and/or to be published under administrative control. Typically, a new CRL will be manually issued when there is an immediate need to make new changes to the list available. Remember, if the list is published to the AD, it will not be immediately available everywhere because distribution relies on AD replication. You might want to publish the list to alternative locations to make sure it is always available in its most current form.

The CRL does not hold expired certificates. The application can tell from the certificate expiration date whether the certificate has expired. The CRL is simply a list of certificates that have been revoked.

The Root CA Certificate Must Be Reissued Before it Expires or the Entire Certificate Services Structure Is Invalid

The root CA certificate has an expiration date. The default is two years; however, it is adjustable. Planning for the renewal of certificates that this CA will issue is the critically important factor in determining the appropriate lifetime for the root CA. In a larger organization, this CA will issue only subordinate CA certificates and will be kept offline. Its Time-To-Live needs to be longer than that of its subordinate CAs. Typically, you will renew the root CA certificate long before its expiration date. A certificate issued by a CA cannot live longer than the CA's own certificate, so you must take the lifetime of your subordinate CAs into account when planning the expiration date and renewal time for the root CA.

The Subordinate CA Certificate Is Reissued Before it Expires or any Certificate that it Issued Is Invalid

Subordinate CAs are often used for either issuing certificates for other CAs or issuing other kinds of certificates for use by applications. Regardless of the types of certificates the subordinate CA will issue, none of the certificates it issues will be valid longer than the subordinate CA certificate. You must regularly renew the subordinate CA certificate. As with the renewal process for the root CA, you renew the subordinate certificate long before it expires.

Certificate Requests Are Made and Can Be Automatically Issued, Placed in a Pending Area for Administrative Approval, or Denied

Certificate request or enrollment and renewal methods include

- **Manual.** Windows 2000 users and computers can use the Certificate Request Wizard to request a certificate from an online enterprise CA. (If the enterprise CA is not online, the wizard cannot be used.) Discretionary Access Control Lists (DACLs) for certificate templates determine which accounts can enroll for a particular type of certificate. This wizard can be accessed from the certificate's console. When the certificate's snap-in is added to an MMC console, you must choose whether it is for the current user or for a computer. This will determine the type of certificate that can be requested.

- **Automatic.** Automatic certificate requests can be configured for Windows 2000 computers. This makes it easier to set up applications like IPSec if you choose to use certificates for authentication. The Automatic Certificate Request Setup Wizard can be used to make this available. This wizard is part of Group Policy (see the section "Group Policy for Public Key Infrastructure" later in this chapter). The next time a computer logs on to the network, the certificate is issued.

- **Web enrollment.** A request form can be completed by visiting special Web pages set up for this purpose. These pages are installed when Certificate Services are installed and are available at <name of web server>\certserv. (Additional management tools are also available via this path.)

- **Smart card enrollment.** Smart card certificates can be requested via the Web interface if smart card hardware and software have been installed. The Web Enrollment Station can also be used by special smart card enrollment agents to request certificates for other users. The enrollment agent uses this facility to prepare and issue smart cards to users.

- **Custom enrollment.** Custom enrollment and renewal applications also can be created.

Certificates Are Used by PKI-Aware Applications

The use of a certificate depends on the type of certificate it is. (A regular user certificate cannot be used for smart card logon or to recover EFS encrypted files.) It also depends on the application that examines it. (Although my smart card user certificate can be used for logon and secure email, if I do not have and use a PKI-aware email client, the certificate will never be used for that purpose.)

A Certificate Can Be Revoked

A certificate should not outlive its usefulness. Likewise, a certificate should not be able to be used if its keys or its CA have been compromised. Although there is no way to ensure that every copy of a certificate can be recalled or somehow marked as invalid, a certificate can be revoked and placed on the CRL. PKI applications should be written to check this CRL before allowing the use of a certificate. Windows 2000 PKI-aware applications do this.

A certificate is revoked by using the Certificate Revocation Wizard in the Certificate Authority console. To do so, you must identify the reason for revocation. The wizard lists the following choices as reasons for the certificate being revoked.

- **Unspecified.** No reason is given.
- **Key Compromise.** The keys for this certificate have been compromised.

- **CA Compromise.** The CA that signed this certificate has been compromised.
- **Change of Affiliation.** The owner of this certificate no longer needs this certificate. (For example, he changed departments, was issued new certificates, or has left this company.)
- **Superseded.** A new certificate was issued for this purpose; perhaps jobs were changed
- **Cease of Operation.** The CA that signed this certificate is no longer in operation.
- **Certificate Hold.** For some reason, this certificate's use is suspended. This is the only revocation status that can be removed to allow the certificate to be used again.

A Certificate Can Be Renewed

A certificate must be periodically renewed; otherwise, it will expire and be of no use. To renew a certificate, users can use the following:

- The Certificate Request Wizard to renew a certificate before it expires
- The Certificate Renewal Wizard to renew a certificate before or after it expires

A Certificate Can Expire

Each certificate is given an expiration date (Valid to...) when it is created. If the certificate is not renewed, its usefulness ends with the expiration date. The expiration date is the result of adding the certificate lifetime to the creation date of the certificate. A certificate lifetime exists for the root CA, subordinate CAs, and other certificates.

Group Policy for Public Key Infrastructure

The use of your PKI can be controlled via Group Policy. The application of the policy follows the standard Group Policy rules for application and inheritance. Most policies are configured under the Computer section of the Group Policy Object (GPO); however, enterprise trust can also be configured at the user level. The items that can be set in Group Policy are

- Enterprise Trust (user and computer configuration)
- Encrypted Data Recovery Agents
- Automatic Certificate Request Settings
- Trusted Root Certification Authorities

Enterprise Trust (User and Computer Configuration)

The Certificate Trust List for a domain, organizational unit (OU), or user is configured here. (To create and sign a trust list, an administrator must have a valid trust list–signing certificate.) The trust list is created to restrict the uses of certificates issued by CAs that are trusted. (Their CA certificates are present in the Trusted Root Certification Authorities Group Policy.)

For example, suppose you want to control a business partner's access to resources within your organization. You initially give him access by placing a copy of his CA's root certificate in the Trusted Root Certification Authority Group Policy, by creating user accounts for him to use, and by importing his certifications and mapping them to the Active Directory accounts. You do not, however, want his certificates to be usable for just any purpose within your organization, so you configure a CTL that specifies valid uses of these certificates. You specify the purpose of the CTL when you create it and then add the root CA certificate. All certificates issued by that root CA will be trusted for the uses specified for the CTL. More than one root certificate can be included. Designated purposes that can be specified are

- Server authentication
- Client authentication
- Code signing
- Secure email
- Time stamping
- Microsoft trust list signing
- Microsoft time stamping
- IP Security end system
- IP Security tunnel termination
- IP Security users
- Encrypting File System
- Windows hardware driver verification
- Windows system component verification
- Key pack licenses
- License server verification
- Smart card logon
- Digital rights
- File recovery

Any new valid purpose can be added by adding an object identifier for that new purpose.

Encrypted Data Recovery Agents

The Windows 2000 operating system does not require that Certificate Services be installed to use EFS. A certificate is issued to the user, and a recovery agent certificate is issued to the Administrator. (By default, the first Administrator account for the domain becomes the recovery agent for the domain.) If, however, you want to have centralized control of recovery agents or additional recovery agents, you must use Certificate Services. You use Group Policy to designate these alternative recovery agents. (You must first issue EFS Recovery Agent certificates to these users.)

Recovery agents published in the Active Directory (or in the case of standalone CAs, available from a file) can be added. To maintain security, you should use file-based certificates and keep the recovery agent private key offline unless it is needed to perform recovery.

Automatic Certificate Request Settings

To ease the administrative burden of requesting computer certificates and to automate the process of configuring PKI-aware applications, the Automatic Certificate Request Setup Wizard can be used to configure auto-enrollment of Windows 2000 computers for domain controller, computer, and/or IPSec certificates. An enterprise CA must be online to process the requests.

You configure the process using Group Policy, and the policy follows normal Group Policy rules. So if you create the policy at an OU level, only computers within that OU will automatically receive the certificates. To configure IPSec to use certificates for authentication in the Accounting OU, for example, run the wizard from the Public Key Policies\Automatic Certificate Request Settings container in a GPO linked to the Accounting OU.

Further granularity (that is, which of the computers within the OU will get the certificate) can be accomplished by setting the DACLs on the certificate template. You should be aware, however, that the DACLs set on the template are not OU-specific.

Certificates granted by this policy are automatically renewed by the enterprise CA that issued them. This means you must remember to revoke these certificates if you no longer want them to be used by the computer.

Trusted Root Certification Authorities

To add certificate trust for third-party CAs (CAs that are not part of your organization), you must add a copy of their root certificate to the Trusted Root Certification Authorities Policy for the domain. The certificate for your organization's root CA is added automatically.

Any root certificates in this policy become trusted root CAs for computers with the scope of the policy. Therefore, if I add the certificate to the peachweaver.me domain Trusted Root Certification Authority Group Policy, only the computers joined in the peachweaver.me domain that will trust this root. If I want computers within other domains to trust it as well, I need to add the CA certificate to the GPO in those domains.

Additional Certificate Services Security Practices

Using Certificate Services to secure your enterprise will be a worthless venture if you do not secure your Certificate Services. Reasonable, default security measures are in place and can be modified. There are several processes and settings that you should use or be aware of to increase your chances for maintaining secure certificate services. This section details several of these processes and settings.

Creating a Secure CA Hierarchy

The issue of taking the root CA offline was first discussed in the "Certificate Hierarchy" section. This practice prevents a network attack on the root CA. To complete its protection, you need to physically secure the CA and implement secure practices when renewing the root CA certificate and when issuing and renewing subordinate CA certificates. A common practice is to lock the root CA in a vault and specify by policy who can enter the vault and operate the CA. The CA, once established, is only used to issue subordinate CA certificates and to renew root and subordinate CA certificate. Subordinate CA certificate enrollment and renewal requests are honored by entering the vault and using a floppy-based certificate request to produce a file-based certificate and key. The certificate and the separate key file are then copied to the floppy and are used to install or renew the subordinate CA.

Care should also be taken to have adequate disaster-recovery plans in place should the root CA be lost. A system can be prepared and waiting if necessary; backup copies of the root certificate can be physically secured in an alternative location. Regular backup of the root CA will also assist the recovery process.

To maintain the root CA offline, the root CA is created as a standalone root CA. A standalone root CA can issue a subordinate CA certificate for an enterprise CA. Figure 17.2 illustrates this concept. The standalone root CA is shown by itself in a vault. Its subordinate CAs and the remainder of the hierarchy are shown with their network connections. User certificates are stored in and CRLs are published to the Active

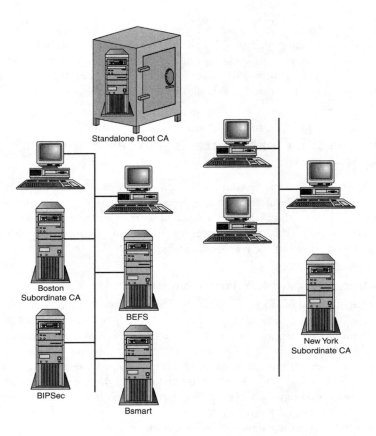

Standalone Root CA

Boston
Subordinate CA

BEFS

BIPSec

Bsmart

New York
Subordinate CA

Directory.

Figure 17.2 Securing the root CA.

CA DACLs

Default CA DACLs and permissions are listed in Table 17.5.

Table 17.5 **Default DACLs and Permissions**

DACL or Permissions	Explanation	Given To/Granted With
Enroll	Request certificates from CA	Given to Local Administrators, Authenticated Users, Domain Admins, Enterprise Admins
Manage	Manage the CA with the Certificate Authority console or run line command programs	Given to Local Administrators, Domain Admins, Enterprise Admins

DACL or Permissions	Explanation	Given To/Granted With
	Includes the Write Configuration, Modify Permissions, Revoke Certificate, Approve Certificates, and Read Database permissions	
Read	Read configuration information for CA	Given to Local Administrators, Authenticated Users, Domain Admins, Enterprise Admins
	Includes the Read Control permission	
Write Configuration	Change configuration data for CA	Granted with Manage permissions
Read Control	View security settings for the CA	Granted with Read permissions
Modify Permissions	Change permissions for CA security	Granted with Manage permissions
Revoke Certificate	Revoke certificates	Granted with Manage permissions
Approve Certificates	Approve certificate requests for standalone CAs	Granted with Manage permissions
Read Database	Gain access to and read info in certificate database	Granted with Manage permissions

As administrator, you can change these permissions to delegate authority for specific management tasks to other groups of users.

Third-Party Party Trust

To enable trust of a third-party CA, you must configure Public Key Group Policy policies. (Refer to the section "Group Policy for Public Key Infrastructure" and see Chapter 18, "Interoperability.")

Backup and Restore Processes and Recommendations

You should back up the entire Windows 2000 server that hosts the CA; however, there are backup and restore wizards that can be used to back up just the CA.

The Certificate Authority Backup Wizard is used to back up the certificate database and the CA private key and certificate. You can selectively back up only portions of the data—such as just the private key and certificate or just the database—or do full or incremental backups. The CA can be backed up to an empty folder on any NTFS or FAT device on a Windows 2000 computer.

Backing up the private key requires using a password, and the key is stored in a password-protected encrypted format. Remember the password; otherwise, you will not be able to recover the key.

The Certificate Authority Restore Wizard can be used to restore the database, the key, or both. If old database logs are still available, the restored CA will automatically be brought up-to-date. If the logs have been lost as well, the CA will be in whatever state it was in at the time of backup.

Logs are placed by default at %systemroot%\system32\CertLog.

Tip

Windows 2000 Certificate Services requires that Internet Information Service (IIS) be running to support the Web enrollment and management pages. When you back up the CA, make sure to back up IIS. You will need to restore IIS when you restore the CA.

Enable Netscape-Compatible, Web-Based Revocation Checking

The Netscape browser–compatible certificate-revocation checking method is different than that used by Windows 2000 Certificate Services. With Netscape, a URL to a Web page that performs revocation checking is included in a certificate extention. (Windows 2000 CRLs are published to the Active Directory, file shares, or Web shares.)

The extension to these certificates includes information that allows Web-based revocation checking. While information on the Microsoft certificates does include the location of the CRL, the Netscape format and process for checking the CRL is different. The revocation check extension holds a URL. This URL is for a Web page that performs revocation checking. This is done by appending the certificate serial number to the URL and thus passing it as a parameter to be used in code on the Web page. The code then contacts the CA to see if the certificate has been issued by it and has not yet been revoked.

If you want the Netscape-compatible extension to be added to every certificate a CA produces, you can do so by using the CertUtil (a command-line tool). The command is

```
Certutil -Setting Policy\RevocationType +AspEnable
```

You must stop, and then restart the service before this will take effect.

Modify Default Certificate Template DACLs

The default DACLs on the CA give authenticated users and others the Enroll permission, which indicates that they can request a certificate be issued. To control which type of certificate they can automatically receive, permissions are set on the certificate templates. Table 17.6 lists the permissions and the associated default grantees for specific templates.

Table 17.6 **Default Enrollment Certificate Template DACLs**

Templates	Default Enrollment Given to
All certificate types	Domain Admins
Exchange User, EFS, Authenticated Session, Exchange Signature Only, User, User Signature Only	Domain Users
All certificate types except Basic EFS, Authenticated Session, Exchange User, Exchange Signature Only, User, and User Signature Only	Enterprise Admins

You can change these DACLs (add other security groups or remove the ones present) by editing the certificate template DACLs. Certificate templates and their default settings are domain specific for the domain where the CA is installed. To allow users from other domains to obtain certificates from a CA in another domain, you must edit the certificate template and give these groups the Enroll permission.

Template DACLs can be edited in the Active Directory Sites and Services console. The View and Show Services Node view must be checked in the console interface. Changes to the DACLs will replicate to other domain controllers in the normal AD replication process.

Certificate/PKI-Aware Applications

A Public Key Infrastructure on its own is like an amusement park in the wintertime. It's certainly fun for those of us who like to figure out how technology works, but it's a mere shadow of itself, and pretty soon even we won't be interested in it until summer comes and some people start using it. Therefore, rather than just implementing a PKI for the joy of implementing a PKI, I'm sure you have in mind some application for its services. PKI-aware applications include

- Smart cards for authentication or secure email
- IPSec over L2TP (which requires Certificate Services) or IPSec Policy using certificates for authentication
- Central control over recovery and recovery agents for the EFS
- Secure email for your Exchange Server
- SSL or TLS and securing Web services
- Code-signing authority for software you are selling or for internal software you distribute in your own company

Several of these applications are discussed in other chapters of this book. See the "For More Information" section at the end of this chapter for specific chapter references.

Best Practices

Microsoft and others recommend the following best practices concerning PKI:

- Leave the root CA offline and physically secured, perhaps in a vault.
- Three or four levels for a CA hierarchy are about the right depth for large organizations with multiple PKI uses and applications. Use breadth to provide additional services or to distribute CAs across the enterprise.
- Renew CA certificates long before they are due to expire.
- Make sure CRL publication is frequent enough to provide current information on revoked certificates but allow time for replication. (You do not want a CRL to expire before it gets replicated to all domains and all domain controllers.)
- Secure a copy of the CA private key and a backup of the database offsite.
- Keep your software up-to-date with service packs and security patches.
- Have a disaster plan in place and tested before there is a disaster.

For More Information

This chapter discussed services for which complementary information exists in other chapters of this book. The following should serve as a referral source for you in locating this information.

PKI is generically discussed in Chapter 4, "Public Key Infrastructure (PKI)."

Using smart cards for authentication is detailed in Chapter 7, "User Authentication."

The use of IPSec over L2TP for VPNs is covered in Chapter 15, "Secure Remote Access Options."

SSL was first described in Chapter 3, "New Protocols, Products, and APIs."

Cryptographic algorithms are described in Chapter 2, "Cryptology Introduction."

Summary

This chapter outlined the features of Microsoft Certificate Services. Several applications provided with Windows 2000 (IPSec over L2TP, centralized control over EFS recovery agents and keys, and smart card integration with Kerberos) require Certificate Services. Others, such as IPSec policies, are enhanced by them. Still other complementary products such as Microsoft Exchange Server can use certificates to produce better security. To use these products, you must understand the operation of and be able to securely manage Microsoft Certificate Services.

Third-party applications can also take advantage of Certificate Services. You might also be required to interface third-party Certificate Services with Windows 2000. Information about doing this is included in Chapter 18, "Interoperability."

18

Interoperability

To EXPLORE ISSUES SURROUNDING SECURING HETEROGENEOUS NETWORKS, you first need to examine the possibilities that exist for interoperability with particular operating systems. Your knowledge of these techniques and the underlying technologies in Windows 2000 will enable you to better evaluate composite interoperability functions such as Single Sign-On (SSO) or directory integration. This chapter will examine interoperability features for Windows 2000 with

- UNIX
- PKI interoperability
- Macintosh
- Novell NetWare
- IBM mainframe and AS400

This introduction to available product-specific utilities and products will be followed by a discussion on SSO and metadirectories. The emphasis in all areas will be on security. Other chapters in this book, as listed in the "For More Information" section at the end of this chapter, provide background in technologies and standards supported by Windows 2000 (such as SSL, IPSec, TCP/IP, Kerberos, and industry-standard common cryptographic algorithms) that enable interoperability.

UNIX Interoperability

Windows NT 4.0 provides minimal integration features with UNIX including a Telnet client, FTP, POSIX compliance, and fewer than a dozen UNIX command-line functions. Services for UNIX, an add-on utility, brought some UNIX tools to NT. The recently released version 2.0 of this product provides many new features that allow for better interoperation of Windows and UNIX networks. Three areas need to be considered:

- Out-of-the box interoperability
- Functionality provided by Services for UNIX
- Kerberos interoperability

Out-of-the-Box Interoperability

Windows 2000 Server provides a Telnet server, and all Windows 2000 systems include a command-line Telnet client. The Telnet server supports NTLM for authentication but only if the session is between Windows 2000 clients and the Windows 2000 Telnet server. UNIX client access through Telnet can be authenticated via cleartext, which is not secure. Two client licenses (simultaneous connections) for the Telnet server are provided. Additional licenses can be obtained by purchasing Services for UNIX. The File Transfer Protocol (FTP) and the Trivial File Transfer Protocol (TFTP) are provided as well.

A smattering of other UNIX commands is available such as rcp (remote copy), which can be used to copy files from Windows 2000 to a UNIX system running the remote shell daemon rshd.

Services for UNIX: Version 2.0

Version 1.0 of Services for UNIX (SFU) was introduced in 1999 with the goals of leveraging UNIX resources and expertise and simplifying network administration and account management. SFU Version 2 continues the process by adding new features and extending others. Several features should be noted:

- Network Information Services
- An additional feature set
- Password synchronization

Network Information Services

One of the major features of SFU Version 2.0 is the addition of Network Information Services (NIS), a UNIX management tool developed by Sun Microsystems as a namespace administration system for UNIX. NIS organizes UNIX systems into administration groups.

NIS is composed of a set of maps or databases of data and sets of computers. NIS clients look up passwords, groups, and hosts on NIS servers instead of relying on local files. Each NIS server holds a database, which is updated when changes are made. Update synchronization is one-way. Changes are always made at the master server and then replicated to the slave server. This replication is similar to the arrangement between Windows NT 4.0 primary domain controllers (PDCs) and backup domain controllers (BDCs). The database is used for authentication and file access.

Figure 18.1 displays the architecture of SFU NIS. The Windows client (using ADSI) can access the NIS server (hosted on a Windows 2000 server) and updates information from the client system. The Windows 2000 server is the master NIS server. The master server replicates the new client information to two NIS slave servers represented by another Windows 2000 domain controller (DC) and by a UNIX slave server. The heavy dark arrows represent replication. A NIS UNIX client (using remote procedure calls, or RPCs) can obtain the information from the UNIX slave NIS server, and another Windows client can obtain information from the Windows 2000 slave NIS server.

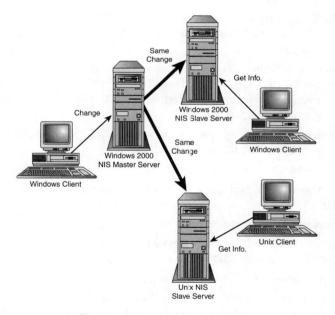

Figure 18.1   SFU NIS architecture.

Note

A Windows server can be a master or slave NIS server to a Windows 2000 master NIS server. A Windows NIS server cannot be a slave server to a UNIX NIS master.

Server for NIS extends the Active Directory (AD) and stores the UNIX attributes. Storing the UNIX NIS data in the AD is a good security choice. Because the Windows 2000 NIS server is the master, only an administrator can change the data directly. Administrators can manage Windows 2000 and UNIX NIS domain using AD.

SFU Version 2 Features

SFU Version 2 provides the following features:

- Perl scripting can be used to automate network administrative tasks on Windows NT or Windows 2000.
- Client for NFS provides access to resources on network file system (NFS) servers.
- Server for NFS enables NFS clients to access Windows NT 4.0 Server or Windows 2000 Server resources via NFS. Default file permission for UNIX clients is (rwxr-xr-x). That is, the owner has Read, Write, and Execute privileges; the UNIX group has Read and execute privileges; and all others have Read and Execute privileges.
- DACLs simulate typical permissions in the UNIX and NFS world. Permission can be set via the NFS Sharing tab and the Permission button on the Windows 2000 file folder.
- Gateway for NFS provides any Windows client access to NFS resources without loading the Services for UNIX client. (This is for light use only.) NFS directories then appear as Windows shared directories, and Windows clients can access them without any NFS software.
- A Windows 2000 or NT Server can serve as a PCNFS server and can provide user authentication for file access to NFS servers.
- MMC consoles and/or command-line functions are provided to manage SFU.
- A NIS Migration Wizard moves NIS network information to AD via NFS or FTP.
- Two-way password synchronization between Windows and UNIX is provided.
- A Windows 2000 DC can act as a primary server for NIS to integrate NIS domains with Windows 2000 domains.
- Additional Telnet server client licenses are provided.
- A subset of the Mortice Kern System (MKS) toolkit, including 60 of the most commonly used Korn shell commands and ActiveState ActivePerl distribution, is part of the package.
- SFU includes the Korn shell, which is POSIX compliant.
- Name mapping associates UNIX and Windows usernames.

- There is a Windows Management Interface for SFU.
- SFU provides simplified network administration via a Telnet client and server, MMC snap-ins, and Perl scripting.
- SFU uses NTLM authentication for client logins on Telnet (Windows clients to Windows Telnet servers only). UNIX clients use username and password in cleartext.

Note

UNIX file permissions are very different from Windows NFS file permissions, and you cannot match them exactly. To ensure resource security, you should be fluent in your understanding of both file systems and should make choices that err on the side of caution in granting access.

Tip

NTLM Telnet connections restrict users to local drives on the machine to which they logged on. To map a network resource, credentials must be provided via the following command:

```
net use g: \\server\share /user:domain\username
```

Password Synchronization Without Windows 2000 NIS Server

One-way password synchronization can also be accomplished with UNIX servers and operated with NIS domains. To do so, pods, or collections of UNIX hosts, are defined on the Windows server. Two methods of password synchronization can be used:

- **Cleartext passwords.** This choice does not require any configuration change on the UNIX host. Password changes are sent to each member of the pod by Windows 2000, and the UNIX rlogin daemon is used.
- **Secure.** A Single Sign-On daemon (SSOD) is available for HP-UNIX, Sun OS, and Digital UNIX. The SSOD collects password changes and sends them to the Password Synchronization daemon on each UNIX host. If the UNIX hosts are part of an NIS domain, the changes are made on the NIS domain master, and the NIS domain master propagates the changes to other hosts in its domain.

Figure 18.2 shows configurations for both secure options. At the top of the figure, the SSOD daemon sends the password changes to all hosts in the pod. In the lower part of the figure, it sends changes to an NIS domain master, which replicates it to the NIS slaves.

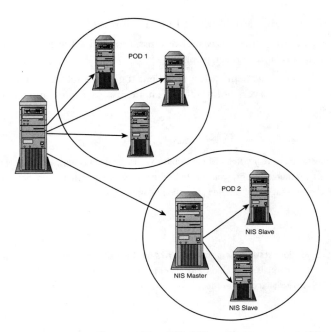

Figure 18.2   SSOD daemon.

Kerberos Interoperability

Kerberos is traditionally implemented in a UNIX environment. Because Windows 2000 follows RFC 1510, you might expect compatibility between Windows 2000 domains and Kerberos realms (the Kerberos standard name for a group of logically connected Kerberos using computers). Although it's not simple, you can integrate Windows 2000 systems and Kerberos realms. (For discussion purposes, I will refer to the traditional UNIX implementation as Kerberos Classic.) To do so, you need to do the following:

- Understand differences (What's different between Windows 2000 and the usual UNIX implementation of Kerberos 5?)
- Investigate Microsoft recommendations (which scenarios work and how to make them succeed)
- Listen to the UNIX community concerns

Understand Differences

First you need to understand the difference between the UNIX and Microsoft implementations.

Realm vs. Domain

A Kerberos Classic implementation uses the RFC designation "Kerberos realm" to define a logical collection of computers that participate in a single Kerberos trust. Microsoft implements Kerberos as the authentication mechanism for the Microsoft domain. These are not exactly the same, but they can be used in a similar fashion when talking about the two systems.

UDP vs. TCP

The Kerberos specification (RFC 1510) defines User Datagram Protocol (UDP) as the transport mechanism. TCP has been suggested as an alternative transport. Kerberos Classic uses UDP. Microsoft uses TCP. Microsoft's reason for using TCP is the limitation in UDP packet size. Because Microsoft uses the Authorization field to contain authorization information (user and group SIDs), the size of the packet could easily exceed the maximum UDP size. When Microsoft Kerberos needs to communicate with Kerberos Classic, this extra authorization information isn't necessary and UDP can be used. This resolves one compatibility issue.

FLAGs

There are more FLAGs in Kerberos Classic than in Windows 2000. The Kerberos RFC states that some flags are optional; however, if a flag is received by a system that does not support it, there often is a prescribed way to react to the flag. One of these flags is the POSTDATED flag used to issue a ticket for use later. The ticket is not authenticated, so it must be resubmitted for authentication at a later time. Microsoft always insists on preauthentication, so this particular flag is not used.

Kerberos Database

Windows 2000 uses the AD to store security principal information and secret keys. Kerberos Classic maintains a database on the Kerberos server.

Installation and Administration

Windows 2000 Kerberos installation is transparent to the user and administrator. When a Windows 2000 server is promoted to domain controller, the necessary files and initialization routines are run. When a Windows 2000 Server or Professional system is joined in a domain, it can immediately begin using Kerberos for authentication. Users do not realize which authentication scheme is being used. Administration of users is also transparent. Users are added and managed using MMCs. Kerberos administration is only required if changes to default policy are required, and this is managed via Group Policy.

Kerberos Classic requires command-line implementation and administration on many systems. Windows 2000 provides several command-line Kerberos utilities used to integrate Windows 2000 Kerberos with a Kerberos Classic realm:

- **kinit.** Log in to the realm using a key derived from the password.
- **klist.** View cached credentials (tickets).
- **kdestroy.** Destroy the credentials cache. (This can be used at logout to keep from any possible use by others. In some UNIX implementations, this might be a necessary tool. Windows 2000 caches credentials in a secure area.)
- **kpasswd.** Change passwords.
- **kadmin.** This is used by the Kerberos Administrator to update accounts.
- **kpropd.** A daemon (a UNIX application similar to Windows service) that accepts changes to a UNIX slave (copy) Kerberos database from a master Windows 2000 Kerberos database.

The first four utilities are standard; however, kpropd is a nonstandard tool. In a UNIX implementation, it is common to provide a master Kerberos Key Distribution Center (KDC) and several slave KDC copies. This allows distribution of essential information to multiple servers. Windows 2000 uses multiple domain controllers, each of which has its own copy of the AD. In an interoperability scenario, the kpropd daemon can be used to update UNIX KDCs from the Microsoft AD.

Microsoft Scenarios

There are three scenarios in which interoperability can be accomplished:

- UNIX clients in a Windows 2000 domain
- Windows 2000 clients in a Classic realm
- Multiclient, Multi KDC

There are also several reasons to anticipate problems in these scenarios.

UNIX Clients in a Windows 2000 Domain

If you want UNIX clients to access resources in a Windows 2000 domain, you must configure the UNIX clients so they can use the Windows 2000 KDC. On the Windows 2000 side, accounts in the Windows 2000 domain need to be established for the UNIX clients to use. UNIX clients can use kinit to log on to the Windows 2000 domain and request a ticket. The Ticket-Granting Ticket (TGT) is returned to the UNIX client by Windows 2000 and can be stored in the UNIX client's credentials cache. The UNIX client presents this TGT to the Windows 2000 Ticket-Granting Server (TGS) to request a session ticket to a Windows 2000 server. Tickets issued to the UNIX clients will include information needed to authorize the UNIX client's access to Windows 2000 network resources. The UNIX utilities kdestroy and klist will also work with Windows 2000–provided tickets.

Windows 2000 Clients in a Classic Realm

For Windows 2000 clients to operate in a Kerberos Classic realm, they must be configured to do so. In UNIX, unless all Windows 2000 users will use a single account, UNIX accounts will have to be created for each Windows 2000 user.

On each Windows 2000 Professional system, the ksetup utility is used to configure an alternative KDC. In a Windows 2000 domain, the process of joining the domain would initialize the Windows 2000 Professional system. Because Windows 2000 would know the name of its own domain, locating the DC would allow it to use Kerberos for authentication to that domain. In the UNIX realm, Windows 2000 needs to be pointed at the UNIX KDC; ksetup is used to do so.

Multiclient, Multi KDC

If your enterprise includes Windows 2000 domains, UNIX realms, and clients from both environments, and if Windows and UNIX clients need to access to each other's resources, you can achieve this. To do so, you must outline the relationships between clients (Windows 2000 Professional or UNIX) and servers (which KDC is used, UNIX or Windows 2000) and then determine your strategy. Two scenarios exist:

- Windows 2000 clients log on to Windows 2000 but want to access resources in both the Kerberos Classic realm and Windows 2000. Establish a one-way trust between the Windows 2000 and UNIX realms.

- Windows 2000 clients and UNIX clients, a Windows 2000 domain and the Kerberos Classic realm want to access both Windows 2000 and UNIX resources. Establish a two-way trust between the Windows 2000 domain and the Kerberos Classic realm. Account mapping must be used, and accounts must be synchronized between the domain and the realm.

Cross-OS Use of Services

The preceding scenarios have dealt with the needs and capabilities of cross-OS access to resources such as files and printers. If UNIX clients need to access Windows 2000 services and vice versa, such sharing can be arranged in some cases.

If trusts have been correctly set up, UNIX Kerberos Classic clients can use Windows 2000 services. For Windows 2000 clients to use UNIX services, the UNIX services must support the GSS-API, and some configuration is necessary on the Windows 2000 side. In the AD, a service instance is created with the ktpass utility provided with Windows 2000.

UNIX Community Concerns

Soon after Microsoft announced that Windows 2000 would support Kerberos, speculation and concern was voiced in many newsgroups. Now that the product is out, the concerns seem fall into three areas:

- Windows 2000's use of the Authorization field

- Microsoft's failure to publish complete details of its implementation
- The perceived requirements for Windows 2000 domains in addition to existing Kerberos servers to authenticate Windows 2000 Professional clients

At first, an individual or organizational position on each concern seemed to depend on whether the speaker already had existing Kerberos implementations, was a strong Microsoft proponent, or was a strong Microsoft critic. Since the product shipped, the lines between positive and negative opinions have shifted. You will find Kerberos Classic proponents who explain some of the issues as nonissues. The validity of each concern can really only be settled as organizations work at integrating Microsoft and UNIX Kerberos implementations and/or use UNIX and Windows clients in the opposite environment.

Use of the Authorization Field

The Kerberos specification includes an authorization field but does not specify how it should be used except to indicate that an implementer can chose to use this field in a way that will support authorization in his environment. Microsoft chose to use this field to transport user and group SID information during the authentication process. This use, it seems to me (and to others), meets the standard; however, many claim that the Microsoft Kerberos implementation is nonstandard, and thus Microsoft Kerberos and Kerberos Classic could not interoperate.

As previously described, the field is not used when providing tickets for non-Windows clients or when Windows clients are using UNIX resources after Kerberos Classic authentication.

Open Source/Closed Source

The open source/closed source debate is not one that anyone is going to win. However, concern with the specification for the Microsoft use of the authorization field led Microsoft to publish those details. Third-party developers of Kerberized applications claimed they needed this information to build applications that could participate fully in the Windows 2000 world.

Microsoft made the specification available for download to anyone who would agree to a nondisclosure. Some open-source proponents scorned this requirement, and the information was published on `http://www.slashdot.com`.

Requirements for Windows 2000 Domains in a UNIX Environment

Some Kerberos Classic proponents would like to be able to access Windows resources using Kerberos authentication without the requirement for a Windows 2000 domain. To allow this would require a complete rewriting of Windows 2000 to subvert the current authentication and authorization schemes. Windows 2000 standalone servers and Professional systems are not able to understand Kerberos unless they are joined in a Windows 2000 domain. Securing Windows 2000 network file shares requires the capability to match user and group SIDs to DACLs.

PKI Interoperability

Interoperability with other Public Key Infrastructures (PKIs) will vary. If the third-party product either has followed proprietary methods of implementing PKI or has implemented current standards in a slightly different way, interoperability might not be complete, might require extensive work, or might not be achievable at all. Four scenarios exist for PKI interoperability:

- **Coexistence.** Windows 2000 and a third-party PKI both exist in your environment.

- **Business partner access.** You want to provide business partner access to your resources using third-party PKI certificates.

- **Third-party PKI only.** You will only be using the third-party PKI and want to know how it will integrate with Windows 2000.

- **Third-party PKI-aware Applications.** You need to use third-party applications that require Certificate Services in a Windows 2000 enterprise.

To determine whether integration is possible, examine PKI goals and determine the standards to which each adheres. Microsoft's goal for PKI in Windows 2000 is to enable the platform for e-business. To this end, Windows 2000 uses Internet-standard protocols such as TCP/IP, Kerberos, SSL, and IPSec. Standard X.509 v3 standard certificates are used, and compatibility with Version 2 certificates is provided. Standard cryptographic algorithms are provided; in addition, the capability to use Cryptographic Service Provider (CSP) interfaces is included.

Windows 2000 PKI follows public key cryptography standards (PKCS) and the PKIX Internet drafts and RFCs (including RFC 2459 from the Public Key Infrastructure working group). PC/SC personal computer/SMART card specifications are followed, and two drivers for third-party SMART card products are provided with the product. You will recall that CSPs perform the encrypting and decrypting, whereas PKI-aware applications need only use the provided API to use their services. Windows 2000 PKI is integrated with AD, and documentation is provided for using third-party certificates with Windows 2000 user accounts in the AD.

Coexistence

If third-party and Microsoft Windows 2000 PKIs are to coexist within your network, how well they do so might depend on the compatibility of many of their parts. You will need to determine which features they support in common and determine whether differences can be worked around or are hopeless causes. Table 18.1 lists common features that might provide interoperability problems. Windows 2000–specific information is included and generic third-party information listed.

Table 18.1 **Interoperability Sticking Points**

Feature	Windows 2000 Support	Third-Party Support
Key import and export.	Yes.	Might or might not exist; might or might not be a factor in your implementation.
Algorithms and key length. If one PKI supports large key lengths and the other does not, you can't exchange symmetric keys. Key exchange and digital signature don't have to use the same key length; symmetric keys do. Symmetric keys are used in PKI to do bulk encryption and to establish secure communication channels.	A number of standard cryptographic algorithms and a range of key lengths are supported.	Compare with Windows 2000 implementation to determine compatibility.
Trust model. If the trust model is different, there might be problems because each might not know the way to create a trust path to be able to determine trust for a specific certificate.	Hierarchical, rooted trust.	Hierarchical, network, or some other model.
Trust path or trust chains.	Trust chains bottom up.	Varies.
Directory requirements. Does the PKI require the presence of its directory for its use? Do all certificates have to reside in its directory?	Takes advantage of AD but a standalone version can be used.	Some require their directory to be present and to be the storage medium for certificates.
The CA can be taken offline.	Yes.	Some require the CA to be online at all times.
A dual key pair is supported.	Both single-key-pair and dual-key-pair support is included.	Some PKIs insist on one or the other.

Feature	Windows 2000 Support	Third-Party Support
Partitioned CRLs (an optional standard) will save hard disk space.	Not supported.	Might or might not be supported.
Optional extensions supported. More importantly, options either present or not present would cause the rejection of a certificate.	Varies.	Varies.
Certificates supported by an application. CA must be online to support a particular type of certificate.	CA is not required to be online to support use of any certificate.	Goes either way.
Certificates and keys can be stored in a hardware device for better security.	Smart card support is provided. Can support additional hardware devices. Hardware abstraction layer allows segregation of application from hardware requirements.	Some are CA dependent.
Encoding formats supported. Name problems can exist if encoding support varies.	Supports those in RFC 2459 and Unicode.	Varies.
Authority Information Access (AIA) field support. This is used in chain building.	Supports and uses if present.	Some PKIs require global directory instead or pushing all certificates to the client.
CRL distribution point (CDP) indicates where to look for CRL.	Published to AD, file system, and Web sites.	Some are easily accessible; CDP for some in field of certificate.
The basic constraints extension identifies which certificates are CA certificates and which are end-user certificates.	Windows 2000 requires this extension and will reject certificates that do not provide it.	Varies.

continues

Table 18.1   **Continued**

Feature	Windows 2000 Support	Third-Party Support
Subject-alternative name extension is used by S/MIME and IPSec to get more information on names.	Uses email name, user principal name, and DNS name.	Varies.
Extended key usage (EKU) extension contains information that describes for what a certificate can be used.	Yes.	Varies.

Business Partner Access

Group Policy is used to establish the trust of a third-party CA. Certificate Trust Lists (CTLs) are signed by Windows 2000 administrators and are given a time period. Each CTL includes a list of uses for which the certificates can be within the domain. After trust is established, certificates from the third-party CA can be imported into Windows 2000 and mapped to user accounts in the AD. Mapping can be

- **One-to-one.** Each certificate is mapped to one account.
- **Many-to-one (subject).** Any certificate with the same subject is mapped to the user account regardless of issuer.
- **Many-to-one (issuer).** Any certificate that has the same issuer is mapped to the same account regardless of the subject.

Remote access can be provided via some combination of Routing and Remote Access Server (RRAS), Internet Connection Services, and VPN tunnels.

Third-Party PKI Only

Using a third-party PKI as the only PKI in a Windows 2000 environment requires careful analysis and testing. You should check to see whether compatibility testing has been done by Veritest, as has been described in previous chapters.

Compatibility Testing/NT Compatibility

Third-party PKIs can be tested for compatibility by submission for logo standard to Veritest. If a PKI works with NT, it should work with Windows 2000, but new features of Windows 2000 (including AD integration) will not be available. These new features include

- **Autoenrollment and renewal of computer certificates.**
- **Windows 2000 PKI management tools.**

- **Roaming profiles** (if applications do not use CryptoAPI).
- **GINA replacement.** If the application replaces the Graphical Identification and Authentication (GINA) component of the Windows 2000 logon process, support for smart card logon is lost. GINA is the graphical component that collects data from the user.
- **Smart card logon certificates.** Smart card logon certificates must be issued by a Windows 2000 enterprise CA and be published in AD for the domain. (This prevents name spoofing.)
- **Issuing CA.** Issuing CA must be a Windows 2000 CA, but its parent or root CA can be a third-party product.

Using Certificates for EFS

Certificates to be used by the EFS file system must contain the enhanced key usage extension for use by EFS, and the CA must use the Microsoft RSA Base Cryptographic Service Provider. Certificates can be issued using this CSP or be imported by using the PKCS#12 file format.

Third–Party PKI–Aware Applications

Third-party PKI-aware applications might or might not interoperate with Windows 2000 certificates and/or Certificate Services. Again, the compatibility logo program can be used to determine whether such compatibility has been tested.

Macintosh

Windows NT has a long history of support for Macintosh access to Windows NT resources through Services for Macintosh (SFM). Windows 2000 continues this tradition by providing a variety of services for Macintosh clients. Although Windows 2000 does not provide a Terminal Services client for Macintosh, Citrix MetaFrame, a third-party product, does. Services supported include

- **File sharing.** Macintosh users and Windows users can store and share files stored to Windows 2000 NTFS volumes that have been initialized for use by Macintosh clients.
- **Printer sharing.** Macintosh users can use Windows 2000 network printers, and Windows clients can use postscript printers on the Macintosh network.
- **Routing.** Support for AppleTalk Phase 2 Routing is provided.
- **Dial-up access.** A Windows 2000 RRAS server can accept dial-up access.
- **Terminal Services.** If a third-party client (Citrix MetaFrame) is used, Windows 2000 application sharing can be used by Macintosh clients.

- **Secure logon.** A Microsoft-provided User-Authentication Module (MS-UAM) provides secure logon.

Three of these items require discussion.

File Sharing

File-sharing support is for Macintosh clients only. Files on Macintosh clients are not available to Windows clients.

File systems are different on Macintosh than on Windows 2000. Windows 2000 Services for Macintosh provides the necessary integration for Windows 2000 NTFS volumes that have been initialized for use by Macintosh users.

Controlling Printer Access

Print Services for Macintosh provides network printer access and print spooling for Macintosh clients. If a Macintosh client can physically access a Windows 2000 network printer across the network, the Macintosh client can print to it. Normal printer authorization methods do not apply.

In the Windows 2000 network, sets of permissions are given to printers. These permissions enable you to deny security groups the capability to print to particular printers. Macintosh users, however, cannot be denied access to specific printers by placing them in such a security group (for example, with restricted access to a check printer).

There is a workaround. If you need to restrict printing at a particular printer, follow these steps:

1. Create a service account for Macintosh services.

2. Use this account to log the Print Services for Macintosh service on to the network.

3. Set DACLs on restricted printers and do not give this account access.

Microsoft-Provided User-Authentication Module (MS-UAM)

Macintosh clients can log on to a Windows 2000 network, but they cannot use Kerberos for authentication. The native Macintosh network client uses a cleartext password. If you do not want to expose the password to network capture and abuse, you can use the Macintosh-provided UAM or the Microsoft UAM. The Macintosh UAM encrypts the password, but the password is limited to eight characters. The MS-UAM password can be up to 14 characters. In either case, the actual password is not sent over the network; it is used in a challenge/response scenario similar to that used by Windows 2000 clients. The Macintosh client, however, requires that the server store the password in a reversibly encrypted form. Normal password storage in Windows 2000 is via one-way encryption. One-way encryption is generally believed to be more secure.

To support Macintosh clients, you must use the reversibly encrypted password format for all passwords in the domain.

Novell

Options for interoperability with Novell can be divided into two tracks:

- Interoperability between Windows 2000 domains/servers/Active Directory and Novell NetWare networks
- Integration of Windows 2000 Professional as clients in a NetWare network

Interoperability Between Windows 2000 and NetWare Networks

Client Services for NetWare (CSNW) and Gateway Services for NetWare (GWSN) can be used with NetWare 2.x, 3.x, and 4.x IPX servers. Windows 2000 Professional can access resources on NetWare servers using CSNW. GWSN includes CSNW and is used on the Windows 2000 server to create a gateway to Novell resources. In either case, Novell server accounts and authorization settings for the server accessed must exist and be used to give access by the NetWare administrator to resources.

Windows 2000 collects these well-known utilities and one new one into a set of interoperability services called Microsoft Services for NetWare v.5. These services provide the following functionality:

- File and Print Services for NetWare v.5 and v.4.
- Directory Services Manager for NetWare (DSMN) can be used to manage NetWare 2.x and 3.x binderies. DSMN is used to provide directory synchronization services between NetWare 2.x, 3.x, and 4.x binderies and Windows NT 4.0.
- Microsoft Directory Synchronization Services (MSDSS).
- The File Migration Utility (FMU) can preserve security permissions while moving large amounts of data from NetWare to Windows 2000. The utility can be used with IPX/SPX- or TCP/IP-based NetWare networks.

The new utility, MSDSS, can be used for bidirectional synchronization of data between the Novell's Directory Services (NDS) and AD. Data synchronization between AD and NetWare 3.x bindery services is one-way, as is password synchronization between AD and DNS. If passwords are administered in the Windows 2000 AD, they can be synchronized with accounts in NDS, and the promise of SSO is fulfilled. Users, however, cannot change their passwords in NetWare and expect them to be synchronized with Windows 2000.

Data that has changed is collected from each directory and then published to the opposite. Figure 18.3 diagrams this action. On the right, Windows applications (including logon) use the Windows 2000 directory. On the left, NetWare applications use NDS. MSDSS sits between the two like a connector, but the data passing between them is made up of directory entries, not file information or email.

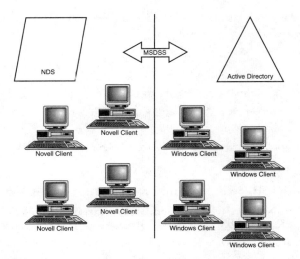

Figure 18.3 MSDSS acts as connector for Directory Services.

Synchronization information is stored securely in the AD, and access to MSDSS is only allowed for authorized users.

An add-on product (not provided with Windows 2000), File and Print Services for NetWare version 5.0 (FPNW5) allows NetWare 2.x, 3.x, and 4.x (in bindery emulation mode) customers to access Windows 2000 files and network printers. To the NetWare client, the Windows 2000 server looks like a NetWare server. File and Print Services 4.0 is the product for use on Windows NT 4.0.

Integration of Windows 2000 Professional in a NetWare Network

Many Windows 2000 Professional features and services can be utilized in a Novell network. Other features are provided by Novell or by third parties. They include

- **Support for VPNs.** Novell's BorderManager supports L2TP and PPTP. Windows 2000 Professional systems using Novell's Client for Windows 2000 should be able to take advantage of this service

- **Client Services for NetWare.** Microsoft's CSNW is NDS-aware and can authenticate to a nonbindery mode NDS server. Unfortunately, it is not compatible with NDS-based applications.

- **The Novell client for Windows 2000 is NDS compatible.** It also supports Citrix MetaFrame, Windows Terminal Services, and the ADSI NDS provider.

- **SAMBA for Novell.** SAMBA makes a Novell server look like a Windows NT server. No additional client software is necessary for Windows 2000 Professional.

- **Novell's Distributed Print Services (NDPS).** Windows 2000 Professional supports and can use NDPS (including providing user credentials for secure access) if provided with the NetWare client. (Legacy print support for NetWare 2.x, 3.x, and 4.x is also included.)

- **Windows Management Instrumentation and WEBM.** WEBM is a Web-based information management initiative that uses WMI (a model of the configuration and status and operation aspects of Windows 2000 Professional) and can be used by Novell's ManageWise IT.

- **Novell's Zero Effort Network (ZENWorks).** ZENWorks is a suite of tools used to manage applications and desktop configuration. Windows 2000 Professional can be registered with ZENWorks, and a workstation record can then be imported into NDS. Then the workstation can be administered. Windows 2000 local computer policy can be created and deployed using the Novell client and NDS.

- **Internet Explorer 5 policy distribution.** Policies can be distributed using IE 5 from a Web share location. The Internet Explorer Profile Manager that is part of the Internet Explorer Administration Kit (IEAK) can be used to save policy settings to a file on a Web server. The .ADM policy template can also be imported using the Profile Manager.

- **Windows Scripting Host (WSH).** WSH enables a Novell administrator to include a VBScript or JScript in a logon. This can be used to create, delete, or modify registry keys.

- **Novell Storage Management Services.** This can back up Windows 2000 Professional.

- **Novell NetWare 5 Public Key Infrastructure Service (PKIS).** This can be used to manage a CA domain using DNS.

- **Novell NetWare Secure Authentication Services (SAS).** This uses SSL to provide authentication support.

- **Smart card support.** This occurs via Novell BorderManager Authentication Services 3.5.

IBM Mainframe and AS400

Microsoft SNA Server is a separate product that has long been used to provide a gateway for use with IBM mainframe and AS400 systems. Data access and SSO can be achieved. Proginet SecurePass is provided with SNA Server. SecurePass provides password synchronization and ensures that an account disabled on one system is disabled on the other. It also makes sure that password rules on both systems are followed. SNA provides the option of encrypting the data sessions between the Windows 2000 client and the IBM host. SNA Server can work with the proprietary security protocols RACF, ACF2, and TOP Secret.

SNA Server will be part of the new Microsoft Host Integration Server. Host Integration Server will provide the following features (some of which are shipping now for use with Windows NT 4.0 and/or Windows 2000; visit www.micorosft.com/sna):

- SNA Server customers can use 3270 and 5250 clients on Windows desktops.

- COM Transaction Integrator (COMTI) for CICS and IMS provides three-tier client/server or a Web-to-host computing environment.

- Websetup for Windows clients provides a downloadable SNA client. Users can then use most emulation products to access the host.

- Telnet support will be provided for 3270 and 5250 clients.

- MMC support will be provided.

- VSAM file transfer will be provided.

- The Host Security Migration feature configures and manages large user populations, creates Windows domain accounts and users into a host security domain, and synchronizes relevant information. It also works with accounts in batch fashion, account mappings, and list mappings in host security domains.

- Complete and direct TCP/IP support will be provided.

- Host Security Integration current services will be provided.

Single Sign-On

Single Sign-On (SSO) is the desired capability to access all network resources via a single authentication. A user presents credentials (a user ID and password, smart card, security token, and so on) once and does not have to enter another to seamlessly access resources across the enterprise, even if the resources are hosted by a variety of operating systems. Whether you can obtain this nirvana and whether you want to depends on many factors. Windows 2000 has a host of interoperability features that might enable you to architect a solution. Remember, SSO does not guarantee authorization and full functionality of every component; it just frees users from having multiple authentication credentials. SSO can be used as the foundation for building other integration features such as authorization (access to resources such as files), administration, and security.

Before you can implement SSO, you must know the following:

- Who can join the extended family (With what OSs you can interoperate?)

- Details (How complete is the meld? Does password synchronization exist?)

- The case against SSO (reasons you might not want to provide this functionality)

Extended Family

SSO allows connectivity with a large range of operating systems including UNIX, IBM mainframe and AS-400, Macintosh clients, and Novell NetWare. Life after SSO (password synchronization, resource access, management) depends on the operating system and the tools available on both sides.

Details

SSO in a pure Windows 2000 network is based on Kerberos and Secure Sockets Layer (SSL) protocols. These protocols can be used to provide SSO in a mixed network, as can other features either provided natively with Windows 2000 or available as additional products. The components available for use are

- Kerberos v.5★
- SNA Server
- Certificate Services including SSL★
- Services for UNIX
- Telnet and other included UNIX applications★
- Gateway Services for NetWare (v2, v3, v4)★
- Directory integration with NetWare 5
- Macintosh★

Items marked with and asterisk (★) are provided with Windows 2000 Server or Advanced Server. Other items must be either purchased or downloaded.

For specific information on each, see the corresponding sections in this chapter.

The Case Against SSO

SSO within a Windows 2000 network provides the basis for providing integrated security. By providing a common user authentication scheme, encryption of the user's network session is more easily accomplished. The elimination of multiple passwords reduces the possibility that passwords will be written down, a common security breech. Disabling a user's account is accomplished in one place.

There are some reasons, however, to hesitate before implementing SSO. The case can be made that achieving SSO in the enterprise will only serve to undermine security. The following arguments should be considered before implementing SSO and should always be kept in mind if the SSO model is adopted:

- If a user has access to multiple systems and only one account, then all a hacker has to do is crack that one account to gain free range over the entire enterprise.
- The security of the enterprise is only as strong as the weakest system. If the weakest system is broken and password(s) are obtained, these passwords can be used to attack the other systems.

- Administration after SSO increases because more attention must be paid to password security. The use of strong passwords and the requirements for auditing account usage become more important. If a user has only one account and the password to his account is compromised, more resources are at risk.

- The complex nature of integration begs the question of unknown security holes in any of the components.

It is also rational to wonder whether a Windows 2000 solution, because it is based on so much new code, is going to present some hacker with possible opportunities.

Directory Integration: The Case for Metadirectories

Synchronization with Novell's NDS is accomplished via the AD synchronization tool, but the Windows 2000 AD will need to meet wider directory synchronization requirements to interoperate with the multitude of directories that exist in the real world. More importantly, the exchange or directory information requires that security concerns be addressed. Specifically, it is through directory synchronization that

- Passwords and other account information can be synchronized and the promise of SSO realized

- PKI certificates for business partners and e-commerce users can be synchronized

- Information about available resources across disparate and discrete networks is made available

To manage multiple directories, the solution might at first seem to be to create a one-size-fits-all directory. Unfortunately, this is probably not feasible. Instead, organizations are looking for ways to integrate their directory information and enable interoperability. Along the way, it seems necessary that some information will have to reside in all directories. Several different functions must be able to interoperate:

- **Connectivity.** Between disparate networks, services, databases, and applications

- **Integrity.** Related data between directories should remain consistent.

- **Change distribution and management.** Every change that affects multiple directories must be distributed to all, and changes must be only made by authorized users.

To this end, Microsoft currently provides several services for managing Windows 2000 Directory and its integration with other directories:

- **Active Directory Services Interface (ADSI) and API used for programming directories.** As currently implemented, it provides access to AD, NDS, Windows NT 4.0 SAM, and LDAP-based directories.

- **MSDSS.** Synchronization services with Novell NDS use LDAP-based DirSync, a tool that can provide connectivity between AD and other directories.

- **Active Directory Connector (ADC) connectivity with Microsoft Exchange Directory.** Proposed connectivity with Lotus Notes and Novell's GroupWise.

- **Metadirectory.** Microsoft acquired Zoomit Corporation, a leader in metadirectory development, and renamed the product Microsoft Metadirectory Services (MMS). With MMS, AD can be used to manage information stored in different directory services.

- **Directory consolidation.** Many Microsoft products, such as Exchange Server, SQL Server, Site Server, COM, and Office, will be updated to use AD. Microsoft will work with third parties to provide help in directory consolidation where desired. Both SAP and Baan have clients that can search for services in the AD. Cisco is extending some products to use information stored in AD.

- **Additional integration.** Additional integration is provided by products such as Microsoft OLE DB data access framework for writing directory-enabled applications using SQL instead of LDAP.

Best Practices

A number of interoperability features carry new risks such as cleartext logon, decryptable password storage, and a larger number of users with potential access to resources. When deploying these features—whether they are Microsoft products, features, or third-party products—use the following guidelines to continue to improve enterprise information system security.

- Use alternatives to cleartext logon.

- Where possible, restrict access to only the resources needed.

- Isolate sensitive files from areas of wide-open access by providing internal firewalled subnetworks.

- Protect these areas using IPSec.

- Remove services and capabilities if they are not or no longer needed. (Example: Do not install Services for Macintosh or Gateway Services for NetWare if you have no Macintosh clients or NetWare servers on your network. Remove them if you no longer need them.)

- Understand the authentication and authorization features of each system before using an interoperability tool. File system DACLs often are not exact matches, and care must be taken to reduce risk.

- Find the new vulnerabilities. Weigh new risks and apply fixes if warranted or provide alternative mechanisms for securing resources.

For More Information

This chapter discussed services for which complementary information exists in other chapters of this book. The following should serve as a referral source for you in locating this information.

To review basic information on Windows 2000 Kerberos and PKI, see Chapter 7, "User Authentication," and Chapter 17, "Enterprise Public Key Infrastructure," respectively.

Information on Active Directory can be found in Chapter 12, "Domain-Level Security," and Chapter 16, "Securing the Network Using Distributed Security Services."

Summary

Not too many years ago, it was exciting work just to establish a connection between two different operating systems. No one was worried about opening up systems to attack; they just wanted their systems open. As customers insisted on and vendors attempted to provide increased connectivity, the possibilities of increased risk also became reality. Connected systems do not have to provide open playgrounds for malicious activity. Better interoperability can also offer opportunities for better security.

This chapter sought to outline possibilities for interoperability and some of the new vulnerabilities that using these options might entail. It purposefully left out the greatest chance for full interoperability—Web services, which will be addressed in the next chapter.

19

Web Security

Protecting a Web server is the ultimate security job. There is a fascinating array of technology, design, philosophy, and personality embedded in a Web site. There is no "one-size fits all." The purpose of a site varies, from intranet to e-commerce and from simple Web presence to business-to-business. Every day brings new challenges and opportunities for disaster or ecstasy. On the roller coaster that is Web security, many elements add to the risk and thus the adventure. The following are some of the problems faced:

- The location of the Web server is advertised.
- Services and protocols in use have been around for a while, and specialized attacks exist.
- New services, protocols, and applications create new security holes and problems.
- There are more areas to configure, and more things can go wrong.
- Some organizations live dangerously: They have the attitude that placing the Web server behind a firewall is all the security you need. (A more prudent organization will continually harden and patch the server and its contents.)
- Newly created attacks are occurring all the time.
- The company might have "bet the farm" on the site. The site might *be* the company.

- Sensitive customer credit and personal information often resides on servers or in databases exposed to the Web.

- Sensitive organization information often resides on databases or servers exposed to the Web.

- Security failures often become public knowledge. An attack on an internal server can often be kept within the corporate family; however, a security breach on a Web server often results in a defaced home page or other evidence of your failure.

Because the risks and opportunities are so great, there is more recognition for the need for security. The issue is how much security and at what cost. There are different ways to secure a Web site and different lengths to which you might want to go depending on risk, monetary restrictions, and policy.

Here are three steps you should take to begin the process:

1. Determine the use of the server. Is it an intranet server that will never be exposed to the Internet? Is it the corporate presence on the Internet? An e-commerce site? Business-to-business? More time should be spent securing an e-commerce site than one that purely exists to provide information to internally located employees. Knowing the purpose of the site will point you in the right direction.

2. Refine and evaluate the potential threat to the site. Is it a small company or organization Web site that attracts few users? Or is it Microsoft, IBM, e-bay, the U.S. government, or some other megalith upon which every renegade will want to leave a mark? Although no Web site should sit unprotected on any network, it just doesn't make sense to ignore social and political factors.

3. Determine the Security Policy of the organization to which the Web site will belong. Determining the level of security to apply might not be up for discussion. You might have a strict policy that prescribes exactly what to do. If a policy does not exist, Web site security is a good place to start defining one. You should also investigate the need for updating any current policy because new risks are discovered all the time.

When you have an idea of the strength of security for which you are aiming, you can begin. To help you in that process, this chapter will address areas of concern and will recommend appropriate steps that need to be taken. In addition, it will outline some tools that Microsoft has provided, either with the product or available for download. Finally, some maintenance tips will be included. After all, Web security does not end when the server goes online; you must constantly monitor and improve security.

The areas I will cover are

- Securing Windows 2000 Server
- Web site essential security
- Security tools
- Monitoring, measuring, and maintaining security

Securing Windows 2000 Server

The first step in Web security is to secure the server. Starting with a solid security approach to the basic system is a must for a strong and impenetrable Web server. You should refer to other sections in this book for more detailed security practices for securing the operating system. Steps that need to be taken in this area include

- Configuring hardware
- Updating the OS
- Removing or disabling unnecessary services and subsystems
- Reviewing and setting Group Policy
- Understanding and limiting logon and user privileges
- Hardening the file system

Configuring Hardware

Depending on your policy and/or risk assessment, you might provide more or less physical security for the server. There are two essential elements here. First, you must make sure the server is in a protected environment that restricts physical access and protects the server from physical elements. Second, you might want to provide security protection by physically disabling CD-ROMs and floppy drives. Once the system is running, you might also want to remove access components such as monitors, keyboards, mice, and so on when you can. You might also want to add security hardware such as encryption boards or accelerator boards, locks, and alarms.

Updating the OS

Install service packs and hotfixes as appropriate. Service packs are regression-tested fixes and usually are safe to add. You should read readme files and look for known issues. Installing on a test system is always advisable. Hotfixes are more immediate and thus are not regression tested. Often they are a response to a security issue. Carefully evaluate each provided fix before installing to see if it is immediately necessary or if you can wait until it is more thoroughly tested. Test any hotfix on a test system before rolling it out to all Web servers. Visit `http://www.microsoft.com/security` for the latest information on fixes that close security holes.

Removing or Disabling Unnecessary Components

Wherever possible, remove parts of Windows 2000 that are not necessary for the Web server to function. Areas you can address are

- Subsystems
- Services and protocols
- Applications

Subsystems

The OS2 and POSIX subsystems support applications written for OS2 and POSIX, respectively. They are installed when you install Windows 2000. You should remove these subsystems. Any part of an operating system can prove vulnerable to attack. By removing excess parts, you are closing potential holes.

Services and Protocols

Services are used to provide additional functionality for the system. Protocols are used for communication between systems. Each service and every protocol, however, is another area that might provide a potential hole. It is just common sense to remove or disable those that are not needed. If the avenues of attack are limited, attacks are limited.

Common services and protocols that are removed or disabled on Web servers are

- Simple Mail Transfer Protocol (SMTP)
- Network News Transfer Protocol (NNTP)
- File Transfer Protocol (FTP)
- Browser
- NetLogon
- Telnet
- Server

In addition to removing unnecessary elements, unbind NetBIOS from TCP/IP on the Internet-exposed interface of the Web server. NetBIOS is used by Windows operating systems to share files. Many well-known attacks can be utilized when NetBIOS is present. NetBIOS over TCP/IP is not necessary for users to access your Web site.

In your search for elements that can be safely removed, do not remove anything until you verify that it is not being used.

Applications

If the server was installed as an intended Web server, you probably will not initially find extraneous application programs on the server. As the Web server is configured and the Web site developed, however, it is often tempting to add the tools necessary to get the job done. Before putting a server into service, review it and look for programs that do not belong there. Look for development tools such as Visual Basic, Visual Studio, C++, and so on and remove them. Make sure to remove applications such as word processing, spreadsheets, and so on.

Reviewing and Setting Group Policy

The application of Group Policy depends on the role of the server. If the server is a standalone server, then the Local Security Policy console can be used to set security options or the Security Configuration and Analysis console can be used to make further changes by applying templates. If the server is joined in a domain, then local policy settings can be overridden by site, domain, or OU Group Policy settings.

Server and Web server settings can be uniformly and centrally applied by using the appropriate tool. Microsoft supplies three sample Web server security templates that can serve as a good place to start. In addition, make sure to use other settings that apply to your circumstances. The Microsoft templates are reviewed in the "Tools" section later in this chapter.

Understanding and Limiting Logon and User Privileges

Access to your Web server is controlled from more than one interface on the server. There are two methods for controlling authentication and one for controlling authorization. Authorization, or the capability to use Web resources such as files, programs or scripts, and printers, is controlled through Discretionary Access Control Lists (DACLs) placed on the files or the printer object. Authorization is discussed in the following section, "Hardening the File System."

Authentication is configured by a combination of settings in the Windows 2000 interface; both Windows logon accounts and Internet Information Server (IIS) authentication mode are used. When the authentication mode is anonymous, a Windows user account is still used.

To access resources on a Windows 2000 server, a user must have an account and prove her identity with a password. Access via HTTP to the Web site is no different; the server authenticates every single browser request. Most Web access does not require that you identify yourself; instead, the Web server anonymous account is used. This anonymous account, the IUSR_*computername* account, is created when IIS 5.0 is installed.

All resource access, as well as programs or scripts that run via the browser, runs under the context of the logon account. This impersonation allows the orderly assignment of access and authority.

Your job is twofold: controlling access via the Internet through Web services and controlling access through any other channel. More information on picking an IIS authentication mode and on the IUSR_*computername* account can be found later in this chapter. To control access via the network or from someone with physical access to the computer, use the local user accounts database and, if applicable, the AD. As in any server, you should do the following:

- Disable the Guest account.

- Set a strong password for the Administrator account.

- Allow only minimal accounts on the Web server.

- Follow the principal of least privilege and give any user accounts as few privileges as possible on the system.

- Thoroughly check user account privileges, group membership, and group privileges.

- Follow standard practices for securing the operating system.

Hardening the File System

Pay particular attention to the permission settings on the operating system files. The default settings protect many critical functions and should not be removed. Note that the root file system setting after installation still provides access to the Everyone group. This is to prevent Windows 2000 from overwriting (through inheritance) any DACLs you might have set for other files on the volume prior to installation. You might want to adjust that setting to something stronger. Additionally:

- NTFS should be the only file system used, and DACLs should be set. There are basic types of files on a Web server: those that support the operating system and those that support the Web site. Although all files should be protected, there will be different settings for both types. Web server files, folders, and appropriate DACLs are discussed in the "File Access" section later in this chapter.

- If the Web server is installed on an NTFS volume, the operating system file and folder DACLs will have the recommended settings. Depending on your policy, you might want to adjust these settings. Auditing should be configured and set to monitor permission changes as well as sensitive object access.

- Remove network shares. Web users should be accessing files through HTTP or FTP, not through file shares.

- The Interactive Users and Network Users implicit groups can be used to aide you. Membership in these groups is not under administrative control; rather, it depends on the nature of the logon, locally or over the network. Web users will be members of the Interactive group. If you use the Interactive User group and give it special Read for File permission, Anonymous User and Basic Authentication modes can access the files. When the Network Users group is given special Read on Files permission, Anonymous, Digest Authentication or Integrated Windows Authentication modes will be able to access the files.

- Turn off NTFS 8.3 name generation. Creating old, DOS-style, short names is a good idea only if you have computers in your environment that need to use such filenames. In the greater world, however, responsible access to your Web site is via a browser; it is not necessary or justifiable for users to be able to browse your directories and see all your files using a command line. Using long filenames prevents utilities that cannot understand long filenames from doing their thing—utilities that often are used by attackers. The long filenames also can slightly improve file system performance.

Securing the Web Site

Securing the Web site requires additional configuration and precautions. In IIS 5.0, there are new features that require understanding and proper applications. Security requires attention to the following areas, which will be discussed in this section:

- Configuring general properties with security in mind
- Setting authentication methods
- Setting virtual directory permissions
- Partitioning the Web application space and applying appropriate folder permissions
- Setting up Secure Sockets Layer (SSL) if appropriate
- Installing scanner/intrusion software and auditing

General Property and Site Configuration

Several items can be configured in the property pages of the Root folder. They include

- **Setting DNS restrictions.** Access can be granted or denied by Internet domain name.
- **Setting IP address restrictions.** You can restrict access to a single or group of IP addresses and prevent access from known or suspected abusers.
- **Validating executable content.** Before loading and running scripts, executables, and so on, you must validate them for trustworthiness. Numerous resources for Web content exist. Before using any code, you should ensure that it does what it is supposed to and that it neither creates new security holes nor affects the operation of the server in any harmful way. In addition, you want to make sure that any code that can be run by or downloaded by the users of your site will not damage their systems. Code should follow all current laws and your organization's ethical standards that involve privacy and so on.
- **Enabling logging.** By default, logging is not enabled. You should always enable logging so you can track usage of your account.

- **Making sure the index service is only indexing documentation, not executables or scripts.** Users of your Web site should not be able to locate executables at their whim.

- **Removing sample applications.** Sample applications are loaded by default when IIS is installed. They are invaluable on a development server; they have no place on a production server. Any executable can offer known and unknown security risks. You should limit the available applications on your servers to those you intend for use.

- **Disabling directory browsing from the snap-in.** This is done to prevent directory browsing at the root and at its parent.

- **Securing FTP.** Unless you require an FTP site, do not install this service. If you require an FTP site, remember that data, including passwords, is sent in the clear. The best practice is not to attempt to authenticate users via Windows authentication, but to make the method of authentication anonymous. Secure FTP site data at the file and folder level by granting appropriate permission to the anonymous user account. Anonymous login asks for a username and email address as the password. The IIS 5.0 FTP service is not installed by default. If installed, it is set for anonymous access by default.

- **Removing FrontPage server extensions.** A server not hosting FrontPage Web sites doesn't need FrontPage; if you plan to use the product later, then set tight security on FrontPage.

- **Setting up auditing.** In spite of all your precautions, eventually someone will be able to intrude and/or administrators will make errors or exceed their authority. You audit to determine whether this has occurred and to track changes in permissions and policy. Specific audit settings are recommended in the "Tools" section later in this chapter.

- **Updating the Emergency Repair Disk.** The ERD should be updated after major configuration changes.

FrontPage

Configuring IIS to secure FrontPage Web sites is beyond the scope of this chapter; however, you should be aware that FrontPage server extensions are installed by default. Unless you need these extensions, you should either not install them or, if they have been installed, remove them. FrontPage Server extensions enable some features of pages created with FrontPage and the direct publishing of Web content from the FrontPage tool to the Web site.

FrontPage Server extensions have no security of their own; you set security by configuring IIS. (FrontPage sets a permission sheet for FrontPage Webs that controls the access a user has to FrontPage Web pages.)

Information on FrontPage security can be found in the Windows 2000 Server resource kit and at `http://www.microsoft.com/security`.

Anonymous User Account

The anonymous user account, IUSR_*computername*, is used to provide access to the Web site when the anonymous method of authentication is chosen. This account is created during the installation of the IIS service. The password for this account is created randomly at this time. The administrator can change the account used and/or the password. If a new account replaces the default, the account name must be entered in the General properties page of the IIS Root folder for the default Web site. The password must be set both in this interface and at the user account level (in Computer Management if the server is standalone, in Active Directory Users and Computers if the server is joined in a domain). Control over password changes can be managed in two ways:

- **Use password synchronization.** Password synchronization enables the IIS Admin to control the password. In the IIS property pages, the permission for IIS Admin to control password changes can be granted. When a change is made in the IIS Admin interface, IIS Admin will make that change to the user account password as well. If this feature is used, the logon type will be a network logon. A network logon can cause problems with some applications or with access to files if you have changed them to rely on membership in the interactive group.

  This feature was first introduced with IIS 4.0 and is possible because of the use of subauthentication DLLs, which can be used with the authentication system. Iissuba.dll is the subauthentication DLL used by IIS 5.0. For more information on subauthentication, see the Visual Studio 6.0 product documentation.

- **Continue to manage the password in both interfaces.** This is the default operation. Logon continues to be interactive. If the password is only changed in one place, no one can access the site through this account.

The characteristics of the IUSR_*computername* can be set differently for different Web sites on the same server and for different virtual directories, directories, and files. This feature means that, even though access to the Web site does not require a user to log on, the user's access to server resources can be controlled at a more granular level. For example, the two Web sites on Server A in Figure 19.1 each use a different anonymous user account. SiteOne uses the UserOne account, and SiteTwo uses the UserTwo account. Access to all files in each directory is restricted. UserOne has no access to any files at the SiteTwo site; UserTwo has no access to any files at the SiteOne site. Even though all files are physically located on the same machine, access is restricted. In the figure, a person has connected to SiteTwo. He can access files on this site that have been given access by the anonymous user account UserTwo. If he attempts to access a file on SiteOne (the arrow with the X), he will be denied access. All files on this site only will give access to the user account UserOne. By compartmentalizing the server in this way, you limit the potential for unauthorized access.

Although access is open to the public, the user would have to move from one site to another. He cannot simply make a connection to the server and then access files anywhere on it. If the Web sites are owned by different companies or departments, each one can determine the level of access the anonymous user has on its Web site.

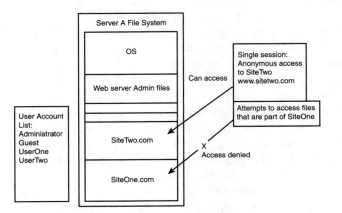

Figure 19.1 Using different anonymous user accounts to control resource access.

Authentication

The first step in controlling access to your Web site is the choice of authentication method or mode. Although every user must log on, you do have a choice of the authentication mode. Modes available are

- Anonymous
- Basic
- Windows Integrated
- Digest
- Client Certificate Mapping

Anonymous

This is the default method of authentication. The IUSR_*computername* account is used by default. This is the method used when access to your Web site is open to the public.

Basic

Basic authentication requires the user to log on, but user account and password information are transmitted in cleartext. This leaves the information vulnerable to network capture and reuse for unauthorized access to the site.

Windows Integrated

To control access by Windows 2000 account name, choose Windows Integrated. Access to sensitive material can be secured, and it will be harder for intruders to obtain user account information via network capture. However, not every browser is able to respond to the Windows authentication challenge. If it cannot, access will be denied.

Digest

Digest authentication is the industry-proposed standard answer to Windows Integrated authentication. User account and password information can be used to authenticate users, and information does not travel the network in the clear.

Client Certificate Mapping

Although SSL is often used to authenticate e-commerce servers to browsers, both SSL and Transport Layer Security (TLS) can also be used to authenticate users to the Web server.

Windows 2000 Certificate Services can be used to issue user certificates for this purpose. Certificates from compatible CAs also can be used if mapped to Windows 2000 user accounts and a Certificate Trust List is created for them. (See Chapter 17, "Enterprise Public Key Infrastructure," and Chapter 18, "Interoperability.")

Virtual Directory Security

Virtual directories also have access rights that can be set in the IIS Administrative console. They are

- Read
- Write
- Log Visits
- Directory Browsing
- Index this Resource
- Microsoft FrontPage Web (for FrontPage Web sites)

Default access is Read, Log Visits, Index this Resource, and if the site is a FrontPage Web site, FrontPage Web. The FrontPage Web setting means that the site can be locally opened (not over the network) using the FrontPage application.

If the location of a virtual directory is a share on another computer, in IIS 4.0, you could not set user authentication on the share because user information could not be passed to the other computer. IIS 5.0 enables you to pass user information through the user account if the underlying authentication mode supports it. To do so, you will have to develop a VBscript.

File Access

Each Web site should have different subdirectories (folders) to contain various content. This way, you can control the access to groups of files. By segregating files, you limit the type of permission required. Once again, you are following the principle of least privilege. Because you might need to grant Write access to some folders, you might not be able to prevent attackers from saving viruses and Trojan horse files to these folders, but you can prevent them from executing them by reducing permission on the folder to Read and Write only. Without Execute privileges, the malicious content cannot be run. Recommended file access permissions are as follows:

- **Root folder.** Protect the Web site by setting the permission on the root folder to Deny Access by the Anonymous User Account, and then override this setting for subfolders by checking the Allow Inheritable Permissions from Parent to Propagate to this Object check box on each directory to which you want to grant access. Permissions set on each directory depend on the type of data within.

- **Executable code.** Executable programs should be kept separate from script files. The executable privilege should only be granted on folders that require it because their content contains authorized executable files. Never give anonymous user accounts Write access to these folders.

- **Script files.** Script files include ASP pages, Internet Database Connector (IDC) scripts and others. Keeping script files separate from executables enables you to keep the permissions on these folders at the execute-script level. Never give the anonymous user account Write access to these folders.

- **Static files.** Static files such as .JPG, .GIF, and .HTM are meant to be Read only. Grant the anonymous user only Read permission on these folders.

The Permission Wizard can be run to set the root permissions. The wizard asks questions and sets permissions according to your answers.

You can further segregate script and executable files into folders that represent different types of executable programs. If you do this, you can set different permissions on each folder. In addition, if some new attack, bug, or fix becomes known, the process of handling the issues will be easier. Table 19.1 introduces the Microsoft recommendations (Windows 2000 Server Resource Kit from Internet Information Services 5.0 resource guide) for permissions on these types of folders.

Table 19.1 **Recommendations for Permissions on Content Folders**

File Type	Directory Browsing Allowed?	Authenticated Users	
		Allow	**Deny**
Statis files: .HTM, .GIF, .JPG, and so on	Yes	Read Anonymous access	Write Execute
ASP pages—scripts only Active Server Pages are used for server-side scripting. They can be used for dynamic Web pages and to build applications. (Certificate Services enrollment pages are ASP pages.)	No	Execute	Read
ASP page includes	No	Execute Read	
Server-side includes	No	Execute (script or execute)	Anonymous access
Common Gateway Interface (CGI) scripts only	Yes	Execute	Anonymous access Read Write
CGI executable applications (CGI bin)	Yes	Execute	Disable anonymous access
Internet Server Application Program (ISAPI) server extensions, scripts only; API for extensions to IIS	Yes	Execute	Anonymous access Read Write
ISAPI filters	No	Execute	Anonymous access
COM and DCOM	No	Execute	Read Write Anonymous access
Downloadables	No	Read	Execute (otherwise, the file will execute rather than download)

Databases should also be stored in separate directories. If the database is on a remote server, then share the directory and enable the guest account for the IIS 5.0 Web server that accesses the share. Security will depend on the database. If the database is an Access database, then it should reside on the Web server. There is no way to secure an IIS connection to Access when Access is located on a network drive.

Delegation of Security Credentials

In previous version of IIS, access to resources on servers other than the Web server was difficult. There was no capability to pass security credentials from one server to another.

IIS 5.0 and Windows 2000 allow delegation of authority. Security credentials, therefore, can be used to secure access to remote databases and to participate in n-tier (multiple-level client server programs in which parts of the code lies on multiple systems). Table 19.2 identifies which type of authentication can be used with this feature.

Table 19.2 **Delegation of Authority and IIS 5.0**

Authentication Mode	Delegation of Security Credentials
Anonymous—IIS controls anonymous account password	No
Anonymous—IIS does NOT control anonymous account password	Yes
Basic	Yes
Windows Integrated when NTLM is used	No
Windows Integrated when Kerberos is used	Yes
Digest	No
Certificate Mapping with IIS 5.0 Mapper	Yes
Certificate Mapping with Windows Mapper	No

To use delegation of authority, you must set the Trusted for Delegation option on each computer you will use. You can override this option on an account-by-account basis.

Tip

Do not allow the Administrator account to be used in a delegation of authority scenario. To do so is to open up too much of a security hole. There will be too many opportunities for abuse.

Using SSL

If you are going to use SSL on this server, you must remember to make sure the Certificate Revocation List (CRL) is available for checking, and you must remember to back up the Web server certificate.

Tools

IIS 5.0 takes advantage of the security facilities offered by Windows 2000. In addition to a specific IIS 5.0 administration snap-in, numerous Windows 2000 security features are used. You have already seen how authentication and file access control can support granular security control of Web site access. Tools fall into two categories: those provided with the Windows 2000 product and those provided afterwards to assist in securing the Web server.

Security Tools and Services Released with the Product

Every Windows 2000 tool and service (security infrastructure) that can be used to secure the operating system, or to secure communications between systems, can be used to support IIS 5.0 security. In addition, there are IIS-specific tools and configurations. Security infrastructure includes

- **IPSec.** IPSec can be used to secure communications between Windows 2000 systems. By setting IPSec policy, you can lock down communications.
- **VPN.** L2TP over IPSec and PPTP can be used to create Windows 2000 VPNs.
- **Certificate Services.** Certificate Services can be used to support user authentication via certificates (smart card support is available) and to support server authentication via SSL or TLS.
- **The IIS 5.0 Snap-in.** The snap-in enables many security-based configurations as identified in previous sections.
- **Security Configuration and Analysis.** Apply security templates based on your policy. Analyze current Web server conditions against this policy.
- **Security Templates.** Review and create templates to be used with Security Configuration and Analysis or Group Policy Objects (GPOs). (Two additional Web-specific templates are provided in the Server Resource Kit.)
- **Group Policy.** Centrally set, maintain and audit settings specific to different types of Web servers, intranets, the Internet, and extranets. Servers can be placed in OUs specific to their usage and a GPO developed for each.
- **Performance tools.** Establishing security can degrade the performance of a server. To determine the affect of various security options, use Performance Monitor before and after applying the security feature or use WCAT, a script-driven, command-line-based tool. (See the section "Security Overhead" later in this chapter.)

- **Active Directory Services Interface (ADSI).** IIS Admin Objects can be scripted suing ADSI. Here are some of the things you can do: You can access and set these com automation-base objects using VB, VBScript, JScript, Java, or C++. You can set access permissions, control the anonymous password, map client certificates, set TTL for passwords retained in the memory cache, set pass-through authentication on network shares, and establish delegation of authority for servers that are part of an n-tier application.

- **Internet Server Security Configuration Tool.** Shortly after the release of Windows 2000, Microsoft provided a downloadable tool that can be used to lock down IIS 5.0 servers. This tool is described and compared to default and resource kit–provided template settings in the following section, "Internet Server Security Configuration Tool."

Internet Server Security Configuration Tool

This tool is downloadable from `http://www.microsoft.com`. The tool can be used to lock down an IIS 5.0 server. Two executables are provided. One is used to interview the user about the nature of the Web site and to prepare a file used in configuration. The other takes the prepared, site-specific configuration file and the provided hisecweb.inf security template and configures security on the site. Although documentation is sparse, a readme file identifies the executables and their syntax and warns the user to review the hisecweb.inf file and modify it to suite his policy before running the configuration tool. No instructions are given for using the tool over multiple servers in any other way than by manually running the tool at each server. In fact, the readme file specifically indicates that the tool cannot be run remotely, although the syntax would allow you to think it might. The tool does not profess to cover every security aspect (it does not deal with multiple NIC cards), it recognizes that policy demands can be different (it tells the user to examine the hisecweb.inf file before running the tool), and it warns the user that he should not assume that the tool is a panacea or permanent solution to Web site security issues. The user also is cautioned that he should understand what the tool is doing and not just apply it blindly because it might not suite the user's requirements.

To use the tool, you should

- Identify the tool files and how to use them

- Understand how Security Configuration and Analysis and Security Templates work

- Compare the hisecweb.inf settings to other possible templates for IIS 5.0 servers

Tool Files and How They Are Used

Tool files and their use are listed in Table 19.3.

Table 19.3 **Tool Files**

File	Function
hisecweb.inf	Security template for Web servers. Is applied when you run the configuration tool.
IISConfig	The executable. Applies the results of the survey and the hisecweb.inf.

Using the Tool

To use the tool:

1. Create the unique policy file by opening default.htm in a Web browser and answering questions appropriate for your site. This creates the security file (default name IISTemplate.txt) and places it on the desktop. Table 19.4 lists the questions and identifies file entries if a "No" answer is given.

2. Review hisecweb.inf and make sure you change any settings that conflict with your organization's policy. You can review the file by creating a database in Security Configuration and Analysis and then using the Analyze feature. (Refer to Chapter 9, "Security Tools," for information on this tool.)

3. Run IISConfig to lock down the server. Test to make sure that applications and services that should work do and that settings have not opened up new holes. Table 19.4 identifies the Web server settings generated as a result of creating the policy file in step 1. Table 19.5 compares the settings in hisecweb.inf to those in secureintranetwebserver.inf and secureinternetwebserver.inf.

Table 19.4 **IIS Configuration Tool Policy File**

Question	File Entry if Answer is No	Result if Applied with IISConfig
Remotely administer this computer using Windows Networking?	Remote Admin = False	Remote Admin services are disabled.
Remotely administer this computer over the Web?	Remote WebAdmin = False	Remote Admin Services are disabled.
Use this server as a File Transfer Protocol server?	FTP = False	FTP service is disabled.

continues

Table 19.4   **Continued**

Question	File Entry if Answer is No	Result if Applied with IISConfig
Use this server as an Internet email server?	SMTP = False	SMTP service is disabled.
Use this computer as an Internet news server?	NNTP = False	NNTP service is disabled.
Use Secure Sockets Layer Transport Layer Security (SSL/TLS) on this server?	SSL = False	SSL is not used.
Use this computer as Telnet server?	Telnet = False	Telnet service is disabled.
Allow files other than static files (.TXT, .HTML .GIF, and so on) and active server pages to be served?	Other than asp = False	Extensions for other scripts are removed.
Use Internet printing?	InternetPrinting = False	Internet printing is not allowed.
Keep the Web samples?	Keepsample = False	Permissions on sample folders are removed.

Web Security Templates

The hisecweb.inf template that comes with the configuration tool will lock down many features of the server. Two other templates are included with the Windows 2000 Resource Kit. Table 19.5 lists the features affected by the templates and shows where they differ.

Table 19.5   **Comparing Web Security Templates**

Entry	hisecweb	Secure Internet Web Server	Secure Intranet Web Server
Password history	24 days	6	6
password age min	2 days	14	14
Password age max	2 days	60	60
Password length	8 char.	7	7

Entry	hisecweb	Secure Internet Web Server	Secure Intranet Web Server
Complexity requirement	Enabled	Enabled	Enabled
Lockout threshold— invalid logon attempts	5 logon attemps	8	8

AUDIT POLICY

Entry	hisecweb	Secure Internet Web Server	Secure Intranet Web Server
Audit account logon	Success/ failure	SF/	S/F
Audit account management	Success/ failure	F	F
Audit logon events	Success/ failure	S/F	S/F
Audit object access	Failure	No audit	No audit
Audit policy change	Success/ failure	S/F	S/F
Audit privilege use	Success/ failure	F	F
Audit system events	Success/ failure	S/F	S/F

USER RIGHTS

Entry	hisecweb	Secure Internet Web Server	Secure Intranet Web Server
Access this computer from the network: puff3\iwam_puff, Administrators, Backup Operators, Power Users, Users, Everyone, PUFF3\iusr_puff3 to Authenticated Users	Authenticated Users	Everyone	Everyone

SECURITY OPTIONS

Entry	hisecweb	Secure Internet Web Server	Secure Intranet Web Server
Additional restrictions for anonymous users	No access without explicit anonymous permissions	Do not allow enumeration of SAM accounts or shares	Do not allow enumeration of SAM accounts or shares

continues

Table 19.5 **Continued**

Entry	hisecweb	Secure Internet Web Server	Secure Intranet Web Server
SECURITY OPTIONS			
Audit use of backup and restore	Enabled	Not defined	Not defined
Clear virtual memory pagefile	Enabled	Enabled	Enabled
Digitally sign client communications (always)	Enabled	Not defined	Not defined
Digitally sign server communications (always)	Enabled	Not defined	Not defined
Digitally sign server communications (when possible)	Enabled	Not defined	Not defined
Do not display last username	Enabled	Not defined	Not defined
LAN Manager Authentication	Send NTLMv2 response only \refuse LM and NTLM	Send NTLM response only	Send NTLM response only
Message text for users attempting to log on	This is a private computer system <add your own text>	Not definied	Not defined
Message title for users attempting to log on	ATTENTION!	Not defined	Not defined
Restrict CD-ROM access to locally logged on user only	Enabled	Enabled	Enabled

Entry	hisecweb	Secure Internet Web Server	Secure Intranet Web Server
SECURITY OPTIONS			
Restrict floppy access to locally logged on user only	Enabled	Enabled	Enabled
Secure channel— digitally encrypt or sign secure channel data (always)	Enabled	Not defined	Not defined
Secure channel— digitally encrypt or sign secure channel data (when possible)	Not defined	Enabled	Enabled
Secure channel— require strong (windows 2000 or later) session key	Enabled	Not defined	Not defined
SETTINGS FOR EVENT LOGS			
Maximum application log size	512 kilobytes	6,144	6,144
Maximum security log size	10,240 kilobytes	6,144	6,144
Maximum system log size	5,112 kilobytes	6,144	6,144
Restrict guest access to application log: enabled	Enabled	Enabled	Enabled
Restrict guest access to security log: enabled	Enabled	Enabled	Enabled

continues

Table 19.5 **Continued**

Entry	hisecweb	Secure Internet Web Server	Secure Intranet Web Server
SETTINGS FOR EVENT LOGS			
Restrict guest access to system log: enabled	Enabled	Enabled	Enabled
Retain application log	7 days	Not defined	Not defined
Retain system log	7 days	Not defined	Not defined
Retention method for application log	By days	As needed	As needed
Retention method for security log	As needed	Manual	Manual
Retention method for system log	By days	As needed	As needed
SYSTEM SERVICES			
Alerter	Disabled	Disabled	Not defined
Clipbook	Disabled	Disabled	Not defined
Computer browser	Disabled	Not defined	Not defined
DHCP client	Disabled	Not defined	Not defined
IPSec Policy agent	Automatic	Not defined	Not defined
Messenger	Disabled	Not defined	Not defined
Net Logon—manual	Manual	Not defined	Not defined
Print Spooler	Disabled	Not defined	Not defined
Remote Access Connection Manager	Disabled	Disabled	Not defined
Remote Registry Service	Disabled	Disabled	Not defined
Simple Mail Transport Protocol (SMTP)	Disabled	Not defined	Not defined

Entry	hisecweb	Secure Internet Web Server	Secure Intranet Web Server
SYSTEM SERVICES			
Task Scheduler	Disabled	Not defined	Not defined
Windows Time	Manual	Not defined	Not defined
TCP/IP NetBIOS helper	Not defined	Disabled	Not defined

Monitoring, Measuring, and Maintaining

A heightened schedule of monitoring and auditing is necessary on any Web server. The Security Configuration and Analysis tool can be used to analyze server settings to make sure the desired configuration is still in place. Audit logs need to be examined on a daily basis. Additional monitoring tools such as intrusion detection programs and the logs and alerts of firewalls should be in place and used.

In addition, performance-monitoring tools can be used to ensure that the server can be upgraded as necessary, or additional servers can be added to ensure acceptable response times and to prevent overloads from taking the Web site down.

Security Overhead

There are two reasons for seeking the answer to the question, "How much performance overhead is incurred when establishing security?" One is to ensure that performance does not suffer by anticipating requirements and adding servers, processors, memory, or other resources that will allow the Web site to both be secure and provide fast, efficient access. The second reason is to allay fears and objections of management. A reason for not applying security is often the imagined performance hit. By measuring systems before and after applying security, you can determine the impact. By continually monitoring your Web site, you will be assured that growth in its use can be met by adding the necessary upgraded or expanded components, not by any degradation in security. A number of counters can provide useful statistics. The following are areas to watch:

- **Processor activity and processor queue.** IP address checking, SSL, and encryption all can increase processor use. Both privileged and user mode processor activity will increase. There will also be an increased number of context switches (changing from user to privileged mode and back again).

- **Physical memory used.** There will be increased storage of user information and retrieval. Physical memory is used in the encryption, and decryption process SSL keys are 40 bits to 1,024 bits. Larger keys will consume more memory.
- **Network traffic.** If Windows Integrated authentication is used, there will be increased activity between the IIS server and the domain controller.
- **Latency and delays.** Encryption and decryption can mean delays. SSL can make downloads 10 to 100 times slower.

Many of the larger increases in activities are due to encryption and decryption processes. Custom and off-the-shelf hardware can be purchased to offset the impact of encryption. Special cryptoboards manage SSL processing. Some network cards have the capability to offload IPSec encryption from the processor to the card.

WCAT is a command-line application. It makes available canned, prepared test workloads, or you can create your own. To estimate the effects of security under various workloads, you run each workload once without the added security and once with it. WCAT simulates clients and Web servers. To operate WCAT you do the following:

- Use at least one client machine, which acts as a host to many virtual clients.
- Use the Web server.
- Use a server to act as a controller, to run the tool, and to collect the statistics.
- Provide a dedicated link for the test. You want to isolate your test results from unrelated network traffic. Although no Web server runs in a vacuum, there is no way to ensure the same amount of "noise" between both cycles of the test except to eliminate all noise during both tests.
- Capture and then analyze data using the WCAT's log, IIS 5.0 logging, and Performance Monitor.

What is Suspicious Activity?

Many tools, including the native Windows 2000 Security Log, the Web Server Log, and third-party products, can provide you with information on your system. The problem, then, becomes how to take that information and determine what types of activity should be inspected closer.

The following are some indications of suspicious activity:

- Multiple failed commands (users attempting to run commands)
- Attempts to upload files to a location where no uploading should occur (especially to any executable or scripts directory)
- Attempts to access Web administration or operating system folders and subfolders
- Attempts to write to executable or script directories
- Excessive requests from a single IP address attempting to overload or cause a denial-of-service attack.

Best Practices

In addition to following best practices for securing the server, you should follow these:

- Review and appropriately modify a higher-security template and then apply it.
- Always use NTFS and use DACLs.
- Review and lock down security on the volume root.
- Review and lock down security on Web server administration folders.
- Shut down unnecessary services.
- Unbind NetBIOS from TCP/IP.
- Segregate types of files (scripts, executables, static) and set DACLs appropriately.
- Use the right authentication model for the purpose of the Web server.
- Place a firewall between the Internet and the Web server and only allow the passage of appropriate connection types (such as port 80 for HTTP) through the firewall to the Web server.
- Apply the appropriate level of security for the purpose of the Web server (for example, intranet vs. Internet vs. extranet vs. a Web server that serves both public and private data).
- Maximize the use of Windows 2000 security features such as Group Policy, Security Configuration and Analysis, IPSec, VPN, IAS, and so on in the design and implementation of your security structure.

For More Information

This chapter discusses services for which complementary information exists in other chapters of this book. The following list should serve as a referral source for you in locating this information.

Information on DACLs can be found in Chapter 6, "Security from the Get-Go."

To review how to use security tools to set and analyze policies, refer to Chapter 9, "Security Tools," and Chapter 16, "Securing the Network Using Distributed Security Services."

For help with Professional, Server, or domain-level policies, see Chapters 10, 11, and 12, respectively.

Chapter 8, "Lifecycle Choices," provides information on auditing and on installation issues that impact DACLs.

Summary

Securing Web servers is a larger topic than one mere chapter can sufficiently cover. This chapter has outlined an approach by breaking the process down into four areas:

- Securing the server
- Securing the Web site
- Using security tools
- Monitoring, measuring, and maintaining security

By discussing securing a Web server, this chapter has completed the task of serving up a smorgasbord of Windows 2000 security components. Your network might use all of these features in various areas. Many people tell me that, after an intensive study of Windows 2000 security features, they feel like they know a lot about many parts but not much about putting it all together. This is akin to knowing how to create great deserts, meats, and vegetables but not knowing how to develop a meal plan that will adequately feed the family. The next chapter pulls it all together by talking about one company's implementation of these features.

Case Study in Interbusiness Access: Distributed Partners

I N THE POST-PC, INTERNET-DRIVEN BUSINESS WORLD, it will be a rare entity that does not have, or at least desire, some business-partner connectivity. Interconnected business entities present a security challenge. How do you keep each organization's data and networks secure while allowing access by the other?

This challenge can be addressed by using the security features of Windows 2000. Remember, however, that additional devices, applications, and especially procedures might be necessary. Business-partner connectivity requires IT to create a security model that expands the protective umbrella to encompass pathways between the corporate network and the network of business partners. In addition, these pathways will not be traditional point-to-point connections established to last a long time; on the contrary, they must be flexible enough to be established on a moment's notice and be gone just as fast. Business partners require more access to each other's corporate data than the public does. Business-partner transactions transcend the mere purchasing done by consumers.

Protection for virtual associations requires attention to every aspect of security, not just the operating system, the file system, or communications on the network. Corporations that are going to share and jointly process data must not only protect their own network, they must also provide protection for each other. This kind of cooperation couples security with connectivity. All partners have to work to protect the entire communication from the outside world and from unauthorized use within their own organizations. In addition, they will need to respect each other's right to privacy.

How could such a cooperative security effort occur? What would it look like? What features of Windows 2000 would be implemented and where? Many companies have formed these sorts of relationships. In the future, many more of us will.

This chapter takes a different approach to Windows 2000 security by designing a secure business-to-business (B2B) operation using the features available with Windows 2000. It will generically reference other products in the mix (such as firewalls, routers, and so on). It will do so by developing the security design for TrainUnion, a fictional B2B cooperative that presents technical training and trainer services via Web and direct-connect interfaces.

This chapter begins with a brief outline of the TrainUnion business model and then describes the security architecture. It will then look at the following:

- The Active Directory architecture backbone
- Authentication and authorization
- Public and private interface processes

Business Model

TrainUnion (www.trainunion.com), our fictional company, is a Web-centric B2B cooperative that offers training-related services to members and nonmembers via the Internet and private dial-up. To understand the company's multilayered business operation and the services it offers, you need a brief introduction to the rationale behind its program.

Rationale

Technical training is considered by some to be a necessary evil; to others, it's a critical part of operations. The industry itself is large and growing, but it is fragmented and varies tremendously in quality. You will hear both good and bad things about the status of technical training from training providers, trainers, and people being trained. Common complaints and needs include the following:

- Training providers have difficulties finding excellent curricula.
- Training providers have difficulty finding and retaining good trainers.
- Training providers have difficulty evaluating contract trainers before contracting with them to teach a class.
- Staff trainers (trainers employed by one company) have difficulty finding training providers that are not sweatshops.

- Independent contract trainers have difficulties getting paid within a reasonable time.
- Independent trainers have difficulties finding common business benefits (insurance, retirement plans) they can afford.
- Purchasers of training services have difficulties evaluating training providers, curricula, and trainers.

Services

In answer to the preceding issues, TrainUnion was formed. It serves as a distributor of training-related services and as a portal to training offered by others.

TrainUnion presents two Web interfaces: one public and one for business partners. The public Web site includes

- Information on its available partner services
- Public catalogs of courses that describe the curriculum, public-training centers, trainers, and scheduling
- The capability to purchase training services either on an individual basis or for a group (for a single class, a training program, or annual training needs)
- The capability to link to and complete transactions directly with the training provider or with TrainUnion

Services available to members (business or trading partners) include the following:

- **Purchase.** Catalogs from more than 500 producers of technical-training curricula are available to the provider online. Customized catalogs can be prepared that enable training providers to make purchases at special rates or to view special components. The catalogs satisfy the curriculum provider that all requirements for purchase (such as a vendor-certified training center) are established.
- **Hire.** Independent trainers can advertise their abilities and post their schedules. Training providers can contract directly with them.
- **Review.** Tables of contents, a sample unit with exercises and questions, and other materials presented by the vendor are available for review online. Entire training courses are made available online if the training partner requests them and the vendor chooses to make them available. This eliminates the need for the vendor to ship review copies and spares the training provider/instructor from having to wait to review the curriculum. When this was first offered, few vendors wanted to expose their materials, but competition has forced the issue, and now 75 percent of vendors offer this capability. Qualified instructors can download and print review copies to use in preparation for certification and teaching.
- **Rate.** If training providers purchase a curriculum and present a class, they can rate the curriculum. If they contract with a trainer, they can rate the trainer. A

trainer can also rate the curriculum and the center. This rating takes the form of a review and is posted to the site, where other training providers and instructors can study it. The ratings can have sections for other training providers as well as for potential students. Instructors and students can also comment on the curriculum. Students and training providers have the opportunity to rate the instructor. Ratings take the form of various evaluation checklists that are then compiled; in addition, the evaluations include comment areas. All content is reviewed before being posted to the Web site.

- **Register.** A class can be registered with TrainUnion, or a link can be provided to the training provider's registration site.

- **Find.** Search capabilities exist to enable trainers, training providers, and customers to find and purchase the services or materials for which they are looking.

- **Trainer services.** Trainers joining the union can obtain insurance (health, dental, business, life) at reduced rates. Business services also are available.

- **Discuss.** Private discussion groups facilitate discussion of training materials. Partners can specify which groups their employees can access.

The users of its services, both customers and vendors, are

- Nonmembers: the public (limited services)
- Public training centers
- Corporate training departments
- Colleges
- Curriculum developers
- Staff trainers (some benefits under employer's membership)
- Independent trainers (can be full partners)

These six types of users operate differently and require distinct sets of services. However, they also use many of the same services.

Network Infrastructure Security

All TrainUnion services are available via the Internet. Training partners and select TrainUnion employees can also use direct-dial facilities. Secured servers handle any purchases (by training partners and customers) and provide private communications between TrainUnion and its business partners. Public Web server transactions are secured via Secure Sockets Layer (SSL), and partner transactions and communications are secured via virtual private network (VPN). Sensitive internal communications, or communications between security infrastructure boundaries, use IP Security (IPSec).

The following TrainUnion security infrastructure description details only the structures on the private network. The business partners' networks might be composed of multiple different operating systems and appropriate defenses. TrainUnion's infrastructure can be described in two ways: logical overview and physical network.

Logical Overview

Figure 20.1 provides a logical overview of the system. The network is organized in three layers as follows:

- An external network, or Demilitarized Zone (DMZ), includes any server that might have requirements for connectivity with the outside world. Servers here are mail servers, Routing and Remote Access Servers (RRASs), Web servers, and the like.

- A middle layer represents TrainUnion's portion of the virtual extranet it has formed with its partners. The middle layer is encapsulated and protected. It has no direct link to the outside world. Every link to a business partner is through the DMZ. Internet connections and dial-up connections do not directly enter the extranet network; instead, they connect to servers within the DMZ.

- A center layer includes all business functions that do not need to have contact from the public or any trading partners. This layer includes financial databases, human resources, executive management, and so on.

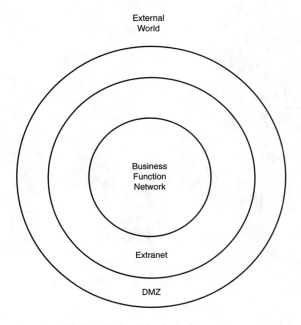

Figure 20.1   The logical overview.

Physical Network

The extranet itself consists entirely of Windows 2000 Server and Professional systems. The business-function network still contains a number of down-level clients and servers as well as a legacy accounting system that resides in a DB2 database on an IBM RS6000.

Figure 20.2 displays the physical network including the location of firewalls and specialized function servers.

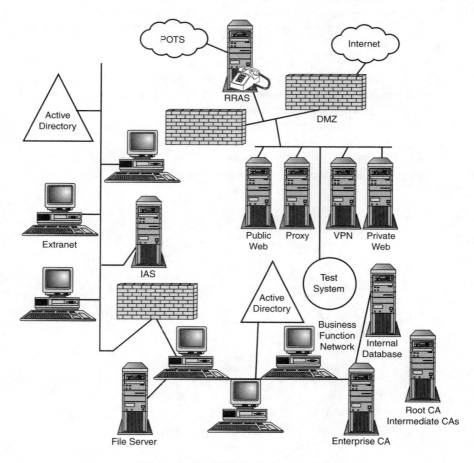

Figure 20.2   The physical network.

Several general restrictions are used to secure the network, and four connection points require special security attention. General restrictions are as follows:

- No employee has access to the Internet except through a proxy server. Level and time of access are restricted dependent on job function. This is accomplished through settings on the proxy server.

- No modems are allowed on any desktop system for access into or out of the network. Some employees are given remote access rights, but that is controlled through RRASs in the DMZ.

- Traffic between the Internet and the DMZ, between the DMZ and the extranet, and between the extranet and the business-function network must pass through a firewall.

Connection points and related security concerns are

- Internet connection to the DMZ
- Dial-up connection to the DMZ
- Connections between the DMZ and the extranet
- Connections between the extranet and the business-function network

Internet Connectivity to the DMZ

Two types of Internet connection to the DMZ exist: pubic and private. The public connection passes through the firewall to the public site. (Each site is represented in Figure 20.2 by a single server but in actuality consists of a server farm.) The public can only browse public areas.

The public can find out a great deal of information about courses including detailed outlines and descriptions of lab exercises. The public also can find a list of training providers that offer the classes. They can view the entire schedule of all training providers that provide this information; alternatively, they can link directly to the training provider site. The public can read course reviews that include ratings on curriculum lab exercises, trainers, and training providers. Information is also presented on various certifications. If a person decides to attend a class, buy a book, or buy other materials, he is transferred to a secure server, and all transactions are via SSL. Customers can subscribe to the service and receive discounts and client authentication (via SSL). Personalized information is kept on customers (with their consent) and is used to provide them with new information when they visit the site and/or via newsletters. If customers purchase a subscription, they receive a certificate that is then mapped to an AD account.

Private extranet connections (those between trainers and the site or between training providers and the site) are via VPN. All tunnel servers use Remote Authentication Dial-in User Service (RADIUS) authentication, authorization, and accounting services. Internet Access Service (IAS) servers provide centralization of Remote Access Policies. VPN tunnels can be either IPSec over Layer 2 Tunneling Protocol (L2TP) or Point-to-Point Tunneling Protocol (PPTP) to accommodate customer requirements.

A system using smart cards for additional authentication security is in test mode with selected customers. Smart-card access is being considered for all transactions and for external authentication (traveling employees, telecommuting employees, and so on). Also being tested are new servers from Microsoft: a commerce server for personalization, payment, and management of catalogs; a Biztalk server for connectivity with customers' ERP systems including business document translation; and an Internet Acceleration and Security Server for caching and firewall services. IAS also provides intrusion detection services licensed from Internet Security Systems.

Figure 20.3 shows an enlargement of the test systems represented by the circle in Figure 20.2. Test systems are within the DMZ but have their own dedicated connection to the external world.

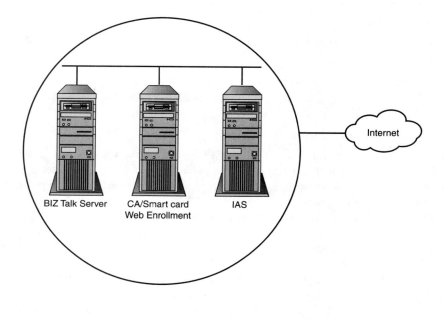

Figure 20.3 The test systems.

Dial-Up Connections with the DMZ

Dial-up connection is provided. A customer can direct-dial to a private (for his use only) or semipublic (available to a group of business partners but not to the public) line. Dial-up connectivity is provided via RRAS servers. All the RRAS servers use RADIUS for authentication. For added security, a firewall is placed between the RRAS servers and the IAS server. After dial-up connectivity is established, a connection is made with a tunnel server for secured communications.

Connections Between the DMZ and the Extranet

A second firewall separates the DMZ from the internal extranet. The only data that passes through this firewall is data redirected by approval of IAS. IAS handles the authentication of access requests. Approved requests from the Internet are referred to tunnel servers (which are located on RRAS servers), and connection is made via tunnel endpoint to the internal extranet.

Connections Between the Extranet and the Business-Function Network

Connections between the business-function networks are always encrypted with IPSec. The exception is Web browsing, which is managed by the proxy server that sits on the extranet. The extranet proxy chains to a proxy on the DMZ.

Active Directory Architecture Backbone

TrainUnion implemented a two-domain, single-tree forest. The top-level domain, bs.TrainUnion.com, is the internal business-function domain. A two-domain approach was chosen for security reasons. Segregating the business functions in a separate domain provides more control over authentication and access. A different account policy can be provided. Extranet functionality is only present in the extranet domain. This also allows a flatter organizational unit (OU) structure in each domain because there is no temptation to provide hierarchical Group Policy Objects (GPOs).

Figure 20.4 displays the Active Directory hierarchy including the OU structure. In the bs.TrainUnion.com domain, three OUs exist: the financial OU, the human resources OU, and the ground0 OU. The ground0 OU represents all basic business functions that are not financial or human resources. Nested within the financial OU are two OUs; one represents people and the other computers. Placing financial computers in a separate OU provides greater control over each. Delegation of authority can be granted appropriately over separate OUs. The financial department, for example, can appoint someone to administer common user functions such as password reset and account creation, while technical administrators can manage databases, networking, and operating system details. Separating human resources, business applications, network employees, and computers into separate OUs allows similar separation of responsibilities and security. Additional control can be applied at this granular level.

The extra.TrainUnion.com domain contains all accounts and resources used to provide services and function to the extranet. All employees who service this function have accounts in this domain. Separate OUs contain RRAS servers (tunnel servers and IAS), certificate servers, databases, Web servers, employees, and customers. The customer OU includes a single nested layer that segregates users into public, training providers, and trainers. In this, the different needs, controls, and security can be applied to user and computer accounts. Further details of the approach are included in Table 20.1.

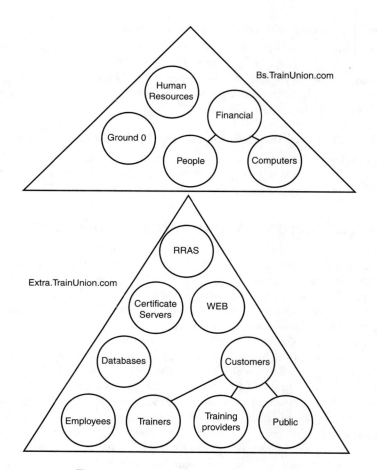

Figure 20.4 The Active Directory hierarchy.

Table 20.1 **Extranet OU Model**

OU	Includes	Provides
RRAS	All RRAS, tunnel servers, and IAS servers	IAS policy controls remote access for RRAS servers (dial-up or VPN). OU GPO locks down the Security Policy, including providing mandatory IPSec communication between RRAS and IAS and between IAS and DCs, restricted groups (Administrators, Power Users), file systems, and registry DACLs.

OU	Includes	Provides
Certificate servers	All CAs in the extranet	Mandatory IPSec communications between all CAs in the TrainUnion hierarchy.
Public Web servers	Public Web server	Secure access to public Web servers is via SSL. Unlike the business-partner access, the server certificate for public Web server SSL is provided by an external, trusted CA. This external service allows transactions and access with the public without investing in providing the public with special TrainUnion CA certificates. Public trust in external CAs is already commonly accepted for Web transactions.
Databases	All catalog content, financial transactions, shipping, and so on	Databases are positioned inside the extranet behind the second firewall. Databases have additional common file system controls.
Employees	All employees that are not part of the business function group	Some administrative control (such as password reset) over employee accounts is delegated.
Partners	Member organizations	No extra privileges. Some administrative control is delegated (managed by different personnel than the employees' OU).

Authentication and Authorization

All authentication is managed by certificates. All users must have at least a user certificate granted by the TrainUnion Certificate Authority (CA) hierarchy; alternatively, their certificate can be imported from trusted trading partner CAs and be mapped to TrainUnion user accounts. All authorization flows from membership in TrainUnion groups and is additionally restricted by controlling for what a certificate can be used. Details for authentication and authorization are in later sections of this chapter.

Public Key Infrastructure (PKI)

As previously mentioned, the TrainUnion PKI consists of two CA hierarchies:

- **Public CA.** Public transactions and other secured access are via SSL implemented via a certificate provided by an external public CA. Public trust in public CAs is well established for financial transactions via the Internet. In addition, no extra processing such as providing certificates to the user needs to be accomplished because a certificate for the public CA already is present in their browser's certificate store.

- **TrainUnion CA hierarchy.** TrainUnion's private CA hierarchy consists of a root CA and is three levels deep. Figure 20.5 diagrams the hierarchy. At the top is a standalone root CA that is kept offline and locked in a vault. Standalone subordinate CAs exist, one for use of the business-function network and one for the extranet. Each of these servers is granted a certificate from the root CA. These middle CAs are also kept offline. Their only purpose is to provide server certificates for the enterprise subordinate CAs. On the business-function network, the enterprise CA provides machine and user certificates for the business-function computers and users. In the extranet network, three enterprise subordinate CAs exist. Division is by function. One exists for the test-system smart-card operation, and one is for the more traditional user and password logon certificate. A third is used for machine certificates.

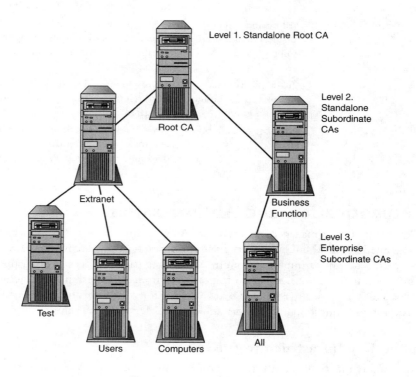

Figure 20.5 CA hierarchy.

Machine certificates are granted automatically to Windows 2000 systems on the extranet and business-function networks. Human resources manages the granting and revoking of generic user certificates as people join and leave the company. Renewal is once a year. Special-purpose certificates, such as administrative, smart card, or enroll-ment certificates, are controlled by IT. No public Web enrollment is allowed. Web enrollment for partners who do not have their own CA is accomplished through a secured server. Partners who have their own CA can have their user certificates imported and mapped to TrainUnion user accounts in the AD.

Business-Function Network Authentication

In the internal network, down-level clients and cross-platform issues exist. Group Policy at the domain level is used to require NTLMv2 or Kerberos for network authentication with Windows 2000 and NT 4.0 servers. AD clients are loaded on all Windows 9x systems. Services for UNIX 2.0 provides connectivity and password mapping between the domain and the RS6000.

Authorization

All access to network resources is controlled through explicit membership in user groups. The Everyone group has no rights on any resource. All Windows 2000 systems are clean-installed and are configured by application of special security templates before they are joined in the appropriate domain. Separate templates exist for each computer function from secure Web server to desktop system. Maintenance of settings is controlled through GPOs placed at the domain and OU levels as appropriate. Full use of file system and registry DACL recording in the templates and the GPO is used. In the business-function network, System Policies are used for down-level clients.

Public and Private Interface Processes

TrainUnion's infrastructure-security design was developed with business-partner secu-rity requirements in mind. While providing connectivity to multiple partners, TrainUnion is able to isolate business transactions from the Internet and, if required, isolate them from other business by providing VPN tunnels to private phone numbers instead of the Internet. At every step, there is consideration of the private part of this connectivity; separate catalog pricing and availability of materials can be provided. The provider can supervise control over access. The architecture is scalable both up (larger systems, more transactions, more partners) and out (private VPN phone numbers, Web sites, catalogs) to support a range of security and privacy concerns.

Summary

The TrainUnion B2B operation design offers many opportunities to explore the appropriate use of Windows 2000 security features. Although every implementation of Windows 2000 will be different, these concepts remain the same:

- Evaluate the business IT needs.
- Evaluate the risks.
- Break down the various areas of operation by the level of security necessary.
- Write or modify Security Policy to reflect the best possible combination of aggressive defense.
- Determine the necessary controls to provide the required level of security for each business function.
- Evaluate the hardware and software necessary to fulfill those controls.
- Determine how best to implement the design using the chosen hardware and software.
- Implement the design.
- Maintain it.
- Be vigilant for unforeseen security issues and modify the design and implementation as necessary.

Resources

THE FOLLOWING RESOURCES SIT ON MY BOOKSHELF or are frequented by me online. I hope they will be as valuable to you as they have been to me.

Books

Abell, Roger, et al. *Windows 2000 DNS*. Indianapolis: New Riders Publishing, 2000.

Adams, Carlisle and Steve Lloyd. *Understanding Public-Key Infrastructure*. Indianapolis: New Riders Publishing, 1999.

Boswell, William. *Inside Windows 2000 Server*. Indianapolis: New Riders Publishing, 2000.

Electronic Frontier Foundation. *Cracking DES: Secrets of Encryption Research, Wiretap Politics & Chip Design*. Sebastopol: O'Reilly, 1998.

Graff, Jon. *Crypto' 101: An Introduction to Modern Cryptography for Poets and Managers and Other Curious but Mathematically Averse People*. KPMG Peat Marwick LLP, 1998.

Krause, Micki and Harold F. Tipton, eds. *Information Security Management Handbook*. Auerbach Publications, 1999.

Lee, Thomas and Joseph Davies. *Microsoft Windows 2000 TCP/IP Protocols and Services Technical Reference.* Redmond: Microsoft Press, 2000.

Martin, Michael. *Understanding the Network: A Practical Guide to Internetworking.* Indianapolis: New Riders Publishing, 2000.

Microsoft Consulting Services. *Building Enterprise Active Directory Services: Notes from the Field.* Redmond: Microsoft Press, 2000.

Microsoft Windows 2000 Professional Resource Kit. Redmond: Microsoft Press, 2000.

Microsoft Windows 2000 Server Resource Kit. Redmond: Microsoft Press, 2000. This resource kit includes

- Windows 2000 Server Distributed Systems Guide
- Windows 2000 Server Internetworking Guide
- Windows 2000 Server Operations Guide
- Windows 2000 Server TCP/IP Core Networking Guide
- Internet Explorer 5 Resource Kit
- Internet Information Server Resource Guide
- Windows 2000 Server Deployment Planning Guide

This book is also a virtual reference. An updated copy of the book can be found at

    http://www.microsoft.com/windows2000/library/resources/reskit/default.asp

The entire book or just updated chapters can be downloaded.

Northcutt, Stephen. *Network Intrusion Detection: An Analyst's Handbook.* Indianapolis: New Riders Publishing, 1999.

Schneier, Bruce. *Applied Cryptography: Protocols, Algorithms, and Source Code in C.* New York: John Wiley & Sons, 1995.

Microsoft Site Information

Technet resources, including links to white papers, training offers, peer group discussions, support groups, and forums, can be found at

    http://www.microsoft.com/technet/

Training and certification information can be found at

    http://www.microsoft.com/trainingandservices/

Windows 2000 white papers and resource kit downloads can be found at

    http://www.microsoft.com/windows2000/library/resources/reskit

Other Web Sites

The Veritest test site (Windows 2000 application compatibility) can be found at

http://www.veritest.com/mslogos/nt98

A hardware compatibility test site can be found at

http://www.microsoft.com/hwdev/winlogo

Developer knowledge can be found at

http://msdn.Microsoft.com/library/default.asp

A large number of links to resources on sites across the Internet can be found at

http://windows.microsoft.com/windows2000/reskit/webresources

A Search page for RFCs by number, keywords, author, or title can be found at

http://www.rfc-editor.org/rfcsearch.html

Information on Public Key Infrastructure can be found at

http://www.pkiforum.org

White Papers

A technical overview of UNIX and Windows NT integration can be found at

http://www.microsoft.com/WINDOWS2000/guide/professional/solutions/unix.asp

A step-by-step guide to Kerberos 5 interoperability can be found at

http://www.microsoft.com/windows2000/library/planning/security/kerbsteps.asp

Information on server for NIS overview can be found at

http://www.microsoft.com/windows2000/sfu/nis.asp

A General Services for UNIX version 2.0 white paper can be found at

http://www.microsoft.com/windows2000/sfu/sfu2wp.asp

More info on UNIX and Windows 2000 is available at

http://www.microsoft.com/windows2000/guide/server/solutions/sfu.asp

Information on interoperability capabilities can be found at

http://www.microsoft.com/windows2000/guide/server/features/interop.asp

The Security Support Provider Interface can be found at

http://www.microsoft.com/windows2000/library/howitworks/security/sspi2000.asp

Index

C

X–Z

Windows 2000 Answers

Building from the author-driven, no-nonsense approach of our *Landmark* books, New Riders proudly offers something unique for Windows 2000 administrators—an in-depth and discriminating book on Windows 2000 Server, written by someone in the trenches who can anticipate your situation and provide reliable answers.

INSIDE
Windows 2000
Server

ISBN: 1-56205-929-7

Architected to be the most navigable and useful reference available for Windows 2000, this book uses a creative "telescoping" design that you can adapt to your style of learning. It's a concise, focused, and quick reference for Windows 2000, providing the kind of practical advice, tips, procedures, and additional resources that every administrator will need.

ISBN: 0-7357-0869-X

Windows 2000 Active Directory is just one of several Windows 2000 titles from New Riders' acclaimed *Landmark* series. Ideal for network architects and administrators, this book describes the intricacies of Active Directory while keeping real-world systems and constraints in mind. It's a detailed, solution-oriented book that addresses the need for a single guide to planning, deploying, and managing Active Directory in an enterprise setting.

Windows 2000
Active Directory

Edgar Brovick
Doug Hauger
William C. Wade III

ISBN: 0-7357-0870-3

Advanced Information on Networking Technologies

New Riders Books Offer Advice and Experience

LANDMARK

Rethinking Computer Books

We know how important it is to have access to detailed, solution-oriented information on core technologies. *Landmark* books contain the essential information you need to solve technical problems. Written by experts and subjected to rigorous peer and technical reviews, *Landmark* books are hard-core resources that get to the heart of what you need to know.

ESSENTIAL REFERENCE

Smart, Like You

The *Essential Reference* series from New Riders provides answers when you know what you want to do but need to learn how to do it. Each title skips extraneous material and assumes a strong base of knowledge. These are indispensable books for the practitioner who wants to find specific features of a technology quickly and efficiently. Avoiding fluff and basic material, these books present solutions in an innovative, clean format.

MCSE CERTIFICATION

Engineered for Test Success

New Riders offers a complete line of test preparation materials to help you achieve your certification. With books like the *MCSE Training Guide*, and software like the acclaimed *MCSE Complete* and the revolutionary *ExamGear*, New Riders offers comprehensive products built by experienced professionals who have passed the exams and instructed hundreds of candidates.

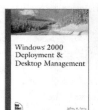

Planning for Windows 2000

By Eric K. Cone, Jon Boggs, and Sergio Perez
1st Edition
400 pages, $29.99
ISBN: 0-7357-0048-6

Planning for Windows 2000 lets you know what the upgrade hurdles will be, informs you how to clear them, guides you through effective Active Directory design, and presents you with detailed rollout procedures. Eric K. Cone, Jon Boggs, and Sergio Perez give you the benefit of their extensive experiences as Windows 2000 Rapid Deployment Program members by sharing problems and solutions they've encountered on the job.

Inside Windows 2000 Server

By William Boswell
1st Edition
1550 pages, $49.99
ISBN: 1-56205-929-7

Building on the author-driven, no-nonsense approach of our Landmark books, New Riders proudly offers something unique for Windows 2000 administrators—an in-depth, discriminating book on Windows 2000 Server written by someone who can anticipate your situation and give you workarounds that won't leave a system unstable or sluggish.

Windows 2000 Server Professional Reference

By Karanjit S. Siyan, Ph.D.
3rd Edition
1800 pages, $75.00
ISBN: 0-7357-0952-1

Windows 2000 Server Professional Reference is the benchmark of references available for Windows 2000. Although other titles take you through the setup and implementation phase of the product, no other book provides the user with detailed answers to day-to-day administration problems and tasks. Real-world implementations are key to help administrators discover the most viable solutions for their particular environments. Solid content shows administrators how to manage, troubleshoot, and fix problems that are specific to heterogeneous Windows networks, as well as Internet features and functionality.

Windows 2000 User Management

By Lori Sanders
1st Edition
300 pages, $34.99
ISBN: 1-56205-886-X

With the dawn of Windows 2000, it has become even more difficult to draw a clear line between managing the user and managing the user's environment and desktop. This book, written by a noted trainer and consultant, provides a comprehensive, practical guide to managing users and their desktop environments with Windows 2000.

Windows 2000 Active Directory Design & Deployment

By Gary Olsen
1st Edition
450 pages, $45.00
ISBN: 1-57870-242-9
September 2000

This book focuses on the design of a Windows 2000 Active Directory environment, and how to develop an effective design and migration plan. The reader is led through the process of developing a design plan by reviewing each pertinent issue, and then provided expert advice on how to evaluate each issue as it applies to the reader's particular environment. Practical examples illustrate all these issues.

Windows 2000 Quality of Service

By David Iseminger
1st Edition
300 pages, $45.00
ISBN: 1-57870-115-5

As the traffic on networks continues to increase, the strain on network infrastructure and available resources has also grown. *Windows 2000 Quality of Service* teaches network engineers and administrators to how to define traffic control patterns and utilize bandwidth in their networks.

Windows 2000 Server: Planning and Migration

By Sean Deuby
1st Edition
450 pages, $40.00
ISBN: 1-57870-023-X

Windows 2000 Server: Planning and Migration can quickly save the NT professional thousands of dollars and hundreds of hours. This title includes authoritative information on key features of Windows 2000 and offers recommendations on how to best position your NT network for Windows 2000.

Windows 2000 and Mainframe Integration
By William Zack
1st Edition
400 pages, $40.00
ISBN: 1-57870-200-3

Windows 2000 and Mainframe Integration provides mainframe computing professionals with the practical know-how to build and integrate Windows 2000 technologies into their current environment.

Windows NT/2000 Thin Client Solutions
By Todd Mathers
2nd Edition
750 pages, $45.00
ISBN: 1-57870-239-9

A practical and comprehensive reference to MetaFrame 1.8 and Terminal Services, this book should be the first source for answers to the tough questions on the Terminal Server VCx2/ MetaFrame platform. Building on the quality of the previous edition, additional coverage of installation of Terminal Services and MetaFrame on a Windows 2000 Server is included, as well as chapters on Terminal Server management, remote access, and application integration.

Windows NT/2000 Native API Reference
By Gary Nebbett
1st Edition
500 pages, $50.00
ISBN: 1-57870-199-6

This book is the first complete reference to the API functions native to Windows NT and covers the set of services that are offered by the Windows NT to both kernel- and user-mode programs. Coverage consists of documentation of the 210 routines included in the NT Native API, and the functions that have been be added in Windows 2000. Routines that are either not directly accessible via the Win32 API or offer substantial additional functionality are described in especially great detail. Services offered by the NT kernel, mainly the support for debugging user mode applications, are also included.

Windows NT/2000 ADSI Scripting for System Administration
By Thomas Eck
1st Edition
700 pages, $45.00
ISBN: 1-57870-219-4

Active Directory Scripting Interfaces (ADSI) allow administrators to automate administrative tasks across their Windows networks. This title fills a gap in the current ADSI documentation by including coverage of its interaction with LDAP and provides administrators with proven code samples that they can adopt to effectively configure and manage user accounts and other usually time-consuming tasks.

Windows 2000 Virtual Private Networking

By Thaddeus Fortenberry
1st Edition
400 pages, $45.00
ISBN 1-57870-246-1
January 2001

Because of the ongoing push for a distributed workforce, administrators must support laptop users, home LAN environments, complex branch offices, and more—all within a secure and effective network design. The way an administrator implements VPNs in Windows 2000 is different than that of any other operating system. In addition to discussions about Windows 2000 tunneling, new VPN features that can affect Active Directory replication and network address translation are also covered.

Windows NT Terminal Server and Citrix MetaFrame

By Ted Harwood
1st Edition
400 pages, $29.99
ISBN: 1-56205-944-0

It's no surprise that most administration headaches revolve around integration with other networks and clients. This book addresses these types of real-world issues on a case-by-case basis, giving tools and advice for solving each problem. The author also offers the real nuts and bolts of thin client administration on multiple systems, covering relevant issues such as installation, configuration, network connection, management, and application distribution.

Windows NT Power Toolkit

By Stu Sjouwerman
and Ed Tittel
1st Edition
800 pages, $49.99
ISBN: 0-7357-0922-X

This book covers the analysis, tuning, optimization, automation, enhancement, maintenance, and troubleshooting of Windows NT Server 4.0 and Windows NT Workstation 4.0. In most cases, the two operating systems overlap completely. Where the two systems diverge, each platform is covered separately. This advanced title comprises a task-oriented treatment of the Windows NT 4 environment. By concentrating on the use of operating system tools and utilities, Resource Kit elements, and selected third-party tuning, analysis, optimization, and productivity tools, this book will show its readers how to carry out everyday and advanced tasks.

Windows NT Performance: Monitoring, Benchmarking, and Tuning

By Mark T. Edmead
and Paul Hinsberg
1st Edition
288 pages, $29.99
ISBN: 1-56205-942-4

Performance monitoring is a little like preventive medicine for the administrator: No one enjoys a checkup, but it's a good thing to do on a regular basis. This book helps you focus on the critical aspects of improving the performance of your NT system by showing you how to monitor the system, implement benchmarking, and tune your network. The book is organized by resource components, which makes it easy to use as a reference tool.

Windows NT Device Driver Development

By Peter Viscarola and
W. Anthony Mason
1st Edition
700 pages, $50.00
ISBN: 1-57870-058-2

This title begins with an introduction to the general Windows NT operating system concepts relevant to drivers, then progresses to more detailed information about the operating system, such as interrupt management, synchronization issues, the I/O Subsystem, standard kernel mode drivers, and more.

Windows NT Shell Scripting

By Tim Hill
1st Edition
350 pages, $32.00
ISBN: 1-57870-047-7

A complete reference for Windows NT scripting, this book guides you through a high-level introduction to the shell language itself and the shell commands that are useful for controlling or managing different components of a network.

Windows Script Host

By Tim Hill
1st Edition
400 pages, $35.00
ISBN: 1-57870-139-2

Windows Script Host is one of the first books published about this powerful tool. The text focuses on system scripting and the VBScript language, using objects, server scriptlets, and provides ready-to-use script solutions.

Internet Information Services Administration

By Kelli Adam
1st Edition
200 pages, $29.99
ISBN: 0-7357-0022-2

Are the new Internet technologies in Internet Information Services giving you headaches? Does providing security on the Web take up all of your time? Then this is the book for you. With hands-on configuration training, advanced study of the new protocols, coverage of the most recent version of IIS, and detailed instructions on authenticating users with the new Certificate Server and implementing and managing the new e-commerce features, *Internet Information Services Administration* gives you the real-life solutions you need. This definitive resource gives you detailed advice on working with Microsoft Management Console, which was first used by IIS.

Windows NT Win32 Perl Programming: The Standard Extensions

By Dave Roth
1st Edition
600 pages, $40.00
ISBN: 1-57870-067-1

See numerous proven examples and practical uses of Perl in solving everyday Win32 problems. This is the only book available with comprehensive coverage of Win32 extensions, where most of the Perl functionality resides in Windows settings.

SMS 2 Administration

By Michael Lubanski
and Darshan Doshi
1st Edition
350 pages, $39.99
ISBN: 0-7357-0082-6

Microsoft's new version of its Systems
Management Server (SMS) is starting to
turn heads. Although complex, it allows
administrators to lower their total cost of
ownership and more efficiently manage
clients, applications, and support operations. So if your organization is using or
implementing SMS, you'll need some
expert advice. Michael Lubanski and
Darshan Doshi can help you get the most
bang for your buck with insight, expert
tips, and real-world examples. Michael
and Darshan are consultants specializing
in SMS and have worked with Microsoft
on one of the most complex SMS roll-
outs in the world, involving 32 countries,
15 languages, and thousands of clients.

SQL Server 7 Essential Reference

By Sharon Dooley
1st Edition
400 pages, $35.00 US
ISBN: 0-7357-0864-9

SQL Server 7 Essential Reference is a comprehensive reference of advanced how-tos
and techniques for developing with SQL
Server. In particular, the book addresses
advanced development techniques used in
large application efforts with multiple
users, such as developing Web applications
for intranets, extranets, or the Internet.
Each section includes detail on how each
component is developed and then integrated into a real-life application.

SQL Server System Administration

By Sean Baird,
Chris Miller, et al.
1st Edition
352 pages, $29.99
ISBN: 1-56205-955-6

How often does your SQL Server go
down during the day when everyone
wants to access the data? Do you spend
most of your time being a "report
monkey" for your coworkers and bosses?
SQL Server System Administration helps
you keep data consistently available to
your users. This book omits introductory
information. The authors don't spend
time explaining queries and how they
work. Instead, they focus on the information you can't get anywhere else, like
how to choose the correct replication
topology and achieve high availability of
information.

Networking Titles

Network Intrusion Detection: An Analyst's Handbook

By Stephen Northcutt
and Judy Novak
2nd Edition
480 pages, $45.00
ISBN: 0-7357-1008-2

Get answers and solutions from someone
who has been in the trenches. Stephen
Northcutt, original developer of the
Shadow intrusion detection system and
former director of the United States
Navy's Information System Security
Office at the Naval Security Warfare
Center, gives his expertise to intrusion
detection specialists, security analysts,
and consultants responsible for setting
up and maintaining an effective defense
against network security attacks.

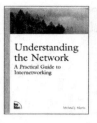

Understanding the Network: A Practical Guide to Internetworking
By Michael Martin
1st Edition
650 pages, $39.99
ISBN: 0-7357-0977-7

Understanding the Network addresses the audience in practical terminology, and describes the most essential information and tools required to build high-availability networks in a step-by-step implementation format. Each chapter could be read as a stand-alone, but the book builds progressively toward a summary of the essential concepts needed to put together a wide-area network.

Understanding Data Communications
By Gilbert Held
6th Edition
600 pages, $39.99
ISBN: 0-7357-0036-2

Updated from the highly successful fifth edition, this book explains how data communications systems and their various hardware and software components work. More than an entry-level book, it approaches the material in textbook format, addressing the complex issues involved in internetworking today. A great reference book for the experienced networking professional that is written by the noted networking authority, Gilbert Held.

Cisco Router Configuration & Troubleshooting
By Mark Tripod
2nd Edition
400 pages, $34.99
ISBN: 0-7357-0999-8

Want the real story on making your Cisco routers run like a dream? Pick up a copy of *Cisco Router Configuration & Troubleshooting* and see what Mark Tripod of Exodus Communications has to say. Exodus is responsible for making some of the largest sites on the Net scream, like Amazon.com, Hotmail, USAToday, Geocities, and Sony. In this book, the author provides advanced configuration issues, sprinkled with advice and preferred practices. By providing real-world insight and examples instead of rehashing Cisco's documentation, Mark gives network administrators information they can start using today.

Understanding Directory Services
By Beth Sheresh and Doug Sheresh
1st Edition
400 pages, $39.99
ISBN: 0-7357-0910-6

Understanding Directory Services provides the reader with a thorough knowledge of the fundamentals of directory services: what DSs are, how they are designed, and what functionality they can provide to an IT infrastructure. This book provides a framework to the exploding market of directory services by placing the technology in context and helping people understand what directories can, and can't, do for their networks.

Local Area High Speed Networks

By Dr. Sidnie Feit

1st Edition

650 pages, $50.00

ISBN: 1-57870-113-9

A great deal of change is happening in the technology being used for local area networks. As Web intranets have driven bandwidth needs through the ceiling, inexpensive Ethernet NICs and switches have come into the market. As a result, many network professionals are interested in evaluating these new technologies for implementation. This book provides real-world implementation expertise for these technologies, including traces, so that users can realistically compare and decide how to use them.

Network Performance Baselining

By Daniel Nassar

1st Edition

700 pages, $50.00

ISBN: 1-57870-240-2

Network Performance Baselining focuses on the real-world implementation of network baselining principles and shows not only how to measure and rate a network's performance, but also how to improve the network's performance. This book includes chapters that give a real "how to" approach for standard baseline methodologies along with actual steps and processes to perform network baseline measurements. In addition, the proper way to document and build a baseline report is provided.

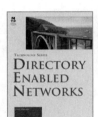

Directory Enabled Networks

By John Strassner

1st Edition

700 pages, $50.00

ISBN: 1-57870-140-6

Directory Enabled Networks is a comprehensive resource on the design and use of DEN. This book provides practical examples side-by-side with a detailed introduction to the theory of building a new class of network-enabled applications that will solve networking problems. It is a critical tool for network architects, administrators, and application developers.

Wide Area High Speed Networks

By Dr. Sidnie Feit

1st Edition

600 pages, $50.00

ISBN:1-57870-114-7

Networking is in a transitional phase between long-standing conventional wide area services and new technologies and services. This book presents current and emerging wide area technologies and services, makes them understandable, and puts them into perspective so that their merits and disadvantages are clear.

Quality of Service in IP Networks
By Grenville Armitage
1st Edition
300 pages, $50.00
ISBN: 1-57870-189-9

Intrusion Detection
By Rebecca Bace
1st Edition
300 pages, $50.00
ISBN: 1-57870-185-6

Quality of Service in IP Networks presents a clear understanding of the architectural issues surrounding delivering QoS in an IP network, and positions the emerging technologies within a framework of solutions. The motivation for QoS is explained with reference to emerging real-time applications such as Voice/Video over IP, VPN services, and supporting Service Level Agreements.

Intrusion detection is a critical new area of technology within network security. This comprehensive guide to the field of intrusion detection covers the foundations of intrusion detection and system audit. *Intrusion Detection* provides a wealth of information, ranging from design considerations to how to evaluate and choose the optimal commercial intrusion detection products for a particular networking environment.

The DHCP Handbook
By Ralph Droms
and Ted Lemon
1st Edition
550 pages, $55.00
ISBN: 1-57870-137-6

The DHCP Handbook is an authoritative overview and expert guide to the setup and management of a DHCP server. This title discusses how DHCP was developed and its interaction with other protocols. Also, learn how DHCP operates, its use in different environments, and the interaction between DHCP servers and clients. Network hardware, inter-server communication, security, SNMP, and IP mobility are also discussed. Included in the book are several appendices that provide a rich resource for networking professionals working with DHCP.

Other Books By New Riders

Quality of Service on IP Networks
1-57870-189-9 • $50.00 US
Designing Addressing Architectures for
Routing and Switching
1-57870-059-0 • $45.00 US
Understanding & Deploying LDAP
Directory Services
1-57870-070-1 • $50.00 US
Switched, Fast and Gigabit Ethernet, Third
Edition
1-57870-073-6 • $50.00 US
Wireless LANs: Implementing
Interoperable Networks
1-57870-081-7 • $40.00 US
Wide Area High Speed Networks
1-57870-114-7 • $50.00 US
The DHCP Handbook
1-57870-137-6 • $55.00 US
Designing Routing and Switching
Architectures for Enterprise Networks
1-57870-060-4 • $55.00 US
Local Area High Speed Networks
1-57870-113-9 • $50.00 US
Network Performance Baselining
1-57870-240-2 • $50.00 US
The Economics of Electronic Commerce
1-57870-014-0 • $49.99 US

SECURITY

Intrusion Detection
1-57870-185-6 • $50.00 US
Understanding Public-Key Infrastructure
1-57870-166-X • $50.00 US
Network Intrusion Detection: An Analyst's
Handbook, 2E
0-7357-1008-2 • $45.00 US
Linux Firewalls
0-7357-0900-9 • $39.99 US

LOTUS NOTES/DOMINO

Domino System Administration
1-56205-948-3 • $49.99 US
Lotus Notes & Domino Essential
Reference
0-7357-0007-9 • $45.00 US

Software Architecture & Engineering

Designing for the User with OVID
1-57870-101-5 • $40.00 US
Designing Flexible Object-Oriented
Systems with UML
1-57870-098-1 • $40.00 US
Constructing Superior Software
1-57870-147-3 • $40.00 US
A UML Pattern Language
1-57870-118-X • $45.00 US

Professional Certification

TRAINING GUIDES

MCSE Training Guide: Networking
Essentials, 2nd Ed.
156205919X • $49.99 US
MCSE Training Guide: Windows NT
Server 4, 2nd Ed.
1562059165 • $49.99 US
MCSE Training Guide: Windows NT
Workstation 4, 2nd Ed.
1562059181 • $49.99 US
MCSE Training Guide: Windows NT
Server 4 Enterprise, 2nd Ed.
1562059173 • $49.99 US
MCSE Training Guide: Core Exams
Bundle, 2nd Ed.
1562059262 • $149.99 US
MCSE Training Guide: TCP/IP, 2nd Ed.
1562059203 • $49.99 US
MCSE Training Guide: IIS 4, 2nd Ed.
0735708657 • $49.99 US
MCSE Training Guide: SQL Server 7
Administration
0735700036 • $49.99 US
MCSE Training Guide: SQL Server 7
Database Design
0735700044 • $49.99 US
CLP Training Guide: Lotus Notes 4
0789715058 • $59.99 US
MCSD Training Guide: Visual Basic 6
Exams
0735700028 • $69.99 US
MCSD Training Guide: Solution
Architectures
0735700265 • $49.99 US
MCSD Training Guide: 4-in-1 Bundle
0735709122 • $149.99 US
CCNA Training Guide
0735700516 • $49.99 US
A+ Certification Training Guide, 2nd Ed.
0735709076 • $49.99 US
Network+ Certification Guide
073570077X • $49.99 US
Solaris 2.6 Administrator Certification
Training Guide, Part I
157870085X • $40.00 US
Solaris 2.6 Administrator Certification
Training Guide, Part II
1578700868 • $40.00 US
MCSE Training Guide: Windows 2000
Professional
0735709653 • $49.99 US
MCSE Training Guide: Windows 2000
Server
0735709688 • $49.99 US
MCSE Training Guide: Windows 2000
Network Infrastructure
0735709661 • $49.99 US
MCSE Training Guide: Windows 2000
Network Security Design

073570984X • $49.99 US
MCSE Training Guide: Windows 2000
Network Infrastructure Design
0735709823 • $49.99 US
MCSE Training Guide: Windows 2000
Directory Svcs. Infrastructure
0735709769 • $49.99 US
MCSE Training Guide: Windows 2000
Directory Services Design
0735709831 • $49.99 US
MCSE Training Guide: Windows 2000
Accelerated Exam
0735709793 • $69.99 US
MCSE Training Guide: Windows 2000
Core Exams Bundle
0735709882 • $149.99 US
Solaris 7 Administrator Certification
Training Guide, Part 1 and II
1-57870-249-6 • $49.99 US

Ⓝ How to Contact Us

Visit Our Web Site

www.newriders.com

On our Web site you'll find information about our other books, authors, tables of contents, indexes, and book errata.

Email Us

Contact us at this address:

nrfeedback@newriders.com

- If you have comments or questions about this book
- To report errors that you have found in this book
- If you have a book proposal to submit or are interested in writing for New Riders
- If you would like to have an author kit sent to you
- If you are an expert in a computer topic or technology and are interested in being a technical editor who reviews manuscripts for technical accuracy

nrfeedback@newriders.com

- To find a distributor in your area, please contact our international department at this address.

nrmedia@newriders.com

- For instructors from educational institutions who want to preview New Riders books for classroom use. Email should include your name, title, school, department, address, phone number, office days/hours, text in use, and enrollment, along with your request for desk/examination copies and/or additional information.
- For members of the media who are interested in reviewing copies of New Riders books. Send your name, mailing address, and email address, along with the name of the publication or Web site you work for.

Write to Us

New Riders Publishing

201 W. 103rd St.

Indianapolis, IN 46290-1097

Call Us

Toll-free (800) 571-5840 + 9 + 7477

If outside U.S. (317) 581-3500. Ask for New Riders.

Fax Us

(317) 581-4663

New Riders \ We Want to Know What You Think

To better serve you, we would like your opinion on the content and quality of this book. Please complete this card and mail it to us or fax it to 317-581-4663.

Name _____

Address _____

City_____State_____Zip _____

Phone _____

Email Address _____

Occupation _____

Operating System(s) that you use _____

What influenced your purchase of this book?
- ❏ Recommendation
- ❏ Table of Contents
- ❏ Magazine Review
- ❏ New Rider's Reputation
- ❏ Cover Design
- ❏ Index
- ❏ Advertisement
- ❏ Author Name

How would you rate the contents of this book?
- ❏ Excellent
- ❏ Good
- ❏ Below Average
- ❏ Very Good
- ❏ Fair
- ❏ Poor

How do you plan to use this book?
- ❏ Quick reference
- ❏ Classroom
- ❏ Self-training
- ❏ Other

What do you like most about this book?
Check all that apply.
- ❏ Content
- ❏ Accuracy
- ❏ Listings
- ❏ Index
- ❏ Price
- ❏ Writing Style
- ❏ Examples
- ❏ Design
- ❏ Page Count
- ❏ Illustrations

What do you like least about this book?
Check all that apply.
- ❏ Content
- ❏ Accuracy
- ❏ Listings
- ❏ Index
- ❏ Price
- ❏ Writing Style
- ❏ Examples
- ❏ Design
- ❏ Page Count
- ❏ Illustrations

What would be a useful follow-up book to this one for you?_____

Where did you purchase this book? _____

_____

Can you name a similar book that you like better than this one, or one that is as good? Why?

_____

_____

How many New Riders books do you own? _____

What are your favorite computer books?_____

_____

What other titles would you like to see us develop? _____

_____

Any comments for us? _____

_____

_____

_____

Windows 2000 Security, 0-7357-0991-2

www.newriders.com • Fax 317-581-4663

Fold here and tape to mail

- -

Place
Stamp
Here

New Riders Publishing
201 W. 103rd St.
Indianapolis, IN 46290